JUL 2 8 2009

Exile to Siberia, 1590–1822

Exile to Siberia, 1590–1822

Andrew A. Gentes

First published 2008 by
PALGRAVE MACMILLAN
Houndmills, Basingstoke, Hampshire RG21 6XS and
175 Fifth Avenue, New York, N.Y. 10010
Companies and representatives throughout the world

PALGRAVE MACMILLAN is the global academic imprint of the Palgrave Macmillan division of St. Martin's Press, LLC and of Palgrave Macmillan Ltd. Macmillan® is a registered trademark in the United States, United Kingdom and other countries. Palgrave is a registered trademark in the European Union and other countries.

ISBN-13: 978–0–230–53693–7 hardback
ISBN-10: 0–230–53693–X hardback

This book is printed on paper suitable for recycling and made from fully managed and sustained forest sources. Logging, pulping and manufacturing processes are expected to conform to the environmental regulations of the country of origin.

A catalogue record for this book is available from the British Library.

A catalog record for this book is available from the Library of Congress.

10   9   8   7   6   5   4   3   2   1
17   16   15   14   13   12   11   10   09   08

Printed and bound in Great Britain by
CPI Antony Rowe, Chippenham and Eastbourne

To my parents

Contents

Preface

This is the first book-length, contemporary history of tsarist Siberian exile. All dates are according to the Julian, or Old Style, calendar, which prevailed in Russia until the 1917 Revolution and was ten days behind the Gregorian calendar as of the mid-seventeenth century, eleven days as of the mid-eighteenth century and twelve days as of 1822.

This book uses a number of Russian-language terms and acronyms with which readers may not be familiar, and so they are encouraged to consult the Glossary.

Finally, transliteration is according to the Library of Congress system, except that in the body of the text I have omitted any diacritical mark that comes at the end of a word so as to facilitate use of the possessive case. Transliteration in the notes and bibliography fully accords with the system.

Acknowledgements

This book is the product of many years' research during which I was assisted by dozens of people and institutions, and so my apologies from the outset if I have overlooked anyone. I wish to thank Stephen Frank for first suggesting the topic to me, and Tom Gleason, Patricia Herlihy and David Kertzer for serving on my dissertation committee. I am especially grateful to Michael Jakobson for reading early versions of these chapters, and to Pavel Kazarian for his advice when I began my archival research in Siberia. Thanks as well to Alan Wood, Vic Mote and other organizers and participants in the British Universities' Siberian Studies Seminar (BUSS) series who took an interest in my research and provided valuable advice. I also appreciate the interest shown by Eva-Maria Stolberg, Sharyl Corrado, Willard Sunderland, Andrei Znamenski, Sheila Fitzpatrick, Lynne Viola, Jane Burbank, J. Arch Getty, Peter Cryle, Robert Elson, Adele Lindenmeyr and Steven Marks. I wish to thank Michael Strang and Ruth Ireland at Palgrave Macmillan, and Ruth Willats for her editing of the typescript. I remain responsible for the final product.

I have benefited from financial or other support from the history departments and graduate studies programs of the University of California at Riverside and Brown University, as well as from the Thomas J. Watson Jr. Institute for International Studies at Brown University; Russian State Humanities University (RGGU), Moscow; Far Eastern State University (DVGU), Vladivostok; the Wilson Center's George Kennan Institute; and the University of Queensland's Faculty of Arts, Centre for Critical and Cultural Studies, and School of History, Philosophy, Religion, and Classics. I greatly appreciate the assistance of librarians and staff at all those institutions where I have either been a student or on the faculty, and particularly the staffs of the Russian State Library and GARF, both in Moscow; RGIA DV, GAPK, OIAK, the Library of the Far Eastern Branch of the Russian Academy of Sciences, and the Gor´kii and Fedoseev public libraries, all in Vladivostok; GAIO and the Irkutsk State University Library's Rare Books and Manuscripts Division, both in

Irkutsk; the Library of Congress; and Harvard's Widener and Law School libraries.

Lastly, I wish to thank my colleagues, students, friends and family who, in their many, often unintended, ways helped bring this book about, and to acknowledge the spirit which embraces us all.

Brisbane, 2008

Glossary and Abbreviations

Arshin (*arshiny*, pl.) – unit of measure equal to 71 cm. or 28 in.

Barshchina – 'labor dues'

Brodiaga (*brodiagi*, pl.) – 'vagabond'

Chetvert´ (*chetverti*, pl.) – 'quarter', unit of measurement roughly equal to 1 liter or 1¾ pints

D´iak – 'chancellor', top *prikaz* official

Desiatina (*desiatiny*, pl.) – unit of measure equal to 1.09 hectares or 2.7 acres

Gorod (*goroda*, pl.) – population point administratively designated as a 'city'

Guberniia (*gubernii*, pl.) – 'province'

Guliashchie liudi – 'wandering people', i.e. early free settlers of Siberia

GUVS (*Glavnoe upravlenie Vostochnoi Sibiri*) – Main Administration of Eastern Siberia

GUZS (*Glavnoe upravlenie Zapadnoi Sibiri*) – Main Administration of Western Siberia

Iasak – 'fur tribute'

IGP (*Irkutskoe gubernskoe pravlenie*) – Irkutsk Provincial Administration

Katorga – 'penal labor'

Kormlenie – 'feeding', i.e. officially condoned graft

Kormovye den´gi – 'foraging money', i.e. funds distributed to deportees to buy food

Litva – catch-all Muscovite term for prisoners-of-war

Masterovye – category of servitor-craftsmen

Meshchane – collective noun for 'urban residents'

Meshchanstvo (*meshchanstva*, pl.) – 'urban communal association'

MVD (*Ministerstvo vnutrennykh del*) – Ministry of Internal Affairs

Oblast´ (*oblasti*, pl.) – '(secondary-level) province'

Obrok – '(peasant) dues (in kind or in money)'

Obshchestvo (*obshchestva*, pl.) – 'peasant communal association'

Okrug (*okruga*, pl.) – 'district' in post-1822 Siberia

OPT (*Obshchestvo popechitel´nago o tiur´makh*) – Prison Aid Society

Ostrog (*ostroga*, pl.) – '(Siberian) fort'

Perevedentsy – 'those transferred between jurisdictions'

Plet´ – 'three-tailed whip'

Pood – anglicization of *pud*, unit of measure equal to 16.38 kg. or 36 lb.
Posad (*posady*, pl.) – 'town' or '(city-administered) village'
Posadskie liudi – 'townspeople'
Posel´shchik (*posel´shchiki*, pl.) – peasant turned over to the state for administrative exile
Poselenie (*poseleniia*, pl.) – 'state-run exile settlement'
Prikaz (*prikazy*, pl.) – '(Muscovite government) department'
Prikazchik (*prikazchiki*, pl.) – '*prikaz* official'
Promyshlennik (*promyshlenniki*, pl.) – 'private fur trader'
Propitannye – category of exiles assigned to be maintained on charity
Sazhen´ (*sazheni*, pl.) – unit of measure equal to 2.13 m. or 6.99 ft.
Sluzhilye liudi – 'service people'
Soslovie (*sosloviia*, pl.) – roughly, 'class' or 'estate'
Ssyl´nye – 'judicial exiles'
Ssylka – 'exile,' esp. 'judicial exile'
Starozhil (*starozhily*, pl.) – 'long-term resident (of Siberia)'
Strel´tsy – '(professional) arquebusiers (later, musketeers)'
Sud´ia – 'judge', a top *prikaz* official
TobPS (*Tobol´skii Prikaz o ssyl´nykh*) – Tobol´sk Exile Office
Uezd (*uezdy*, pl.) – 'district' in pre-1822 Siberia
Ulozhenie – '(1649) Law Code'
Verst – anglicization of *versta*, a unit of measure equal to 1.06 km. or 0.66 mile.
Voevoda (*voevody*, pl.) – '(Muscovite Siberian) military governor'
Voevodstvo (*voevodstva*, pl.) – Muscovite territorial and administrative designator
Volost´ (*volosti*, pl.) – roughly, 'canton'
Zavod (*zavody*, pl.) – 'fortified industrial township'

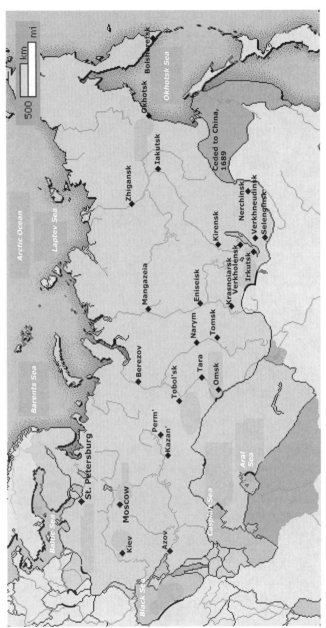

Russia and Siberia, c. 1590-1822

Introduction: The Universal Experience of Exile

Exile is among the oldest of punishments. The prospect of being expelled by one's community or dispatched by the authorities evokes profound and universal dread across time and place. Literary traditions from around the world recount how both gods and men have used exile. When Zeus defeated his father Cronus he also banished the other Titans, save Ocean, Hyperion and Mnemosyne. In the Japanese creation myth *Nihongi* the gods Izanagi-no-Mikoto and Izanami-no-Mikoto give birth to the particularly cruel Sosa-no-wo-no-Mikoto, whom they expel saying, 'Thou art exceedingly wicked.... Certainly thou must depart far away to the Nether-Land.' Sosa is banished to the Rock-cave of Heaven, where she is imprisoned behind the Rock-door.[1] Sophocles uses the exile motif in *Oedipus at Colonus*, sending the blind and outcast Oedipus to wander with his daughter Antigone through foreign lands. When Oedipus confronts two people he had known when he was king he cries:

> These were the two
> Who saw me in disgrace and banishment
> And never lifted a hand for me. They heard me
> Howled from the country, heard the thing proclaimed!

> And will they say I wanted exile then,
> An appropriate clemency, granted by the state?
> That is all false! The truth is that at first
> My mind was a boiling cauldron; nothing so sweet
> As death, death by stoning, could have been given me...[2]

Exile is also fundamental to the monotheistic literary tradition. In *Paradise Lost* Milton uses Lucifer's expulsion from Heaven to introduce the battle between Good and Evil:

> Th' infernal Serpent; he it was, whose guile
> Stirr'd up the Envy and Revenge, deceiv'd
> The Mother of Mankind, what time his Pride
> Had cast him out from Heav'n, with all his Host
> Of Rebel Angels, by whose aid aspiring
> To set himself in Glory above his Peers ... [3]

For aspiring to usurp God, Lucifer and his followers became the first of many political exiles banished from the realm. Indeed, the Old Testament's God is punitive and later banishes from Paradise the first humans, Adam and Eve, for disobeying him and succumbing to the Serpent's temptation. 'Therefore the Lord God sent [Adam] forth from the garden of Eden,' records Genesis, 'to till the ground from whence he was taken. So he drove out the man; and he placed at the east of the garden of Eden Cherubim, and a flaming sword which turned every way, to keep the way of the tree of life.'[4] God also uses exile to punish the first crime committed by one human against another, for after slaying Abel, Cain is rendered

> a fugitive and a vagabond ... in the earth. And Cain said unto the Lord, My punishment is greater than I can bear. Behold, thou has drive me out this day from the face of the earth; and from thy face shall I be hid; and I shall be a fugitive and a vagabond in the earth; and it shall come to pass, that every one that findeth me shall slay me.[5]

Like Oedipus, Cain finds exile a punishment that is worse than death. In the Talmudic tradition, first Egypt then Babylon serve as a place of exile for the Jews, whose banishment Yahweh uses to test the legitimacy of His Chosen People. As for Mohammad, himself a one-time exile, he believed his own punitive expulsion of the Jews of the tribe of Banû An-Nadîr to be an act of 'the All-Mighty, the All-Wise. He it is who drove out the disbelievers among the people of the Scripture from their homes at the first gathering .... And had it not been that Allâh had decreed exile for them, He would certainly have punished them in this world .... '[6]

Well before Russians were first deported to Siberia in 1590, exile, with its attendant fears of banishment and solitude, was already associated with basic notions of justice, punishment and penitence. Indeed, when community is synonymous with survival, exile is an especially lethal threat, and so its recurrence in foundational myths and literature is but one explanation for the terrible power it exerts over our imagination. For many of those in modern cultures, the promotion of individualism and autonomy has combined with technology to render 'community' something of a quaint notion; yet exile as a global phenomenon is more prevalent today than at any time in history. Over the last century two world wars, numerous civil wars, genocides and globalization have pushed to almost all corners of the earth 'displaced persons', whose very ubiquity has inspired the burgeoning field of exilic studies, as well as research on social displacement and exclusion.[7] In his essay 'Reflections on Exile' Edward Said, himself an exile, distinguishes between 'exiles, refugees, expatriates and émigrés', yet notes that all share 'decentered, contrapuntal' existences. 'The pathos of exile,' he writes, 'is in the loss of contact with the solidity and the satisfaction of earth: homecoming is out of the question.'[8] It is this pathos which is the first point I wish to make about exile to Siberia, yet one for which analogies are necessary, since sources for the period 1590–1822 are largely silent concerning individual exiles themselves. Beginning in the 1860s, Dostoevskii and others produced an exilic literature of great historical value; but with only rare exceptions no firsthand accounts were written during the earlier period of exile. Most exiles were illiterate and could leave no written records, and so we are left to imagine the thousands of personal tragedies that occurred. Tapping into what may be called the 'universal experience of exile' helps in this effort.

To further define the topic of this book something should be said about terminology. 'Exile' is often used to describe the condition of Russian ex-patriots living abroad;[9] but whereas Russians often considered Siberia to be 'outside' their country, this study does not consider those sent beyond national borders. As established by George Kennan in *Siberia and the Exile System*,[10] 'exile' is used here to refer to deportation to Siberia and what is sometimes distinguished as the Russian Far East. In a more conceptual vein, Gabriele Griffin has written:

Exile is . . . always the effect of force exerted upon a person or a people, resulting in a condition which is not freely chosen but inflicted, an experience where the subjecthood of the individual is called into question as s/he becomes the object of a displacing power which s/he is unable to resist.[11]

Exile to Siberia certainly objectified thousands; but unlike Griffin, I have found that many were able to resist the 'displacing powers' which, during 1590–1822, included the sovereign, various state agencies, the church, serf owners and self-regulating rural and urban collectives (*obshchestva* and *meshchanstva*). Irrespective of any criminal guilt, exiles were certainly victims in a sense; but a considerable body of scholarship demonstrates that even victims possess agency and may carve from their surroundings spaces in which to exercise personal autonomy and resistance.[12] Said accordingly observes that despite its disordering effect, exile allows for reinvention of the self. This theme figures alongside that of pathos in this study and reveals that many banished beyond the Urals transformed their fates through personal agency. Lastly, note should be made that whereas these and all other 'displaced persons' discussed here are referred to as 'exiles' or 'deportees', not all those deported were judicially sentenced to exile (*ssylka*) nor were they exiles (*ssyl´nye*) by legal or administrative definition. This book defines several categories of deportees, though it should be clear when I am using 'exile' in the broader or narrower sense.

Griffin also writes, 'The experience of exile produces cultural expressions of that condition, both by those who have actually undergone or been in a state of exile, and by those affected by the exile they observe or experience indirectly.'[13] Because exiles were coincident with Siberia's first settlers, a discrete exilic culture quickly developed and went on to significantly influence the hegemonic cultures of both Siberia and Russia. These cultural expressions can be conceived of on both the macro and micro level. At the macro level, exile contributed to what Immanuel Wallerstein and others have described as the emergence of a world economy,[14] when during the sixteenth century human migration combined with a military technological revolution[15] to allow Europeans to impose exploitative relations on non-Europeans on a scale previously impossible. Historians writing on this global development often overlook or understate the impact of the Russians' eastward expansion, despite their having acquired in less than a century a landmass equal to North and South America combined;[16] and no historian has fully demonstrated exile's role in Russia's commercial domination of Siberia.

A less concrete but no less important macro-level cultural expression was exile's function in commodifying the human body – another phenomenon which, like international trade, characterizes modernization. 'Exile becomes an essentially somatic experience' for the displaced person, write Wendy Everett and Peter Wagstaff, in which the subject's own body, or image, is appropriated by an external agency. Just as forced migration – mass or otherwise – threatens the autonomy of individuals by defining them in terms of economic value, so the commodification and expropriation of an individual's physical reality deprives her or him of the ability to live on her or his terms.[17]

In Russia a combination of autocracy, patrimonialism and statism commodified all subjects, with exiles being an egregious excrescence of the whole. Such materialistic use of subject populations was not unique to Russia: Portugal imported 200,000–300,000 slaves during the sixteenth century.[18] The point is that Siberian exile had a primarily economic rather than punitive function within the systematizing Russian state. For this reason, during the period before 1822 economics and statecraft rather than penology and law best account for exile's development.

Commodification also introduces Michel Foucault's notion of the bourgeois state's disciplining of the human 'soul' (a word he typically used idiosyncratically) for purposes of normalizing and maximizing productivity during the industrial age.[19] Tsarist Russia hardly qualifies as a bourgeois state. Nonetheless, it was transformed after the mid-1600s – coincident with a significant expansion of exile to Siberia – into a highly regulated mercantilist state where, as Marshal Poe explains, the autocrat capitalized on the polity's profound religiosity (expressed primarily via humility and suffering) to demand a degree of state service greater than anywhere else in Europe.[20] Simultaneously, the autocratic imagination blended developments in cartography, conceptions of the body politic and corporeal displays of majesty to arrive at a synonymy between sovereign and state – a duality genealogically linked to what Ernst Kantorowicz has shown was the medieval doubling of the king's body into 'the body natural and the body politic'.[21] This synonymy inspired metonymical associations between the map and the subject's body, to the extent that the latter became another text on which the sovereign could *de*-scribe his authority. Hence the significance of the public spectacles of torture and execution, for if a subject asserted control over his self he was seen to be usurping both realm and ruler, and such usurpation rendered his body a contested space on which it was necessary to stake a claim. Like those in Europe, the authorities in Russia would scourge this body with flame, rod, brand, knout, knife, lash or any number of other instruments;[22] and also like their European counterparts they often excised this now mutilated body from the larger social body as if it were a pestilence or bacillus so it could neither offend nor infect others. As such, the malfeasant body was banished beyond the ruler's body-realm. However, possession of Siberia as a cartographically ill-defined region both outside yet also very much inside the realm allowed the state to keep this body within manipulatory reach and use it purposefully.[23]

The modernizing state's demand for usable bodies largely explains why, beginning in Western Europe during the mid-eighteenth century, penality evolved away from retribution and towards rehabilitation. Science, not spirituality, became the key to understanding the criminal, for deviants were no longer seen as minions of the Devil but as products of society and its discontents. The focus shifted to knowing the offender's mind rather than his heart. Of course, belief that a deviant could be rehabilitated and normalized was itself an act of faith that is now beginning to crumble alongside many other Enlightenment verities. Nevertheless, with evil no longer resident in the heart (or anywhere else), the virtuous sovereign's desecration of the criminal's body in a public spectacle began to lose its *raison d'être*. At the same time, new-found faith in rehabilitation, though seemingly progressive, resurrected approaches which for millennia had been intended to cure the soul – thus the Quakers adopted the anchorite cell as their model for the basic unit of the modern penitentiary. In contrast to medieval dungeons with their racks and wheels for releasing the soul from its earthly vessel, the penitentiary would challenge the conscience by providing no other outlet save solitary introspection. This gave birth to one of Western penology's essential conceits.

Given the above, the history of Siberian exile shows medieval and modern penalities to have been coeval in Russia after the early seventeenth century. Scourging miscreants satisfied the punitive and significatory requisites of a retributive, pre-modern penality whose primary benefactor was the sovereign, whereas exiles' assignation to various *ostroga* (forts), settlements and industrial sites served a quintessentially modern penological goal to discipline and perhaps even rehabilitate deviants into what are blandly called 'useful members of society'. In Russia, the disjuncture between these two penalities rendered the exile himself something of a bifurcated subject: on one side, his body was beaten, mutilated and otherwise debilitated; on the other, it was expected to perform services newly demanded by the state. The irony was that if this body did not expire during scourging, deportation or fulfilment of assigned functions, it stood a good chance of obtaining in Siberia a level of autonomy impossible anywhere nearer the Leviathan's head. Nonetheless, because these various forms of retribution satisfied different masters (scourging – the sovereign;

exile – the state) tsarist Russia was never able to resolve what were mutually irreconcilable penalities (nor for that matter have many other states). Analysis of Siberian exile therefore highlights the anachronistic relationship between a modernizing state demanding service and a medieval monarchy demanding recognition and obedience.

On the micro level, exile's cultural expressions can be subdivided into push and pull factors. Among the latter influencing exile's development were the fur trade, land availability and personal autonomy, whereas the former included imperial expansion, warfare and the state's and the elites' increasing control over the peasants. Well into the seventeenth century Russia was a warrior society in which the best soldiers held the most important government posts. George Yaney writes that the fur trade Muscovy inherited from the Mongols established a continuity with Asian nomadic empires whose 'characteristic form of "government" ... was essentially a protection racket ... in which a gang (horde, *druzhina*) of warriors transcended the simple quest for booty and reorganized themselves as "protectors" to extort tribute and/or slaves from their "subjects" on a more or less regular basis.'[24] Whether or not such a racket was characteristically 'Asian' (Yaney overlooked the druzhina's existence in pre-Mongol Rus), this notion helps account for the state's exceedingly exploitative relationship to the polity and explains its obsession, especially from the seventeenth century onwards, with knowing the locations of those within the realm and monitoring or stabilizing their movements. That developments in Siberia directly reflected state–society relations in the motherland is demonstrated by the 1649 *Ulozhenie* (Law Code), which codified both serfdom and Siberian exile. Yet, despite eventual transformation of European Russia's power constellation into a government run by servitors and bureaucrats on behalf of a most un-warlike landed elite, the Siberian apparatus remained militarized until the end of the old regime, so that with the important exception of Mikhail M. Speranskii, all Siberia's top officials were military officers. Admittedly, frontier life to a large degree necessitated martial administration. Siberia was a brutal, unforgiving place where the accouterments of modern civilization were (and sometimes still are) few and far between; survival depended on self-discipline, strategy and foresight, each of which favored a warrior ethos that abjured those softening European cultural influences increasingly conditioning the post-Petrine nobility; and violence was prevalent, with the Chukchi fighting their occupiers for years and the Tatars, Kazakhs, Kirghiz, Chinese and Manchus fielding powerful armies. In addition, the region's small but unruly population of cossacks,[25] indigenes, trappers, soldiers, state peasants, schismatics, fugitives and criminals led Moscow and later Petersburg to believe that only a military government could keep it in check. Nonetheless, their military ethos also conditioned local administrators to deal harshly with those under their control. John Stephan writes that the military governor 'Golovin used meat hooks on Yakuts, but he did not shrink from employing hot coals, pliers, and the knout on his own men and their wives.'[26] Such brutality was an amplification of the center's service-state ethos that commodified the subject population.

*   *   *

Siberian exile therefore relates to broader themes. The scholarly literature bearing more directly on exile and Siberia will now be considered. By way of a brief comparison between tsarist exile and the more thoroughly researched Soviet GULag, I will simply note the latter was a much larger phenomenon in terms of the number of deportees and physical plant. Accounts by Solzhenitsyn, Shalamov, Ginzburg and others, as well as a visual archive, render the GULag a much more immediate and viscerally horrifying spectacle than the tsarist system. That said, tsarist exile blighted society over many more generations, and its worst features inspired and were perfected by Stalin's camps. Studies of the GULag nonetheless lack detailed information on pre-Soviet exile,[27] and so the present study helps contextualize the Soviet experience.

Several excellent books on exile were written before 1917. Following the 1864 judicial reforms, increasing attention was devoted to Russia's penal history amid a political debate about the probity and efficacy of Siberian exile. Sergei V. Maksimov's *Siberia and Penal Labor*[28] and Nikolai M. Iadrintsev's *Russian Society in Prison and Exile* and *Siberia as a Colony*[29] are free-ranging though indispensable ethno-historical accounts packed with detail. Ivan Ia. Foinitskii's *Studies on Penology in Connection with Prison Management*,[30] Grigorii S. Fel´dstein's *Exile: Its Genesis, Significance, History and Contemporary Existence*[31] and the government publication *Exile to Siberia: Essays on its History and Contemporary Situation*[32] are more methodologically rigorous works, each of which criticizes exile as a penal institution, but also draws a distinction between its arguably better management during the 'Muscovite era' (c. 1590–1725) and inchoateness during the 'Petersburg era'.

The best works from the Soviet period include those published by the All-Union Society of Political Penal Laborers and Exile-settlers (which also published the journal *Penal Labor and Exile* between 1921 and 1935);[33] F. G. Safronov's studies of exile and peasant life in Iakutiia;[34] and a series of collections which appeared during the 1970s and 1980s, edited by L. M. Goriushkin of Novosibirsk University.[35] Exile was, however, a fraught topic in the USSR, and most historians writing on the period before the 1825 Decembrist Uprising confined themselves to fitting Siberian events into officially condoned stages of economic development. This produced ideologically fettered works that ignore most of the questions posed here about administration, penality and the exile population, though these publications are largely based on archival sources and so proved quite useful. The post-Soviet period has seen some work on Siberian exile, most notably by P. L. Kazarian and G. V. Shebaldina,[36] though the focus, if not the methodology, remains fixed on political and other notable exiles despite their having accounted for only a fraction of the exilic population.

English-language literature on tsarist Siberian exile is limited. Kennan's work is the best known, but does not concern the period covered here. This leaves several articles by the British historian Alan Wood and me, as well as my doctoral dissertation. However, a number of scholars, including Robert Kerner, George Lantzeff, Terence Armstrong, Donald Treadgold, James Forsyth, Marc Raeff, Yuri Slezkine and G. Patrick March, have written more generally on Siberian history. Basil Dmytryshyn's documentary collection and Janet Martin's study of the fur trade also proved especially useful.[37]

Keeping with the theme of Siberian history generally, a number of Russian language works provided necessary context as well. These include Gerhard F. Müller's *History of Siberia*, first published in German in the eighteenth century. Müller (1705–83) accompanied the 1733 Kamchatka Expedition and pored over hundreds of manuscripts he found in Siberian monasteries, many of which were subsequently lost or destroyed, so that the copies he made remain the only extant versions. A recent, excellent three-volume edition of his *History* includes hundreds of pages of supplementary notes and documents.[38] Ivan V. Shcheglov's *Chronology of the Most Important Dates in Siberian History: 1032–1882* proved similarly useful, since it is not just a compendium of events but also a collation of essays drawn from numerous sources.[39] Mention should also be made of M. N. Gernet's five-volume *History of the Tsarist Prison*, first published in the 1940s, and which, despite its focus on political prisons, contains some information on exile.[40] Ancillary works on settlement, administration, demographics and economics by S. V. Bakhrushin, V. I. Shunkov, N. I. Nikitin, V. M. Kabuzan, M. A. Braginskii and Z. G. Karpenko were especially useful, as was the five-volume *History of Siberia* (1968–9) edited by A. P. Okladnikov.[41] Also notable is the series begun by L. M. Goriushkin and continuing since his death entitled *History of Siberia: Primary Sources*, which as of this writing includes several well-edited volumes reproducing and transcribing into modern orthography documents from Siberian archives. Issue 7, *The First Hundred Years of Siberian Cities: The 17th Century*, edited by N. N. Pokrovskii and others, was particularly useful.[42]

Scholarly literature on penality proved helpful, though it deals overwhelmingly with prisons rather than exile. While there are definite similarities between exile and prisons, and while the exile system did include prisons of a sort, differences outweigh the similarities, largely because exile essentially took the place of prisons during the tsarist period. Exiles in Siberia led very different lives from those of inmates in European dungeons, jails or prisons. Nonetheless, I have made use of studies by Pieter Spierenburg, David Garland and David Rothman. Of the few works on exile *per se*, Robert Hughes' *Fatal Shore*, concerning the history of transportation to Australia, suggested that a history of Siberian exile might prove similarly interesting; and Joanna Waley-Cohen's study of exile in Xinjiang Province provided some basis for comparison. Yet, despite parallels with other systems, Siberia's exile system was unique. Unlike New South Wales and New Caledonia, Siberia was not separated from the motherland by thousands of kilometers of ocean; and although Xinjiang was similarly a frontier contiguous to central China, it received far fewer exiles, who were moreover much more closely administered than those in Siberia.

Foucault's *Discipline and Punish* is the best known work on penality, as well as perhaps his most studied publication. I will only note for now that some have been misled by the book's subtitle 'The Birth of the Prison'. Despite claims to the contrary,[43] Foucault was not attempting a *history* of the prison in the generally accepted sense of the word; rather, he was using techniques of metaphor and poeisis to describe a modern mentality (*episteme*) which threatens to result in the construction of a panopticon society (something also habitually taken all too literally).[44] The more perceptive commentators recognize that Foucault was exposing a conceptual paradigm rather than documenting the genesis of the modern prison.[45] It is however true that Foucault sometimes fancied himself sufficiently informed to comment on Russian penality. He wasn't.[46] And so his influence here has been more theoretical than historiographical.

Foucault's work introduces the notion of power and how the state works. His influence has already been acknowledged in my discussion of sovereign and subject bodies, which also owes a debt to analyses by Evgenii Anisimov, Valerie Kivelson, Christine Worobec and Georg

Bernhard Michels, who have each explored conflicts between various belief systems and within state–society relations. Equally influential have been more conventional studies of Russian statecraft by John P. LeDonne, Marc Raeff, Richard Pipes and especially George Yaney, whose brilliant analysis of the systematization of the tsarist state informed my overall conceptualization of the factors influencing exile's administration. Although I disagree with Yaney's positivist interpretation of Russia's administrative development, his work led me to recognize exile as having consistently played a role in systematizing efforts at the highest level, despite its hindering efforts to reform not just the government apparatus but society as a whole. This study builds upon Yaney's and Foucault's quite distinct approaches in order to demonstrate how the modernizing Russian state incorporated penology into a larger systematizing process whose ultimate goal was universal discipline.

This is therefore the first English-language history of tsarist Siberian exile, and the first of three volumes on the topic. In this volume, I owe much to secondary sources but have tried to use archival and other primary sources whenever possible. Documents in *fond* 435 (Kirensk City Government, 1784–1867) of the Irkutsk State Archive (GAIO) provided much of the material for chapter 4; and a wonderful copy of the 1822 Reforms found for me by the staff of Irkutsk State University Library's rare books and manuscripts division informed chapter 5. Hopefully, this book will provide a framework for future research and debate on a long-ignored topic.

* * *

My first argument is relatively simple and essentially similar to that expressed by the nineteenth-century juridical historian N. D. Sergeevskii:

> As a punishment, exile served the Russian state as an inexhaustible source from which labor was derived for those locations where it was necessary, for civilian and military service, for settlement and the strengthening of boundaries, for the production of food supplies to maintain service people, and so on.[47]

Some qualification is needed, insofar as exile was actually not an 'inexhaustible source'. With the exception of short-lived and vain efforts by Catherine II and Alexander I to reduce the number of exiles, between 1590 and 1822 the government used various strategies to increase the numbers deported to Siberia to make up for a lack of free settlers. Such efforts in fact distinguish the pre- from the post-1822 period of Siberian exile, when the government generally tried – again in vain – to *reduce* the number of deportees. Sergeevskii and others were nonetheless correct to see exile as a tool of economic policy wielded by authorities who lacked a coherent penology.

My second and more far-reaching argument is that dependence on Siberian exile significantly retarded development in Russia of legal and judicial systems similar to those in the West. I hasten to note that I am not necessarily proposing those in the West were more advanced in any qualitative sense, simply that they were quite different, despite sharing with Russia origins dating as far back as the Classical Age.[48] What kind of development would have occurred had Russia never annexed Siberia is difficult to say, but the lack of a huge repository for society's human refuse would probably have necessitated establishment of a series of prisons in European Russia similar to those in the West, and such prisons would have had a more immediate impact than did exile on general society. In Western Europe and the United States, where deviants were not so readily banished but instead consigned to prisons and workhouses, civilians' familiarity with prisons and sympathy for prisoners prompted reforms which, as Bruce Adams has shown, little influenced Russia until the late nineteenth century, and made only a marginal impact on the exile system. Questions of penal reform intertwined with those of judicial reform, but prior to 1864, writes Peter Solomon, 'The typical judge was uneducated in law, depended on his clerks to explain cases, and accepted bribes.'[49] Improvements followed, but there was still much to do before the Bolshevik coup railroaded all reform efforts, and so Russian judicial institutions' immaturity helped allow the legal casuistry of the pre-Reform era to return. The tsarist state's possession and use of Siberia therefore influenced Russia's long-term legal development.

These arguments are developed in the chapters that follow. For now, this introduction will conclude with a brief outline. Chapter 1 details the Slavs' initial advances into Siberia and encounters with native Siberians. Many have written on this topic, but the stress here is on its relevance to exile's subsequent development. This chapter accordingly describes economic conditions which precipitated Russia's advance and rendered exile from its very beginnings an economic tool of the state. Exile's punitive origins in Russia are discussed next, before looking at the first groups deported to Siberia and an analysis of Muscovy's exilic population based on category of offence (criminal, political or religious). Chapter 2 uses a different model based on social estates to analyze this population, before discussing administrative reforms from Peter the Great's reign to the beginning of Catherine the Great's and concluding with an overview of Petrine penality.

Together, these first two chapters cover the Muscovite era which, like Sergeevskii, Foinitskii viewed favorably: 'The tasks of Muscovite exile were many-sided, but the government pursued it with laudatory caution and significant success.' Foinitskii went too far in claiming that 'in a majority of instances, [exiles] had the opportunity to choose positions that largely corresponded with their inclinations and abilities,'[50] but it is safe to say that Moscow administered exile better than did Petersburg. '[T]here was a carefully worked out program behind the Russian expansion in western Siberia,' observe George Lantzeff and Richard Pierce of the Muscovite era,[51] and evidence supports this. But as the government apparatus grew increasingly complex it increasingly mismanaged the exile system. Reluctant to credit either Moscow or Petersburg tsars with efficiency, Soviet historians covering this period tended to focus on the Siberian peasantry, thereby creating an impression that most of those banished were assigned 'to the land' (*na pashniu*). Sources are problematic, but strongly suggest that prior to 1649 most deportees were actually assigned 'to service' (*na sluzhbu*), usually as cossacks to collect furs. In any case, few of those assigned to the land remained in their locations and instead escaped to join the servitor estate or *posadskie liudi* (townspeople).

After Peter's assumption of power in 1689, the traditional use of exiles as servitors or peasants was eclipsed by a new penal regime which owed its existence to the burgeoning service-state ethos and was more ruthlessly administered so as to foster economic productivity. Over the next several decades *katorga* (penal labor) largely replaced *ssylka* (exile) as the preferred penal mechanism, and functioned as a version of exile insofar as it removed convicts from civil society and assigned them to labor sites which, prior to Catherine II's reign, tended to be in European Russia rather than Siberia. During the Muscovite era exiles had been incorporated into already existing social estates in which they lived much as non-exiles; but *katorga* put an end to this, creating a netherworld of brutality, unrelenting labor and death. Prior to the mid-eighteenth century most penal laborers (*katorzhnye* or *katorzhane*) were sentenced indefinitely and worked until they either dropped dead or became incapacitated. Some received fixed terms but most had no hope of returning home, and their sentences prohibited contact with their families and rendered them legally dead. The Petrine state used *katorga* as both a crushing punitive measure and a means to generate a malleable workforce to build through sheer numbers what Russia, given its lack of technology, could not otherwise accomplish. That thousands died in the process was irrelevant to an emperor whose numerous construction projects and wartime demands required such a labor force at the very time that serfdom was increasingly tying down the population. He therefore promoted what Fel´dstein calls a 'casuistic' justice system to 'produce' convicts assignable to *katorga* sites. Following completion of the Baltic port of Rogervik in 1767 the locus of *katorga* permanently shifted to Siberia. Henceforth, *katorga* and exile (*ssylka*) developed an intimate relationship given that the former also became a colonizing tool. Conditions associated with *katorga* improved during the late nineteenth century; but Peter's legacy was profound.

The proliferation of *katorga* sites throughout European Russia actually constituted something of an interregnum between exile's Muscovite and Petersburg eras. The remaining chapters deal with the latter. Chapter 3 concerns exile's development from the time of Peter's death in 1725 to the end of Catherine II's reign in 1796. This period is important because numerous measures were taken to regulate and increase the exile population. *Katorga* expanded particularly under Catherine (1762–96). Chapter 4 discusses a 'grandiose project', initiated by Paul I and gamely continued by his son, Alexander I, to populate eastern Siberia with thousands of exiles. Alexander tried as well to honor Catherine's memory by imposing limits on what was by then a runaway exile population. The chapter then discusses the nexus between exile and official corruption which became so detrimental that even Petersburg finally paid attention, thus initiating Speranskii's 1822 reforms.

In sum, chapters 3 and 4 show that convicts' primary role began to change from that of laborers to colonists during Anna Ioannovna's reign (1730–40). But Anna also inaugurated what Foinitskii characterizes as a long-term oscillation between these two service functions, an oscillation perhaps conditioned by Enlightenment notions of humane and rational penality, though probably owing more to the lack of a consistent penology. That new invention the prison was still a long time coming to Russia, and so falls outside the period covered here, but the processes leading to Russia's incomplete adoption of it, including the influence that Locke, Montesquieu, Beccaria and other theorists had on Catherine, are noted with regard to exile. Catherinian legislation undoubtedly reflects this Western influence, though Isabel de Madariaga errs in claiming that Catherine was the first Russian autocrat to be so influenced.[52] Early in her reign Elizabeth Petrovna (1741–61) amnestied a group of soldiers sentenced to have their nostrils slit and to be sent to *katorga*, and banished them instead to 'distant cities' for life. Under her adviser Petr

Shuvalov's direction she largely abolished capital punishment and created the category 'exile to settlement' (*ssylka na poselenie*) as a means to incorporate penal laborers into the peasantry upon completion of their *katorga* sentences. Finally, late in her reign, she sought to regulate deportation procedures and to abolish both the slitting of nostrils and the branding of the face as ways to mark criminals. This and other legislation counter dismissals of Elizabeth's adherence to penal reform by John LeDonne and Evgenii Anisimov, while supporting the conclusion reached by A. B. Kamenskii, W. Bruce Lincoln and Cyril Bryner that her reign, precisely because it was so influenced by the Enlightenment, was a watershed in Russia's administrative history, distinct from Anna's despotism and presaging Catherine II's enlightened absolutism.[53] Therefore, rather than being its initiator, Catherine perpetuated this trend by issuing amnesties, abolishing torture, calling for workhouses to replace exile and requiring medical assistance for those who fell sick during deportation. Also, she was the only sovereign to abolish (albeit very briefly) Siberian exile. It is true that her decisions reflected statist concerns as much as (if not more than) humanitarian ones; nonetheless, it is clear that no later than the 1740s compassion for the condemned as well as a belief that human nature could be modified were emerging in Russia consonant with similar trends in the West. The struggle to put these ideas into practice, however, took a very long time, and the persistence of its moribund penality contributed to Russia's vilification by Western writers.

Another factor conditioning post-Petrine Russia's oscillatory penality was the centre and periphery's evolving relationship. As before Peter's death Siberia continued to provide the center with natural resources, but Petersburg increasingly viewed it as a colony (and indeed described it as such) for exploitation rather than infrastructure development. This is one reason why as imperial Russia's borders expanded so did its use of exile. In contrast to the Muscovite era, when exiles served primarily as state servitors or food producers, the autocracy now began a series of efforts lasting until nearly the end of the imperial era to use exiles as colonists for securing far eastern territories, though the continued presence of a large population of non-food producing servitors as well as proximity to China meant agricultural and trade considerations remained. The Russian court first heard about Zabaikal´e's agricultural potential from exiled Swedish prisoners-of-war, and by 'the second half of the eighteenth century,' writes Marc Raeff, 'the combined demands of trade and of physiocratic doctrine resulted in a renewed stress on the advantages of agriculture and the desirability of its expansion into Siberia.'[54] Plans to colonize Siberia encountered obstacles, however, for whereas freemen and runaway peasants had earlier comprised the largest proportion of Siberian immigrants, their numbers were now being limited by expanding enserfment. Thus Petersburg turned increasingly to its reservoir of involuntary migrants – the deportees.

Exile expanded also because the autocracy used it as a release valve to minimize European Russia's mounting social problems. Siberia's seemingly infinite expanses absolved the state from having to build a network of prisons to accommodate its growing convict population; moreover, when landowners and village communes obtained exilic authority in the 1760s, they enthusiastically embraced it as a way to rid themselves of unproductive serfs and other undesirables. Siberia therefore became a geographical analogue of the multifarious asylum then being discovered (in David Rothman's words[55]) in the West: a vast dumping ground for society's detritus, for tens of thousands of criminals, beggars, cripples and elderly to whose welfare and impact on Siberia's nascent society Petersburg gave little heed. By the middle of Catherine's reign Siberian exile had therefore assumed a life of its own, dictating the government's actions rather than being efficiently administered by it. Distant and indirectly affected by the damage wrought on an enormous and increasingly important region, Petersburg decision-makers were content to let it remain the empire's carceral. Petrine *katorga* had been brutal, but at least reflected a coherent administrative and penological approach. Exile and *katorga* after Peter were brutal as well, yet not so much by design but rather because competing and self-defeating objectives resulted in a penal system so poorly administered that it not only failed to stand up to that of the Muscovite era but presaged a future of irresolvable problems.

Chapter 5, the final chapter, consists of a textual analysis of the 1822 Siberian reforms and, to some extent, their impact on exile. Although Speranskii is recognized as the reforms' principal author, close reading reveals internal inconsistencies which reflect the influence of the Siberian Committee's conservative members. Discussion of some post-1822 developments demonstrates that many committee recommendations were impractical or simply ignored. Nonetheless, the 1822 reforms highlight the role envisaged for exiles within a systematizing government apparatus and reinforce the conclusion that exile was primarily a tool of economics and statecraft, and only secondarily concerned with penal justice.

1
'To where the Sovereign Chooses. . . '

When the Russians arrived in Siberia in the late sixteenth century 230,000 indigenes were there speaking 120 distinct languages. This population declined by as much as 15 per cent over the next century due to the disease and alcohol introduced by Europeans, but rose steadily after 1700. The so-called small peoples of the north fall into two major linguistic groups: the Uralic (Finno-Ugric and Samoedic) and Altaic (Turkic and Tungusic). The Tungus (modern-day Evens and Evenks) were native to almost all of eastern Siberia with the exception of the far northeast, where the Chukchi and Iukagirs, among others, lived. Their neighbors, the yurt-dwelling Iakuts, proliferated throughout what is today the enormous Sakha Republic. Besides the Tungus and Iakuts the Buriats, situated around Lake Baikal, and the Oroks, Giliaks and Ainu, all on Sakhalin, are those 'small peoples' who figure most prominently in the history of Siberian exile.[1]

The Tatars were located farther to the south and were exceptional among Siberia's indigenes for being quasi-sedentary and possessing fortified settlements. Beginning in the earliest centuries CE, Turkic nomads left the steppe for the western Siberian forest. During the eleventh century Kipchak Turks migrated there from present-day Kazakhstan and intermarried with the Mansi, Khanty and Bashkiri already settled there. Two centuries later the Mongols arrived to join this ethno-linguistic stew and produce the people known as Tatars. Mongol authority eventually reached far west of the Urals to dominate the Slavs of ancient Rus. But with the collapse of the Khanate of the Golden Horde in the fifteenth century two major political constellations emerged to fill the vacuum: the Principality of Muscovy in the northwest; and the lesser khanates of Crimea, Astrakhan, Kazan and Sibir in the southeast.[2]

With its capital Isker at the confluence of the Irtysh and Tobol rivers Sibir Khanate denoted the marshy lands just east of the Urals. It first appeared on a Russian map in 1367 and next on one dated 1459. Russian chroniclers referred to all the territories east of the Urals as 'Siberia land' (*Sibirskaia zemlia*), in tacit recognition of the khanate's subjugation of tribes in the central Urals and Ob watershed who provided tribute, mostly in the form of sable and fox furs. The Tatar (originally Turkic) word for this tribute was *iasak*, and would be adopted into Russian.[3] The khanate's many vassals, several fortified cities and cartographical iteration should not, however, disguise the fact that by the mid-sixteenth century it was a society exhausted by civil war. During the preceding 150 years internecine violence had periodically erupted as contenders vied to become khan. In 1547, the same year Ivan IV was officially crowned tsar of Muscovy, Ediger, a member of the Taibuga clan, was named khan of Sibir. But Ediger's hold on power was tenuous; and in 1555, after learning of Ivan's defeat and annexation of Kazan Khanate, he dispatched ambassadors to Moscow to declare his vassalage to the tsar. Ivan responded by dispatching the courtier Mit´ka Kurov to Isker, who returned to Moscow the following year with 700 sable pelts and a Tatar ambassador named Boianda, who delivered a letter from Ediger in which he acknowledged the pelts were only a portion of those Ivan had demanded, but explained 'that the [Kazakh] prince of Shiban had been waging war against them and captured many people'.[4] Angered by this insolence from his newly declared vassal, the tsar kept Boianda as a hostage and dispatched the loyal Tatars Devlet Kozia and Sabania Riazanov to the Irtysh, where they apparently made Ediger an offer he could not refuse, for on their return with yet another hapless ambassador they also brought 1,000 black sables and an especially valuable gift of 169 white sables. This time another letter from Ediger acknowledged Ivan's full authority and promised never to come up short on the tribute again. But he was unable to keep this promise, for in 1563 the prince of Shiban, otherwise known as Shibanid Kuchum, a Kazakh fuelled by a fervent belief in Islam who had formed an alliance with the Nogai Tatars, overthrew Ediger and proclaimed himself Sibir's new khan. Kuchum set about spreading Mohammed's teachings while planning a *jihad* against the infidels to the west.[5]

*   *   *

These infidels had been a long time coming. Although Russia's 'conquest' of Siberia dates from 1582, Muscovites and Novgorodians began crossing the Urals centuries earlier, with the latter trading for furs, walrus tusks and other goods in western Siberia by the ninth century. In 1079 they encountered Nentsy and Ostiaki at the mouth of the Ob, in the northern trans-Uralic region they called either Zavoloch´e, 'the clouded (land)', or Iugriia, 'land of the Iugriians'. Eventually, 'Iugriians' came to refer to several different tribes.[6] Although Novgorod claimed Iugriia as its own, its hold was always weak. In 1198, for instance, a five-week siege of a Iugriian settlement abruptly ended when most of the Novgorodian commanders were murdered through subterfuge. As Novgorod declined during the fifteenth century Muscovy began to assert itself in Iugriia. In 1465 Ivan III (1462–1505) ordered the first Muscovite sortie against Iugriians. He launched another invasion in 1483; and the next year, despite continuing resistance, made Russia's first claim to Siberian territory by annexing Iugriia and adding 'Prince of Iugor' to his already prolix royal title. However, Moscow like Novgorod exerted little real authority over Iugriia, and had to invade twice more before the indigenes finally agreed to pay tribute in 1502. Moreover, the Russians established no permanent settlements in a region regarded simply as a source of furs. 'Moscow's annexation of the northwest tip of Siberia,' writes Donald Treadgold, 'was merely part of the annexation of Novgorod and was not intended as the beginning of an advance to the Pacific.'[7] Eighty years would elapse before Slavs of any sort advanced deeper into Siberia.

Iugriians paid tribute in the form of furs, the importance of which in Russia's conquest of Siberia and exile's early development cannot be overstated. Furs had for a long time provided the state enormous revenues. 'In Kievan Rus,' notes James Forsyth, 'furs probably constituted the biggest single item of export, except perhaps slaves ... '[8] While still autonomous, Novgorod Principality exported furs to the southern Slavs, Byzantium and other states in the Hanseatic League; but a shift in consumption tastes during the mid-fifteenth century away from the squirrel furs it specialized in significantly undermined its stability. In the meantime, Muscovy's geographic position allowed it to take over the more valuable trade in sable and fox furs, which the disintegrating Golden Horde could no longer maintain. Widespread demand throughout Europe and western Asia rendered exporting these furs a necessity for a polity set on imperialist expansion. As the papal legate Paulus Jovius observed during the reign of Vasilii III (1505–33), Muscovy's lack of precious metals was 'recompensed with an abundance of rich furs, whose price ... is grown to such excess, that the furs pertaining to one sort of apparel, are now sold for a thousand crowns.'[9]

Increasing its number of fur-paying vassals and facilitating access to markets were themselves major reasons for Muscovy to expand. Ivan III's annexation of Novgorod, Smolensk and other territories to the west, as well as Ivan IV's (1533–84) incorporation of Polish lands and his granting of the trading port of Arkhangel to the English, gave Muscovy vital access to land and sea routes, though growing competition from England and the Netherlands, not to mention Lithuania and Poland, pushed Muscovy's attention towards overland routes leading east. Having formally renounced the 'Mongol Yoke' in 1480, the Kremlin hoped to secure routes that proved key in establishing the world economic system. Muscovy's location between Europe and Asia promised it considerable leverage within this system.[10]

A desire to access markets in Ottoman Turkey and Persia helped push Muscovy into conflict with Kazan Khanate. Ivan IV believed the costs for this and other expansionist wars would be more than offset by the wealth gained from these new markets – and on strictly monetary terms, he seems to have been correct. 'Moscow, in replacing Novgorod as the chief fur trade center and in substituting luxury fur for squirrel pelts, also broadened the scope and increased the gross income from the fur trade,' writes Janet Martin, who adds: 'By the mid-sixteenth century, inflation had raised fur prices just over two times their fifteenth-century levels.'[11] Far from being 'dispensable',[12] the fur trade proved the bedrock on which Muscovy established its economic might. England's representative Giles Fletcher learned in 1591 that the crown 'receiveth yeerely in furres . . . a great value out of *Siberia, Pechora, Permia*, and other places, which are solde or bartered away for other forreine commodities to the *Turkish*[,] *Persian, Armenian, Georgian* and *Bougharian* [Bukharan] Marchants that trade within [these] cou[n]tries . . . ' These furs' value, he reported, 'may be gessed by that which was gathered the last yeere out of *Siberia* for the Emperours custome, vz. 466 timber [1 timber = 40 furs] of Sables, five timber of Martrones [martens], [and] 180 [timbers of] blacke Foxes . . . '[13] By 1595 Muscovy was wealthy enough to finance the Holy Roman Emperor's war against the Ottomans, sending him what Forsyth describes as a mountain of pelts 'which caused wonderment and was valued at 400,000 rubles'.[14] The historian Robert Kerner has illustrated the value of such pelts:

> [T]wo black fox pelts in 1623 brought 110 rubles. With these 110 rubles the owner could buy fifty-five acres of land, erect a good cabin, buy five horses, twenty head of cattle, twenty sheep, several dozen fowl, and still have half his capital left.[15]

The Kremlin obtained its furs from state servitors, private traders and middlemen (*promyshlenniki*), some of whom were trappers, though '[i]t was not so common for a Russian to hunt and trap the animals', writes Terence Armstrong. 'He hunted the natives.'[16] Both servitors and *promyshlenniki* employed cossacks to compel natives through kidnapping, torture and other coercive measures to hand over much of their caches; and by the mid-sixteenth century most of the Bashkiri, Cheremi and other peoples along the Urals' western slopes, in addition to the Samoedy and Nentsy in the north, were delivering *iasak* to the Russians. This was not a new arrangement: the Russians simply took over the tributary system once managed by the Golden Horde. But the amounts they demanded were far in excess of their predecessors', so that during the seventeenth century the number of pelts from Siberia reached more than 100,000 a year. As best it could, the crown taxed *promyshlenniki* in kind, even going as far as to establish sentries along the border between Russia and Siberia. But many *promyshlenniki* escaped the taxman and became fabulously wealthy in turn.[17]

Muscovy's subjugation of its vassals deprived Sibir of a major source of income and betokened conflict. Ediger tried to avoid this by paying *iasak* to Moscow, but Ivan IV used the threat of force to increase his demands, and so when Kuchum became khan he seems to have been in no mood to broker a deal, especially with those he may have considered heathens. Religious zeal possibly blinded him to the reality of Muscovy's military strength, though what he could have known about this is difficult to say. In any case, this impasse coincided with a decline in the overall fur market that began in the 1560s, largely because European fashion tastes switched to silk and other fabrics. There was little Muscovy could do about this. Another reason for the decline was that Russia's caravan trade with Turkey became virtually impossible. Between 1568 and 1574 not a single caravan traveled from Ottoman Turkey to purchase furs in Moscow[18] owing to internal disorder caused by the *oprichnina*, hostilities between Muscovy and the Crimean Khanate, and, most significantly with regard to later developments in Siberia, Don Cossacks' pillaging of caravans. Ivan knew that to remedy this situation Muscovy needed to open new markets in Persia and Central Asia; monopolize the fur supply to these markets so as to maximize profits; and use a combination of military strength and diplomacy to protect eastern supply routes. A permanent Russian presence east of the Urals was imperative to achieving these goals.

$$* \quad * \quad *$$

In addition to the fur trade, another development leading to Russian dominance over Siberia involved the entrepreneurial Stroganov family.

The Stroganovs launched their mercantile empire during the fifteenth century in Sol'vychegodsk, a town 800 kilometers northeast of Moscow at the confluence of the Dvina and Vychegda rivers. Nearby was a saline lake, and this allowed them to grow rich producing salt for Muscovy, which until then depended almost entirely on foreign supplies. The family patriarch Anika Stroganov built an enormous wooden block-house in Sol'vychegodsk modelled on western Europe's medieval castles and from which he oversaw something of his own fiefdom. Following Muscovy's annexation of Kazan he sought to increase his holdings by sending his eldest son, Grigorii, to appeal directly to Ivan IV. In April 1558 the tsar granted Grigorii a 20-year charter for territory along the Kama River, just west of the Urals near today's city of Perm. A decade later Anika's second son, Iakov, obtained a ten-year charter extending these holdings eastward along the Chusova River. Ivan acknowledged in both charters that the brothers planned to establish salt works and collect furs in these regions and their workers would be free from serf-dom and Crown taxes. The Stroganovs thus acquired almost 13 million square kilometers of land formerly part of Kazan Khanate. This espe-cially vexed Sibir's Khan Kuchum, who because of religious and ethnic connections considered the land his inheritance. Insult became injury when the Stroganovs began enserfing and enslaving the Komi and other peoples who were paying *iasak* to Kuchum. Moreover, part of the land Ivan gave the Stroganovs had once formed the khanate of the Nogai Tatars, Kuchum's ally in overthrowing Ediger. Nogai Khanate was in disarray by the time the Stroganovs arrived, but the Nogai people remained and were still to be reckoned with. Fighting ensued, as made clear by Ivan's 1568 charter authorizing Iakov to hire soldiers with 'cannons and arquebuses . . . for attacks by the Nogai people and other hosts'.[19]

Kuchum welcomed and possibly ordered these Nogai attacks, which were the first in a series of escalating measures by which he sought to protect his khanate from the Russians. In 1571 – the year Crimean Tatars so devastated Moscow that nearly everything save the Kremlin was burned to the ground and most of its population died or was enslaved – Kuchum formally renounced Sibir's vassalage and began ordering Mansi, Khanty and other proxies to rid the Kama of the Stroganovs and their kind. Their raids caused such havoc that three years later Ivan, in the words of one chronicler, 'recognizing their thievery and vile recalcit-rance',[20] granted another charter giving the Stroganovs the right to attack Sibir directly. Ivan clearly wanted to wipe the khanate off the map, for he promised the Stroganovs a 20-year lease on Sibir's territory if they defeated Mametkul, variously described as either Kuchum's brother or nephew, and who undoubtedly commanded his army. The 1574 charter permitting the Stroganovs to colonize and build factories and fortresses in Sibir however said nothing about the army necessary to achieve this – an omission seemingly explained by the tsar's ongoing Livonian War and struggle against the Crimean Tatars. Kuchum's vassals therefore continued to raid the Stroganovs' settlements throughout the next decade, for as wealthy as they were, the Stroganovs did not have the means to hire and equip the troops needed to defend them. By 1580 both Grigorii and Iakov Stroganov were dead and their family's hold on the region was looking grim.

Cossacks now entered the drama to begin their historic association with Siberia. For decades Don Cossacks had been raiding caravans bound for Persia and Bukhara, and so in October 1577, as part of his securing of trade routes, Ivan dispatched a large force under the courtier Ivan Murashkin to deal with these bandits. Murashkin soundly whipped the Cossacks, then pursued a group estimated at between 500 and 1500 north towards the Kama River. Led by Ermolai Timofeev, who came to be better known as Ermak Timofeevich, these fugitives arrived at a small town named Orël on the banks of the Kama, where they were warmly greeted by Maksim Stroganov, son of the recently deceased Iakov. Whether Maksim was expecting or had even sent for them is uncertain, but he helped them settle in.[21]

For several years Ermak and his people lived quite peacefully alongside the Kama, albeit with an occasional raid for booty. Why, then, did he invade Sibir Khanate on 1 September 1582 in command of a combined force of 840 'dangerous, courageous, and skilful warriors from among the Lithuanian, German, Tatar, and Russian peoples ...'?[22] Lack of documentation allows only for speculation. On the one hand, Ermak was still a wanted criminal. On 16 November 1582 Ivan, unaware that Ermak had already crossed the Urals, sent an instruction (*gramota*) to the new heads of the Stroganov family, Maksim and Nikita, forbidding them to allow Ermak and his Cossacks to advance 'against the people of the Siberian sultan'[23] because, in Müller's words, the tsar considered them 'brigands, who had already caused great mischief, particularly as a result of their attacks against the tribute-paying Voguls'.[24] It is possible that Ivan simply did not want Ermak's raiders stirring up trouble in a major locus of fur collection, and to emphasize his point he literally threatened the Stroganovs' lives if they allowed this. Yet the tsar wrote in the same instruction that he intended to suborn Ermak's Cossacks to Russian commanders for use against Kuchum's vassals. Ermak, for good reason, may have seen this as a ploy to take him prisoner and hence sought to escape the tsar's crooked staff by moving east.

On the other hand, Ermak was an inveterate freebooter and adventurer. Possibly having learned of Sibir's structural instability, he may have devised a plan to establish himself as regional warlord and master over Kuchum's vassals. There is some evidence that the Stroganovs supported this daring plan (if it existed), establishing what sources call 'certain agreements' with Ermak that included supplying him with weapons and additional soldiers. This helps explain chroniclers' cryptic references to Lithuanians, Germans and other apparent mercenaries. The Stroganovs certainly hoped for Sibir's destruction, since only this would allow them to take full advantage of the 1574 charter. However, for his part, Ermak may have planned to renege on any arrangements after he captured Isker. Whatever his motives, Ermak and his men ransacked several of the khanate's towns before defeating Mametkul in open battle and capturing Isker on 25 October 1582. He immediately imposed tribute on the surrounding tribes, and within a short time was able to send ataman Ivan Kol´tso to the tsar with a gift of 2,400 sables and a plea for mercy. Ivan pardoned him and his retinue for their crimes, but also dispatched 500 troops under Prince Semen Bolkhovskii to keep Ermak in check.

What followed is debatable. Janet Martin argues that Ivan did not intend to defeat and annex Sibir Khanate because he feared that eliminating it would flood the fur market and depress prices.[25] This argument seems implausible. First, it fails to acknowledge Ivan's limited ability to support the Stroganovs militarily. By 1582 Muscovy was on the verge of economic collapse, and the Kremlin was trying to invigorate the fur trade not by limiting output but rather by increasing its number of *iasak*-paying vassals and opening up new markets. Annexation of Sibir would give the Russians greater access to Persian and Central Asian markets, which in turn would boost Muscovy's economy. (Martin acknowledges this in fact happened.) Ivan's initial hesitation should therefore not be read as a lack of intention but rather the result of financial constraints and requirements imposed by other military commitments. Second, Martin's argument credits Ivan with too much economic wizardry, for the possibility that Sibir's fall would depress the fur market was itself dependent on several variables recognizable only in hindsight. Ermak's invasion took place amid great turmoil in Russia caused by 'the ravages of the *oprichnina*, the casualties of war, the flight of the peasant population, harvest failures, increasing taxation, epidemics, rising prices and famine',[26] and so few, including the tsar, could know what would happen next. But even if he did fear that the khanate's collapse would depress fur prices, it is hard to believe he would not have welcomed the elimination of yet another enemy khanate. Kuchum's bellicosity towards the Stroganovs, one of Muscovy's most important merchant families, had after all been growing for a number of years. Finally, Ivan's diplomatic efforts to reach an agreement with Kuchum and which Martin favorably cites pale beside evidence of repeated Russian incursions into Sibir's territories. Rather than peaceful, Ivan's moves towards Sibir tended to be aggressive, and as early as 1554, in a letter to Edward VI of England, he dubbed himself 'ruler of Siberia'.[27] Michael Khodarkovsky observes that 'Russia's expansion to the south and east was anything but haphazard, spontaneous, and uncontrolled',[28] and so the most that can be said is that Ivan may not have welcomed the *timing* of Ermak's invasion, but he doubtlessly welcomed the outcome.

Ermak's early success was nonetheless ephemeral. Despite losing Isker and other principal sites, Kuchum and his Tatars remained unbowed, and the Russians hit a string of bad luck. Perhaps because Moscow misjudged the distance, Bolkhovskii's troops were insufficiently provisioned, so that by the time they arrived in Isker in early November 1584 they were half-starved and of little use, and Bolkhovskii soon died. Moreover, Ivan himself had died in March. Then, in 1585, the 'Conqueror of Siberia', supposedly weighed down by the suit of armour Ivan had sent as a gift, drowned in the Irtysh while trying to escape a Tatar ambush.

This lapse in Russian fortunes proved brief, however, and by late summer 1586 government troops under Ivan Miasnoi and Vasilii Sukin managed to establish an *ostrog* (fort) at the site of the former Tatar city of Chimgi on the Tura River, thus founding Tiumen, the Russians' first permanent settlement in Siberia. A garrison of 300 cossacks and *strel´tsy* (arquebusiers)[29] secured the environs. Construction of subsequent *ostroga* – Tobol´sk (1587), Mangazeia (1601), Tomsk (1604), Eniseisk (1620), Iakutsk (1632), Okhotsk (1649), Irkutsk (1652) – would mark the Russians' meteoric advance eastward, each *ostrog* serving as a nodal point for military domination and *iasak* collection, as well as to coordinate both free and compulsory settlement. As of 1622, 23,000 Russians and other foreigners were in Siberia; 40 years later the figure was 105,000; and as of 1709 it was 229,227 and rapidly growing.[30] Because of this population influx and cossack explorers' amazing pace, by the late seventeenth century Russia could lay claim to almost all of Siberia to do with as it wished.

Actually, continual warfare, military impressment and the collapse of economic and social institutions were pushing migrants across the Urals many years before Ermak's invasion, though numbers were small compared to those that arrived after 1582. During the fifteenth century Novgorodians crossed the Urals to escape Muscovy's annexation of their city; Tatars later similarly fled the Kazan and Astrakhan khanates. By the early 1580s there was considerable demographic fluidity throughout Muscovy as people fled increasingly onerous circumstances. The flight from the countryside was so large that in 1581 landowners successfully lobbied the crown to prohibit peasants' right of movement on St George's Day, the last of the holy days during which peasants had been able to leave their masters' lands and thus exert some degree of autonomy. Hereon serfdom would steadily expand until the 1861 emancipation. A destination for peasants fleeing landowners and government impositions, Siberia therefore became a foil to serfdom, with its immigrants known as *guliashchie liudi* (wandering people), in contrast to those serfs tied to the land. So it was that in the mid-seventeenth century Muscovite officials acknowledged 'that many peasants had recently moved from Russia proper to Siberia'.[31] They told Siberian officials to register these people, but nevertheless leave them where they were. Such freemen formed a significant portion of Siberia's early population, helped establish towns and villages, worked in the fur trade and served as cossacks or state servitors. And so a picture emerges of what might be called a colonization of Siberia from below in the decades immediately after Ermak. In his history of Russian vagabondage Iadrintsev argues that the *guliashchie* laid tracks the state later followed into the East. Detailed evidence on trans-Uralic demotic migration is in fact lacking, but Ermak's invasion would seem to mark the final stages of this phenomenon prior to the state controlling migration. As we shall see, it was a period in stark contrast to Siberia's later colonial history.

Despite scattered instances of tribal resistance, no organized polity stood between Muscovy and the Pacific Ocean after Sibir's collapse. Geographically and figuratively, this absence created the largest power vacuum in the world at that time, which in turn necessitated rapid development of an administrative apparatus to govern, defend and exploit the region. The extent to which Russian state and society were shaped as a result of expansion into Siberia is nevertheless debatable. Eva-Maria Stolberg has argued that Frederick Jackson Turner's frontier thesis can be applied to European Russia's relationship to Siberia. She notes that in 'Imperial Russian literature' *prostor*, meaning both 'spaciousness' and 'freedom', was often used to describe Siberia.[32] *Prostor* certainly captured *nineteenth-century* Russian writers' imaginations, yet Russia's administration and settlement of Siberia differed significantly from those of the American West. For example, the American tradition of independent pioneers finds little similarity in the Russian experience. Despite the early *guliashchie* and a few other groups, European Russian dwelling patterns were for the most part replicated in Siberia. It is true that serfdom barely existed in Siberia, where almost all peasants were state peasants and therefore quite different from serfs,[33] though it needs to be mentioned that monasteries such as the St Nikolai in Verkhotur´e, which obtained a land charter in 1622, and Tobol´sk's Sofiisk Monastery, chartered in 1628, did acquire serfs, in part by enserfing *guliashchie liudi* already living on what became their lands. Eventually, some 35 monasteries were established in Siberia (e.g. Dolmatov Uspenskii, Tobol´skii Znamenskii, Nev´ianskii Bogoiavlenskii), each of which obtained the right to enserf peasants on their lands, whether they were freemen or fugitive serfs. As of the early eighteenth century Siberian monasteries possessed 1,082 peasant households, and by 1762 owned more than 14,000 male serfs.[34] Small numbers of privately owned serfs also existed in Siberia; but truly exceptional is an instruction dating from the mid-1640s in which Tsar Michael rules that the *guliashchie* Mishka Chashchin and Seluianko Nikonov be assigned to debt servitude (*kabala*) in Verkhotur´e *uezd*.[35] All of which is to say that even if the typical Siberian peasant was more economically autonomous than his European Russian counterpart, he tended like him to live within a village commune that dictated both his existence and *Weltanschauung*. As for Siberia's urban centers, after their initial incarnations as *ostroga*, they developed to resemble European Russian cities – Irkutsk, one of the oldest, being a sterling example (Chekhov called it the 'Paris of Siberia'). Moreover, government administrators established a presence in Siberia much more quickly and decisively than did their counterparts in the American West, delimiting areas of settlement and imposing military authority over indigenes and migrants alike. Yet the most decisive factor distinguishing the Russian from the American frontier experience is the exile system, for which there is no parallel in American history, save the deportation of comparatively small numbers of Native Americans.

The earliest Muscovite agencies responsible for administering Siberia suggest that despite Ivan's claim to be its ruler, the government still considered it a foreign territory. *Posol´skii prikaz* (Department of Embassies), which was headed by Ivan Vakhrameev between 1596 and 1599, actually devoted little attention to Siberia, which possibly explains why jurisdiction was transferred to *Kazanskii prikaz* after Vakhrameev's term. A number of different figures, most notably Prince Vasilii Cherkasskii, ran *Kazanskii prikaz* between 1599 and 1610. All must have been adept administrators, for despite the chaos that befell Muscovy during these years the *prikaz* managed to steadily extend authority over western

Siberia. During the three years before Michael Romanov assumed the throne in 1613 *Kazanskii prikaz* was, like the country itself, leaderless, though that year Aleksei Shapilov, the *prikaz's* former *dumnyi d'iak* ('chancellor'), resumed his position for an undetermined period. In 1619 Prince Aleksei Sitskoi became *sud'ia* (literally, 'judge'[36]) of *Kazanskii prikaz*, followed by Prince Dmitrii Cherkasskii (1624–32) and, in 1635, Prince Boris Lykov. These administrators' prominence indicates the seriousness with which both the declining Danilov and new Romanov dynasties viewed their foreign acquisition.

With cossack explorers pushing ever onward and seemingly without end, and with trade between Siberia and European Russia growing, the Kremlin realized this enormous territory needed its own governing agency. On 19 February 1637 Tsar Michael established *Sibirskii prikaz*, which began operating in early April. The *prikaz* would move its headquarters from the Kremlin to Moscow's Kitai-gorod district in 1670, where it remained until being abolished in the 1760s.[37] Like other *prikazy*, *Sibirskii prikaz* was headed by a *sud'ia*; and similar to those in charge of *Kazanskii prikaz* the men appointed to run *Sibirskii prikaz* were all top officials. Boris Lykov, while still in charge of *Kazanskii prikaz*, served as *Sibirskii prikaz's* first *sud'ia*, from 1637 to 1643. He was followed by Nikita Odoevskii (1643–6), Aleksei Trubetskoi (1646–62), Rodion Streshnev (1663–80), Prince Ivan Repnin (1680–97), the Dutch merchant and chairman of the Boyar Council Andrei Vinius (1697–1703) and Fedor Romodanovskii (1704–5), previously in charge of *Preobrazhenskii prikaz*, Peter the Great's major police organ. *Sibirskii prikaz's* last *sud'ia* was Prince Matvei Gagarin, who became Siberia's first governor when it was reorganized as a *guberniia* (province).[38] Despite its mandate, *Sibirskii prikaz* did not exert unrivalled control over Siberia, and such other *prikazy* as *Razriadnyi prikaz* (Department of Ranks) interfered in administering both Siberia and exilic affairs. When first colleges then ministries came to replace *prikazy* a completely salient Siberian administration was still lacking. The absence of a single administrative agency for Siberia and particularly the exile system would plague the whole of the tsarist era.

Moscow initially divided Siberia into *kraia* – unorganized territories that when sufficiently populated or if slated for development became *uezdy*. Over time, these *uezdy* were subsumed into larger administrative units called *voevodstva*, whose top officials (*voevody*) were typically nobles with bureaucratic or military experience. As the tsar's plenipotentiaries, *voevody* often ignored *Sibirskii prikaz* officials and provoked jurisdictional conflicts. Siberian *voevody's* functions were limited at first; yet by the late seventeenth century they had acquired significant power. Initially, no restrictions were put on the lengths of their terms, but in 1621 Tsar Michael reduced them to two years in an effort to curtail corruption. Term lengths doubled in 1653; and in 1695 Peter fixed them at between four and six years.

So heavily did the tsars rely on *voevody* to govern Siberia that their relationship was quasi-feudal. Much of the *voevody's* power turned on the absence in Siberia of landowners who elsewhere normally staffed organs of self-government. In Siberia, almost all non-clerical positions were staffed by military officers, and until 1917 civil society there remained more regimented than elsewhere in Russia. During the seventeenth and eighteenth centuries *voevody's* major responsibility was to provide furs for the state. All other duties were organized around this. They were required to explore, survey and designate lands for peasant settlement and oversee agricultural production to provision soldiers and administrators. Moscow authorized *voevody* to raise their own military forces of cossacks and *strel'tsy* from among local peasants and natives; to adjudicate legal disputes; and in some cases even to conduct diplomacy with the Mongols, Kazakhs, Kalmyks and Manchus. Individual Siberian *voevody's* powers varied greatly depending on the issues and personalities involved, but as a group they possessed greater authority than their European Russian counterparts.

Compounding jurisdictional conflicts between *voevody* and *prikaz* officials was corruption. 'Siberia was the sore spot of the provincial administration,' writes Robert Crummey. 'Given the great distance from Moscow, the central bureaucracy could not exercise any measure of effective control over local officials, and scandals were common.'[39] How often *voevody* abused their authority is in fact difficult to ascertain given the patchy documentation. Basil Dmytryshyn believes they generally conducted their responsibilities as ordered. Pointing out that Moscow could exert leverage by sending investigators and controlling supplies, he argues for a strong link between center and periphery.[40] But whereas numerous instructions sent by the tsars to *voevody* are to be found in the archives, it is quite another matter to determine whether or not *voevody* faithfully executed them. Moreover, their clandestine activities would have for the most part escaped documentation. Referring to all Muscovite *voevody*, J. Michael Hittle writes, 'Many became, in the space of a few months, local satraps, greedily gouging their hapless subjects';[41] and Lantzeff and others insist Siberian *voevody* were exceptionally problematic in this regard. In the end, it can be safely said that when Eniseisk *voevoda* V. Ia. Golokhvastov was dismissed in 1665 for misappropriating funds and abusing natives, his was not an unusual case.[42]

The major impetus for corruption was the practice of *kormlenie*, by which the Kremlin expected *voevody* 'to feed' themselves by skimming off a percentage of the taxes and dues they collected for the state. Given that it was an officially condoned practice, *kormlenie* renders the question of corruption something of a semantic argument; nevertheless, successive tsars were willing to tolerate only so much graft. Siberian *voevody* saw *kormlenie* as a perquisite and compensation for having to serve in Siberia, despite a considerable average annual salary of 250 rubles. In addition, bribery, though not sanctioned, was like *kormlenie* part and parcel of Siberian bureaucratic life. A typical court edict (*nakaz*) promised *voevody* that if caught accepting bribes to allow prisoners to escape, they would be exiled in their stead; and at some point the Kremlin began appointing dual *voevody* in the hope they would police each other.[43]

Corruption nevertheless proved contagious, with Ivan Zheglov a case in point. Assistant to Iakutsk's *voevoda*, Zheglov was typical of several local officials in leading a gang that pillaged settlers. His particular reign of terror lasted several decades, though it is documents from the early 1660s which detail how he and his thugs assaulted and extorted peasants and *promyshlenniki*. Zheglov's racket was cornering the beer market. At one time he stole 110 poods of rye from *promyshlennik* Iakunka Savvin so as to ferment the brew, and another time stole casks of beer from innkeeper Ivan Pivovarov ('Ivan-of-the-Brewers'). He would coerce peasants into buying his beer by parading cartloads of hostages past their *izbas* and shouting that if they did not come out and pay, he would kidnap them as well. Apparently not a pious man, Zheglov even 'stole 24 rubles and 20 gold pieces from the chapel' of one village. Like many a corrupt official he got off scot-free, which perhaps induced his son to carry on the family tradition.[44]

Irrespective of such monsters as Zheglov, Siberia's Muscovite administrators demonstrated an efficiency and *ésprit de corps* which distinguish them from their successors. Borivoj Plavsic has shown that prior to 1700 a genuine meritocracy allowed those with ability, not necessarily rank or wealth, to occupy important positions within the administration, and he points out that malfeasance does not always lead to maladministration.[45] Communications between Moscow and Siberia show a bureaucracy functioning surprisingly well only a few decades after Ermak. Indeed, had this not been the case, Russia could never have accomplished what it did in Siberia. In a manner of speaking, the state was so efficient at expanding *iasak* that by 1700 Siberia's supply of 'soft gold' was nearly exhausted. More to the point, the Muscovite apparatus made of exile something quite different from what it later became. Although administrators certainly committed their share of mistakes and violations, conditions for Siberian exiles as a group were generally better during the seventeenth century than at any later time.

To understand why this was so, attention must first be given to the non-exiles who settled in Siberia. Aside from those state servitors less than thrilled to be assigned to places like Tara or Tiumen the first persons compulsorily sent to Siberia were peasants. Those transferred for the purpose of settlement and not as punishment were not, strictly speaking, exiles (*ssyl'nye*), but their treatment at the hands of the state makes them crucial to understanding Moscow's exilic policies. Quite simply, Moscow forcefully relocated peasants because other efforts to colonize Siberia were failing. So desperate was the Kremlin for free settlers that at one point the self-proclaimed tsar Vasilii Shuiskii (1606–10) offered '[f]unds for the land and all necessities, as well as financial assistance for buying horses and constructing outbuildings',[46] but there were few takers. Given that serfdom was already limiting migration and that *guliashchie liudi* were showing a marked proclivity to 'go native' or otherwise elude state control, the tsars began to use their patrimonial and proprietary authority to relocate peasants to Siberia.

Despite 1593 being acknowledged as the year exiles first arrived in Siberia, 1590 denotes the beginning of compulsory settlement in Siberia, when Moscow relocated 30 peasant families from Sol'vychegodsk *uezd* (location of Anika Stroganov's first salt works) to either the Ob or Irtysh river in the former Sibir Khanate. The Stroganovs may have requested this transfer so as to populate the territory with 'their people' (recall the 1574 charter), though it was the Kremlin that supplied each male householder (*khoziain*) with a considerable number of livestock and other farm animals, a year's worth of provisions, a wagon and sledge, tools and utensils, and 25 rubles. These and similar outlays to later deportees indicate the leadership's interest in seeing these settlers thrive, and moreover contradict the claim of an autocracy 'disinterested' in Siberia during this period.[47] The result of this first deportation remains unknown, though the state's transfer two years later of another group of peasants, this time originating around Perm and Viatka, suggests it was considered successful. The Perm/Viatka group is known to have been assigned to build Pelym *ostrog* on the river of the same name just east of the Urals. During the next four decades Moscow relocated peasants from around Kazan and other southern regions, typically assigning them as food producers to *ostroga* built throughout western Siberia.

Not all those transferred were assigned as agricultural laborers, how-ever. Some were relocated because they were artisans. For example, Tsar Michael issued an ukase specifying that the blacksmiths Ivan Barshen and Vikhor Ivanov be 'sent from Ustiug to live in Tomsk in Siberia'.[48] In 1637, as *Sibirskii prikaz* was being established, Moscow transferred from the northern trade and crafts centers of Vologda, Tot´ma, Zheleznyi Ustiug and Sol´vychegodsk 300 families, including 150 'girls' (*devki*) who were to serve as brides for cossacks and servitors.[49] This seems to have been the same group known to have arrived at the Lena River the following year and to whom the Kremlin referred when it ordered local servitors to '[p]urchase in Siberian cities supplies of various grains... one hundred *arshiny* of cloth [*sermiaga*], six hundred *arshiny* of canvas, twenty poods of butter... [and] ten reels of wool, for persons of the male and female sex...'[50] Once again, the government's keen interest in these matters is unmistakable.

Available evidence suggests this 1637–8 deportation was the last of its kind, though neither Shunkov nor other experts on this period explain why. At first glance it would seem voluntary migration and natural population growth had, by the mid-1600s, alleviated the need for large deportations of food producers and artisans, though servit-ors continued to depend on supplies originating from European Russia for some time after 1638.[51] Another possibility is that such transfers proved too costly or damaging to the local economies where deportees originated. This may have been what Tsar Alexis had in mind when, after 1645, he cancelled any future such operations. Another possibil-ity involves the impact of the 1649 *Ulozhonie*, whose institutionalizing of serfdom limited the numbers available for transfer. A less likely pos-sibility, though one particularly relevant to the deportation of exiles, is that mortality rates associated with these deportations were high enough for Moscow to revisit its strategy. This is purely conjectural, since evidence on overall mortality rates is lacking. But it is clear that in some instances large numbers of deportees died. Thus Tomsk ser-vitors wrote to Tsar Michael, in a petition dated several years after the fact:

Sire, in the year 1607, 100 agricultural peasants were sent from Moscow to Tomsk to cultivate your Tsarist lands. However, Sovereign, some of the peasants were killed by treacherous Kirghiz, and others died of other causes, so now there is no one to do the work of farming on your Sovereign lands.[52]

Such raids were a serious threat in western Siberia for many years, as *voevoda* reports show. In 1618, for instance, Ostiaki killed 60 peasants along the Ob. Even without the threat of native retaliation, surviving this harsh environment was exceedingly difficult. 'We are mounted streltsy, cossacks, Litva, foot cossacks, gunners and obrok peasants,' reads a petition addressed to Tsar Michael. 'Sovereign, we are dying of hunger and fever on [*sic*] your Tsarist service.'[53] As of the early 1620s native resistance had subsided enough to allow western Siberia's immigrant population to stabilize and grow, though its dispersion remained uneven because peasants tended to cluster for safety as well as goods and services around Tobol'sk and Tiumen.

Such clustering led officials to redistribute peasants already living in Siberia. Officials' use of the term *perevedentsy*, roughly 'those transferred between jurisdictions', illustrates the statist goals conditioning their treatment. *Perevedentsy* were by definition state peasants or *guliashchie* already living in Siberia prior to removal. The first group was transferred as early as 1624, when officials removed peasants living near Tobol'sk and Tiumen to nearby Nitsa. Other small-scale transfers followed. That same year, Pelym's *voevoda* Ivan Vel'iaminov informed Verkhotur'e's *voevoda* that the tsar had authorized the transfer of 20 peasants to Pelym *uezd*, so as to 'augment the new settlement [*usadishche*] in the Gari [forest]'.[54] Later that decade Tsar Michael sent 300 cossacks 'selected from Tobol'sk and other Siberian towns' under Prince Andrei Khovanskii to establish Eniseisk *ostrog*. In addition to providing them with weapons and ammunition, Tobol'sk *prikazchiki* loaded flat-bottomed boats with 'five chetverts of flour and groats and one of oats per man'.[55] Yet, having arrived at the Enisei River these servitors were dependent on a supply line thousands of kilometers long, and so in 1632 *Sibirskii prikaz* ordered 142 *perevedentsy* to be transferred to the Eniseisk and Krasnoiarsk *ostroga* to serve as local food producers.[56]

Moscow apparently sent no *perevedentsy* to eastern Siberia for almost 50 years: during the interregnum it attempted to convert exiled criminals and other deviants into peasants. But continued reliance on supplies from Tobol'sk[57] is just one indication of these exiles' failure to conform to government plans and moreover explains why, in 1682, Moscow resumed transferring *perevedentsy* to this region. These later transfers were quite large. In 1687, for example, *Sibirskii prikaz* ordered Tobol'sk *voevoda* A. Golovin to transfer *all* peasants in his *uezd* – a total of 589 households and 1,494 persons (a figure which probably refers to adult males only) – for resettlement near Irkutsk and Eniseisk. The following year Golovin accordingly prepared what must have been an enormous flotilla of flat-boats to convey *perevedentsy* along the complex riverine network.

Twenty-five *perevedentsy* managed to escape en route from their so-called escorts (*provozhaty*); that more did not indicates they had nowhere to go but the taiga. How many perished by the time the party arrived on the Bela and Oëk rivers is unknown. Another large operation occurred in 1701 when Moscow ordered Irkutsk *voevoda* N. F. Nikolaev to transfer 100 families from Verkhotur´e *uezd* to Nerchinsk. Large transfers of *perevedentsy* continued until the late eighteenth century.[58]

As it had those peasants deported from European Russia, the state viewed Siberian *perevedentsy* as a labor force to be assigned as the situation demanded. During the Muscovite era the primary function of both groups of deportees was to serve as food producers for cossacks and servitors busy subduing natives and collecting *iasak*. In tune with mercantilist economics, these peasants fulfilled a secondary role that supported acquisition of real, tangible wealth in the form of furs. That the autocracy's exploitation of this human capital would incur debts it would one day have to repay was literally inconceivable at the time. This essentially bureaucratic approach to the use of human capital is therefore important as a precedent for the administrative exile introduced in the mid-eighteenth century. Like *perevedentsy*, administrative exiles were not exiles (*ssyl´nye*) *per se*; nonetheless, in common with all deportees, they suffered loss of their homeland and relocation to an unfamiliar and inhospitable environment. It should also be noted that servitors were hardly freer than the people they deported, and referred to themselves as the tsar's 'slaves' (*kholopy*). The meanings behind this word have been debated, with some writers are at pains to make clear Russians were not like slaves in the antebellum American South.[59] But a stark indication of what they took their status to mean is a missive which reported that, while trying to deliver to Moscow a 'Sovereign sable treasury' consisting of a mere 30 pelts, 27 servitors under Mikhail Kashinets 'died from privation and starvation on the Tugur portage and on the Olekma River' between Lake Baikal and Iakutsk.[60] The conditioning reflex behind the Kremlin's use of all these pawns on the enormous chessboard that was Siberia could not but influence its treatment of exiles; the major difference, however, was that its deployments of non-exiles were usually better planned and executed. Exiles were, after all, criminal offenders and other deviants, and so their welfare demanded less attention.

* * *

As of the sixteenth century two types of social expulsion existed in Muscovy. The first, *izgnanie* (banishment), was similar to the Roman Empire's *relegatio* in that it signified removal beyond the country's borders. This particular punishment faded out during the seventeenth century. The second, *ssylka* ('sending away' or 'exile'), evolved out of *vybitie* ('beating away'), a punishment common among townspeople and villagers alike, though descriptions of persons being 'beaten away from the land' (*vybitiia iz zemli von*) suggest that peasants most often suffered it. Civil and religious, as opposed to state, authorities tended to use *vybitie*. There is a record from 1549 of Kirillov Monastery near Lake Beloe using *vybitie* to punish offenders, though whether these were monks, parishioners or serfs is unclear. Despite the distinction made by Fel´dstein and others between *izgnanie* and *vybitie*, those punished with *vybitie* seem not to have been sent to specified locations but probably migrated to other communities or ended their days as vagabonds or street beggars.

In 1582, the year Ermak took Isker, Ivan IV issued a supplement to his 1550 Law Code (*Sudebnik*) identifying exile (*ssylka*) as part of the state's punitive arsenal. For lodging false complaints in court and sowing sedition among minor-boyars (*deti-boiary*), the tsar replaced execution with exile to such 'border cities' (*ukrainnye goroda*) as Sevsk and Kursk. This supplement marks the first legal recognition of exile's existence in Russia,[61] though Ivan was not responsible for introducing the practice of exiling political opponents. While Ivan was still a boy dynastic struggles raged within the Kremlin walls, and Prince Ivan Obolenskii managed to have his rival, Prince Mikhail Glinskii, exiled to the far north. Prince Ivan Shuiskii similarly exiled Metropolitan Ioasaf to a 'distant monastery' in the north before repaying Obolenskii in kind. Nonetheless, it was Ivan who significantly expanded this practice, sending many to waste away on the coasts of the White Sea, the northern lakes of Onega and Beloe, and along the Northern Dvina and Mezen rivers. Other opponents were removed to such peripheral cities as Uglich, Galich and Iaroslavl in the north, Viatka, Nizhnii Novgorod and Perm in the east, and Kazan and Astrakhan in the south. Almost all these exiles were assigned to monasteries that had dungeons specially built to house them. In 1555 the tsar exiled Father Artemii, who had been in charge of Trinity Monastery, to Solovetskii Monastery on charges of heresy. Seven years later he dispatched Prince Dmitrii Kurliatev and his family to Chel´msk Monastery in Kargopol in the Arkhangel region. Jailer-monks relished their roles as dual instruments of God and tsar and tortured and starved their prisoners, though sources are vague as to how many died. By contrast, a small number of Ivan's enemies were treated comparatively well. When Prince Mikhail Vorotynskii and his family were exiled to Voskresenskii Goritskii Monastery in Beloozero, 500 kilometers north of Moscow, he was allowed to bring twelve servants, and Ivan gave him a stipend and ordered the monks to provide a diet of fish, fruit and berries.[62] Thus, before the first exiles arrived in Siberia a duality was inherent in the punishment of exile. Many suffered in full the sovereign's vengeance; but a small number found that banishment to the periphery, far from the Kremlin's watchful eyes, brought surprising benefits.

Siberian exile therefore had antecedents in both Russia's punitive traditions and the state's relocation of subjects across the Urals. These two developments – one involving reprisals against political opponents, the other geared towards achieving statist goals – began to dovetail in 1591 when nine year-old Tsarevich Dmitrii, Ivan's designated heir, was found with his throat slit in the courtyard of his home in Uglich. Dmitrii's Tatar mother's family, the Nagois, became convinced a local cabal was guilty of the murder, and rang the cathedral's 300-kilogram copper bell to summon townsfolk who subsequently rioted and murdered several officials. Boris Godunov, by now acting in place of the mentally incompetent Tsar Fedor, sent *strel´tsy* from Moscow to restore order, and later convened an investigatory commission under Prince Vasilii Shuiskii, which reached the ludicrous conclusion that Dmitrii had accidentally killed himself with his own knife during an epileptic seizure. Claiming to be punishing them for rioting and killing state officials, Godunov exiled to Siberia those Uglichians not executed or imprisoned. Yet he only did so a full two years after the murder. Why the delay?

Historians today doubt claims made at the time that Godunov ordered Dmitrii's murder as part of his machinations to succeed the throne. But these charges, however unfounded, help explain his decision to exile the Uglichians. Although rumours of his involvement in the assassination began soon after Dmitrii's death, a span of two years may have been needed before they coalesced to pose a real danger to Godunov. He may also have needed time to lay the groundwork for what seems to have been a large deportation (some sources claim all Uglich residents were exiled). Whatever the case, in 1593 a large number of Uglichians arrived at Pelym *ostrog*. Godunov even punished the church bell the Nagois rang, first silencing it by having its 'tongue' removed (soon common among human victims), then 'exiling' it to Tobol´sk, where it sat alongside the Great Siberian Road until the nineteenth century, a mute reminder to the hundreds of thousands of exiles who passed by that they owed their fate to an implacable autocracy.[63]

A legitimate question nonetheless remains as to whether or not the Uglichians can be considered Siberia's first *political* exiles. That the state began transferring subjects from Russia's north to Siberia three years before the Uglich deportation suggests they were not. Officials were already assigning some deportees as peasants and others as artisans to Siberia's nascent settlements and surrounding lands. Uglich, center of Iaroslavl principality (*kniazhestvo*), was renowned for its artisanate, and so Godunov's exiling of its inhabitants injected into Pelym a readymade stratum of townspeople, or *posadskie liudi*. In addition, some exiled Uglichians appear to have been peasants, for we know that '30 Uglichians' (*uglechan 30-t´ chelovek*) were among a group Godunov ordered from Pelym and Tara to fields near Turinsk *ostrog* in February 1603,[64] and that 60 Uglichian families were among *perevedentsy* relocated from Pelym to Turinsk and Tiumen no later than 1622.[65] Hence these Uglichians' treatment perpetuated the trend begun in 1590 and was moreover distinct from that meted out to political exiles sent to monasteries.

Supporting a view of the Uglichians as victims of political repression, and as such unique within Siberia up to that point, is that Godunov, according to Maureen Perrie and others, clearly saw their rumor about him as a political threat. Moreover, the Nagoi family's residence in Uglich and the region's status as a principality rendered it a locus of political opposition. Lastly, the Uglichians had, whatever their political allegiance, rioted and murdered state officials, which alone made them, in a manner of speaking, political dissidents and thus different from any group previously sent to Siberia. The Uglichians' deportation, even if it simultaneously served statist goals, was therefore a turning point, marking the first retributive use of Siberian exile.

*   *   *

The nineteenth-century Siberianist Petr A. Slovtsov calculated that as of 1662 Siberia's Russian and European population totaled 70,000, with peasants accounting for 34,500. In addition, he estimated there were 7,400 exiles, 3,000 of whom were settled along the Enisei with the rest along the Angara and Lena rivers or in Zabaikal´e. Slovtsov's figures, however, appear not to include either *Litva* (which signified all prisoners-of-war, not just those from Lithuania) or exiles assigned to western Siberia. Using somewhat more reliable data, Slovtsov calculated that 19,856 men and 8,728 women were exiled during the period 1662–1709, by the end of which Siberia had a Russian and European population of 152,778 men and 76,439 women.[66]

Despite these figures, lack of data renders any effort to identify the class origins and crimes of those exiled during the Muscovite era difficult. Archival records are so disparate, vague and full of imprecise and unclear terminology that historians of this period admit to difficulty even in identifying who was and was not an exile. An ethnography of the exilic population is further hindered by the fact that many originally assigned to one function, say farming, ended up performing another, such as soldiering. The taxonomy which follows, while being nominally sound, therefore forms something of a proximate model of Siberia's exilic population.

I have categorized exiles according to the general nature of their offences: political, religious or (usually violent) criminal acts. For heuristic purposes, 'political exiles' include notables perceived by the sovereign as threatening; prisoners-of-war (i.e. Litva); and participants in such popular uprisings as those led by Ivan Bolotnikov and Stenka Razin. 'Religious exiles' include clerics deemed to have violated either church or state law, as well as non-clerics charged with violating church law. The final category of 'criminal exiles' is rather loose and includes those who broke state laws as well as all those who do not conveniently fit into the first two categories. I refer to exiles in this latter category as 'criminals', but this is a nominative and not necessarily descriptive term. Sources make distinguishing between outraged peasants, townspeople and Cossacks who supported Bolotnikov, on the one hand, and bandits who robbed caravans, on the other, nearly impossible because the state typically charged both groups with 'brigandage' (*razboistvo*); but where context strongly suggests those exiled as brigands were at least partially motivated by opposition to the state, I tend to consider them 'political exiles', to which category we now turn.

Political exiles

Several years after ridding himself of the residents of Uglich, Boris Godunov, now tsar, exiled the first nobles to Siberia in an effort to clear the political playing field. Hence Ivan and Vasilii Romanov, uncles of Godunov's eventual successor, Michael, and brothers of Moscow's patriarch Filaret, joined the Uglichians in Pelym in 1599. Elite status resulted in their being treated much more harshly than their forebears: Godunov ordered both to be held in dungeons, where Vasilii perished in 1601; Ivan was, however, allowed to return to Moscow that same year, where he held important government posts until his death 40 years later.

Godunov personally banished minor figures as well. In 1604 he exiled to Tobol´sk the *strelets* (arquebusier) Stepan Kachalov who, according to Müller, was related to 'Nikita Kachalov, one of those whom Boris had gotten to agree to the murder of the tsarevich', but who had since fallen out of favor. The royal formula 'in our disfavor' (*v nashei opale*) appears frequently in sources from the Muscovite era and denotes political repression. It was given as the reason for banishing 35 individuals to Tomsk *uezd* in 1608.[67]

After Godunov the Romanovs expanded the practice of exiling political opponents. In 1620 the Kremlin exiled the Poles Samson Nawatskij and Anton Dobrynskij to Tobol´sk. Ordered into 'the sovereign's service' (*gosudar´evo sluzhba*), they participated in expeditions along the Lower Tungus and Lena rivers.[68] Nine years later Tobol´sk's dual *voevody* A. N. Trubetskoi and I. V. Volynskii sent Tsar Michael a long list of men and their families who had been exiled either to the peasantry or to serve as cossacks, including:

> Fedka Sholomov with his wife, son, and brother Mishka; Larka Grigor´ev with his wife, son, and nephew...the immigrant [*vykhodets*] Circassian Oleshka Liatskovskoi and the Circassian Senka Mikitin...the Don Cossack Optiushka Zotov [etc., were removed] from Moscow to Tobolesk [Tobol´sk], to Siberia, by a *d´iak*.[69]

Some on this list, including Zotov, were previously held in jail. Following Tsar Alexis' ascent to the throne in 1645 'Siberian *ostroga* little by little began to assume an importance as state prisons,' writes Sergei Maksimov, 'and by the end of this ruler's reign possessed a large supply of political exiles.'[70] Indeed, in January of that year Eniseisk ataman Nikifor Galkin reported, 'in the new Iakutsk *ostrog* there are seven prisons, and in these prisons are many servitors, traders, and *promyshlenniki*, more than 100 people, and all the prisons are full.'[71] Two years later Alexis ordered Mangazeia *voevoda* Fedor Baikov

> to establish an *ostrog* and strengthen...the prison to incarcerate local Mangazeians of all types and travelers, as well as traders and *promyshlenniki*, not just for a year but as is possible considering the affairs there, so that there be no more offences [*oskorbleniia*] by the servitors in the city and *ostrog* of Mangazeia.[72]

Political exiles suffered more during the seventeenth century than at any other time under the tsars. In 1668 Tobol´sk *voevoda* P. I. Godunov sent a personal appeal to Tsar Alexis on behalf of the former *strelets* and now cossack Iakov Shul´gin, who with his family had been in Iakutsk *ostrog* for several years. 'Iakov,' he wrote, 'with his wife and children...now, without you, great sovereign, without money and without bread and salt and without a daily ration...goes from house to house begging for alms, dying of starvation.'[73] When the same tsar exiled Old Believers Senka Alekseev and Vaska Novogorodtsov to Iakutsk on charges of mutiny, he ordered them 'kept under heavy guard and chained in an earthen prison, so that no one can visit them and their evil knowledge cannot be spread'.[74] (During the Muscovite era particularly threatening offenders were incarcerated in earthen dugouts. Hence the archpriest and schismatic Avvakum, discussed below, spent many years in one in Pustozersk, in Russia's far north.) Descriptions of Russian monasteries suggest that conditions were similar for political prisoners in Siberian monasteries, some of which operated veritable prisons, though most incarcerated prisoners in small cells located either above or below ground. Safronov writes that Godunov imprisoned Mikhail Nikitich Romanov in a small cell with a single window, low ceiling and walls dripping with moisture located behind the iconostasis of Nyrobskoe selo church near Perm; and ordered Fedor Romanov to a similarly tiny cell, albeit one located beneath a church in Antonievo-Siiskii Monastery. Sometimes exiles were locked inside small *izbas* (log huts) on church property. Whatever their accommodations they often died of starvation or malnutrition. For example, Novgorod archbishop Feodosii Ianovskii, imprisoned in Nikol´skii Karel´skii Monastery at the mouth of the Northern Dvina River, finally succumbed after seven months on bread and water.[75]

Tsar Alexis' government strove to weed out those who even hinted at dissent, significantly increasing the number of political exiles. For disobedience and 'rude words' (*nevezhlivye slova*)[76] the Tatar chief Mikhail Naumov was knouted and exiled in 1655. Twenty years later Ukraine's hetman (military commander) Dem´ian Mnogogreshnyi ran afoul of the Kremlin when, in a speech emphasized as also being abusive towards the tsar, he declared his alliance with the Ottomans. Upon learning of this the putative 'Quietest One' responded with alacrity, exiling Mnogogreshnyi and his family to Tobol´sk, then later transferring them to Iakutsk and finally to Selenginsk *ostrog* near Lake Baikal, where the former hetman was forced to serve in a cossack foot regiment. Mnogogreshnyi's successor, Ivan Samoilovich, would later be exiled by the regent Sofiia in 1688. Given this prickly state of affairs, even peasants might find themselves exiled for offending the sovereign. The Boyar Duma cleared Mit´ka Demidov and Pershka Iakovlev of the more serious charge of impersonating the tsar during their village drinking bouts, but nevertheless found them guilty of causing 'an affray' and therefore had them flogged, mutilated and sent to Siberia.[77]

Moscow's seventeenth-century border wars resulted in the deportation of hundreds, possibly thousands, of prisoners-of-war, virtually all of whom were assigned to the Siberian cossacks. One of the earliest of these was 'the Lithuanian captain Bartosz Stanislavov' who, in 1613, 'was sent with state servitors from Tobol´sk to the upper Irtysh to search for a salt lake; he found the salt lake and Tobol´sk began to get salt from it.'[78] Captured soldiers account for over half the 560 persons known to have been exiled during the decade ending in 1624; and between 1614 and 1622 Moscow, desperate to protect new settlements and expand *iasak*, assigned all such captives to the cossacks. In 1633 and 1645, *Sibirskii prikaz* assigned 83 and 140 foreign soldiers respectively to the cossacks.[79] 'During the 1650s and 1660s a significant portion of exiles assigned to the service were former prisoners of war,'[80] writes Kazarian, who elsewhere notes that 'the first stage of Polish exile to Iakutiia' began in the mid-1640s.[81] Indeed, within a year of the end of the Russo-Polish War of 1654–67 Tsar Alexis repatriated 37 Poles earlier exiled to Iakutsk. A roster compiled by *Razriadnyi prikaz* in 1666 or 1667 enumerates 41 Polish and Latvian prisoners 'sent to Siberian cities in the service of the great sovereign', including Tomsk, Tobol´sk, Verkhotur´e, Kuznetsk, Uzhum and Krasnoiarsk and other points along the Enisei River.[82] Despite peace between Poland and Russia, as late as November 1668 Moscow was still deporting Polish prisoners and their families: hence Jezop Hrochovskoj and his wife Anjutka, originally from Lwow (L´vov), found themselves east of the Urals. Many prisoners-of-war seem to have been condemned to the tsar's service for the rest of their lives. The same year as the Hrochovskojs' deportation a group of Poles led by Martyn Bartitskij that had been fighting 'in Kazan, Ufa, and other Kazan settlements against the Bashkir and Kalmyk peoples', was sent further east 'to serve the city of Tomsk'.[83] Moscow's repatriation of captives seems to have been selective, though it is true a small number of foreign soldiers were either mercenaries or chose to stay after being exiled.[84]

Not all political exiles accepted their lot. Nikifor Chernigovskii, who, Maksimov claims, was the 'first exiled Pole' but Soviet scholars believe was a Russian exiled with his family in 1637 'for attempting an escape from Tula to the Lithuanian lands,'[85] was responsible for a celebrated chapter in Siberia's history, leading in 1665 one of the most successful exile uprisings ever. Following the murder of authorities at the Ilimsk salt works, to which he and others were assigned, Chernigovskii led a makeshift but capable army of convicts and cossacks to the Amur River, where they captured and razed a Chinese town and built the small fortress of Albazin. Chernigovskii founded his own satrapy, imposed *iasak* on surrounding Tungus and, interestingly, forwarded tribute to the *voevoda* in nearby Nerchinsk. This arrangement lasted until March 1672 when Chernigovskii, his son and 46 associates were captured, sent to Moscow and sentenced to death. However, Chernigovskii reportedly gave Alexis 'choice' furs and pleaded for mercy and so the tsar 'forgave their crime and absolved them of sin, and on top of this awarded them two thousand rubles'.[86] Chernigovskii's conquests were incorporated into the tsar's lands and his followers allowed to become landowners. Like many a political exile who came later, Chernigovskii was enamored of the East, exploring the upper Amur and earning in Maksimov's estimation a place alongside the better known explorers Erofei Khabarov and Vladimir Atlasov.

The peasant and Cossack uprisings that began in the seventeenth century and culminated so spectacularly in the *Pugachevshchina* during Catherine II's reign also provided Siberia with many exiles, as did the *strel´tsy* rebellions. The majority of those exiled as a result of the state's ongoing war against the peoples of the periphery, the countryside and disfranchised social estates comprise a faceless mass about which little is known. There is a record of an exile convoy from 1682 including *strel´tsy* and soldiers, who would almost certainly have been punished for the uprising in Moscow of that year; and these same elements are known to have accounted for half of a group of 86 deported two years later to eastern Siberia. But other documents indicate military deserters were sometimes punished with exile, and so these *strel´tsy* and soldiers may have been guilty of nothing more than leaving their posts. Some colorful characters nevertheless emerge from this faceless mass. During Ivan Bolotnikov's siege of Kaluga the German mercenary and physician Friedrich Fiedler informed Moscow that he would pose as a traitor, infiltrate the rebel camp and poison Bolotnikov. But once in the charismatic leader's presence Fiedler revealed his plan in return for a handsome reward. After Bolotnikov's eventual defeat Tsar Vasilii Shuiskii exiled Fiedler as well as 52 other German mercenaries.[87]

Religious exiles

In 1625 Tobol´sk archbishop Makarii informed the tsar that Pavel Korovnik, a monk from Nizhnii Novgorod who had been charged with heresy and exiled to Tobol´sk, was being held in the city's Znamenskii Monastery under the supervision of Archimandrite Tarasii, who had 'assigned him to hard labor and ordered him held under strict guard, so that he could not leave the monastery and spread his evil to anyone'.[88]

We have seen that exile to a monastery and the rhetorical formula about preventing the spread of evil were not unusual in Muscovite Russia, but this monk's case is exceptional. A survey of the literature reveals only one other figure, Prince Semen Shakhovskoi, exiled to Siberia for heresy prior to the Great Schism, and as Paul Bushkovitch explains, Shakhovskoi's exile was brief and as much the result of a political dispute as a religious one.[89] It is known that in 1622 Tsar Michael ordered Tobol'sk archpriest Kiprian to send cossacks to Moscow to retrieve several clerics earlier sent to Tobol'sk but who had since 'come from Siberia to Us in Moscow without Our orders'.[90] These men obviously did not want to be in Siberia, but there is nothing to indicate they had been sent there for any wrongdoing.

During the seventeenth century church and state authorities became especially vigilant against witches and sorcerers, and this may have produced some religious exiles. Like Europe's Protestant Reformation, Russia's religious schism was accompanied by a widespread campaign to find and punish those in league with Satan. Owing to Nikon's and other hierarchs' political prominence, the bureaucratic apparatus played a major role in prosecuting those who violated religious law. Subjects could be punished merely for thinking evil thoughts about the tsar. Functionaries tortured witches and sorcerers until they confessed, then usually burned them at the stake or beheaded them. Witch-hunts in Muscovy however differed from those in Europe insofar as more men than women were victimized. Another difference was that Muscovy's witch-hunts peaked in the late seventeenth century, 50–100 years later than those in the West. That said, despite widespread persecution, few witches and sorcerers appear to have been exiled to Siberia. Valerie Kivelson writes that while exile was among the punishments meted out to such individuals, most of the cases she has surveyed involved exile to Ukraine, not Siberia; and of those witches and sorcerers Evgenii Anisimov mentions in his study of investigations and torture, only one was exiled to Siberia and that was in 1733.[91] Unfortunately for historians, records from this period typically do not distinguish between those exiled as schismatics and those exiled for mundane religious offences, a fact that renders exceptional the deportation of several individuals to Iakutsk for robbing churches (*za tserkovnye tatby*) during Tsar Fedor III's reign (1676–82).[92]

It is well known that Old Believers were germane to Siberia's development; but the state deported large numbers of them only during the eighteenth century, and so this group will be discussed below. The schismatic colonies that originated in Siberia during the seventeenth century resulted not from deportation but from entire Old Believer communities 'voluntarily' fleeing European Russia. Kazarian mentions several schismatics exiled to Iakutiia during the Great Schism; and soon after the Nikonian Reforms a priest named Lazar and an ecclesiastical clerk and 'heretic and apostate' named Fedor Trofimov were removed from Borisoglebsk Monastery and deported to Siberia, though exactly where is unknown. But with the partial exception of the removal of the Vtorogo clan in 1682, there were no large deportations during the Muscovite era, and the Kremlin sent most Old Believer leaders to Pustozersk *ostrog* (later named Mezen), 215 kilometers northeast of Arkhangel. In short, Muscovy exiled few Old Believers to Siberia.[93]

Nonetheless, Muscovy's most famous exile was Old Believer archpriest Avvakum Petrovich (c. 1620–82), whom Tsar Alexis ordered to Siberia in 1656. Avvakum's *The Life*, written after he had returned from Siberia and was being held in an underground cell at Pustozersk appropriately called a 'grave', both recounts his heroic struggle and marks the beginning of Russian secular literature.[94] The tsar originally sent Avvakum and his family to Tobol´sk, where the archbishop assigned him a subordinate role. The headstrong Avvakum soon formed an uneasy relationship with the archbishop's secretary, a man named Ivan Struna, and when back in Moscow Nikon learned that Avvakum had assaulted Struna in the church during vespers (of all times), he took advantage of the tsar's temporary absence to order him further removed to the Lena region. En route to his new destination Avvakum was diverted to Eniseisk, where his family was assigned to a cossack unit led by Afanasii Pashkov preparing to explore Dauriia, as Zabaikal´e was then known. In a bizarre relationship by turns sadistic and masochistic, Pashkov and Avvakum spent the next six years in each other's company.

Pashkov was a vicious tyrant. 'One day he built a torture chamber and stoked a fire – he wanted to torture me,' writes Avvakum.[95] On another occasion Pashkov planned to rape two elderly nuns his men encountered along the Tungus River. When Avvakum vehemently forbade this he flew into a rage and savagely knouted the priest, reportedly delivering 72 blows. Half-dead by the time the party reached its winter quarters in Bratsk *ostrog*, Avvakum was tossed into the dungeon:

> I lay among the straw like a puppy: sometimes I was fed, sometimes not. There were lots of mice and I'd hit them with my skullcap – the idiots hadn't given me a stick! I lay always on my stomach: my back was rotting. There were lots of fleas and lice. I wanted to shout 'Farewell!' to Pashkov, but the power of God forbade this and I was meant to suffer.[96]

In June 1658, two years after leaving Eniseisk, Pashkov finally settled his several hundred cossacks and their families, along with Avvakum and his own, on an island in the Nercha River as part of an operation to relocate Nerchinsk *ostrog*, built several years earlier. These fighting men failed to sow enough crops, however, and when supplies from Tobol'sk did not arrive some grew so desperate they forced pregnant horses into premature labor so they could devour the fetuses and afterbirth – a crime the well-nourished Pashkov enthusiastically punished with the knout. Some 500 persons, including one of Avvakum's young children, died. The group abandoned Nerchinsk after two years, but remained in Dauriia. Avvakum and his family stayed with Pashkov until 1662, when Tsar Alexis granted him permission to return to Russia. Over the course of their relationship Pashkov's hatred for the Old Believer gave way to admiration, and shortly before Avvakum's departure he formally submitted himself to the archpriest's spiritual authority. Transformed, he died in 1664. 'Ten years he tormented me, or I him – I don't know,' Avvakum remarked of their odd relationship, 'God will figure it out in the end.'[97] Soon after his return Avvakum was condemned to several years in a 'grave' at Pustozersk, where he was eventually burned at the stake as part of the reprisals following the 1682 *strel'tsy* uprising.

Indeed, so apocalyptic was the overall religious struggle during the late seventeenth century that as many as 20,000 Old Believers killed themselves in mass conflagrations across Russia, the first occurring in Tiumen in early 1679, when some 2,700 schismatics immolated themselves along the banks of the Tobol. A decade later 400 Old Believers locked themselves behind the doors of their church in the village of Kamenskoe, near Tiumen, and set it alight.[98] Such protests suggest the futility many sectarians felt in the face of continued persecution after fleeing to Siberia.

Juraj Križaníc (c. 1618–83) was a religious exile very different from Avvakum and the schismatics, though as Dmytryshyn admits, 'No one really knows why Križaníc was exiled to Siberia.' A Croat who attended university at Graz and Bologna and trained as a Catholic missionary at the College of St Athanasius in Rome, he earned his theology doctorate in 1642, dedicated himself to spreading the faith among Orthodox Slavs and accordingly travelled to Moscow 18 years later. Various explanations have been suggested for his deportation, including court intrigue, an ukase banishing all bachelors and newly arrived foreigners and a 'foolish word' (*glupo slovo*) he uttered about Tsar Alexis. Perhaps his identity as a missionary was revealed. The *Prikaz* of Lifland Affairs, which had jurisdiction over matters concerning Poland, Sweden and the Baltic region, is known to have instigated Križaníc's banishment, and so it may have labeled him a spy or *agent provocateur* at a time when the crown was becoming increasingly xenophobic. Whatever the case, *Sibirskii prikaz* agents delivered Križaníc to Tobol´sk in March 1661. He spent 15 years in Siberia, apparently never leaving Tobol´sk, which by then was a small city possessing the usual amenities. Križaníc's situation forms an instructive contrast to Avvakum's, insofar as he was well maintained and more or less allowed to do what he pleased, which was mainly to write. Unlike his predecessor, Križaníc was not concerned with telling his own story but with writing about history, science, grammar, politics and other intellectual topics. He completed 16 of his 17 known works in exile, and after being released in 1676 moved to Vil´no to complete his *History of Siberia* in 1680–1. He made only two brief references to exile in all his works, describing the system as fair in its treatment of 'undesirables'. This may reflect the influence of his own, highly atypical term in exile or a desire to ingratiate himself with his captors. Križaníc eventually joined the Polish army and died defending Vienna against the Turks. Dmytryshyn writes that he may have been 'the only cultured individual in Siberia in the 17th century'.[99] He was at least a prototype of those exiled *intelligenty* who during the revolutionary period would produce a number of works, and so it is tempting to regard him as a political rather than religious exile. But there is little evidence he was plotting against the Kremlin or promoting anything other than a religious agenda.

The examples of Avvakum and Križaníc, as well as those of certain nobles and many Litva, show that, from the beginning, exile did not necessarily constitute permanent banishment. Despite the fact that Avvakum was subsequently exiled again and eventually executed, the state occasionally regarded exile as a temporary expedient. This indicates that in some cases exile had a rehabilitative function, as well as that exiles' fortunes might shift depending on political winds in European Russia. When Muscovy and Poland-Lithuania enjoyed peaceful relations, exiled Litva were exchanged for Russian prisoners; and although a boyar might fall out of the favor of one tsar, his successor might allow repatriation. Ordinary criminal exiles, however, derived few benefits from such political variables. Exiles in this category fared better during the Muscovite era than later, but almost always remained in Siberia for life, unless they managed to escape. For them, there were no pardons. Their sheer numbers and long-term presence render criminal exiles more significant than the religious.

Criminal exiles

Concerning the Muscovite era, criminal exile can be divided between that which occurred before and after the 1649 *Ulozhenie*. Only scattered references exist of criminals being exiled during the earlier period. The nineteenth-century scholar P. N. Butsinskii estimated that the state exiled only 1,500 persons to Siberia between 1593 and 1645, and that more than a third of these were banished during 1614–24. Moreover, virtually all appear to have been prisoners-of-war and not convicted criminals. Safronov considers Butsinskii's figures too high, though gives no reason to support this; but even if Butsinksii was mistaken, it is clear that comparatively few exiles ended up in Siberia prior to 1649. What documentary evidence there is suggests criminal convictions account for the deportation of some 40 people to Tomsk *uezd* in 1608. In 1633 Verkhotur'e *voevoda* Boiashev dispatched 73 exiled criminals eastward to help build Eniseisk and Krasnoiarsk *ostroga*. And between September 1641 and April 1642 more than 100 criminal exiles arrived in Tobol'sk bound for the east.[100] Further information on criminal exile during this period is lacking.

Records for the period after 1649 are not much more consistent, but do at least make clear that the number of criminal exiles significantly increased as a direct result of the *Ulozhenie*. The *Ulozhenie* itself came in response to Moscow's popular uprising of the previous year, when thousands were killed and half the city burned to the ground. Designed to empower an expanding bureaucratic apparatus the *Ulozhenie*, writes Kivelson, 'marks the state's commitment to bind the Russian peasantry inescapably and permanently to serfdom... [and] to crush the varied population into fixed strata...'[101] This and subsequent regulations from the late seventeenth century chart an autocracy increasingly at odds with those it ruled. 'By the middle of the seventeenth century,' explains Paul Avrich, 'the Russian empire had become a vast armed camp, over-burdened with taxation and military recruitment and living under the harsh regimentation imposed by an increasingly centralized and bureaucratic regime.'[102] This situation grew more extreme as time went on, with the conflict between state and society generating a *grande peur* among the populace that expressed itself in the Great Schism and apocalyptic interpretations of natural and man-made events. Paranoia also characterized the view from inside the Kremlin, such that a simple denunciation was enough to convict someone of treason. One could be exiled merely for being suspected of untrustworthiness; and later, a 1690 ukase codified the practice of deporting those who spoke negatively about the sovereign. Fears that sorcerers and witches were constantly mixing potions, incanting spells and using the evil eye (*sglaz*) 'to strike the tsar with melancholia' or with hexes (*porcha*) and other pollutants (*skvernenie*) were rife throughout the court well into the eighteenth century, when it fell to the *Sysknoi prikaz* (Department of Investigations) to torture into confession those charged with practicing black magic or consorting with the Devil.[103] Satan was everywhere, plotting behind the walls of princely palaces as well as in the dark corners of peasant huts.

Such irrationality forms a striking contrast to the development of a rational bureaucratic state striving to maximize its use of human resources, and as such highlights what may be seen as Russia's uneven development. In fact, every society develops unevenly, with varying admixtures of rationality and irrationality. Moreover, development itself is not necessarily rational. In the case of Muscovy, a marriage between the autocratic imagination and an increasingly monolithic state apparatus led to the sovereign's anthropomorphic identification with the state, so that laws designed to protect the social order came to be seen as protecting the sovereign's personage as well. Legal discourse from this period associates specific crimes and retributive uses of exile with the person of the tsar. The *Ulozhenie* held that even the pettiest crime against one's neighbor was a threat to the state and hence the tsar. Punishing offenders therefore became intimately associated with protecting the sovereign, who at any time could override his own ukases to spare a life or take one away. Foucault once observed that post-medieval Western Europe's legal systems dealt 'essentially with the King, his rights, his power and its eventual limitations'.[104] The same was true of Muscovy after the Time of Troubles, though autocracy's persistence and the Enlightenment's limited influence allowed this rhetoric to continue for longer. Ukases issued during a autocrat's reign also reveal his or her psychology, with punitive extremes suggesting high levels of anxiety.

Part of the 'crush' Kivelson refers to in writing about the *Ulozhenie* involved creation of a juridico-penal mechanism that produced convicts the state then used to realize its goals in Siberia. The *Ulozhenie* codified legal decisions that, *inter alia*, legitimated exile's usage and laid the foundation for its expansion. A dozen of the code's articles refer to exile, albeit only one (art. 13, ch. XIX) specifies Siberia (literally, 'the Lena river') as a destination. Two articles (art. 198, ch. X; art. 16, ch. XXV) associate exile with the formula 'to where the Sovereign chooses' (*kuda Gosudar ukazhet*). Hence, those caught in possession of tobacco (the so called *tabashniki* who either smoked or sold the forbidden substance) were to be knouted in the marketplace, have their nostrils slit or noses cut off, and then be 'exiled to distant cities chosen by the Sovereign'.[105] Such cities included Arkhangel, Pustozersk and Kazan, though the numbers sent to these locations paled in comparison to those sent to Siberia.

The *Ulozhenie* also demonstrates the bifurcated nature of Russian penality – that is, between a pre-modern one demanding corporal punishment to satisfy the sovereign and a modern one involving rehabilitation and use of the criminal to benefit the state – insofar as it almost wholly substituted scourging and exile for the death penalty.[106] Mutineers, murderers and thieves were to be tortured, knouted and then exiled instead of being beheaded or drawn and quartered – the traditional punishment. The death penalty was retained in some instances: women who murdered their husbands were to be buried alive; forgers were to be doused in molten metal; heretics, witches and warlocks were to be burned at the stake. Such hideous methods were consonant with punishments throughout Europe at that time, the spectacle of executions in public squares and marketplaces serving not only as a warning and gruesome form of street theater, but also affording rulers the opportunity to demonstrate in full their awesome authority by using the convict's body as a tableau upon which to imprint a gory text. The tale thus told became public evidence as to why the divine monarch, one step removed from God, occupied the throne. If execution was the most extreme manifestation of royal might, then the scourging and mutilation now substituted by the *Ulozhenie* represented only a slight diminution in spectacular impact. Yet mutilation also served an identificatory function that reflected rational bureaucratic norms. For instance, a severed right ear marked a thief, a left one a brigand. During Alexis's reign the severing of ears seems to have been the preferred way to designate exiles, whereas under Peter I the slitting of nostrils, earlier reserved for more serious criminals like murderers and *tabashniki*, became common. Late in the seventeenth century officials began to tattoo a convict on five different places on his body with the Cyrillic 'B' for *vor*, which strictly translated means 'robber', but more generally designated any type of criminal. The method involved using a razor-sharp instrument to make incisions into which ink was rubbed. Tattooing became common during Catherine II's reign, though convicts were still knouted before being sent to Siberia.

Besides detailing tortures and mutilations, the *Ulozhenie* emphasizes as no other document how all subjects, even convicted murderers or thieves, were deemed necessary to the state. Economic rationalism motivated its codifying of both serfdom and exile, and because deviants now acquired hitherto unrecognized value, after 1649 a criminal was more likely to keep his life following conviction, for exile both cleansed society and ensured his usefulness for the state. Subsequent legislation specifying deportation as the principal form of punishment for crimes ranging from the serious to the petty shows the state's increasing reliance on this policy. Between 1649 and 1696 a total of 1,535 acts further defined the legal code and many broadened exile's applicability, often stipulating convicts' families be deported as well to shore up the Siberian population. 'Those thieves and robbers who through their own fault would have been sentenced by previous ukases to death . . . ,' reads a 1653 ukase, 'will instead of the death penalty be knouted, have a finger cut from their left hands, and be sent to the borders with their wives and children, to Siberian and lower [*ponizovye*] and border cities.'[107] Subject to exile were artisans who failed to register with Moscow's neighborhood authorities; receivers of stolen goods; and counterfeiters and their families. Heretics and schismatics were still being burned at the stake as late as 1684; but long before that those discovered concealing them were being sentenced to exile and the knout (*ssylka s knutom*). As of 1679 those convicted of two or more robberies, instead of having their hands, feet or fingers cut off, were simply deported along with their families. A decade later exile became the standard punishment for those making false assertions about the 'words and deeds of the sovereign'. A 1691 ukase initiated the practice of replacing the death sentence for a third robbery conviction with exile and the knout, while another that year ordered exile for *all* convicts who would previously have been sentenced to death. So wide-ranging was the penalty of exile that in 1699 officials prescribed it as the punishment for those who committed larceny during a fire.[108]

If exile's expanding application reflected a more modern penology it nonetheless served a pre-modern function as well. Both the *Ulozhenie* and subsequent ukases discursively portray it as a sovereign reprieve (*pozhalovanie*) or act of mercy (*milost*). One ukase reads: 'His Great Majesty has issued a reprieve, replaced the death sentence, and given [you] life; instead of death – exile'; another more simply states: 'instead of the death penalty, We have sentenced you to exile.'[109] Such formulations in the aftermath of the 1648 uprising and during the Great Schism were important in presenting the tsar as merciful and pious. The use of the plural first person to express what was essentially an administrative decision erased the distinction between sovereign and state, while the illustration of his awesome power to decide between life or death confirmed the tsar's godliness.

These putative reprieves permanently altered Russian penology: exile replaced execution to such an extent that the latter became a rarity in Russia long before 1753, when Elizabeth Petrovna largely abolished it. From cradle to grave, the subject now owed his life to the state such that even banishment to distant cities on the border could not alter this fact. Late Muscovy's nearly wholesale and *de facto* abolition of the death penalty reflected the emergence of a service-state paradigm requiring popular acceptance of, or at least obsequiousness to, government-dictated behavioral norms. And it was by this device that a pre-modern penology also became modern.

*   *   *

If this was the situation in European Russia, what impact did criminal exile have on Siberia? As mentioned, overall figures for those exiled during the seventeenth century are hard to come by. Nonetheless, as early as the 1640s and 1650s *voevody* along the Lena River and in the Iakutsk, Ilimsk, and Eniseisk *uezdy* began petitioning Moscow not to send more exiles and to transfer those already there. These officials were probably exasperated more with the behaviour rather than quantity of exiles, but numbers were increasing to an alarming degree. In 1686 *Sibirskii prikaz* assigned 86 exiles to Irkutsk and Nerchinsk *ostroga* alone,[110] and by 1698 local officials were reporting: 'Siberian cities and villages are everywhere filling up with many exiled people.'[111] Between 1640 and 1700 *Sibirskii prikaz* exiled 1,150 convicts and 1,880 of their relatives to the upper Lena region near Ilimsk *ostrog*.[112] Documentation for this period is hit or miss, and so more than that were almost certainly sent; but this suggests the proportion of family members among exiles and points to government efforts to create a regional peasantry.

Posol'skii prikaz and its successor in administering Siberia, *Kazanskii prikaz*, were originally responsible for organizing parties destined for Siberia. There is some evidence that a separate agency for overseeing deportations briefly existed, but in any case the removal of exiles to Siberia remained haphazard until the end of the old regime. It should be borne in mind that exile was only one of *Sibirskii prikaz*'s many responsibilities, and at first it did not even administer exile so much as provide, according to Fel'dstein, 'a central location to which various reports and messages were sent from locations of Siberian exile, where petitions were being observed and created according to the necessary requirements'.[113] Nevertheless, an exile administration of sorts evolved as ad hoc departments (*vedomstva*) were created to provision exiles and oversee their distribution.

Siberia's *voevody* were primarily responsible for delivering exiles to their locations. They and their soldiers occasionally transported exiles individually, especially if they were important figures; but more often exiles traveled *en masse* chained to each other in a convoy. Vast distances, poor planning and officials' carelessness could render deportations disastrous. Although much of the journey was accomplished by boat along river systems, this could prove more harrowing than on foot. Many died from illness, fatigue or starvation. Few escaped. Many in these parties were convicts' spouses and children, and so if the convict died, their future depended on a combination of luck and charity. In 1685 only nine of a party of 19 arrived at their destination of Iakutsk; four years later a party of 15 lost two members; and five years after this a party of 90 lost almost 10 per cent of its number. Not all who failed to arrive necessarily escaped or died. While in transit convoy commanders often received ukases ordering delivery of some or all of their charges to other destinations, usually as a result of intercessions by benefactors in Moscow. The story of one party destined for Ilimsk *ostrog* in 1698 illustrates each of these factors. Of 26 exiles originally in the convoy, only 14 arrived in Ilimsk: among those who did not, three managed to escape; the peasant Onashka Grigor´ev died in Vologda; a certain Ivashko Stepanov also died there, leaving his widow Nenil´ka to settle (and remarry) in Tobol´sk; the taxpayer (*kadashevits*) Il´ka Kalmyk, his wife Kovroshka and son Grishka were rerouted to Tobol´sk; someone simply described as a 'man' named Vitevskii was redirected to Eniseisk along with his wife Vasiliska and daughter Parashka (all were servants of Princess Paraskov´ia Romodanovskaia); and Vas´ka Blokhin, a scrivener from Nikitskii Monastery accompanied by his wife and son, never saw Ilimsk because someone in Moscow got the family assigned to the more salubrious Tobol´sk.[114]

A major problem facing criminals arriving in the nether regions east of the Enisei was local officials' inability or refusal to meet their needs. Those *voevody* who begged Moscow to stop sending exiles complained they had neither food nor arable land to offer them. Their excuses may actually have been valid, given that agriculture was slow to develop in eastern Siberia, local indigenes refused to become farmers and servitors are known to have remained dependent for years on supplies originating in Tobol´sk, though even Tobol´sk and other sites in western Siberia were often unable to produce sufficient food surpluses, and so the logistical connection sometimes extended all the way to European

Russia. Moscow's 1653 order to Tomsk *voevoda* Nikifor Nashchokin to buy draught horses for both his and the Lena region reflects the center's cognitive dissonance regarding the periphery. Nashchokin's eloquent response: 'There's no money in the Tomsk treasury.'[115] That arable land could be lacking in a region so enormous may seem perverse; but land suitable for agriculture was what counted, and besides, officials had to survey and designate plots before exiles could be assigned to clear and sow. While the bureaucracy threw its weight around red tape hampered efforts to settle Siberia, and *voevody* with exiles on their hands had to await Moscow's approval before settling them on land right in front of their eyes. Quite unlike the American, the Siberian frontier was closed, not open, and so *voevody* in such locations as Ilimsk and Iakutsk *uezdy* sought to conserve good land and maximize agricultural production through such draconian measures as expelling bachelors or families with too many sick or elderly members. These outcasts sometimes made a life for themselves by joining other estates (bachelors typically joined the servitors), but many succumbed to the elements.

An account of the first exiles sent to the Lena region shows how dire the situation could be.[116] In 1641 *Sibirskii prikaz* cobbled together a group of 188 Ukrainians (*cherkasy*), 93 of whom were men (apparently criminals), and exiled them to Sviiazhsk, Kurmysh, Iadrin, Tsarev-Sanchiurskii, Kokshanskii, Chebokasary, Koz´modem´iansk and Iarensk – all in the Kazan-Volga region, which the state wanted to populate with Slavs to offset the indigenous Tatar population. Once there, the married men went to work in the fields while the bachelors filled the ranks of the *strel´tsy* and other servitor positions. In February 1642 Tsar Michael ordered Iakutsk *voevoda* Petr P. Golovin to transport these people to the Lena River and fix them up as that region's first peasants. This was no spur-of-the-moment decision, for in 1638, the year Iakutsk *voevodstva* was established, Moscow was told:

> It is possible to procure great wealth for the Sovereign from these distant and inaccessible lands. It would be possible to introduce agriculture in areas along the Lena, Angara and Oka rivers, and a detachment of troops could bring these settlements into eternal servitude under the mighty hand of the Tsar.[117]

As ice broke on the Volga, Golovin readied the Ukrainians and delivered them to Kazan, whence by following the Kama River they were passed

on to Verkhotur´e *voevoda* Prince Nikifor F. Meshcherskii and his assistant Semen Zviagin, who forwarded them along the Tavda to Tobol´sk.
Tobol´sk's dual *voevody* Prince Petr I. Pronskii and Fedor I. Lovchinov
provisioned the exiles with tools, food and money, then delivered them
to Eniseisk. The group was proceeding fairly well but, observes Safronov,
'excruciatingly slowly'. The effects would be felt soon enough.

A year and half after leaving Kazan the exiles arrived in Eniseisk in late
1643 to begin the crucial phase of their saga. In Eniseisk, *voevoda* Osip G.
Anichov settled the exiles 'in the corners' of local homes while two assist-
ants traveled east to survey the land, set up food caches and arrange for
the draught horses they would need. In summer 1644 Anichov delivered
them to the portage between the Lena and Ilim rivers near Ilimsk. For
some reason, only now did Iakutsk *voevoda* Golovin, the man initially
responsible for organizing the deportation, realize Tobol´sk had provided
the exiles with just 220 *chetverti* of grain, a quantity sufficient for just six
months, and only 200 rubles, not enough to purchase all the draught
horses they would need. Why this was not realized earlier is unclear,
though somewhere along the line mis-communication must have played
a role. Unable to continue, the exiles were forced to winter in the portage before returning to Eniseisk, where according to documents they
'lived on alms...among the households'. Anichov cancelled a transfer of 20 of these families, some 77 persons, planned for spring 1645,
because Golovin was now refusing to have anything to do with them.
Perhaps he did not want the responsibility for these charges, riddled as
they were by sickness and entirely without means. With nowhere to go,
the refugees (who included Ivan and Ovdot´itsa Oskutin's newborn son,
an eleven year-old girl named Annitsa Moiseeva and many other children) remained in Eniseisk on a food stipend of 1½ poods of grain per
month for adults and ½ pood for children. That summer, after Tobol´sk
sent more grain, barley, oats and tools (the exiles had probably traded the
originals for food), Iakutsk *voevoda* Vasilii N. Pushkin led 20 families (66
persons) into the Lena portage once again. During the 13-week journey
along the Enisei, Verkhniaia Tunguska and Ilim rivers oarsmen managed
to lose half their supplies overboard. This and their late arrival in September forced the exiles to winter yet again in the portage, where, according
to official reports, many 'died of hunger, with nothing to eat or drink'.

When May arrived and the rivers were again navigable Pushkin
pushed his charges 110 kilometers further east to the Ust´-Kut block-
house (*ostrozhek*). Here, he transferred ten families to commander Kurbat
Ivanov, who brought them to the Kulenga River and founded a settlement. Pushkin then took the other ten families down the Lena all the

way to Iakutsk, apparently to obtain supplies or to learn what to do next, for after the exiles arrived the servitor Oksenk Anikeev led them back in the direction from whence they had come to establish three settlements in the Nizhniaia Tunguska portage near the upper reaches of that river. Wherever they settled, each family received a horse-and-harness (which administrators purchased from local servitors and *promyshlenniki* at a cost of 10–15 rubles apiece) and additional seed and tools (sent from Tobol´sk and Eniseisk to replace those lost). These exiles managed to become the Lena region's first peasants, and were eventually joined by most of the families left behind in Eniseisk.[118] The latecomers undoubtedly benefited from the lessons learned transporting their predecessors, but faced the same harsh conditions once they arrived. Nonetheless, the upper Lena's first exilic settlements appear to have prospered, which made them the exception rather than the rule.

To summarize discussion of the criminal exile category, two main developments, intertwined in terms of cause and effect, increased the use of Siberian exile. One was the 1649 *Ulozhenie* and subsequent legislation which greatly broadened the number of crimes punishable by exile. The other was the need to establish, especially in eastern Siberia, a local peasantry that would free servitors and *posadskie liudi* from the need to produce their own crops. Early efforts to establish exiles in the Lena region were fraught with mismanagement and an unknown number of fatalities, but proved trial runs from which servitors learned much. Problems certainly remained and there would be more tragic episodes: for example, a 1697 effort to resettle 624 runaway peasants and their families in Nerchinsk was so poisoned by incompetence that a third starved to death along the Ob and Ket rivers.[119] But it is significant that this tragedy took place during Peter's reign. Prior to this, servitors were for the most part competent in at least delivering exiles to their locations. There were problems with keeping them there, but this introduces another topic, for as we shall see, once Muscovy's exiles arrived in Siberia they became virtually indistinguishable from non-exiles.

2
'Exile to the Service in which he will be Useful'

If the nature of the offence dictated to some extent an exile's situation in Siberia, his social origins were more determinant. Analysis of the social estates to which exiles were assigned shows they lived quite similarly to non-exiles in Muscovite Siberia. As with efforts to categorize exiles according to their offences, identifying individuals or groups according to social estate is made difficult by incomplete data. Nonetheless, an approximate demographic model of the exilic population *in situ* is possible.

The types of crime punishable by exile as well as urban dwellers' proximity to state authorities would seem to have rendered this group more susceptible than others to deportation. But the data suggest that it was peasants and soldiers who made up larger numbers of exiles during the seventeenth century. For example, a 1682 convoy of 18 deportees included a serf from Kostroma's Ipat´evsk Monastery; another serf owned by a landowner named Samarin; a nondescript 'person' owned by Prince Odoevskii and another owned by a scrivener named Molchanov; several *strel´tsy* from the Moscow garrison; some regular soldiers; and others. Similarly, of the 86 exiles known to have been assigned to Irkutsk and Nerchinsk *ostroga* in 1684, 36 were state or landowners' peasants or domestic serfs, but 39 were *strel´tsy*, artillerists (*pushkari*) or soldiers. Half this group originated in Moscow.[1]

Exiles were juridically defined by the estate (and, *mutatis mutandis*, the function) to which they were assigned. Such phrases as 'exile to the service in which he will be useful' and 'assign to the rank [*chin*] in which he will be useful' appear in the *Ulozhenie* and other legal documents.[2] Broadly speaking, Moscow assigned exiles to one of three estates: state peasantry (*gosudarstvennye krest´iane*); townspeople (merchants, artisans and workers, collectively known as *posadskie liudi*);

servitors (*sluzhilye liudi*), including administrators, cossacks, *strel´tsy* and soldiers. These estates emerged during the sixteenth century as discrete 'fiscal-administrative units' and had evolved into generally recognized social designators,[3] though in practice their functions often overlapped, especially in Siberia, where individuals did whatever was necessary to survive. Exiles were given their assignments at the time of their conviction; but over time officials in Siberia increasingly ignored judicial guidelines under the pressure of administrative exigencies, and so a wide gap emerged between the letter of the law and practice. All Siberian exiles were funneled through Tobol´sk, whose administrators distributed them first to new and sparsely populated sites, and second as 'cadre replacements' for existing communities of peasants and servitors. Between July 1642 and May 1643, for instance, officials assigned 70 per cent of new exiles to either Krasnoiarsk, the most recent *ostrog*, or the Lena region, where agricultural settlement was just beginning.[4]

Per its utilitarian goals Muscovite exile was not so much a punishment as 'a consequence of punishment, given that it followed the torture, mutilation, and internment of the individual'.[5] Muscovy's exiles became hardly distinguishable from non-exiles after arriving in Siberia: if assigned to the land, they were expected to become state peasants and turn over a set amount of grain to officials; if assigned as cossacks or administrators, they entered the lowest rank and were generally paid and enjoyed the same privileges as non-exiles; if assigned to townships (*posady*), they were expected to provide those essential services which form the basis of any complex urban society. Such assignations rendered Muscovy's penology modernistic, for as Foucault observes of Western Europe's development: '[during] the seventeenth and eighteenth centuries a form of power comes into being that begins to exercise itself through social production and social service. [Power becomes] a matter of obtaining social productive service from individuals in their concrete lives.'[6] Punishment became a more fine-tuned instrument of power, one activated through bureaucratic knowledge of the purposes a criminal could serve. In Russia, the *Ulozhenie* instrumentalized Siberian exile insofar as the punitive phase of punishment concluded with the convict's knouting or mutilation. Having endured this, the convict expiated his crime; yet as the tsar's subject still had to serve the state, albeit in a distant location. Deportation was the transmission belt linking the sovereign's punitive vengeance to the state's utilitarian exploitation. Owing to its early replacement of the death penalty and ever-increasing use of exile, Russia therefore experienced 'a veritable technological take-off in the productivity of power'[7] that put it ahead of the West.

'Exile to the land'

Muscovy's assigning of exiles to the land (*na pashniu*) reflected an effort to supply Siberia's non-food producers rather than a colonial policy as such. Yet barely able to survive let alone thrive, criminals rarely proved to be productive peasants. Harsh natural conditions were exacerbated by the shortages of goods and supplies *voevody* used as excuses for not providing assistance, though evidence that *perevedentsy* were more usually well-supplied suggests that discrimination also played a role. Officials assigned convicts to buttress existing peasant settlements and to create new ones, and registered such exiles as state peasants. They settled and cultivated land which in practice became theirs, but were obliged to cultivate state-owned fields as well. Like regular peasants they were at local officials' beck and call. For example, *voevody* could conscript them into the private armies they used to subjugate natives and to police the countryside.

Prior to Siberia's agricultural development Moscow increased *barshchina* for state peasants in northern Russia so as to create 'food-aid supplies' (*pomoshnye zapasy*). These supplies would arrive in Verkhotur´e, just east of the Urals, whence officials would transport them downriver to Tobol´sk for distribution. The challenges confronting this supply network were immense, and goods were often spoiled or lost. Embezzlement was also a problem. Soon after assuming the throne, Tsar Michael informed Verkhotur´e *voevoda* Belianitsa Ziuzin that for three years the 'bread ration' for Verkhotur´e's 60-man garrison had been insufficient, and ordered him 'to give them Our bread ration for the current year 1614 according to the pay-scale...and written order'.[8] Sometimes private contractors rather than officials were to blame. In 1650 Tsar Alexis complained to Eniseisk *voevoda* Afanasii Pashkov (soon to be paired with Avvakum) about the merchant Aleshka Men´shoi, who, despite being paid 4,000 rubles, failed to deliver salt ordered for Eniseisk's cattle.[9] In addition to problems of spoilage and embezzlement, European Russian peasants designated to produce surpluses increasingly fell into arrears. For all these reasons, the state very quickly sought to create an indigenous agricultural peasantry that would support Siberian servitors in their functions. To do so it relied on exiles.

In his studies of seventeenth-century Siberian agriculture the Soviet historian V. I. Shunkov comments sparingly on the role exiles played in western Siberia. He argues that most who arrived in the Verkhotur´e-Tobol´sk region were bound for points east, and so few settled there permanently. Those who did disappointed officials. For example, in

1600 Moscow exiled 43 Latvians and Russians to work the fields around Tara; 24 years later, only ten peasants were living in the area. As early as 1608, and certainly no later than the 1630s, Tobol´sk *prikazchiki* began assigning exiles to the Tomsk-Kuznetsk region further east. But as in the Verkhotur´e-Tobol´sk region most failed to conform to a peasant lifestyle. Tomsk *voevoda* S. Klobukov-Massal´skii reported that those assigned to him formed bandit gangs and began pillaging local peasants. They became so noxious that servitors, peasants and townspeople collectively petitioned the tsar to urge him to limit deportations to their region. By 1648 not a single exile was working the land in Tomsk *uezd* because most had absconded or become beggars. Shunkov concludes that with regard to western Siberia, exiles contributed to the agricultural development of only those more remote regions in Kuznetsk *uezd*, though he provides no figures on how many settled there.[10] Müller's account supports Shunkov by showing that peasants who had been settled along the Tagil and Mugai rivers in Verkhotur´e *uezd* refused to remain there. It is not clear if they were exiles or not, but their proximity to both European Russia and the nearby Murzinsk settlement, where several fugitive exiles were reportedly captured, seems to explain why in the mid-1600s officials were still complaining that 'settled peasants have run away from the Tagil [River] in Verkhotur´e *uezd*'.[11] Another factor limiting settlements' sustainability during these early decades was the presence of bandit gangs and natives, who made life in the former Sibir Khanate anything but peaceful. Nevertheless, as early as the 1620s a sufficient number of freemen and state peasants were in place to overcome western Siberia's dependence on penal agriculturalists.

Whereas exile made a negligible impact on western Siberian agriculture, the situation in eastern Siberia is more difficult to assess. According to Shunkov, Eniseisk *uezd* had only 27 peasants as of 1626.[12] Between 1621 and 1630 just nine peasant families voluntarily settled there; and between 1650 and 1671 only 125 did so. Given such disappointing figures – in themselves reflecting both the undesirability of living in Siberia's wilder east and the dampening impact serfdom was having on migration – the state used a mix of *perevedentsy* and exiles to establish agriculture in Eniseisk *uezd*, sending the first group of exiles, a total of 20 families, to Eniseisk in 1621. However, it assigned only ten more before 1630; and a total of only 57 families of *perevedentsy* and exiles between 1650 and 1671.[13] The decline in the number of exiles assigned to the land was partly because most deported east of the Enisei originated as Litva, *strel´tsy* or townspeople rather than peasants, though many in these groups ended up living as farmers. Although the overall number of exiles assigned to the Enisei region grew during the seventeenth century and they were dispersed to such locations as Balagansk, Bratsk and Irkutsk, according to Shunkov they made no positive impact on agriculture in these areas. During the 1680s Eniseisk's *voevoda* began to relocate some to the south to serve as peasants for Nerchinsk and Albazin *ostroga* east of Lake Baikal. By the turn of the century Nerchinsk *uezd* had a population of 134 peasant householders (exiles and non-exiles) who supplied soldiers battling the Manchus and Buriats. Yet Shunkov discounts exiles' influence on agriculture here as well. A brief comment by Slovtsov to the effect that during this period 'one and a half thousand [exiles] perished on the Amur [river]' would seem to support Shunkov's conclusion.[14] However, the Soviet historian may have discounted too much exiles' impact on these regions' agriculture.

Shunkov nonetheless believed exiles benefited agricultural development in the Lena region, though Safronov later persuasively argued that the benefit was restricted to the river's upper reaches, in what after 1648 was known as Ilimsk *uezd*. The origins of this region's development date from 1633 when Andrei Palitsyn, *voevoda* of Mangazeia, informed Moscow that 'along the upper Lena and along the Oka and Angara it is possible to establish agriculture'. The Kremlin waited almost a decade before deporting the first exiles there (the 188 Ukrainians described in the previous chapter), but when it did so it was to 'provide food to Lena servitors, soldiers, and *obrok* peasants... [so that] Tobol´sk will not have to send food to these... people'.[15] Because of the Lena portage's importance, its Slavic population grew rapidly. By 1647 local administrators were begging Moscow for additional *voevody* and authorization to survey new fields because 'the upper and lower Lena portage is filled with exiled Ukrainians [*cherkasy*] and Russian people, and no one can establish themselves there'. Exiles accounted for almost a third of the peasants assigned to Ilimsk and Iakutsk *uezdy* during the 1640s. In 1650 Ilimsk's *voevoda* reported assigning 41 persons, including 17 exiles, to land along the Lena and Ilim rivers. During the period 1653–6, 120 peasant families were assigned to the upper Lena, more than a third of whom were exiles. Despite the increase in their numbers, exiles still seem to have been outnumbered by non-exiles who, if not assigned to the peasantry, nonetheless lived off the land. For example, *promyshlenniki* accounted for 39 of the 64 agriculturalists known to be living in Ilimsk *uezd* during the mid-1650s; exiles made up just 21 of this total.[16] In the end, the distinguishing factor between those exiled along the upper Lena and Ilim rivers and those 'assigned to the land' elsewhere in Siberia was that the former stayed where they were. Why they did so is not clear. They may simply have had nowhere else to go and moreover found it possible to survive where they were.

By contrast, nearly every one of those assigned north of Ilimsk to Iakutsk *uezd* refused to serve as peasants. No matter how many exiles the administration sent they fled in droves, usually to participate in the still lucrative fur trade. These exiles were so wilful that Iakutsk's *voevody* repeatedly asked Moscow to send them *perevedentsy* instead. Moscow refused, probably because it did not want to waste its more valuable state peasants on a region renowned for its low agricultural yield. During the late seventeenth century it persisted in increasing the number of exiles assigned to Iakutiia's virtually nonexistent peasantry while at the same time reducing those it sent elsewhere. As of 1700 Iakutsk *voevody* oversaw five peasant villages containing a total of only 600 male and female 'souls' cultivating a mere 40 *desiatiny* of state land and 300 of their own. Traders, *promyshlenniki* and others who traveled to Iakutiia knew to bring with them a year's supply of foodstuffs, which they often procured from the more productive (exile-) peasants of Ilimsk *uezd*.[17]

What was life like for exiles assigned to the land? If they did not flee, they generally lived like other Siberian peasants. Much of Siberia's landscape is forested and mountainous and poses a challenge to agriculture, especially east of the Enisei. *Sibirskii prikaz* would assign land on the basis of its *probable* suitability for farming – suitability later confirmed or denied after exiles (sometimes *perevedentsy*) were delivered to these locations. Success betokened more deportees; though failure, as in the case of Iakutsk *uezd*, did not necessarily rule out sending more. Administrators kept a firm grip over land allocation, and settlement was tightly regulated if not always well planned. However, some freemen did settle outside state control; and the landscape's sheer breadth combined with the small number of authorities meant that peasants, exiles or not, could often leave assigned locations with impunity. In addition to the landscape, violence hampered agricultural development. Because they were typically the first to settle in remote areas exiles were more likely than non-exiles to suffer attacks by indigenes. In August 1634, 1,000 Kirghiz descended by water and land routes on Krasnoiarsk. Most of the garrison had gone to procure supplies in Eniseisk and so only 120 men were left to defend the *ostrog*, but they staved off the assault and lost only twelve servitors and four exiles. The surrounding countryside, however, fared much worse. '[S]everal villages were burned to the ground, 30 agricultural peasants and 40 Tatars were killed, and many others were taken prisoner,' writes Müller.[18] Indeed, as late as 1653, Kuchum's grandsons Bugai, Kuchuk and Kansuer were raiding peasant villages around Tiumen, the first area the Russians settled.[19]

Aside from human factors, a site's accessibility and the quality of its soil were major determinants in a settlement's fate. Rye was Siberia's principal crop, though oats, barley, cabbages and potatoes were also grown. In eastern Siberia tracts along the Enisei River between Eniseisk and Krasnoiarsk and along the Verkhniaia Tunguska, Angara and Ilim rivers proved most fecund. 'By the end of the seventeenth century,' writes A. P. Kopylov, 'there were 928 state peasant and 84 monastic peasant householders in Eniseisk *uezd*'. The success of Eniseisk agriculture was not immediate, however, for these peasants faced greater challenges than those in western Siberia. For instance, Eniseisk peasants sent a petition to Tsar Michael in 1641: 'for 7 years our grain has not grown, and last year the seeds did not sprout.' Yet shortly thereafter they 'achieved their first successes', according to Kopylov, and by 1646 Eniseisk had become the center of food production and trade in eastern Siberia, supplying 'Iakutsk, Ilimsk, Daursk *ostrog*, Krasnoiarsk, and Mangazeia'.[20]

Local market forces combined with access to supply lines originating in Tobol´sk or European Russia also influenced peasants' lives. Both agricultural and material goods were more expensive along the Lena than anywhere else in Siberia, and peasants benefited and suffered accordingly. Because agriculture hardly existed downriver, peasants along the upper Lena profited handsomely from the rye they sold to servitors and *promyshlenniki* travelling north. Whereas Eniseisk's peasants earned 50 kopeks per pood of rye, the Lena's got three times as much. The difference between Eniseisk's and Iakutiia's economies is also evident when comparing prices for horses. During the late seventeenth century a horse cost 3–4 rubles in European Russia and 5–6 in Eniseisk; but in Iakutsk *ostrog* they sold for 15–20 apiece, and in the Lena portage, where draught horses were especially valuable, a horse cost as much as 30 rubles. Iakutsk officials complained to Moscow in 1646 that Eniseisk's prices were exorbitant, but little seems to have changed since Eniseisk horse dealers knew they controlled the market.[21]

Although not serfs, Siberia's peasants had to fulfil service obligations for the state. In general, writes L. M. Goriushkin, the seventeenth-century Siberian peasant had to sow 'one *desyatina* (1.09 hectares) of land out of five for the benefit of the treasury'.[22] Other sources indicate the ratio of state plots (*desiatinnye pashni*) to those of peasants varied widely between regions. In the Lena portage, because of its lower yields, the average peasant sowed three *desiatiny* for the state and nine for himself. Moscow may have demanded each peasant work state lands of this or another size, but in eastern Siberia especially, peasants neither strictly observed nor did administrators consistently enforce this. As a result, in Iakutsk *uezd*, where agriculture was more difficult than anywhere else, peasant plots outnumbered state plots by more than seven to one. There were instances when the state reduced its demands. The Kremlin sometimes allowed exiles to work just half a *desiatina* of state land instead of the full *desiatina* mentioned by Goriushkin. Fel´dstein approvingly notes that this allowed exiles 'to free themselves in the first year from economic demands and in succeeding years from the incidents of bad harvests', though few remained long enough for these meliorations to take effect.[23] Even when exiles remained, their livelihoods, like those of regular peasants, were hobbled by 'especially oppressive... service and labor obligations (*naturalnye povinnosti*),' according to Goriushkin,

> such as upkeep and repair of roads, bridges, and ferries; provision of horses for transport of official personages; supervision of and furnishing of supplies to exile convoys and transit prisons; fire-fighting services in crown- and state-owned forests; and the gathering and storage of grain in case of poor harvests.[24]

Particularly during the eighteenth and nineteenth centuries officials managed these obligations poorly, sending peasants as many as 100 versts from home to perform tasks for which they were ill prepared. Not only was peasant labor used inefficiently, but an individual's time away caused his own production to suffer. On the one hand, by offering tools, farm animals, seed and reduced *barshchina* (and possibly even loans and grants[25]), *Sibirskii prikaz* clearly made efforts to transform exiles into productive state peasants; yet, on the other, service obligations and requirements that exiles devote even a small part of their labor to state fields undermined these efforts. This, combined with the absence of a single agency for exilic affairs, highlights not so much the lack of a coordinated policy as the relentlessness of the service-state ethos which came to bear during the seventeenth century. Tellingly, exile's administrative problems would only worsen over time.

Ultimately, exile to the land during the Muscovite era was successful only in removing undesirables and russifying Siberia's population. Administratively and economically it was a failure, with the important exception of the upper Lena region where exiles were critical to agriculture. Many exiles fled their assigned locations to take up vagabondage or banditry, while probably greater numbers joined the servitors or *posadskie*. Especially in eastern Siberia, where Moscow exerted less control and regional administrators were more likely to ignore orders, agricultural exiles wandered off to participate in the fur trade. This helps explain why many of Siberia's mammals were nearing extinction as early as the late 1600s. In conclusion, Soviet historians' view that 'exiles' role in the formation [of the Siberian peasantry] was insignificant'[26] would seem correct. What remains questionable is why, given such limited success, the state refused to abandon 'exile to the land'. Allowing for variations on the theme, this exilic category was coeval with tsarist Siberian exile from beginning to end.

'Exile to service'

Siberian chronicles record that, in 1585, a military detachment led by *voevoda* Ivan Mansurov along with 'Volga ataman Matfei Meshcheriak and his cossacks established Obskii *gorodok* [settlement] at the confluence of the Irtysh and Ob, and lived there in the *gorodok* for a long time'. Mansurov and his men had arrived in autumn, just as ice was forming on the rivers, and this harbinger of winter's approach impelled them to settle in. 'Within several days,' according to one chronicler, 'many Ostiaki who had been living along the great Ob and Irtysh came to the settlement ... [but] the pagans were kicked and beaten for a whole day and at night expelled from the settlement.' When they returned the next morning the Ostiaki set a wooden idol in a nearby tree and supposedly began praying for the Russians' demise. Some *strel´tsy* left the camp and shot the idol out of the tree so that it shattered at the natives' feet. Afraid of the *strel´tsy's* powerful 'bow' (*luka*), the Ostiaki retreated to the woods to consider their options. Chroniclers write that this incident decided the Ostiaki to begin delivering *iasak* to the Russians, though in actuality their subjugation was a decidedly more complex and bloody affair.[27]

Mansurov and his men serve as specimens of the so-called 'serving people' (*sluzhilye liudi*), or state servitors. Their action against the Ostiaki was replayed a thousand times during the next hundred years as Russians continued their inexorable advance across Siberia. The servitor class, or estate, included many other types of individuals, and so it should be noted in this context that 'class' and 'estate' are imperfect translations of the Russian *soslovie*. As Gregory Freeze has pointed out, in the European sense of the words neither classes nor estates can be said to have existed in Muscovy.[28] This is made clear by Muscovite writers' use of '*sluzhilye liudi*' to refer to a vast human spectrum extending 'from

exalted boyars to the great mass of service gentry to the specialized
contract servitors'.[29] Indeed, within the Siberian context, according to
Fel´dstein, 'exile to service' (*ssylka na sluzhbu*) initially meant 'exile for
the fulfillment of any task benefiting the state, excluding field work'.[30]
'To service' however soon came to refer more narrowly to the bureaucracy and military, though sometimes even the clergy as well. 'Any man
below top official rank might be a servitor on some special assignment,'
adds Dmytryshyn.

> Cossacks and promyshlenniks often joined the ranks of government
> servitors on expeditions, and on occasions even natives might be
> admitted into service, particularly if they had been baptized and taken
> the oath of loyalty to the Tsar. A low-ranking Russian government
> employee, military or civilian [could be a servitor].[31]

While it is important to keep all this in mind, a focus on *function*
rather than further digression into nomenclature best highlights what
the service estate did and the roles exiles played within it. The Kremlin and *voevody* assigned servitors to both urban and rural locations and
controlled their movements much as they did those of peasants. Servitors' earliest tasks involved exploration and establishment of *ostroga*,
blockhouses and winter encampments, principally along water routes
and primarily for collecting *iasak*. Thus Iakutsk *voevody* Vasilii Pushkin
and Kiril Suponev reported to the tsar:

> On July 12 of this present year of 1646, we, your humble servants,
> Sire, sent men from Iakutsk ostrog to distant rivers on assignments
> of one year or more to collect your iasak, Sire, and to subdue new
> hostile lands. We sent 40 men to the new lands on the Lama and
> on the Ulia and Okhotka rivers. Sixteen were sent to the Sobachia
> and Indigirka, and 20 to the Kolyma. Sire, God willing, your iasak
> collection for the year 1647 will be as large as the one for 1645 which
> we sent to Moscow, if you will send eighteen servitors to the Viliui
> River in addition to the three who are presently there; fifteen to the
> middle zimov´e [winter encampment] on the Viliui River; ten to the
> mouth of the Viliui; fifteen to the zimov´e on the upper Maia; six to
> the zimov´e on the middle Maia [etc.].[32]

As this quotation suggests, the state required increasing numbers of servitors. Lantzeff calculates that 2,735 servitors were in Siberia as of 1625

and nearly twice that number a decade later.[33] Drawing on seventeenth-century pay rosters (*okladnye knigi*), N. I. Nikitin has shown that western Siberia's 'military-servitor population' more than doubled from 2,181 in 1624 to 4,655 in 1699.[34] As for eastern Siberia, Safronov found that 236 military servitors were assigned to Ilimsk *uezd* in 1660 and 173 in 1695. Figures for Iakutsk *uezd* range from 445 in 1648 to 956 in 1701 (though 104 of the latter were listed as 'killed').[35] In 1642 Iakutsk's customs house (*tamozhennaia izba*), which processed furs for the entire northeast region, employed 839 men. Figures are lacking for the total number of military servitors in Mangazeia *uezd*, which included Krasnoiarsk and Eniseisk *ostroga*; but in Mangazeia *ostrog* alone some 1,000 *sluzhilye liudi* were processing the state's furs during the mid-1600s.[36] With some extrapolation, aggregate data indicate a total of 6,000–8,000 military servitors in Siberia by the late seventeenth century; and that the total number of all state servitors approached 10,000. The percentage of exiles among servitors varied across time and place, and definitive numbers are lacking overall. Nonetheless, it is clear they played a significant role.

Nikitin and others have used pay rosters to distinguish nine categories of military servitor in Siberia: 1) state servitors and commanders (*sluzhilye po otechestvu i nachal'nye liudi*); 2) Lithuanians and other prisoners-of-war (*Litva*); 3) baptized Tatars and other indigenes (*novokreshcheny*); 4) Ukrainians (*cherkasy*); 5) horse cossacks; 6) foot cossacks; 7) *strel'tsy*; 8) artillerists (*pushkari i zatinshchiki*) and 9) 'yurt-dwelling Tatar servitors'. Like the Litva, Ukrainians tended to be prisoners-of-war and therefore members of the category of political exiles already discussed. Nikitin, like Lantzeff before him, concludes that 'exiles from the borders – Lithuanians, Ukrainians, and Germans – played a significant role in manning Siberia's first garrisons'.[37] As of 1630 Lithuanians accounted for over 15 per cent of Tobol'sk's military servitors; and in 1699 Lithuanians and Ukrainians together accounted for 28 per cent of Tara's military servitors.[38] D. Ia. Rezun has similarly found that most of the servitors who founded Achinsk *ostrog* in 1641 'were called "Litva," signifying Ukrainians, Belorussians, Lithuanians, and Poles'.[39] Nikitin elsewhere writes that such foreigners were more numerous than ethnic Don Cossacks among Siberian cossacks, but that even the Don Cossacks in Siberia 'normally did not end up beyond the Urals by their own volition: followers of Bolotnikov and Stenka Razin and participants in other Cossack disturbances were exiled…'[40] Probably few exiles were assigned to the *strel'tsy* or artillerists because of the more rigorous training needed for these positions. By contrast, the lowest military servitor rank, that of 'yurt-dwelling Tatar servitors', may be considered an exilic category, since most would have been forced to abandon their way of life for military service. The overall importance of exiles to the servitor estate is indicated by Tobol´sk's decision to so assign 80 of 108 exiles whose destinations were recorded between September 1641 and April 1642.[41]

Safronov's figures make no distinction between cossacks and Litva, but are more precise than Nikitin's in that they show the percentages of exiles among military servitors assigned to Iakutsk and Ilimsk *uezdy* each year. Prior to the 1680s exiles accounted for between 20 and 50 per cent of those assigned to Iakutsk *uezd*; and during the period 1649–57 made up 35 per cent of those assigned to Ilimsk *uezd*. 'One reaches the general conclusion,' he writes, 'that exile played a significant role in populating the ranks of *sluzhilye liudi* within the borders of Ilimsk *uezd* until the end of the 1650s, and within the borders of distant Iakutsk *uezd* until the end of the 1680s.'[42] But raw numbers were small. For example, only 21 exiles were assigned to Ilimsk during 1653–7; and only 37 arrived in Iakutsk in 1691. As of 1690 a certain Tit Tret´iakov was the only exile in all of Ilimsk *uezd* still assigned to service; and ten years later Iakutsk similarly had only one exile so assigned.[43]

This sudden decline in exile-servitors' numbers in Iakutiia is difficult to explain, but may have resulted from two factors. First, the near-extinction of sable and other animals during the late seventeenth century began to have a telling effect on the amount of *iasak* collected. For example, in 1629 *promyshlenniki* in Eniseisk *uezd* delivered 33,334 sable furs to customs houses; 50 years later they delivered just 900. In 1629 in Mangazeisk *uezd* they delivered 54,600 furs; 50 years later this was down to 7,656, after which the government prohibited collection there. The situation was no better farther east: in Irkutsk *uezd* in 1685 *promyshlenniki* delivered only 1,307 sable furs – a mere 40 years earlier they had delivered 65,652.[44] No matter how many indigenes cossacks took hostage or slaughtered they could not pump blood from a turnip, as it were, and so servitors' numbers may have dwindled simply because they were not needed. Second, even when collecting *iasak* instead of laboring in the fields, exiles were not always the most reliable of servitors. Eniseisk exile-servitor Liubimir Pavlov brought discredit to his ilk when, as *prikazchik* Onufrii Stepanov reported, 'he tried to escape by going down the Amur River, but he had difficultly finding anything to eat and he fell ill'. In summer 1650 Iakutsk *voevoda* Dmitrii Frantsbekov humbly reported he could not meet Moscow's *iasak* quota for that year 'because of the shortage of servitors and the desperate need for them'. Frantsbekov did have 56 servitors in Iakutsk *ostrog*, but refused to send them to collect *iasak* because 'these are men who have been exiled and have no weapons'. The *voevoda's* reluctance to arm and release a group of exiles suggests mistrust and fear, an interpretation supported by a similar instruction from 1663, in which Iakutsk *voevoda* Ivan Golenshchev-Kutuzov urges jailers to 'exercise extreme caution and vigilance with prisoners day and night, so they cannot tunnel out of prison and escape'. Chained to their cell walls and denied both ink and quill, such prisoners could hardly be trusted with the sables of the Great Sovereign.[45]

For the most part, however, exiles blended in with non-exilic servitors. They entered the lowest rank and were eligible for promotion. The yearly pay scale of 6 to 12 r. 25 k. for Litva assigned to the Tobol´sk garrison during the mid-1600s was the second highest, after those of minor boyars and commanders, among the nine servitor categories identified by Nikitin, though it is true that most Litva were actually paid 7 r. 25 k., the same as most horse cossacks.[46] The state presumably offered Litva a higher pay scale in order to dissuade them from escaping, which they could easily do and undoubtedly often did. Nevertheless, military service was not a lucrative career path for anyone save *voevody*. 'Most cossacks received 4 to 8 rubles, 30 to 50 poods of grain, and 1.5 to 2 poods of salt per year,' writes Nikitin.[47] Moreover, although Litva's salaries were potentially high, their allotments of rye, oats and salt were no different from those given the lower ranks. An exiled prisoner-of-war earning 7 r. 25 k., for example, received 6.5 units [*khlebnye*] of rye grain, 4 *chetverti* of oats, and 1.5–2.25 poods of salt (probably depending on whether or not he had a horse). Despite earning less money, *strel´tsy* and artillerists received virtually the same quantity of provisions. Although a few Tatar servitors assigned to the Tobol´sk garrison earned 12 rubles, the majority were paid between 3 and 6 rubles and received no provisions other than a pood of salt.[48]

Salaries were often not paid or were insufficient to cover living expenses, and so rank-and-file servitors were habitually hungry, often died of starvation or sometimes even resorted to cannibalism. At one point during the 1630s a group of cossacks had to spend their entire annual salaries and sell their coats to purchase mounts costing 15–20 rubles apiece.[49] Servitors were constantly petitioning for their pay. Lena cossack Ivashko Erastov addressed a letter to *voevoda* Ivan Akinfov, *d´iak* of Ilimsk *uezd* Osip Stepanov, and Tsar Alexis asking to be paid for the many services he enumerated, from exploring the Iana River to extorting *iasak* by capturing 'young and old hostages' from among 'the Alazeia [River] Iukagirs'. He asked for compensation 'for my service to you, Sovereign, for my wounds and my blood, for the hostages I took, for the killing of [my] horse.... Sovereign tsar, please have mercy.'[50] In 1657 servitor Fedor Maksimov sent the tsar what amounted to a bill for services rendered by his two brothers who 'served you, Sovereign, on the Amur River for four years without receiving any pay from you, Sovereign'. Both had been killed by natives and Maksimov honored their debts to the tune of 60 rubles, which amount he was now asking Alexis to authorize as a disbursement from the Iakutsk treasury, though, like many an honest petitioner, he admitted '[t]here are receipts for some of these [debts] but not for others'.[51] *Voevody* and other commanders often embezzled underlings' pay, thus necessitating the tsar's personal intervention. In 1648 Alexis informed Iakutsk *voevoda* Dmitrii Frantsbekov that 'the foot cossack Mikifor Agramakov reported . . . Our salary has not been paid him for the four years he served on the Lena River.'[52]

Perhaps on the basis of these petitions Fel´dstein concludes that many servitors fell into 'a weak-minded dependency' and became little more than 'wards of the state'.[53] Such a view implies that servitors had a choice, when in fact the all-embracing paradigm under which they operated meant they could be nothing other than wards of the state. Hence the servitor's reference to himself as the tsar's *kholop*, that is, both his 'vassal' and 'slave'. But if Siberia was in a sense ideologically colonized by late Muscovy's service-state ethos, this did not preclude individuals from exerting personal autonomy beyond the Urals. One way to free oneself was to join the *guliashchie liudi*, though this essentially meant becoming either a hermit or an itinerant constantly in fear of the authorities. 'Free people existed before the Muscovite Ivans, *guliashchie* during their reigns and until that of Peter,' Maksimov ruefully observed.[54]

A less extreme way for a servitor to win some measure of autonomy was to become a landholder. To a certain extent, cultivating the land liberated one from the state's salary and provisions mechanisms, though it bonded one to natural vicissitudes. Beginning in the sixteenth century the crown paid state servitors with land grants, and over time these servitors came to exercise *de facto* ownership of their lands to become the powerful gentry which displaced the boyars. In Siberia the percentage of military servitors who received land as part of their remuneration varied between regions, and in comparison to their western counterparts their hold over their land was tenuous and ephemeral. This, combined with the small number of Russian women, largely accounts for the absence in Siberia of dynastic landed families similar to those in Russia. State efforts to address the shortage of women will be discussed below; but for now Nikitin's figures serve to demonstrate the nature of servitor landholding in western Siberia. These figures fluctuate wildly according to time and location,

but this very fluctuation indicates the transience of Siberian landholding. Of five locations including Tobol´sk, Tiumen, Tara, Verkhotur´e, and
Turinsk the latter three generally had the highest percentages of landholding servitors. Yet because the absence of Litva and cossacks among
the categories listed for Verkhotur´e and Turinsk prevents consideration
of any possible exiles in these regions, only Tobol´sk, Tiumen and Tara
will be looked at here. A comparison of data for the years 1630, 1650 and
1699 shows that 1650, early in Tsar Alexis' reign, was the low point of
servitor landholding in each of these locations. In Tobol´sk the percentage of landholders among servitors was as follows: 23.4 per cent (1630),
9.2 per cent (1650) and 11.4 per cent (1699). Corresponding figures for
Tiumen are 55 per cent, 21.6 per cent and 49 per cent; and for Tara
27.6 per cent, 9 per cent and 42.7 per cent. The resulting U-curve for
the period 1630–99 indicates that during Alexis' reign the government
provided few land grants and sought to exert leverage over servitors
through salaries and supplies. Mounted troops were in most years and
locations more likely than foot soldiers to receive land grants: 69 per
cent of mounted cossacks in Tiumen possessed land as of 1699, as did
60 per cent of those in Tara that same year. These figures compare to 34
per cent for minor boyars and commanders and 39 per cent for *strel´tsy*
in Tiumen, and 32 and 25 per cent for these groups in Tara. Most significantly, data show Litva were just as likely as non-exiles to obtain land
grants.[55]

Therefore, while exiles contributed little to Siberia's peasant stratum,
they appear to have contributed to the formation of a quasi-independent
yeomanry which did foster agricultural development in Siberia. Shunkov
observes, for example, that Kuznetsk *uezd*'s early agricultural success
hinged on such servitors and other non-peasant farmers. Other historians have shown that agriculture accounted for the livelihoods of 22 per
cent of Tobol´sk servitors prior to 1700 and that the corresponding figure
for Tomsk *uezd* was as high as 40 per cent. By the early eighteenth century one out of every five Siberian servitors possessed land from which
the state expected him to derive a living.[56] A firm conclusion cannot be
made about exiles' roles as landowners, but in this area they appear to
have performed indistinguishably from non-exiles.

'Exile to a suburb'

'Exile to a suburb' (*v posad*)[57] was generally reserved for taxpayers (*tiaglye
liudi*) deemed for one reason or another too troublesome to remain in
their original locations. Officials occasionally banished such offenders to

the outskirts of their own or a nearby city. But if banished to Siberia they assumed within this, the most innocuous of Muscovy's exilic categories, a (sub)urban existence among the small numbers of *posadskie* inhabiting at this stage primarily Tobol´sk, Tomsk, Eniseisk, and Irkutsk.

It should be noted that these nevertheless remained garrison cities well into Peter I's reign. 'Around the city [of Tobol´sk] is the *ostrog* made of logs both broken and cut,' reports a 1701 tax manifest of Siberian cities,

> [with] an eight-sided tower with a guard bell, an entry bell, and a canonical bell, two lines of pointed stakes, a four-sided tower, and a six-sided tower. The *ostrog* with towers extends 259 *sazheni* around the old city. Inside the city wall is Ascension Cathedral and the *prikaz* chamber. It is 440 *sazheni* from the six-sided tower to the remote outer tower.[58]

The manifest goes on to describe numerous other battlements and towers. Although the threat of attack had receded considerably, few *posadskie* lived in these cities. In 1701 Tobol´sk contained 2,000 military servitors but only 546 *posadskie*. Elsewhere in western Siberia *posadskie* numbered 445 in Tiumen, 270 in Tomsk and 143 in Verkhotur´e. Eniseisk was exceptional in having more *posadskie* than soldiers: 632 as compared to '515 servitors, soldiers, and *obrok*-people'. Nonetheless, eastern Siberia's *posad* populations were generally smaller than those in the west: only 110 *posadskie* lived in Irkutsk, 65 in Mangazeia, 65 in Ilimsk, 59 in Krasnoiarsk and 46 in Iakutsk. Nerchinsk *ostrog* near the Chinese border had a garrison of 470 servitors but only six *posadskie*. Several settlements listed in the manifest including Ket and Narym *ostroga* had no *posadskie* whatsoever.[59]

In contrast to servitors and peasants, *posadskie* appear to have had minimal contact with the state or its representatives. Functioning primarily as artisans in a region sorely in need of their services, they paid their taxes and hoped for peace. *Posadskie* were not, however, immune to the predations of servitors and cossacks who, aggravated by their duties as *iasak* collectors and soldiers, periodically rolled into town to blow off steam by drinking and whoring. Their bacchanalia, especially when brawling and murder were involved, terrified many residents, though a 1623 report by Tobol´sk *voevoda* Matvei Godunov indicates that '[p]eople from all walks of life', including *posadskie* and even monks and nuns, not only tolerated but often joined in 'this scandalous behavior in all the towns'. From their very beginnings Siberian towns and cities had been havens for all kinds of 'illegal [and] un-Christian behavior' according to Godunov, whose list of outrages ranged from binge drinking and concubinage to incest and child sexual abuse. He also relates that, besides the usual goods and services, *posadskie* made available alcohol, women and tobacco smuggled from China.[60]

Their existence as loci of immorality and criminality may explain why the Kremlin refrained from exiling large numbers of convicts to Siberian *posady*, despite sending many political exiles to work as servitors in city garrisons. O. I. Vilkov has found that during the period 1614–24 the state exiled only two convicts to Tobol'sk *posad*, five in 1643, seven in 1661 and two in 1698.[61] No further information exists on them. Similarly obscure is an instruction dated May 1625 showing the tsar sent (*posylka*) a coke-oven specialist (*tsarevokokshaiskii chelovek*) named Meleshka Leont'ev, who was registered in Kazan *posad*, to Mangazeia to become customs chief there.[62] Whether Leont'ev was being promoted or punished is unclear. Virtually no exiles were assigned to *posady* in eastern Siberia, where exiles were prominent only in forming Iakutsk *posad*.[63] Like servitors, *posadskie* often worked the land. As of 1624 more than 40 per cent of *posadskie* held land, even in those Tobol'sk-affiliated *posady* where soil quality was poor. As of the early eighteenth century 30 per cent of Eniseisk's *posad* population and almost all of Tomsk's were engaged to some degree in agriculture.[64]

*   *   *

In concluding this overview of the Muscovite era we may ask, How did exile influence Siberia's development prior to 1700? '[E]xile during the Muscovite Era made, more or less, a huge impact in the expansion of state boundaries and the strengthening of the Russian monarchy in the territories,' concludes Fel'dstein. Iadrintsev finds that fugitives from exile were, like *guliashchie liudi* and runaway serfs, instrumental in settling the Central Asian and Siberian frontiers and thereby rendering Moscow's annexation of these regions that much easier. Alan Wood has argued that despite administrative inefficiency and 'mass escape and desertion',

> [s]o great was the need for all kinds of personnel in the new territories that the exile population in seventeenth-century Siberia played just as important, if not so numerically large, a role in the colonization and settlement of the country as the free immigrants and government servitors.

Dmytryshyn agrees with Wood, insofar as he sees exiles as part of the polyglot vanguard which settled Siberia prior to the eighteenth century.[65] In addition, the reader will recall Slovtsov's statistics for the seventeenth century. His figure of 35,000 deportees for the period 1662–1709 combined with that of a Siberian Russian population of 230,000 as of 1709[66] suggests exiles comprised at least 10 per cent of the non-indigenous population well into Peter I's reign. While not insignificant, this figure in no way qualifies all of Muscovite Siberia as a penal colony. For purposes of comparison, Great Britain deported 50,000 convicts to North America prior to 1776; and according to L. L. Robson, 'Transportated [sic] convicts made up most of the population of Australia in its early years. As late as 1841, approximately one-fifth of the population of New South Wales was described as "bond," and twenty years previously the proportion of transported convicts had been only slightly less than that described as "free".'[67]

Did exile constitute a success if measured by the Kremlin's own standards? As we have seen, exile made a greater impact on the service estate than any other. Exiles, most especially the Litva, played key roles in the suppression of indigenes and collection of *iasak*, but were negligible in the overall development of the peasantry and *posadskie*. This distinction further suggests the overwhelmingly male exiles had little impact on the long-term growth of Siberia's Russian population, since many refused to adopt a sedentary peasant existence and raise offspring with either Russian or non-Russian women. Those deported along with their families are obviously an exception, but they were a minority among exiles. Writing in 1900, the authors of *Exile to Siberia* observed: 'Even the most impassioned worshippers recognized that [exile during the Muscovite era] was rife with serious deficiencies.' In these authors' opinion one of the most serious deficiencies concerned women, whose very absence, they believed, proved them necessary for the establishment of civilized society, since without them 'incest, illegal cohabitation, illegal marriages, and all forms of lechery occurred ordinarily in Siberian life at that time, attracting the special attention of even the upper hierarchy of the church'. This conclusion mirrored the complaints made 200 years earlier by *voevoda* Matvei Godunov, and to solve the problem officials then 'demanded from the local population...their daughters and female kin and threatened disobedient persons with "large fines"'. But this was of little help. However, *Exile to Siberia* ultimately cites exiles' personal characteristics to explain their failure to contribute substantively to Muscovite Siberia. Regardless of government measures and 'even indulgences', the 'great majority of exiles' did not want to live by their own labor but preferred to rob and steal. None was useful for work in the cities and there was massive flight to the countryside, where they often formed bandit gangs. Ironically, however, '[i]t happened that such campaigns [*pokhody*] worked to the state's advantage' by helping to decimate the native population through the diseases these fugitives spread. This was supposedly why authorities did little to suppress exilic gangs.[68]

Litanies of the incest and other 'forms of lechery' presumed to have regularly occurred in Muscovite Siberia probably reflect these nineteenth-century writers' fantasies more than anything else; but their comments about what essentially constituted genocide and biological warfare resonate today, and prompt the cold-blooded conclusion that even if exiles did not *contribute* much to Siberia's population by propagation, they managed to pathogenically *reduce* the indigenous population in such a way that this helped prepare the ground for Russians' ascendancy.

Another consideration is that although Muscovy's exilic population was small, its exiles could exert considerable leverage because the state was in various circumstances quite dependent on them. For this reason, as well as to stave off the always dreaded popular uprisings, *voevody* generally adopted a diplomatic attitude towards exiles. According to Sergeevskii, 'it was necessary to take care of the exile population; it was necessary to get along with them. This they understood in Moscow; but even more so, local *voevody sensed* this.'[69] But this should not lead us to discount the trauma caused by deportation. If not social outcasts beforehand, persons uprooted from ancestral homes and banished to the wilderness often became so upon entering a truly inhospitable environment, both natural and man-made. Many were exiled in the first place because they could not or would not earn an 'honest living' in European Russia, and so when called upon to do so in a land where the stakes were much higher, they failed to meet the challenge. The expansive frontier did allow some to find a niche and survive. But a more common outcome is suggested by *Exile to Siberia*'s characterization of exiles as irredeemable failures, a characterization lacking the subtlety of modern criminological analysis but nevertheless essentially correct within the value structure of the service-state ethos. Like many social deviants in prison today these exiles, regardless of the many so-called indulgences offered them, proved generally incapable of fulfilling those services the state demanded of them. During the eighteenth century the autocracy would put even more energy into hammering its convict population into an efficient labor force, to serve what had now officially become an empire. For some, the resulting tension proved unbearable.

*   *   *

Peter the Great's reign (1689–1725) changed exile and Siberia, as it did much else in Russia. This section begins by looking at the administrative changes Peter oversaw with regard to Siberia and, for the sake of continuity, follows them through to the end of Paul I's reign (1796–1801), before moving to a discussion of punishment under Peter.

It is clear from the changes he made that Peter wanted to more closely integrate Siberia with the rest of Russia. On 18 December 1708, as part of a systemic reform affecting the entire empire, Peter replaced the five *razriady* (divisions),[70] which until that point had territorially defined Siberia, with a single administrative entity, Sibirsk *guberniia*, which incorporated the *razriady*'s various *uezdy*, each of which was centered on an *uezd* city (*gorod*). Separate administrative apparatuses were established for the *uezd* and its counterpart city, a division that would hamper implementation of exilic policies until the end of the old regime. As of 1726 Sibirsk *guberniia* (which then included the Perm and Viatka regions west of the Urals) contained a total of 26 cities (*goroda*).[71] Two years after establishing Sibirsk *guberniia* Peter subordinated *Sibirskii prikaz* to the new *guberniia*'s Moscow Chancery. *Sibirskii prikaz* continued to exist, but all Muscovite-era agencies previously associated with Siberia lost influence over the region. This move indicates efforts to incorporate Siberia into the central bureaucracy, but also formed part of a broader scheme to streamline the bureaucracy and compel each *guberniia* to bear the expense of quartering and maintaining troops on its territory. However, Peter's creation of first eight and later twelve *gubernii* succeeded only in decentralizing authority and inflating the bureaucracy. The issue of quartering troops mattered little in Siberia, since few soldiers were stationed there, but the administrative reorganization did make a significant impact, involving as it did the installation of a governor (*gubernator*) in Tobol´sk who superseded the *voevody* as Siberia's chief executive. There was just one central agency, the Moscow Chancery, to which this new governor had to answer, yet even still, its authority was weak due to the dismantling of the Muscovite apparatus and Tobol´sk's distance from Moscow.

Peter's frequent absences from the capital and his obsession with military affairs further undermined the chancery's authority.

Gazing east, Siberia's governor would have recognized that he alone controlled an expanse of ten million square kilometers, for there was no senior official anywhere between Viatka and the Pacific Ocean. Vasilii Kliuchevskii once observed that Peter's '[p]rovincial reforms showed neither forethought nor wisdom'.[72] This was certainly the case for Siberia, since decentralization allowed a succession of ambitious governors to transform their jurisdiction into the world's largest personal fiefdom. This tendency was established by the very first governor, Prince Matvei P. Gagarin, who formally assumed his role in Tobol´sk in March 1711. Gagarin had the right résumé for the job: he had been Nerchinsk's *voevoda* and *sud´ia* of *Sibirskii prikaz* before being named governor of Moscow. An exiled Swede, Philipp Johann von Strahlenberg, later met Gagarin and wrote that he 'had already experience'd the Art of extorting Mony from the *Siberians*', but was able to avoid the gallows 'by Means of a great Sum of Mony which he had raised in *Irkutski*'.[73] Once bitten did not, however, leave Gagarin twice shy, and just eight years after taking up residence in Tobol´sk he was recalled to the capital, tried and eventually executed in 1721.

In 1719, again as part of another empire-wide reform, Peter subdivided Sibirsk *guberniia* into three provinces (*provintsii*): Viatka, Sol´kamsk, and Tobol´sk. His decision to create the separate provinces of Viatka and Sol´kamsk foreshadowed the 1727 designation of the Urals as the border between Siberia and Russia proper. To counterpoise as much as to assist new governor Aleksei M. Cherkasskii, the emperor assigned a vice-governor to each province. Shortly before he died, Peter created the two additional provinces of Eniseisk and Irkutsk from out of Tobol´sk province.[74]

The Petrine reforms also established new designations (e.g., *kameriry, zemskie komissary, rentmeistery, fiskaly*) for officials serving at the provincial and *uezd* level, who themselves were grouped into regional departments corresponding to the center's newly created colleges (*kollegii*). These terms reflect not only the adoption of European terminology but also an attempt to conform to Western European administrative norms and procedures,[75] yet the transition was awkward and resulted in an apparatus more injurious to Siberia than the Muscovite system. Peter's judicial reforms as well affected Siberia, insofar as its provinces received a supervisory role over juridical matters and *uezdy* acquired lower courts (though supervisory courts were not established in what became Irkutsk province). Finally, Peter's urban reforms of

1721 and 1724 allowed Siberian cities the right of self-governance (*samoupravlenie*), though their autonomy was limited following his death. As did the separation between *uezd* and city governments, resultant struggles between municipalities, governorships, and the judiciary for control over Siberia's cities undermined operation of the exile system.

Following Peter's death Siberia's administrative landscape changed frequently. In 1730 the Senate resurrected *Sibirskii prikaz* and placed it under the leadership of Pavel I. Iaguzhinskii, Peter's procurator-general of the Senate and survivor of the purges that followed Anna Ioannovna's succession. Iaguzhinskii's appointment reflected a trend whereby the new empress resurrected defunct *prikazy* to dispense as gifts to faithful courtiers, though because Iaguzhinskii again became the Senate's procurator-general it was this body, rather than *Sibiriskii prikaz*, which probably decided Siberian affairs. A mere three years after Iaguzhinskii's appointment Anna divided control over Siberia among various colleges, thus replicating the pre-Petrine competition between different *prikazy*. The capriciousness animating these and other moves reveals how favoritism and court intrigue rather than statecraft were dictating policy at the time. Characteristically, Anna gave the Mining College responsibility for deporting exiles, but failed to allocate funds necessary to its task; gave the Admiralty College supervision over gold mining at Nerchinsk's *katorga* sites, but put the Senate's Convict Bureau (*Ekspeditsiia o kolodnikakh*) in charge of the *katorga* sites of Azov and Rogervik; and granted *Sysknoi prikaz* (Department of Investigations) and various local bureaux exilic authority, which only further allowed arbitrariness (*proizvol*) to determine judicial procedures. The sum total was chaos, not just because too much responsibility was dispersed too widely among competing organs but also because neither the empress nor any of her advisers appear to have evinced much interest in penal affairs. The empire as a whole consequently suffered, while Siberia and its exiles were left to the mercy of satraps far worse than Gagarin. Indeed, there really was no exile *system* to speak of between 1725 and the early nineteenth century, which explains Fel´dstein's description of those departments that had any relationship to exile as being reduced to 'fictions'. It is therefore all the more remarkable that *Sibirskii prikaz* not only remained intact but actually re-emerged after Anna's death, if not shortly before, to resume primary authority over Siberia.

Besides changing the central administration, Anna altered the territorial schema of Sibirsk *guberniia* by dividing it in January 1736 into what her ukase simply called 'two parts' (*dve chasti*).[76] The western half was to be administered by the governor in Tobol´sk, the eastern by a vice-governor in Irkutsk. How these 'two parts' corresponded with the provinces Peter had earlier established is unclear, but the move presaged Speranskii's creation of the Western and Eastern Siberian governor-generalships.

Following Ivan VI's brief reign (1740–41) Elizabeth Petrovna took the throne. Although she oversaw important legislation concerning exile (discussed below), she does not appear to have tampered with either the territorial or administrative revisions Anna introduced, with the exception, as noted, of allowing *Sibirskii prikaz* to resume administering Siberian affairs.

Catherine II, however, instituted a number of changes affecting Siberia, fancying herself as she did a ruler in the Petrine mould. John LeDonne has described these changes in detail[77] and so it is necessary to note here only those which particularly influenced exile. One of her first acts after disposing of husband Peter III (1761–2) was to abolish *Sibirskii prikaz* forever and to divide yet again its administrative duties among various organs serving all Russia. Raeff argues that this marked a change in the autocracy's view of Siberia from that of a colony to an integral part of the empire,[78] but as we have just seen it was Peter who first evinced such a view. Nevertheless, Siberia became in practice little more than a colonial appendage of European Russia, as Iadrintsev and its other champions would later show.

What may be called the 'integration argument' by Raeff and others should however be discussed, since this impinges directly on the explanation for Siberian exile's expansion. LeDonne provides evidence that would seem to support Raeff. Arguing that what tied Siberia to the center were the patronage networks of the Naryshkins and Trubetskois, on the one hand, and that of the Saltykovs, on the other, he writes: 'The Orenburg territory and Siberia did not really form a world apart, despite the great distances.'[79] But his own and other evidence suggests distance as well as several other factors did indeed keep Siberia separate from the rest of the empire. First, LeDonne argues that it is more correct to speak of an elite rather than a state controlling Russia during the late eighteenth century. Because this elite was divided between these two major patronage networks and, within these, among clientage spheres which 'privatized public power', any cohesive, overarching power structure that might have arisen was instead atomized into ineffectiveness. This atomization had a geographical corollary, insofar as certain sections of the empire fell under the control of separate and competing power constellations. Second, he observes that many of the governors-general on the eastern frontier were so corrupt they actually 'provided abundant spoils for members of both [patronage] networks'. Hence these officials 'were more than mere brokers' between the center and periphery, '[t]hey were also proconsuls with their own agenda'.[80] All this seems evidence of the autonomy of Siberia's governors-general rather than subordination to one of the patronage networks.

Further evidence adduced below will support this interpretation. But for now, it is necessary to pause and ask, If Siberia was a virtual colony ruled by an aristocratic elite, which in any case had connections to the center's patronage networks, who were the officials within this elite? To quote Brenda Meehan-Waters's characterization of the administrative elite in general, almost all 'were middle-aged officers "retired" into civil positions'.[81] Writing on this same class of retirees during Catherine II's reign, Robert Givens has noted:

> Men whose training and experience had emphasized the arts of warfare could hardly be expected to be at home with legal procedure.... Distance also contributed to these attitudes, so that laws were probably disregarded most often in outlying regions of the empire where supervision tended to be lax [e.g. Siberia].... As long as the nobles [among them] hewed to the well-trodden path of state service it was unlikely they would be concerned about the operation of Russia's provincial government.[82]

Siberia was from the beginning ruled by a military administration; but the Muscovite military administration had demonstrated less corporate autonomy than its successor, either because it accorded the sovereign greater reverence or because a chauvinistic understanding of 'Russianness' had not yet developed to the point that the military looked down on the non-Russian regions and peoples it administered. By contrast, the type of administration that emerged in Siberia during the eighteenth century resembled those that subsequently dominated the empire's other 'foreign' or 'occupied' territories – Poland, Central Asia and the Caucasus. The notion of Siberia as occupied foreign territory allowed for excesses to be committed there which were becoming obsolete in European Russia, and given their tenuous connections to Petersburg, Siberian officials were largely autonomous actors who exhibited little regard for either local society or the center's procedural norms. Catherine II acknowledged as much when, soon after taking the throne, she wrote to Siberia's newly appointed governor D. I. Chicherin: 'Because of Sibirsk *guberniia*'s remoteness, you may sometimes find it impossible to implement those ukases sent to you from Us ...'[83] She went on to grant him authority to develop his own policies provided he informed her about them. This and other evidence incidentally provides an instructive contrast to China's administration of Xinjiang Province, over which central Qing officials exercised direct control. During the eighteenth century the sophistication and rationality of the Chinese bureaucracy was utterly lacking in Petersburg's governance of Siberia.

Further evidence of Petersburg's colonialist orientation is Catherine's re-mapping of Siberia so as to facilitate exploitation of its natural resources. In 1764–5 she detached Irkutsk province from Sibirsk *guberniia* (which continued to comprise the Tobol´sk and Eniseisk provinces) and established it as a *guberniia* in its own right, naming as its governor the former commander of the Siberian Line Karl L. Frauendorf. In 1782–3 she applied the Organic Laws of 1775 to Siberia so as to create *namestnichestva* (lieutenancies) to replace the *gubernii* established by Peter. Under this new arrangement two governor-generalships (*general-gubernatorstva*) headquartered in Tobol´sk and Irkutsk split administrative duties. The Tobol´sk and Irkutsk *namestnichestva* were subdivided into *oblasti* ('provinces' in this context) which included the still extant *uezdy*. The Tobol´sk governor-generalship also administered the Perm *namestnichestvo*, while the Irkutsk governor-generalship had responsibility for the Kolyvansk *namestnichestvo*. Perm is not important here, but Kolyvansk is. As later became the case with Nerchinsk, Kolyvansk was a metallurgical region in the Altai Mountains which the Romanovs owned as a *votchina* (dynastic fiefdom), and so the Imperial Chancery directly administered and absorbed all Kolyvansk's profits.

The final administrative reform and territorial realignment to be considered here are those of Paul I, who on 12 December 1796 re-established the Tobol´sk and Irkutsk *gubernii*. He appointed a governor-general over each; but four months later 'liquidated their responsibilities' and invested command over all Siberia in a single military-governorship headquartered in Irkutsk. The *gubernii* nonetheless remained, as did their governors-general, albeit with responsibilities undefined throughout Paul's brief time on the throne.

Eighteenth-century Russian governments therefore maintained the exploitative relationship with Siberia earlier established by Muscovy, but took a large step *back* from the previous century in terms of administrative efficacy, regardless of Siberia's nominal integration with the rest of the empire. Their expanding use of Siberia as a penal dumping ground provides further evidence of this counter-productive relationship between center and periphery, a relationship essentially akin to the early relationship between England and Australia. Indeed, Russia's overall attitude to Siberia was quite similar to that which England and Spain had to their territories in the New World, that is, Siberia was to provide raw materials the mother country would then transform for domestic consumption or export.

As a result of the many changes just outlined, Siberia's administration was chaotic from Peter through Paul. Yet if the primary source for this chaos was the center, where decisions were (supposed to be) made, it bears repeating that the peculiarities of Siberian society were a contributing factor. A major problem was the slow growth of the non-native male population, which between 1719 and 1795 rose from 169,000 to 412,000. This may at first appear a significant increase; but it remained steady at just over 2 per cent of the empire's total male population during this same period. Furthermore, distribution of this population remained uneven, with four-fifths of these males located in western Siberia even at the end of the century. The Siberian population's composition also presented a challenge for administrators. For one thing, it included a large proportion of indigenes who often resisted Russian control. In 1719 indigenous men comprised 30 per cent of Siberia's male population of 241,000; at the close of the century, when the total male population was 595,000, their percentage was the same.[84] This consistency (so at odds with the American and Australian experiences) further evidences the government's failure to colonize the subcontinent. Then there was the uniqueness of Siberia's Russian population. As in European Russia, peasants eventually claimed the majority, climbing from 42 per cent of the non-native male population during Peter's reign to 87 per cent at the beginning of Paul's. But in contrast, almost all were state peasants rather than privately owned serfs, since landowners were virtually nonexistent. There were only 2,595 serfs in all of Siberia in 1795.[85]

Siberia was also distinguished by its pattern of settlement. A larger percentage of Siberians lived in cities than that of the empire's inhabitants generally. During the eighteenth century the peak (numerically and as a percentage) for non-native males occurred in 1744, when 74,067 (37.7 per cent) were assigned to city estates (*gorodskie sosloviia*). During Anna Ioannovna's and Elizabeth Petrovna's reigns the military built many fortified cities in the south as part of the Siberian Line to defend against Kazakhs and Kirghiz, and this concentration of frontier garrisons may help explain this exceedingly large 'urban' population. Under Catherine II Siberia's urbanites fell to around 10 per cent; yet even this figure was two-and-a-half times greater than that for the empire as a whole in 1795.[86]

Another difference with European Russia was that despite living in fortresses and *uezd* cities, few urbanites belonged to the *meshchane*. By the end of Catherine II's reign only half of all city dwellers in the Tomsk and Eniseisk regions were registered as *meshchane*; the rest belonged to either the peasant or servitor *soslovie*. This helps explain why the 'rulers/ruled' dichotomy was so entrenched in Siberia, in contrast to the autonomy *meshchane* in Russia were gradually asserting at the time. The small number of *meshchane* as well as the atomized nature of urban society hindered development of an autonomous civil society for a long time. Further inhibiting development of Siberian society, particularly during the eighteenth century, was the small number of merchants and the public's disdain for them. In 1797 fewer than 400 were enrolled in the merchantry (*kupechestvo*) in both the Tomsk and Eniseisk regions.[87] This combined with Russians' traditional hatred and mistrust of merchants, as well as the absence of a landed nobility, retarded the growth of those civic institutions on which local self-government could be established. As a result, Siberia's local administrations remained staffed largely by military bureaucrats rather than civilians, in striking contrast to the empire in general, for which, as Yaney explains, Catherine II was trying 'to set up a civil administration in the countryside to replace the army'.[88] In Petersburg, various senatorial departments with little idea of what was actually happening thousands of versts away issued orders to subordinate Siberian personnel (victims as much as progenitors of *formal´nost*, or 'mind-numbing bureaucratism'[89]), who proved unable or unwilling to reconcile their orders with local realities. Add to this Catherine's abolition of *Sibirskii prikaz* as well as her decision that governors-general answer no one but herself, and the way was cleared for the center's orders to be ignored or contradicted outright. Similarly counterproductive was Catherine's inane establishment of the post of lieutenant (*namestnik*), which saddled governors-general with a jurisdictionally competing twin to no discernible benefit, and moreover demonstrates why the very patronage network LeDonne credits with tying Siberia to the rest of the empire actually fostered dual and equally malfeasant hierarchies within the region itself.

Whereas Siberian officials were loath to initiate constructive programmes either because of *formal´nost* or contempt for the center, they managed to embrace corruption with a fervour remarkable even for Russia, thereby perpetuating a Muscovite tradition that now, however, was an especially corrosive anachronism in the age of systematization. Distance and poor communications allowed them to dissimulate and deceive Petersburg; and local civilians found it all but impossible to impress on the center how thoroughly corrupt the administration was because it controlled postal routes and most other services. Even when

Petersburg did receive information about what was happening, the ministers and senators who conspired with Siberian officials rendered it moot. 'With the collapse of central supervision,' writes Foinitskii,

> abuse of the Siberian people became chronic. The first Siberian governor, Gagarin, was executed. Irkutsk vice-governor [I. V.] Iakobi was on trial for several years. [Siberian governor D. I.] Chicherin left quite a heavy legacy. The villainies of Irkutsk investigator [P. N.] Krylov were a blow to Catherine II and are remembered by Siberians to this day.[90]

Let us look more closely at Foinitskii's gallery of rogues. A. I. Glebov, procurator-general of the Senate, was infamous for having sent Petr N. Krylov to Irkutsk to extort wine revenues from local merchants. In what became known as the Krylov Pogrom of 1758–60, Krylov arrested and imprisoned 120 merchants and extorted hundreds of thousands of rubles in bribes and property from them. In 1761 Governor F. I. Soimonov had Krylov arrested and sent to Petersburg where, according to one version, he was knouted and exiled to *katorga*, but according to another was freed thanks to Glebov's intervention. After Soimonov resigned his post in 1763 Catherine II appointed Denis I. Chicherin to replace him. Following the empress's letter quoted above, Chicherin took her permission to act autonomously to the *n*th degree by establishing a veritable satrapy. An investigatory commission later found that he was 'never present' at government offices in Tobol´sk and willfully ignored his duties. He preferred instead to stay at home, a place the investigator G. M. Osipov described as 'untidy' and 'impossible not to be disgusted by',[91] where criminals were either knouted or made to serve alongside hussars and foot soldiers in a pathetic palace guard. Catherine removed Chicherin two years later but refused to bring charges against him for fear of publicizing the scandal. A similar case involved Ivan V. Iakobi, governor-general of the Irkutsk *namestnichestvo* from 1783 to 1789. Catherine removed him on evidence that he planned to start a war with China from which he hoped to profit. He also had designs against Japan. Corruption charges against Iakobi were finally dropped in 1793, possibly because of the Naryshkin-Trubetskoi clan's intervention.

Throughout all this mayhem the aptly named Sibiriakov family was busy establishing Irkutsk's most powerful merchant dynasty. Having survived the Krylov Pogrom they managed to have one of their own, Mikhail Sibiriakov, named city mayor in the late 1700s. Sibiriakov sent numerous complaints to Petersburg about Irkutsk *guberniia's* then governor Boris B. Letstsano (Lezzano). Among other things, Letstsano failed to apportion the correct amount of land for peasant villages; forced peasants 'to transport grain to remote places'; suborned convicts to repair his mansion; rendered Irkutsk unsafe by establishing a *katorga* distribution center outside the city gates; and prohibited use of Lake Baikal for the transport of goods, requiring instead use of the region's poor road network, probably to increase toll collections.[92] There is more of Letstsano's corruption to be discussed, but the examples above make clear that the Golden Age of the Russian nobility was also the heyday for those embezzlers, extortionists, enslavers and other crooks with official titles who ran Siberia like the mafia once ran Italy. Small wonder, then, that those exiled to this massive den of thieves met with little resembling humane treatment.

*   *   *

Evgenii Anisimov has characterized Peter's reign as laying the foundations for the modern Soviet totalitarian state,[93] and so far as such a thing as totalitarianism may be said to have existed, his assessment seems fair. More so than even his father Alexis, Peter identified himself with the state, to the extent that he cultified and fetishized it and *ipso facto* himself. That his rules concerning facial hair and chimney dimensions may not immediately strike the reader as pathological indicates the extent to which the ubiquity of official regulations has become accepted as part of the natural order. Every one of Peter's subjects had to serve what has correctly been characterized as the 'mythical common good'. Given the emperor's *idée fixe*, it became necessary to eliminate once and for all the freedoms still held by *guliashchie liudi* and others who did not fit neatly within newly defined social castes. Passports, first introduced under Alexis, became under Peter the fixative glue for a police regime seeking to abolish unregulated movement. Subjects who could not produce a passport when required were deemed *brodiagi* (vagabonds), and soon formed a huge new criminal caste subject to military police arrest and punishment by assignation to the army, navy or *katorga*. Also adding to the number of criminals was Peter's encouragement of denunciations and his expanding definition of what constituted a state crime (*gosudarstvennoe prestuplenie*). All offences committed or even contemplated were to be reported—failure to do so was itself a crime. Any act not legislatively approved in advance risked being interpreted as a major violation, and so Petrine justice was at the 'highest levels casuistic', as Fel´dstein writes, with defendants' guilt determined by chance rather than the 'text of the ukases'.[94] In short, statist goals ran roughshod over legal justice. Among Peter's many legacies, this subversion of law was perhaps most damaging to Russia's subsequent development.

More than any other European ruler Peter marshaled human capital for the service of the state. Having come to power at the end of Europe's most belligerent period in history, when 95 per cent of the years between 1500 and 1700 witnessed a war somewhere on the continent, Peter inherited a legacy of insecurity in a polity which had utterly collapsed a century earlier during the Time of Troubles (1598–1613). Poland remained a powerful enemy to the west; but Peter's greatest nemeses were Sweden and the Ottoman Empire, both of which controlled vast territories Russia eventually annexed after years of fighting. These and other powers benefited from a head start in the military technological revolution that began in the sixteenth century and which partly explains Peter's early capture by the Ottomans and humiliating defeat by Sweden at Narva. The increasing mercantile competition associated with the development of the world-wide economy also put pressure on the tsarist state.[95] These external threats translated into increased pressure on society to conform, and rendered Peter's service-state ethos as much a part of his grand strategy as the navy or metallurgical industry. His was a do-or-die philosophy by which even the lowliest of subjects was made to serve in one capacity or another. As serfdom embraced growing numbers of peasants and the military and bureaucracy called for ever more recruits and officials, the new epistemology subjected society to the state and commodified human relations as never before. In its efforts to improve tax collection the Petrine government assigned every subject to a social estate, and for this reason specifically targeted the *guliashchie*. 'The struggle with "the free and the itinerant" became part of a whole system of combating fugitives,' writes Anisimov.[96] As Adele Lindenmeyr has shown in her study of poverty in Russia, government efforts to order society continued through the eighteenth and nineteenth centuries with laws against vagrancy and begging,[97] all of which involved a 'de-sanctification of the poor' (to borrow A. L. Beier's words).[98] 'Holy fools' once honored as recipients for pietistic almsgiving now became deviants and louts to be excised from general society and put to use as soldiers, penal laborers or exile-settlers. Were they unable to perform these services satisfactorily – perhaps because they were mentally ill, physically disabled or enfeebled – Siberia's vast expanses offered a solution and thus became their home for as long as they could survive, though the march into this freezing hell probably killed most before they arrived.

As codified in the 1649 *Ulozhenie*, punishments remained various and ghastly, but we are concerned here only with Peter's use of exile and *katorga*. How many the government exiled during Peter's reign is not known, though it is clear that exile to Siberia continued despite the diversion of many convicts to *katorga* sites throughout European Russia. Peter continued the use of exile to remove political rivals; and in comparison to other exilic categories political exile seems to have expanded rather than contracted during his time. He exiled the printer Grigorii Talitskii and others for the state crime of producing criminal publications (*vorovskie pis´ma*) identifying him as the Antichrist. Colonel Semen Palei was sent to Eniseisk *ostrog* as a traitor for his dealings with Charles XII of Sweden and Ukrainian hetman Ivan Mazepa, though in what seems a rare act of clemency the emperor allowed Palei to return to Russia in 1708. Soon thereafter Mazepa himself was captured and exiled. Peter also exiled a Prussian named von Freik (Fon-Vrekh) who served under Charles XII and was captured during the rout following the battle of Poltava. Von Freik went on to found a private school in Tobol´sk in 1713, presaging the Decembrists' and other political exiles' philanthropic activities. Mazepa's nephew Andrei Ia. Voinarovskii had been captured but managed to escape for a time to Europe where he lived in Vienna, Breslau and Hamburg before Russian agents recaptured and brought him to Petersburg in 1716. He sat in the Peter and Paul fortress for six years until the Senate finally exiled him and his family to Siberia in 1723. Voinarovskii died in Iakutsk during the early 1740s.

By far the largest deportation during Peter's reign was that of the Swedes captured after Poltava in 1709. G. V. Shebaldina's recent excellent study, which draws on both Swedish and Russian sources, details this chapter in Siberian history. The most accurate figures indicate approximately 20,000 Swedish soldiers, non-combatants, and women and children were taken prisoner. Most were initially assigned to Moscow and other locations in European Russia, where they imposed a heavy burden on local residents and administrators. Despite some historians' claims that the 1711 mass deportation of Swedes to Siberia was a response to a planned uprising by Swedish officers in Kazan and Sviiazhsk, Shebaldina convincingly argues that it actually resulted from Peter's considerations as to how this large and technically skilled labor force could best be utilized. 'Such a utilitarian approach,' she writes, 'completely coincided not only with the spirit of the time and universally accepted practice, but also the practicality of the principal constructor of Russian power – Peter the Great.'[99] Indeed, on 11 July 1709, a mere two weeks after Poltava, Peter ordered 3,000 Swedes sent to reinforce the Voronezh garrison and help build the Black Sea fleet. As of March 1710, that is, before the Swedish officers' conspiracy was discovered, as many as 7,000 Swedes had been sent to Voronezh with a similar number assigned to Azov.

On 30 December 1710 Peter gave the first order transferring these and Swedes held in other locations to Siberia. What Shebaldina does not mention is that this order eventuating in the deportation of 20,000 Swedes was addressed to *Sibirskii prikaz's* Matvei Gagarin a mere three months before his appointment as governor of the newly created Sibirsk *guberniia*. Could this deportation have been the cause of Siberia's administrative and bureaucratic reconfiguration? Based on the available evidence it is difficult to say one way or the other, but Peter's government was constantly reacting to military exigencies, and so this may be another example of the impact war had on Russia's internal development. In any case, during late winter and spring 1711 twelve separate parties of Swedes were convoyed to the following destinations: Tomsk, Kuznetsk, Eniseisk, Turukhansk, Krasnoiarsk, Irkutsk, Nerchinsk, Iakutsk, Selenginsk, Ilimsk, Kirensk, Viatka, Solikamsk, Cherdyn, Kai-gorodok, Iarensk, Tiumen, Turinsk, Pelym, Verkhotur´e, Kosmodem´iansk, Surgut, Narym, Berezov, and Tara. Gagarin and his assistant, courtier Gerasim Pleshcheev, looked after the Swedes as best they could. The officers were for the most part kept separate from the soldiers, presumably to forestall a mutiny, and both groups were provided with *kormovye den´gi* ('foraging money'). Nonetheless, these prisoners' journeys took many months and conditions were harsh. The group in which cornet Barthold Ennes found himself took almost five months to complete its march from Simbirsk to Tobol´sk. Of another group of 200 which left Ufa and was later joined by 105 officers originating out of Sviiazhsk, 21 died en route, six were either killed or seriously injured when they tried to escape, and only one successfully escaped. Of another group of 97 which left Simbirsk, 20 were lost.[100]

In Siberia, officials requisitioned in each town to which Swedes were assigned one out of every 100 houses to quarter the prisoners. Because an average of one guard was assigned to every two or three prisoners, officials were forced to hire retired soldiers, *posadskie* and peasants for this purpose. Residents responded to this influx of foreigners in various ways. Some charges were starved, beaten or even murdered; others benefited from sympathy and largesse. Almost immediately after his defeat Charles XII had formed a field commission to liaise with the Russians and see to his countrymen's treatment. Peter's government allowed this commission to transfer funds from Sweden to prisoners, though over the years sometimes withheld or prevented such transfers. Despite instances of embezzlement by Russian officials, Shebaldina concludes: 'Siberian governor M. P. Gagarin played the largest role in the fate of the Siberian prisoners. Material aid and moral support on his part saved the lives of many hundreds of prisoners.'[101]

A small number of Swedes joined the Russian army. Figures are lacking for the lower ranks, but 56 officers are known to have entered the service during 1709–21. A few others, such as Jan Gottfried, proved resourceful in earning money through various trading and bartering schemes, while some like Joachim Lut hired themselves out to peasants. Most Swedes depended on support from Gagarin and the Swedish commission. Despite considerable numbers being assigned to Siberia's fledgling metallurgical industry, this valuable labor force was largely left to its own devices. With the exception of initially assigning prisoners to Voronezh and Azov, Peter, fearful of concentrating too many in one location, dispersed them throughout Siberia and failed to use them efficiently. The reasons for this are not clear, though his involvement in other matters may have distracted him from dealing more coherently with them. Perhaps Gagarin failed to assign them as ordered. But the most likely explanation is that Siberia's economy was too underdeveloped to incorporate the Swedes on a large scale, given that this was something of a transitional period, what with the fur industry declining and the metallurgical industry in its infancy.

Early in the Northern War both Russia and Sweden sought to convert prisoners, but a 1702 agreement acknowledged their religious rights. As early as 1710 Gagarin assigned a pastor to administer to the small number of Swedes already in Tobol´sk; and over the years the prisoners received donations from co-religionists in Sweden and Germany sufficient to build churches, a school and a hospital in the same city, as well as to put together a library of religious texts. Shortly before his death, Peter allowed them to marry Russian women without having to convert to Orthodoxy, but a synodal ukase of 23 June 1721, entitled 'On Permitting Them [Orthodox women] to Marry Foreigners', prohibited wives from converting to Protestantism and ordered that their children be raised as Orthodox. This ukase effectively prevented wives and children from accompanying husbands and fathers to Sweden after the 1721 Nystad Treaty, and as a result broke up many families.[102]

Despite his sympathy for the Swedes, Gagarin continued to serve his tsar, at one point passing on to subordinates the emperor's warning 'that Swedish prisoners are secretly receiving and sending letters' and should be watched closely.[103] Similar warnings and measures nonetheless failed to prevent commission officials routinely smuggling letters between prisoners and Sweden that gave information on their conditions and locations. A number of Swedish officers enjoyed considerable freedom, served in official capacities or participated in regional explorations. Lorenz Lange even made several trips to China as a Russian trade representative. Lieutenant-colonel Ivan Bucholz's expedition to the upper reaches of the Irtysh River near Lake Zaisan included several Swedish mining experts, in particular Johan Gustav Renat, who with his wife Brigitta Scherzenfeldt was captured by local Kalmyks. Renat taught the Kalmyks how to make rifles and cannon, and on his return to Sweden in 1734 brought with him two Kalmyk maps of Central Asia that have since proved invaluable to researchers. He is less heralded for also bringing three slave girls, one improvidently named 'bad girl' in Turkish. The earlier mentioned Strahlenberg similarly mapped Siberia and, on his return to Stockholm, published a massive study of the region in which he described the Stroganovs as having been very supportive of Swedish officers during captivity.[104] Virtually all Swedes exiled to Siberia returned home after the end of the Northern War, though a few remained, especially if they had married and managed to establish themselves. Despite their relatively brief presence in Siberia, Swedish prisoners left a legacy of technical knowledge and cultural sophistication.

Peter also used exile to remove his political enemies the *strel´tsy*. During suppression of their 1698 rebellion those not executed were knouted, branded on the right cheek and exiled, mostly, it seems, to Astrakhan. Maksimov provides figures showing that while the young tsar preferred to have most *strel´tsy* beheaded, broken on the wheel, hanged, quartered, disembowelled or otherwise eliminated, he spared with sentences of exile or *katorga* especially young *strel´tsy* aged 15–20 and colloquially known as *maloletki* (youngsters). On one day alone (19 September 1698) he ordered 100 *maloletki* knouted, branded on the right cheek and exiled to Siberian cities. Another 285 *maloletki* were knouted and sent to *katorga* in early 1699. On 9 February 1700, of the 40 *strel´tsy* punished that day, 25 were sentenced to *katorga* and nine were banished to Siberia. By the time the Northern War ended 'there was not a single fortress or *ostrog* even as inconveniently far removed as Udsk, Anadyrsk, Kolymsk, Okhotsk, Bratsk, Ilimsk, Balagansk, or Tunkinsk without *strel´tsy*'.[105] Those banished in 1698 to Astrakhan later joined up with local Don Cossacks to incite the massive uprising of 1705, which Peter crushed with the help of some 300 executions as well as deportations to winter encampments in the Anadyr Peninsula. Once there, *strel´tsy* formed bandit gangs and began pillaging local (presumably native) villages. Such activities may have predicated the 'state of mutiny from 1707 through 1717' about which James Gibson writes with regard to those Don Cossacks exiled to Kamchatka after their mass uprising in 1707.[106] Eventually, these maddened *strel´tsy* were transferred south and held under guard, apparently in Okhotsk, a wind-swept *ostrog* established on the Pacific coast during the mid-1600s.

In contrast to his deportation of soldiers and personal enemies Peter ordered few criminals exiled to the land. An instruction dated February 1695 and bearing both his and co-tsar Ivan V's names informs Tomsk's *voevoda* of the arrival of a group of exiles, some to be assigned to cossack foot regiments and the rest 'to be settled on our agricultural lands'.[107] Two years later Peter exiled 624 runaway peasants and their families to Nerchinsk, a third of whom starved to death on the way there. But for the most part he showed little interest in Siberian agriculture and therefore assigned most offenders to *katorga*. This altered for several decades the convict population's primary constituency from that of exiles to that of slave laborers in what were, to borrow William Blake's words, the 'dark, Satanic' factories, mines and other sites of Russia's nascent industrialization.

*   *   *

Katorga comes from the Greek and originally meant 'galley'. Andrei A. Vinius, Peter's Dutch confidant who later headed *Sibirskii prikaz* and oversaw the birth of the Urals iron industry, is credited with first recommending that criminals be used to man galleys he proposed would comprise a Caspian fleet. His ideas caught Peter's attention in 1695, though by this time Azov was the sea of choice. Having previously failed to take by land the Turkish fortress of the same name, the tsar planned to capture it by water, as occupation would give Russia not only control of the Azov Sea but, more importantly, access to the Black Sea and Anatolian coast. Peter accordingly launched a ferocious campaign to build Russia's first navy in four shipyards established along the lower Don. He levied 26,000 laborers from Riazan, Ukraine and the Belgorod Military District, but '[n]one of the four shipyards actually saw its full complement of workers because "no-shows" (*netchiki*) and runaways dramatically reduced the labor force,' writes Edward Phillips in his history of the fleet.

> The example of the Dobryi yard is indicative of the problem's scope. Of the 4,743 workers drafted according to Peter's second decree [of 31 January 1696], 1,244 (26 percent) did not appear; of the remaining 3,499 men, 1,878 (54 percent) ran away at some point during the construction.... The labor shortages caused by runaways plagued the enterprise at all four of the yards.[108]

Nevertheless, the fleet was built and Azov taken that spring. Tagan-rog, 55 kilometers upriver from Azov, later became the fleet's moorage, while Voronezh, largest of the four shipyards, contributed mightily to building the numerous barks, bombardes, Barbary ships and galleys that characterized the Black Sea fleet.

Long before his reliance on Swedish shipbuilders it was this labor short-age which, in 1696, led Peter to first assign convicts to, in this case, 'Azov *katorga*' (*azovskaia katorga*), where they appear to have served for the most part as common laborers. As of 1702 Russia's Black Sea and Baltic fleets totaled 23 galleys, each of which required 100–130 oarsmen, in which capacity convicts reportedly also served, though sources provide no information on their numbers. During the period 1704–9 Azov's and Taganrog's total labor force averaged 8,500; and *Sibirskii prikaz* was still exiling criminals to Azov in 1709; but the percentage of penal laborers there is similarly unknown. Phillips writes that some 3,000 Swedish pris-oners and unspecified others dissembled the Voronezh yard and its works when the fleet found new moorings to the south, an operation that pos-sibly occasioned a letter that year to Peter from Azov's governor I. A. Tolstoi, who complained: 'I now do not have enough laborers with which to build [a salt works in nearby Bakhmuta]'.[109]

Exile to Azov, Taganrog and other lower Don sites ended abruptly in 1712 when defeat at the hands of the Ottomans obliged Peter to cede the territory and destroy his fleet. Yet Peter had already begun using penal laborers to build St Petersburg, Kronshtadt, the Baltic port of Rogervik, fortresses in Riga and Reval, and the Urals' first metallurgical works. He may also have assigned them to build fortresses in southern Siberia. In September 1703, as many of these projects were beginning, the tsar wrote to Moscow's governor: 'Several thousand criminals (specifically, if pos-sible, 2 thousand) should now be made available for future years. Get them immediately from all the *prikazy*, town councils, and towns.'[110] Des-pite their status as memorials to Petrine brutality, little information exists on these *katorga* sites. Nikolai Karamzin poetically wrote that Petersburg was built on 'tears and corpses', but sources are silent as to how exactly these tears and corpses ended up as part of the fundament of its archi-tectural wonders, though it was reported that on any given day 500–800 penal laborers were working in the city for the navy, which is also known to have punished fugitive sailors by exiling them to its mines near Azov. Beginning in 1722 Rogervik reportedly received 600 penal laborers a year; and Strahlenberg, writing in 1730, states that '10,000 Men have, for some Time, been constantly employ'd [at Rogervik]'.[111] The port was Russia's single largest *katorga* site until completion in 1767. All this, as well as figures suggesting the navy may have used up to 15,000 convicts as oarsmen (though this number is probably too high), suggests the Admiralty College benefited more than any government agency from the new penal apparatus, at least until the first years of Catherine II's reign.

Besides suborning legality to statist goals, Peter's fevered demand for 'several thousand criminals' highlights the relationship between his massive projects and *katorga*'s emergence. Penal laborers were part and parcel of Russia's transformation from principality to empire, but *katorga* cannot be said to have been *sui generis*. Rather, it evolved out of the post-1649 notion that even criminals should continue to serve the state. By the early 1700s mining and construction were fast displacing fur collection as the major sources of Russia's empowerment, and the greater rigidity of the industrial workplace led to a more systematic use of labor as the goal of economic autarky linked the Petrine to the Muscovite era and ensured a continuing commodification of imperial subjects.

In addition to Peter's revolution from above, certain events in Siberia suggest another explanation for *katorga*'s eclipse of exile as the state's preferred way to deal with criminals. In 1690 Iakutsk *voevoda* Petr P. Zinov´ev learned that local cossacks were conspiring to mutiny. He responded mercilessly, executing the two ringleaders and torturing, knouting and exiling their followers to Nerchinsk, Irkutsk and elsewhere. Siberian cossacks had a well-established tradition of mutinying; but Zinov´ev's brutal suppression combined with other indignities to spark an unprecedented series of revolts that paralysed eastern Siberia between 1695 and 1700. The most serious of these began in Krasnoiarsk in May 1695 and was not quashed until five years later. Nerchinsk, Udinsk, Selenginsk and several other locations experienced uprisings that also involved not just cossacks but servitors, *posadskie*, peasants, natives and exiles. At least one revolt, originating in Bratsk, is known to have been coordinated by an exiled peasant named Kopytov. By the time loyal troops re-exerted control the state was assigning most new convicts to *katorga* sites west of the Urals, possibly to avoid fueling the Siberian conflagration.[112]

During Peter's reign there existed only two categories of *katorga*: permanent (*vechnaia*) and temporary (*vremennaia*). Unlike those sentenced to permanent *katorga*, penal laborers sentenced temporarily lost neither status nor property and were spared corporal punishment; some were even allowed to visit their families. After completing their sentences they were free to resume their former lives. In some ways, then, temporary *katorga* was similar to indentured servitude or the short-term slavery arrangements Richard Hellie describes.[113] Temporary *katorga* may even have replaced short-term slavery arrangements. By contrast, convicts sentenced to permanent *katorga* were publicly knouted and typically had their nostrils slit, as well as their money and property distributed to their neighbors and contact with their families permanently severed. The sum total of these measures consigned the individual to 'civil death', legally speaking. In recognition of this, Peter in 1720 allowed the wives of such men to remarry, enter a monastery or return to their parents. If while serving their sentences penal laborers became enfeebled, disabled or senile they remained in assigned locations supported by tax revenues; but if disabled during either incarceration, corporal punishment or removal to labor sites they were sent to monasteries to receive what little charity was available. Women sentenced to *katorga* were assigned to Russia's burgeoning textile manufactories. While this labor was less demanding than that encountered in a mine or a galley, it similarly destroyed a person's health over the long term.

Textiles were key to the development of Russia's navy, and Peter's visits to Holland may have led to this use of female convicts. In 1597 Amsterdam had opened its *spinhuis*, an asylum exclusively devoted to reforming woman prisoners by engaging them in textile production. '[A]s a separate prison for women it remained virtually unique,' writes penal historian Lucia Zedner. 'Throughout Europe, women were generally housed within male prisons and often herded alongside men with little concern for the likely results.'[114] Anisimov notes that a similar 'spinning house' (*priadil'nyi dvor*) existed in Petersburg in 1723 employing 30 female convicts and owned, tellingly, by a Dutchman, Jan Tammes. Peter had put Tammes in charge of all Moscow's linen factories as early as 1706, and so may have begun assigning female convicts to them as well. Tammes reportedly employed only attractive young women, and it would be of little surprise, given the general history of women's incarceration, if his factories did not also serve as brothels.[115]

That the Petrine *spinhuis*, like its Amsterdam predecessor, incarcerated women separately from men renders it something of an example of progressiveness in Russia's penological development. However, this is not to say penal conditions were much more progressive elsewhere. Prior to the mid-1800s women's prisons were rare in both Western Europe and North America, too; but as time passed Russia's treatment of female convicts diverged from practices in the West. One reason for this was the succession of malfeasant administrations already mentioned; another was that within the service-state ethos female convicts were not as valuable as males. Not until 1827 did the Senate designate another facility specially for woman convicts – the Tel'minsk linen factory, outside Irkutsk, which nevertheless excluded women convicted of murder, robbery or brigand-age, who apparently continued to be mixed in with the male convict population. Tel´minsk's distinction as a women's carceral did not last long; as early as 1839 more male than female convicts were being held there.[116]

Under Peter the state began to control its convict population more directly than during the Muscovite era. *Katorga* segregated convicts from society, in contrast to the earlier policy of incorporating them into Siberian society. This renders *katorga* analogous to the asylum then emerging in Western societies and whose 'dual purpose', writes David Rothman, was to 'rehabilitate inmates and then, by virtue of its success, set an example of right action for the larger society'.[117] Rehabilitation cannot be said to have been the primary goal behind Petrine *katorga*, but temporary penal laborers were returned to civil society presum-ably because authorities considered them better adjusted to their roles as state subjects. Moreover, studies of the fear engendered by modern prisons[118] suggest the dispatching of persons to Rogervik or elsewhere would have been effective in providing a cautionary lesson to others. It is this disciplinary function of *katorga* which connects Foucault's observations with the second part of Rothman's formulation, insofar as Russia's expanding penologico-administrative apparatus served the larger goal of subordinating society to the will of the state. Such a goal necessitated altering the relationship between power and the indi-vidual – the corporeal body – to create a new paradigm in which, writes Foucault,

> power relations have an immediate hold upon [the body]; they invest it, mark it, train it, torture it, force it to carry out tasks, to perform ceremonies, to emit signs. This political investment of the body is bound up, in accordance with complex reciprocal relations, with its economic use; it is largely as a force of production that the body is invested with relations of power and domination; but, on the other hand, its constitution as labor power is possible only if it is caught up in a system of subjection (in which need is also a political instru-ment meticulously prepared, calculated and used); the body becomes a useful force only if it is both a productive body and subjected body.[119]

Such was the creed that would condition Russia's administration of both convicts and Siberian exile for the next two centuries. In the process, the struggle between state and society was exacerbated.

3
'Punishment for Insignificant Crimes'

Little information exists concerning exile during the period 1725–62,[1] but it is clear that whereas both exile and *katorga* expanded, the balance shifted in the direction of the former as Peter's successors focused on colonizing Siberia. During this period, the penological distinction between exile (*ssylka*) and *katorga* grew almost imperceptible as the state shuttled convicts between settlements and labor sites with little regard for judicially imposed sentences. Elizabeth Petrovna attempted to systematize and regularize the use of exile and *katorga*, introducing a scale of punishments for the first time in Russian history; however, the administration of these punishments rarely coincided with the regulations.

Exile was the primary implement for the house-cleanings that became a feature of court life during this period. Examples abound. Grigorii Skorniakov-Pisarev, former procurator-general of the Senate under Peter, was knouted for his part in a conspiracy against Catherine I and sent to Zhigansk, a winter camp on the lower Lena. For four years he lived there with rough-and-tumble cossacks assigned to collect *iasak* from local Tungus. His fortunes changed when Anna Ioannovna ascended the throne and put him in command of the entire Okhotsk-Kamchatka region. But Skorniakov-Pisarev soon ran afoul of the Iakutsk *voevoda*, who sent him back to Zhigansk. In November 1733 the Senate reversed the *voevoda's* decision and restored Skorniakov-Pisarev's command. He failed to learn from his experiences and by 1739 his corruption, drinking and orgies had grown so infamous he was arrested and imprisoned at Okhotsk. When Elizabeth assumed the throne the phoenix-like Skorniakov-Pisarev again found favour and bid the cossacks and fishermen goodbye to return to Petersburg.[2]

Following Peter II's assumption of the throne, Prince Aleksei Dolgorukii managed to get his old enemy, Aleksandr Menshikov, who after Peter I's death was perhaps the most detested man in Russia, exiled in December 1727 to Berezov *ostrog* on the lower Ob. Exile was a transformative experience for Menshikov: in the two years before he died he became renowned for his piety, a characteristic captured by Vasilii Surikov in his canvas 'Menshikov at Berezov'. Dolgorukii later got his when Anna took the throne and, in a perverse twist of fate, banished him, his wife Praskov´ia and their seven children and one daughter-in-law to the same *ostrog* that witnessed Menshikov's conversion to the simple life. Like his predecessor, Dolgorukii soon died there. After the elder Dolgorukii's death his son Ivan was returned to Petersburg and broken on the wheel. Ivan's widow Natal´ia Borisovna and their two sons were allowed to reside in Moscow during Elizabeth's reign; but when Catherine II took over she sent them to Florovskii Monastery in Kiev, where Natal´ia died in 1771 under the name Nektariia. Anna removed another of Aleksei Dolgorukii's sons further to Kamchatka, where he served in the navy, and ordered his remaining two brothers knouted and, after having their tongues cut out, sent first to Okhotsk then to Kamchatka. She re-assigned his daughters to various Siberian monasteries.[3]

Indeed, Anna worked diligently to rid Moscow of enemies. Her German lover Ernst-Johann Biren (Biron) unleashed a wave of terror known as the *Bironovshchina* which involved exiling many. Between August 1730 and January 1731 he supervised the torture of 425 people, eleven of whom died; executed another eleven outright; and exiled 57 to Siberia. Another 44 were 'exiled' to military service. In 1731 a total of 1,151 persons were tortured: 58 died as a result; 47 were ceremoniously executed; 54 were exiled to locations in Siberia; 155 were assigned to *katorga* at the Okhotsk salt works; and 101 were 'resettled' in Tara in western Siberia. The military claimed another 213 victims. Aleksandr Kamenskii writes that the Secret Chancery (*Tainaia kantselariia*) persecuted some 10,000 victims during the 1730s.[4] Many, if not most, were probably exiled to Siberia.

The chronicler I. V. Shcheglov relates an interesting story about Fedor I. Soimonov, Admiralty College vice-president who, in 1740, was exiled to the Okhotsk salt works after being knouted and having his nostrils slit. The story goes that 'a skilled doctor in Siberia re-grew [his nose] with a chunk of flesh cut from the innocent victim's left arm'. If so, this may be the first case of plastic surgery on record. When Elizabeth Petrovna took the throne she recognized Soimonov's innocence and welcomed him back to Petersburg. But he preferred to remain in Siberia and spent the next 16 years exploring the Shilka and Amur river valleys. In 1757 he was named governor of Siberia, which post he held for six years.[5]

Elizabeth is popularly thought to have been kinder and gentler than Anna; in fact, she could be every bit as ruthless. During a ten-year period beginning in late 1740 (about a year before she took over) 20,000 nobles and state officials were exiled.[6] Baron Karl Ludwig Mengden, who had directed the Commerce College during Anna Leopol'dovna's regency, was one of Elizabeth's early casualties and serves as an example of her use of political exile. Commuting his execution in 1742 she had him, his wife, son, daughter, sister-in-law and a servant couple named Iogan and Luiza exiled to Nizhnekolymsk on the Arctic Ocean, about as far from Petersburg as one could go and still be in Siberia. No guards were assigned to watch these seven exiles, who managed to obtain several head of cattle and establish a small trading concern selling goods delivered from Iakutsk. But then Mengden's wife died, followed by his daughter and the servant Luiza. After Mengden himself expired in 1760 the rest were allowed to return to Russia.[7]

As sobering as are the cases of Mengden, Menshikov and other notable victims of court politics, a tragedy of much larger proportions involved the commoners exiled during the period 1725–62. Precise figures are lacking, but the Secret Chancery re-established at the beginning of Anna's reign is supposed to have exiled at least 1,500 people.[8] Yet this was a drop in a very large bucket to which other state agencies were contributing. Iadrintsev estimates that Anna exiled 2,000 annually and that during her reign Elizabeth banished 80,000 criminals. Iadrintsev sometimes exaggerates, but this latter figure is not improbable as it likely includes many exiles' families and, moreover, accords with another source stating that 20,000 from the privileged classes were exiled during the first half of Elizabeth's reign. Whatever the exact numbers, exiles certainly came to account for a greater proportion of Siberia's Russian population, which as of the beginning of Catherine II's reign stood at 400,000.[9]

The state's increasing reliance on exile after Peter I's death indicates on the one hand maintenance of the service-state ethos, and on the other an interest in developing Siberia as a colony that would deliver raw materials. Other factors attest to Siberia's growing importance as a colony, such as the Treaty of Kiakhta (1728), which among other things settled the border with China; the Great Northern Expeditions of the 1730s, which involved Vitus Bering's discovery of the strait which bears his name and the establishment of Russian settlements in California; Alaska's annexation; increased trade with Persia and China; and development of the Kolyvansk and Nerchinsk metallurgical regions. The reorganizations of Siberia's administration and territory previously discussed further demonstrate that Russia's relationship to Siberia was modifying with each succeeding decade, albeit in rather haphazard manner as the government groped towards the systematization that Yaney and others have documented. Each of these developments represented the state's deepening penetration into Siberia rather than absorption of it as an integral part of Russia. But even if Petersburg was content to treat Siberia as a colony, substitutes needed to be found for the settlers now disappearing thanks to serfdom, and so the government began to focus on the use of exiles as colonists.

On 5 October 1731, with an ukase deporting 153 debtors to the Okhotsk seaboard, Anna launched Russia's first attempt to develop a colony composed solely of exiles. Skorniakov-Pisarev, whom Anna had just placed in charge of the region, was supposed to employ these exiles as either craftsmen or unskilled laborers. The colony's main purpose was to provision Bering's and others' regional expeditions. Okhotsk had been founded much earlier, in 1649, but the coastline remained a forbiddingly barren place. Skorniakov-Pisarev assigned the debtors to both mining and agricultural work, but the colony failed: the salt-ridden soil yielded almost nothing and officials failed to adequately provision the exiles, who either died or escaped, though a few stuck it out as trappers or fishermen. In July 1733 the Senate ordered an indeterminate number transferred to Kamchatka to found an agricultural colony there. As with Okhotsk, this Kamchatka experiment soon failed. Despite this, in 1738 and 1744 Petersburg sent more exiles as well as *perevedentsy* to southern Kamchatka, where agricultural endeavors came to naught and the unwilling colonists died, escaped or turned to other pursuits. There may also have been an earlier attempt to establish an agricultural colony on Kamchatka around the time of the Okhotsk colony. Shcheglov writes that in 1732 the government transferred 30 families from the Lena region to Kamchatka to grow wheat and other grains. Perhaps some of these *perevedentsy* were descendants of Lena's seventeenth-century exiles, but like all the other colonies described – and like a joke without a punch line – this one failed as well.[10]

Anna assigned convicts to western Siberia also, though their numbers were few and they were not organized into exilic colonies *per se*. M. M. Gromyko provides figures from Anna's reign showing exiles accounted for only 259 of Tara *uezd*'s 7,978 Russian males; and that in 1743 exiles headed only four of Turinsk's 339 households.[11] Beginning in late 1736 Petersburg sent the first of a somewhat larger number of exiles to colonize the border between Samara and Orenburg, as part of the Orenburg Expedition initiated two years earlier. Historian Iu. N. Smirnov quotes an ukase dated 11 February 1736 as the basis for this decision: 'instead of Siberia, send exiles to Orenburg for assignment to the cossacks, the fields, and the mines; yet assign supernumerary ones to Siberian *zavody* [industrial townships].' As of June 1737, 548 exiles comprised 18 per cent of those cossacks assigned to a series of fortresses and settlements built to keep the Kazakhs at bay; and figures from 1741 show exiles similarly accounted for up to a third of the Orenburg Expedition's 726 administrative personnel.[12]

The effort to colonize Siberia continued after Anna's death. Writing in the journal *Russian Wealth* at the end of the nineteenth century, Sergei Dizhur argues that Elizabeth's reign witnessed the creation of 'the so called "state *poseleniia*"'.[13] Strictly translated, *poselenie* means 'settlement', but would later signify a type of exilic status, as in the juridico-penological phrase *ssylka na poselenie* or exile to settlement.[14] Initially, however, a *poselenie* was a settlement for exiles operated along military lines replete with cossacks and overseers. Despite Dizhur's claim that such highly regimented camps emerged under Elizabeth, he offers no evidence. Smirnov writes that such camps were actually established in Orenburg during Anna's reign. 'However, there were few izbas and the penal laborers and exiles assigned [to forests around Krasnosamarsk fortress] were "kept in earthen dugouts and, as a result, many died".'[15] An early Soviet history of political exile in Eniseisk *guberniia* claims *poseleniia* were established there, in Turukhansk, Kemchug and Kargat, as early as 1754.[16] But aside from these allusions in secondary sources, confirmation of *poseleniia*'s existence prior to Paul I's reign has not been established.

Besides those *poseleniia* which may or may not have come to be in Eniseisk *guberniia*, the only other examples of Elizabeth's colonization efforts date from late in her reign. In 1760 she ordered the Foreign Affairs College to settle exiles along the Uda, Gluboka and Irtysh rivers to secure the border and populate the Kolyvansk region, already characterized by a series of fortifications, but which may have included *poseleniia* as well. Either way, exiles assigned to Kolyvansk appear to have been kept under heavy guard. Two years later, the state began settling exiles in Baraba Steppe, an inhospitable region between Omsk and present-day Novosibirsk, to strengthen the border further to the west and establish local agriculture.

Like their Muscovite predecessors, Elizabeth's officials believed a major hindrance to developing permanent, productive colonies in Siberia – populated or not by exiles – was the lack of Russian women. To remedy this situation they deported female convicts expressly for the purpose of serving as wives for the male populace. In 1759, 77 women between the ages of 19 and 40 – one third of whom had murdered their husbands, ten their children and one her father – arrived in Omsk. K. L. Frauendorf, the garrison's commander and later Irkutsk *guberniia's* first governor, divied up the women among officers, cossacks, soldiers and bureaucrats. A similar plan existed to distribute some female exiles who had ended up in fortresses along the Irtysh, but '[d]ue to . . . the licentiousness of the "women and girls",' contends Fel´dstein, 'the settled population carefully avoided them.'[17]

Similar to compulsory colonization was exile to the army, since many so exiled either served on Siberia's borders or became exile-settlers if they proved unfit for soldiering. Convicts have formed a part of the world's armies from earliest times, and in Russia it was Peter I who began the practice of exiling convicts to the military. This continued into the nineteenth century. A 1733 ukase prescribing punishments for young clerics guilty of 'wicked deeds, quarrelling, fighting and drunkenness' ordered them lashed with the *plet*[18] and exiled to the military; if unfit for service they were to be knouted, have their nostrils slit and be exiled to Siberia. A few years later Anna sought to prevent the practice of hiring substitutes for army recruitment by ordering both parties lashed with the *plet* and exiled to the Orenburg garrison; if unsuitable for service, they were to be lashed then exiled to Okhotsk, presumably to serve as colonists or to labor in the salt works there. During the Seven Years' War Elizabeth ordered runaway serfs captured in Poland or Lithuania assigned to bring military regiments up to strength; if unfit for service or over 50 years of age these serfs and their families were deported as settlers.[19]

Peter had made the military a top priority, and as the type of punishments handed out under Anna and Elizabeth show, his successors maintained this emphasis. In addition to efforts to colonize Siberia using exiles, the state increasingly sentenced convicts to 'exile to fortresses for labor' (*ssylka v kreposti dlia raboty*). Juridically speaking, such convicts were petty criminals (*malovazhnye*) sentenced to exile, not *katorga*, but were nevertheless used to build fortifications along the Baltic littoral, on the Kola Peninsula, and in Novorossiia and Orenburg and Astrakhan *gubernii*. As for convicts sentenced to *katorga* during the period 1725–62, they were most likely to be assigned to Rogervik; to repair roads around Okhotsk; to man state distilleries or ironworks such as Iakutsk's Tamginsk works (where in 1753 they comprised 45 per cent of the workforce); or, if female, to labor in such linen mills as the Tel´minsk near Irkutsk or the Kutkinsk near Tobol´sk, where they produced sails and other military accouterments. Both sexes labored in shackles.[20]

The metallurgical industry was of growing importance for *katorga* during this period, though complete symbiosis between the two would not occur until Catherine II took the throne. The first ironworks in Siberia was established near Tomsk in 1623. This was a very small operation: an instruction dated 1625 shows that during a five-month period it smelted only eleven poods of slab iron. However, the crown held the works dear, for the first items produced there were muskets and cannon. The Tomsk works was followed a few years later by the opening of iron ore mines in Verkhotur´e *uezd*; and by mid-century ore was being mined in eastern Siberia in Ilimsk, Eniseisk and Balagansk *uezdy*. In 1700 the state opened an ironworks in Nev´iansk, a town 100 kilometers south of present-day Ekaterinburg in the Urals. This works would soon become the famous Demidov family's *entrée* into Siberia. That same year a weapons manufactory was established in Tobol´sk. The first copper mines, in Tomsk and Kuznetsk *uezdy*, followed in 1718; and a year later the entrepreneur S. Kostylev began operating in the same region a series of mines for extracting various metals. A 1724 ukase indicates the high value Peter placed on these mines, since he expressly ordered fortresses to be built along the Chinese border to protect them.

The most important metallurgical location with regard to *katorga* was Dauriia, which under Peter became known as Zabaikal´e. Mining began there in the late seventeenth century, and in 1704 Russia's first silver smeltery opened in Nerchinsk. A year later Peter transferred 626 captured male and female fugitive peasants from Tobol´sk to Nerchinsk. Twenty servitors under the command of Petr Meleshin convoyed the party, only 403 of whom reached Nerchinsk: 164 died along the way, 41 were too sick or injured to continue and 18 escaped. Many who died were beaten to death by convoy guards. Undaunted by these and other fatalities Peter continued to assign subjects to Nerchinsk. For example, in 1710, 78 peasant families arrived there. It is unclear if these or certain other groups were exiles or *perevedentsy*, or if, once they arrived, they worked primarily as laborers or as peasants, yet the manner by which they came to be there indicates almost no voluntary migration to Zabaikal´e. From early on the regime necessarily depended on penal laborers and exiles to settle the region. Nerchinsk remained the empire's only silver-producing region until the 1740s, though output was low before the 1760s.[21]

Although penal laborers were significant to Siberia's metallurgical development they accounted for a minority of the industry's total workforce. Initially, the state tried to use Tungus, Buriats and Tatars to work the mines and smelteries, but this proved futile. It later assigned to the service of particular works whole peasant villages for certain periods of time, alternating one village with another on a rotating basis.

In 1704, when Peter put Nikita Demidov in charge of the Nev´iansk works, he also gave him his own peasants, making him the first commoner to own serfs. The Demidov works eventually supplied most of Peter's weaponry, its iron becoming so valuable that by '1745, nearly seven out of every ten tons of metal that came from the ironworks were being sold abroad'.[22] The state also assigned a caste of skilled workers called *masterovye* (sing. *masterovoi*) to these industries. *Masterovye* tended to be young bachelors from Russia transferred to Siberia for obligatory service, similar to the craftsmen of the Muscovite era. The length of this service was entirely at the discretion of the government, and *masterovye* seem more times than not to have ended their lives in their new locations. Like peasants assigned to particular factories they were not convicts, but unlike peasants were subject to greater discipline and tied more permanently to their particular locales. *Masterovye* became a self-generating skilled labor force: local administrators would train their sons then enroll them at age 15 in the *masterovye*, which *soslovie's* compulsory labor ended only with serf emancipation. Examples of the use of both peasants and *masterovye* can be found early in Peter's reign. In 1702 he transferred *masterovye* belonging to the Tula weapons factory, which Nikita Demidov also owned, to the newly established factory in Tobol´sk; ten years later he transferred *masterovye* from the Urals to Zabaikal´e.[23]

Some evidence suggests that Peter assigned convicts to the Siberian metallurgical industry at the same time he first used them at Azov. An article by Vasilii Otemirov in the journal *Siberian Messenger* in 1822 describes how, in response to a letter of June 1695 from the Greek entrepreneur Aleksandr Levandian, Peter ordered '50 or 100 persons from among [Tobol´sk's] homeless exiled population' to dig for silver along the Kia River not far from Tomsk. Otemirov gives no further details on the Kia mine, and if one existed it remains unclear whether or not exiles ever worked there.[24] Penal laborers were more likely sent to Nerchinsk soon after silver mining began there. Anisimov writes that large groups of exiles, including political exiles, were sent, but provides neither figures nor precise dates for the Petrine period. Beginning in 1711 Governor Gagarin assigned Swedish prisoners as *masterovye* to the Tobol´sk weapons factory, to which other exiles were later assigned. When Peter learned these exiles were cursing him by name he ordered Gagarin's replacement Cherkasskii to fine and punish them. At some point Peter exiled Old Believers to Nerchinsk but, alarmed by reports that they were proselytizing throughout Siberia, began to assign them to Rogervik instead.[25]

The Seven Years' War (1756–62) brought both an expansion of *katorga* and a relocation of its major operations. Desperately in need of silver, lead and iron to finance and fight its wars, Petersburg strove to develop Nerchinsk's industries. Prior to 1740 Nerchinsk's works smelted only 200 poods silver; but during the succeeding decade smelted 364 poods; and 1,073 poods between 1750 and 1761. Peter's successors continued transferring subjects to the region to serve as laborers or peasants. In 1759 Elizabeth sent *posadskie* from Tomsk and other *uezdy* there; and the following year began transferring penal laborers of both sexes from Rogervik to work in Nerchinsk's mines. Over the next seven years, as the Baltic port finally neared completion, officials siphoned off penal laborers and sent them to Nerchinsk, making it, rather than Rogervik, Russia's largest *katorga* site during Catherine II's reign.[26]

* * *

For every ukase issued between 1725 and 1762 that designated the use of exiles as colonists there seems to have been one or more that assigned them to fortresses, factories or mines. The jumble of contradictory legislation indicates this period's inconsistent penology compared to that of Peter's reign. The government probably did not even know where the majority of exiles were located, what with *Sibirskii prikaz's* lack of record-keeping (one reason we have so few statistics for this period) and the large number of escapees. Nevertheless, an important development during this time was Elizabeth's systematizing of penal sentences and categories. Cyril Bryner has written that whereas it cannot be confirmed that Elizabeth actually promised God she would abolish capital punishment if her bid to seize the throne proved successful, she was nevertheless motivated to do so by religious conviction.[27] Bryner, however, overlooks the significance of the simultaneously established scale of punishments, which suggests that abolition was part of a general reform of the procedures established by the 1649 *Ulozhenie*. Most likely initiated by Elizabeth's favorite, Petr I. Shuvalov, both the tariff of punishments and abolition of the death penalty reflected attempts to more systematically utilize convicts. The emphasis here is on *attempts*, for shortcomings inherent in the legislation of both Elizabeth and her successor Catherine, combined with the severity of extant punishments and administrative problems, negated much of these reforms' intended benefits. 'The most benevolent person will probably entertain no extraordinary veneration for this boasted abolition of capital punishment,' wrote the Englishman William Coxe, who visited Russia in the late 1770s,

[w]hen he reflects, that though the criminal laws in Russia do not *literally* sentence malefactors to death, they still consign many to that doom through the medium of punishments, in some circumstances, almost assuredly, if not professedly, fatal, which mock the hopes of life, but in reality protract the horrors of death, and embitter with delay an event which reason and humanity wish to be instantaneous. For when we consider that many felons expire under the infliction, or from the consequences of the knoot [*sic*]; that several are exhausted by the fatigue of the long journey to Nershinsk [*sic*], and that the forlorn remnant perish in general prematurely from the unwhole-someness of the mines, it will be difficult to view the doom of these unhappy outcasts in any other light than that of lingering execution. In effect, since the promulgation of the edict [abolishing capital punishment], a year has never passed in which many atrocious criminals, though legally condemned to other penalties, have not suffered death. And indeed, upon a general calculation, perhaps it will be found, that notwithstanding the apparent mildness of the penal code, not fewer malefactors suffer death in Russia, than in those countries wherein that mode of punishment is appointed by the laws.[28]

Prior to reforming judicial sentences the government had hoped other legislation would help to manage colonization and labor in Siberia. Thus, a 1733 ukase punished with exile those who counterfeited anything made of silver; soldiers who deserted or purposely injured themselves were to be exiled; and until 1767 defaulters on loans and those in arrears to the government (*kazennye nedoishniki*) were to be exiled. Exile became the standard punishment for begging and vagabondage, crimes suffi-ciently common to produce many more unwilling colonists. Yet the state wanted to profit from these exiles' labor as well, and so in 1732 Anna condemned to corporal punishment and labor in Siberian factor-ies monks who fled their monasteries disguised as laymen; three years later one of her ukases condemned criminals to exile for life in state factories; and towards the end of her reign Anna considered the thorny issue of using Old Believers in factories and mines while making sure they did not proselytize among their co-workers. In 1750, presaging her abolition of capital punishment, Elizabeth ordered all political criminals facing execution to be sent to *katorga* instead. Five years later she issued an ukase warning directors of state factories they would be fined if any workers escaped, something which suggests the state's reliance on both penal and peasant laborers as well as a high escape rate.[29] Eighteenth-century legislation, in other words, perpetuated the trend established by the 1649 *Ulozhenie* of producing convicts and exiles for utilization by the state.

In separate ukases dated 25 May 1753 and 30 September 1754, Elizabeth abolished capital punishment except for treason and other very serious crimes; officially replaced the death sentence with *katorga* for life; and designated three main categories of exile. 'In fact,' argues LeDonne, 'the death penalty was never abolished, but it remained mandatory for a large number of offences, and the "courts" continued to impose it as a matter of course in accordance with the *Ulozhenie*, the Military Articles of Peter the Great, and other laws.'[30] LeDonne's source, the *Collected Laws* (*Pol´noe Sobranie Zakonov*), is however misleading, for while laws prescribing capital punishment for a number of offences remained after 1753–4, the government had been routinely substituting exile or *katorga* for the death penalty since 1649. This is not to say that many did not die as a result of *corporal* punishment – they did. But with the notable exception of the *Bironovshchina* during Anna's reign, relatively few executions were carried out in Russia between the mid-seventeenth century and the monarchy's final years. Indeed, as Sidney Monas notes, the hanging of five Decembrists in 1826 represented 'the appearance of a scaffold in Russia for the first time in fifty years'.[31] Between 1876 and 1905 Russia experienced only four executions per one million subjects – an execution rate significantly lower than those of other European countries and the United States.[32] Certainly, Siberian officials often ignored finer legal distinctions, failed in practice to distinguish between penal laborers and exile-settlers and, because of general mismanagement, perpetuated a brutal penal system. But the 1753–4 ukases were not without effect.

Of the categories created or further defined by Elizabeth, that called 'exile to labor' (*ssylka na rabotu*) did little more than rename *katorga*. In place of the death penalty the numerous chanceries with judicial authority were now to sentence convicts to life or fixed terms within this category. Convicts were still to be knouted, but the excruciatingly painful slitting of the nostrils was replaced by the branding of the forehead and cheeks, usually with the Cyrillic letters 'B-O-P' (*vor*, 'thief'), or 'Б' if the convict was a *brodiaga* (vagabond). At some point those sentenced to *katorga* began receiving a 'К' on their foreheads, in a practice that continued into the mid-nineteenth century.[33] Despite Elizabeth's prohibiting the slitting of nostrils, this and many other rulings limiting scourging were routinely ignored. William Coxe reports seeing a convict's nostrils 'torn with pincers' well after Elizabeth's death. But if the women who occupied the throne during this period truly did oppose such scourges, then it must have been those officials who stood somewhere between sovereign and executioner, and who adopted the sovereign's need to demonstrate power and authority by desecrating the subject body, who were responsible for perpetuating them. Such usurpation represents both a weakening of sovereign authority and a diffusion of power – which nevertheless still found expression in traditional modes of punishment – and as such frustrated development of a coherent modern penology based on discipline and rehabilitation.

Second on the scale of punishments was 'exile to permanent settlement' (*ssylka na vechnoe poselenie*), which the relevant ukase characterized as an administrative procedure and pardon from *katorga*. Although the ostensible purpose was colonization, the law now called for each convict to serve a term of several years in a state factory or mine before being sent to a settlement. Ideally, therefore, the same convict would serve the state as both laborer and colonist. But if the rigors of the march to Siberia did not ruin his physical health, then conditions in factories and mines often did, thereby rendering him useless for tilling the soil. Many exiles escaped before they completed their labor terms and could even be sent to the countryside; and poor record-keeping and exiles' and prison officials' shared ignorance and illiteracy resulted in others remaining in labor sites for years longer than those specified by their sentences. In addition to assigning exiles to *preliminary* terms of labor, the 1753–4 legislation also called for exiles (*ssyl´nye*) to be *permanently* assigned to state industries, thus confounding the very notion of 'exile to settlement'. Under this scheme, the treasury could assign exiles to one of four categories after they completed preliminary labor terms: 1) to build *poseleniia* from scratch in remote and under-populated regions (e.g. Turukhansk *uezd*); 2) to reside in villages of long-term residents (so-called *starozhily*), either permanently or until relocated to state *poseleniia*; 3) to replenish factory labor forces; or 4), if aged or otherwise unfit for work, to be assigned as so-called *propitannye* ('those-being-maintained') to peasant villages, where they were expected to survive as best they could, or incarcerated in prison (though with so few prisons at that time very few exiles met this fate).

The third category effectively transformed *ssyl´nye* into penal laborers (*katorzhnye*), the only difference being they were spared corporal punishment before deportation. 'Permanent exile to settlement' would nonetheless expand much faster than 'exile to labor': '[L]ittle by little,' writes Foinitskii, 'individual ukases began to assign [to settlements] those incapable of military service, or used this as a punishment for insignificant crimes – thus, by 1775, all those convicted of a first offence of theft [were so sentenced].'[34] Both 'exile to labor' and 'exile to settlement' were accompanied by a loss of rights that deprived the convict of his property and essentially nullified his existence as a member of civil society. Such exiles were not allowed to return home without the sovereign's permission.

The third main category of exile designated by Elizabeth was 'exile for residence' (*ssylka na zhit ë*), a much less stringent punishment than the others. Theoretically, the categories to which convicts were assigned depended on the nature of their offences rather than their social rank, but sources agree that 'exile for residence' largely involved the nobility, and during the nineteenth century this association was made official. The crown (as opposed to the treasury) determined locations for convicts who received this sentence and who, after 1770, tended to be sent to locations closer to rather than farther from Petersburg. Unlike those in other categories, convicts exiled for residence did not serve a labor sentence, and in 1799 even obtained the right to enter the merchant *soslovie* after a certain number of years.

In practice, these exilic categories were often confused or ignored as a result of haphazard administration, local officials who could not read or understand their orders, and a justice system which did not properly supervise exiles' distribution after dispatching them to Siberia. Other detrimental factors were the ukases' vagueness and inherent contradictions, which themselves reflect the autocracy's inattention to detail. The overlapping definitions of *katorga* and 'exile to settlement' were replicated in ukases from 1760 until the end of the century that often assigned exile-settlers to labor in the same locations (e.g. Nerchinsk, Ekaterinburg) as penal laborers. When both groups of convicts arrived at such locations officials gave little heed to legal niceties and simply assigned them to the same hard labor regime. Nevertheless, this legislation's content – if not its impact – demonstrates an effort to lessen Russian penality's arbitrariness and cruelty and to systematize the employment of convicts for statist goals. Further evidence of this is a 1755 ukase ordering that documents detailing crime and punishment (*spiski* – essentially, rap sheets) accompany each deportee to Siberia. These *spiski* ideally forestalled confusion over convicts and their sentences, though were no guarantee against sloppiness and malfeasance.

Elizabeth's legacy concerning exile is therefore a mixed one. She sought to maximize the state's use of exile as an institution and to rationalize the system, while at the same time curb its barbarity. Nonetheless, the eighteenth century's single most important ukase concerning exile, also issued during her reign, reflects the arbitrariness that undermined the development of legalism in Russia.

On 13 December 1760 the Senate promulgated an ukase allowing landowners and monasteries to turn over their serfs to the state. By drawing on lists typically prepared by village headmen, landowners could now choose men and women labeled 'indecent', 'obscene' or of 'rude conduct' for removal to Siberia. In return, males over the age of 15 counted against serf owners' military recruitment quotas, and for each male under the age of 15 they were paid 20 rubles and 10 rubles for those under the age of five. Female serfs fetched half price. The same ukase also granted communes (both *obshchestva* and *meshchanstva*) the right to banish members to Siberia. Three subsequent ukases – one in 1761, two in 1762 – reiterated the substance of the original while further extending civil authorities' exilic powers.[35] Serfs and state peasants exiled under these ukases were called *posel´shchiki*, a diminutive of the word for settlers (*poselentsy*). Most *posel´shchiki* were assigned as colonists, though Alan Wood and V. N. Dvorianov have separately pointed out that prior to issuing the December ukase, the Senate debated for months how best to drum up laborers for the Nerchinsk mines, and they have on this basis argued that like *ssyl´nye posel´shchiki* were used as laborers.[36] However, it would seem only a small minority of *posel´shchiki* were so used.

Serf owners and communal leaders expeditiously used this new method of 'exile by administrative order' (*ssylka po administrativnomu poriadku*) to rid themselves of troublesome serfs and neighbors in much the same way military recruitment was often used. Moreover, the monetary inducements facilitated a Gogolian speculation in living souls. 'Some landlords,' writes Jerome Blum, 'to save good workers from the army draft, banished inefficient and infirm serfs whose only offence was their ineptitude or incapacity.'[37] In fact, the large numbers of *posel´shchiki* suggest a great many landlords did just that. Administrative exile resulted in the deportation of hundreds of thousands of persons never convicted by a court and therefore not criminals by any legal definition. Civilian use of administrative exile would grow so widespread that by the second quarter of the nineteenth century administrative exiles accounted for half the exilic population, a proportion that remained constant until the end of the century. At a time when the crown was considerably weaker than during Peter's reign, it invited subjects to participate in the already oft-abused business of exile. The lowliest of subjects, far from exercising this terrible authority with equanimity and prudence, eagerly exceeded the arbitrariness and improbity of their rulers.

*   *   *

Following Elizabeth's death in December 1761 and Peter III's violently foreshortened reign, Catherine II won the throne in 1762. For her, the punishment of exile served essentially the same purposes it had her predecessors: it removed political contenders; was a form of social control and repression against criminals, Cossacks, Old Believers, Poles and rebels; and colonized Siberia and built an industrial workforce. During her reign the number sent each year to Siberia steadily grew, though as with earlier periods, quantitative evidence is disparate. At the same time, and more than any of her predecessors, Catherine took steps to lighten the punishment meted out to criminals. Hers were baby-steps by today's standards, but nonetheless reflected the meliorating influence of such Enlightenment humanists as Beccaria and Montesquieu.

'It seems to us,' write the Soviet demographers V. M. Kabuzan and S. M. Troitskii, noting the upward spike in Siberia's non-indigenous male population from 261,000 to 389,000 during the first 20 years of Catherine's reign, 'that this may be explained by the increase during this time in the number of peasants escaping to Siberia, and also the growth in the number of exiles.'[38] Both peasant flight and deportation can in turn be explained by serfdom's enormous growth and spread into Ukraine, Belorussia and newly annexed territories, for as Nikolai Novikov exclaimed at the time: 'Stupid serf owners! These poor slaves seem to you more like horses and dogs than people.'[39] Peasants fleeing to Siberia, however, failed to increase its Russian population *as a percentage* of the empire's total population, in part because they tended to be single males who produced no offspring. Though Siberia's Russian population was growing, it was doing so too slowly for Petersburg. Whereas serfdom caused many peasants to flee, it limited more the number of persons who might have migrated to Siberia. This lack of voluntary migrants and the need to pacify the serf-owning nobility by allowing and even assisting them to reclaim runaway serfs presented two major obstacles to colonizing the region. Catherine responded in several ways, including advertising across Europe for foreigners to settle Siberia; expanding the number of crimes punishable by exile; and increasing civilian authorities' powers of administrative exile and even offering them inducements to use it. None of these efforts had the desired effect. What the empress did achieve was a significant increase in the exile population and in promoting both official and civilian authorities' greater reliance on deportation as a punitive measure.

The first of these steps, advertising for foreign settlers, does not concern us, so let us begin with Catherine's legislative efforts to expand exile's use. Several examples suffice. A 1763 ukase prescribed that if charged with theft, robbery or harboring criminals, defendants who could not post bail would be exiled for life to Siberia as 'unreliables' (*neblagonadezhnye*). In 1767 this self-styled Minerva who claimed to be enlightening her benighted people revived an article from the 1649 *Ulozhenie* forbidding petitions to the sovereign unless they reported treasonous acts; violators were to be knouted and exiled to Nerchinsk *katorga*. In 1792, one year after Tobol´sk's first production of *The Brigadier* – Denis Fonvizin's parody of official life and one of Catherine's favorite plays – she ordered exiles assigned to the state distilleries there. Finally, thanks to her promotion of administrative exile, landowners banished so many *posel´shchiki* in 1773 that the army lost an estimated 7,000–8,000 potential recruits. 'All these persons,' observed Coxe,

> are transported in spring and autumn from different parts of the Russian dominions. They travel partly by water and partly by land, are chained in pairs, and fastened to a long rope. When the whole troop arrives at Tobolsk, the governor assigns the colonists who are versed in handicraft trades, to different masters in the town; others he disposes as vassals in the neighbouring country. The remainder of the colonists proceed to Irkutsk, where they are distributed by the governor in the same manner. The felons are then conveyed to the district of Nershinsk [*sic*], where they are condemned to work in the silver mines, or at different forges.[40]

Despite her naked expansion of *katorga* and exile, Catherine, like Elizabeth before her, sought to improve the exile system. Her legislation permitting landowners to exile serfs so as to satisfy recruitment quotas clearly stated that only able-bodied peasants no older than 45 were acceptable; that those who were to be beaten as part of their punishment were not to be incapacitated by said punishment; and that serf owners could not use the law to rid themselves of the elderly, crippled or sick. Her intention was to ensure that what were in essence the state's chattels would be fit on delivery. But despite Catherine's simultaneous expansion of the police apparatus, enforcement of these restrictions seems to have been nonexistent, as this was indeed the nobility's 'Golden Age' and they brooked no interference with a policy that essentially allowed them to bilk the state. Thus landowners violated these restrictions with impunity, capitalizing on Elizabeth's and Catherine's enormous extension of their rights to purge their estates of old and useless serfs they could not otherwise expunge via the military draft.

Catherine's other legislation concerning the exile system met with similarly mixed results. She addressed problems resulting from the absence of guidelines specifying how exiles were to be transported by ordering, in 1769, and more precisely four years later, that military personnel be assigned to convoy exile parties. Exiles were to be marched shackled to each other *seriatum* (*na kanatakh*). The ratio of guards to prisoners is suggested by a party of 170 Poles known to have been escorted by ten soldiers and one officer. However, convoy regulations also called for local indigenes to be pressed into duty for up to two years if soldiers were unavailable. Such shanghaied natives exacerbated exiles' misery. Bashkirs and Meshcheriaks in the Kazan region became especially notorious for their corruption and abuse of prisoners, many of whom died or fled for their lives. Furthermore, administrators tended to ignore the rap sheets legislated under Elizabeth, and treated indiscriminately *posel´shchiki* and those exiled to *katorga*, settlement or residence. The only Catherinian ukases which positively affected operation of the exile system were quite specific. For example, in 1785 the empress ordered that exiles who fell sick during the march not be moved any further until they received medical care; and she granted a general amnesty to penal laborers who had worked no less than five years in the Nerchinsk factories and shown 'improvement' – they were to be rewarded by being sent to labor 'in the fields' instead.[41] This last act reflects the growing view of exile as a rehabilitative punishment and suggests that Catherine was broadly influenced by Enlightenment notions of penology.

Such notions also played a role in Catherine's becoming the only Russian autocrat to abolish Siberian exile. The background to this abolition is as follows. In 1770 she exiled 150 Zaporozh´e Cossacks to the Siberian Line and directed that others caught avoiding military recruitment be exiled to Siberia for 20 years. Petersburg's persecution of Cossacks in the years leading up to the Pugachev uprising not only helped create the font of rebellious subjects from which the tsar-impersonator readily drew his following, but most importantly for us here, it served to overwhelm the exile system. On 30 November 1773, in the midst of the *Pugachevshchina*, Catherine issued a manifesto abolishing exile. This is worth quoting at length since it demonstrates, first, the complexity characterizing deportation procedures by this time; second, the autocracy's reliance on exile; and finally, the sheer volume of prisoners:

Her Imperial Majesty – having learned that in Kazan there are up to 200 criminals sentenced to exile in Orenburg; that there are up to 700 persons en route there under the Moscow Investigative Bureau

[*Moskovskaia Rozysknaia Ekspeditsiia*]; that on top of this, there are in the same place [Kazan] still more than 4,000 people from various locations sentenced to exile to Siberia, and not an insignificant number of Poles and returnees from Siberia awaiting resettlement to their homelands – has deigned to order that henceforth those sentenced to exile in Orenburg and Siberia, as well as those [to be assigned] to *poseleniia*, proceed no further, and that the Senate consider other places to which those who have already proceeded and those who have accompanied them can be distributed. All criminals, instead of going to Orenburg and Siberia, shall be dispersed [as follows]: [convicts originating] from Smolensk, Belgorod, and Slobodskoi *gubernii* [shall go] to the new line at Aleksandrovsk fortress; [those] from Moscow, Kazan, Voronezh, Nizhegorod [*gubernii*], and other places in the Moscow region [shall go] to Azov and Taganrog; [those] from Arkhangelogorod *guberniia* [shall go] to fortress labor in Finland[;] and [those] from Petersburg and Novgorod *gubernii*, and points between Moscow and Petersburg, and from Moscow itself, [shall go] to Riga and to labor along the Dvina [*Dvinskaia rabota*].... Until further notice, this ukase forbids [the exile] to settlement of those brought to and currently in Kazan, [and orders] their redistribution to their previous residences in the same manner in which they were brought [to Kazan or Siberia].[42]

This manifesto appeared two and a half months after Pugachev issued his first edict in the guise of Peter III and launched his devastating campaign against Orenburg, and so the impetus behind what proved a brief suspension of Siberian exile was Catherine's recognition that deporting more convicts east would simply swell Pugachev's army, which already contained large numbers of exiles. That the uprising was a veritable civil war which the empress needed to take seriously is shown by the fact that when it ended in 1774 it had claimed 20,000 Russian lives, more than were lost during the Seven Years' War. The same month as her manifesto, Catherine announced a 1,000-ruble bounty on Pugachev's head.

But if the uprising itself and the need to deny fuel for the fire were what initially provoked the manifesto, several ukases issued in 1775 ordering creation of work- and strait-houses (*rabochie* and *smiritel´nye doma*) support an interpretation that Catherine genuinely intended to abolish exile once and for all. Both work- and strait-houses seem to have been modeled on the workhouses that proliferated throughout Western Europe beginning in the late sixteenth century and which were designed to eliminate begging and vagrancy by cultivating productive work habits. Foinitskii assumes Catherine's model was the strait-houses Peter I had created for 'holding in permanent labor persons of an indecent and intemperate [*nepotrebnago i nevozderzhanago*] lifestyle...'[43], which phrasing probably refers to groups similarly targeted in the West. Catherine undoubtedly knew of Peter's plans, though Foinitskii himself admits that few such institutions were ever built and that Peter preferred to send indecent and intemperate persons to *katorga*. M. N. Gernet is probably more on the mark in citing Voltaire's letters to Catherine as well as Beccaria's writings as being most influential.

Whatever her inspiration, Catherine had both humanitarian and disciplinary motives for ordering such institutions built in each *guberniia* capital. In March 1775, shortly before ordering the workhouses, she allowed Siberian exile to resume, and so must have realized that they would not immediately replace the exile system, but nevertheless seems to have believed that some convicts could better serve the state in these institutions than through exile. Yet, as with so many of Catherine's projects, there was a lapse between word and deed, and despite a 1781 Senate ukase replicating the substance of those issued several years earlier, only one strait-house appears to have ever been established, on Petersburg's Vasil'evskii Island that same year, for after her initial rapture Catherine neglected to finance the project. There is some indication that attempts were made to construct additional strait-houses towards the very end of her reign. But when Paul I ordered all such institutions demolished in September 1797 there was really nothing to tear down, since with the exception of that on Vasil'evskii Island none had been built. Curiously, Paul reversed himself two years later, opening the way for the construction of a workhouse near Irkutsk, to be discussed below.[44]

Nevertheless, in the immediate aftermath of the November 1773 abolition of exile, the Senate responded by returning some exiles to their homes and redirecting others to fortresses, though the prisons to which Catherine fancifully wanted to send most convicts were too few and too small to contain those removed to them. Coxe, who later visited prisons in Petersburg and Moscow in 1778, provides descriptions of overcrowding and disease that suggest they must have been hell-holes when the exiles were earlier sent to them. Gernet supports Coxe's account by showing just how small these prisons (really, jails) were: Petersburg's main prison held only around 150 inmates; Kronshtadt's around 250; and Tambov's a maximum of 200. And these were among the largest in Russia at the time. The Shlissel'burg and Peter and Paul fortresses also incarcerated (usually political) prisoners, who were held in thick-walled casemates. The former's capacity was around 100, the latter's probably no more than 300—400. By comparison, Rogervik's *katorga* barracks held 1,000 penal laborers.[45] These prisons' limited capacity combined with failure to establish the workhouses quickly made apparent that if exile were permanently abolished, Russia would have no means with which to address its convict population.

Within a year and a half of its abolition exile to Orenburg and Siberia resumed. This allowed the state to banish what Iadrintsev estimates were the 5,000 arrested at the height of the Pugachev uprising, some of whom were distributed to *katorga* sites throughout the empire. Anisimov claims that during the 1770s the regime was exiling 10,000 criminals a year to Siberia, a figure that would seem too high were it not for the repressions both preceding and following the uprising. As for Pugachev himself, it was necessary he be made an example of. Hearkening back to the traditions of the seventeenth century, yet with a slight nod towards Beccaria, Catherine allowed Pugachev to be beheaded *before* he was quartered on 10 January 1775. The bearded and pockmarked head of this man-who-would-be-king was put on a stake, the four quarters of his body mounted and burned on wheels posted at the four corners of Moscow. Catherine's desecration of Pugachev's body was doubly necessitated by the sovereign weakness his uprising had exposed.

In sum, Catherine's administration proved unable to develop effective alternatives for the huge numbers of exiles now being generated by her and previous rulers' legislation. Nor was the management of exile significantly improved, overwhelmed as the system was by greater than ever numbers. After the failure to definitively abolish exile, the penal system slipped out from under autocratic control to assume a life of its own, like tubers choking their host.

*   *   *

Political and religious exile continued apace under Catherine. She exiled, for instance, the peasant Chernyshev, another Peter III impersonator, first to Nerchinsk then to Mangazeia in the far north. Kondratii Selivanov, founder of the *skoptsy*, a self-castrating Old Believer sect, was exiled to Irkutsk in 1774. Years later, after he had awarded himself the title of emperor, Selivanov was brought to Petersburg and personally interrogated by Emperor Paul. In 1772, in response to the murder of General von Traubenberg and others in the Orenburg garrison, Catherine ordered that dozens of Iaik Cossacks have their nostrils slit and be exiled with their families.[46]

Early in her reign Catherine struck particularly harshly against Old Believers. In 1762 the Senate issued what was essentially an amnesty for Old Believers who had crossed the border into Poland to escape persecution, but this was never acted on, probably because of confusion over the succession at the time. A couple of years later Catherine sent troops across the border to capture thousands of Old Believers whom she then exiled to the Altai and Zabaikal´e. She was motivated not by religious zeal but statist concerns, for around this time she also ordered that Old Believers caught trying to avoid the double poll tax imposed on them since Peter I's reign be exiled to Nerchinsk *katorga*. Catherine also continued the practice, begun under Peter, of exiling Old Believers to the Caucasus. Raeff, apparently in the belief that the Senate's 1762 amnesty for Old Believers was a general policy, claims that Old Believers from Poland who ended up in Siberia went there voluntarily.[47] Yet even if some did avail themselves of the amnesty before the Russians launched their punitive cross-border raids, they did so in the knowledge that if they refused, they faced harsh reprisals. It seems fair to say that they faced an invidious choice between living the life of refugees under constant threat of persecution or migrating thousands of kilometers from their homeland to avoid the long arm of the autocracy. Being skewered on the horns of such a dilemma hardly represents freedom of choice.

According to later chronicles the first Old Believers exiled to the Irkutsk region arrived in December 1756. Prior to this comparatively few were exiled, though many had been escaping since the Great Schism to Siberia, whose remoteness allowed separatists to thrive. Old Believer missionaries, especially from the Kerzhenskii and Brynskii monasteries, spread their belief throughout the countryside. As early as 1681 the government responded by dispatching a Nikonian clergyman 'good and skilful in teaching, for educating disbelievers with Christian law'. It is not clear how many such clergymen went to Siberia, but in any case they were unable to impede the spread of pre-Nikonian Orthodoxy. Old Believers were sober and hard-working, and their penchant for having children made them perhaps the fastest growing of all Siberia's religious or ethnic groups. The Old Belief also spread to the cities and as such gained protection from local officials, who falsely reported an absence of Old Believers to Petersburg. Protection was probably not a reflection of the officials' piety but rather the universally held conviction that Old Believers were a necessary antidote to the exiles, who generally detracted from, rather than contributed to, regional economies. Hence the Sibirsk *guberniia* chancery prematurely concluded in 1727 that virtually no Old Believers were left in the Urals, though the contemporary historian

V. N. Tatishchev, a resident of the region, believed the 'core' of these 'superstitious persons' was rooted in the forests surrounding the Demidov works. These and other Old Believers had their own clergy who clandestinely existed within the official church and its monasteries. So it was that in the early 1800s, in Zabaikal´e, Chikoiskii Monastery's senior priest, a man named Izrail, established together with a woman merchant from the region a secret sect in the nearby Kiakhta Hills. The sect turned into something of a cult, with its own versions of God, Christ, the apostles, and ceremonies and hymns based on Old Believer poetry. After the authorities raided the community, Izrail was convicted of heresy and cohabitation with the woman and exiled to Solovetskii Monastery, where he died in 1863.[48]

The greatest influx of Old Believers occurred during Catherine II's reign. In 1772, the German zoographer P. S. Pallas counted 2,520 Old Believers living in eight settlements along the Selenga River in Zabaikal´e, where they were colloquially known as *semeiskie* (an adjectival noun connoting both 'family' and 'seed'). A Nordic doctor travelling with the Russian military in 1776 described the villages of Bobrovskoe and Sekisovskoe, located on the Irtysh River in the Altai, as being populated exclusively by exiles from Poland, though in fact these would have been the Old Believers mentioned above. Bobrovskoe and Sekisovskoe numbered between 200 and 300 households each and, according to the doctor, had been founded at the end of the previous decade, which would correlate with Russia's 1767 annexation of parts of Poland. He characterized the inhabitants as 'honest and hard-working farmers' in contrast to 'the negligent, debauched, so called *posel´shchiki* exiled from Russia'. Other early nineteenth-century investigations revealed thousands of Old Believers – Catherinian deportees and their descendants – living in communities in the Altai and Zabaikal´e. A total of 8,000 Old Believer males lived in a 400 verst-long series of villages in Zabaikal´e's Verkhneudinsk *okrug*, where most engaged in cattle-raising. When the Decembrists Nikolai and Mikhail Bestuzhev settled in this region after their *katorga* terms, they found that, with the exception of the native Buriats, Old Believers accounted for the majority of the population.[49]

If the Old Believers were exiled for their religious affiliation, many under Catherine were exiled because of their political links. As far as political suppression went, exile was a comparatively humane weapon in Catherine's arsenal. Stepan I. Sheshkovskii, secretary-general of the Senate and director of the Secret Bureau (*Tainaia ekspeditsiia*), was valued by the empress for his inquisitorial skills. A major concern of the autocracy at this time was Freemasonry, which Sheshkovskii colorfully termed 'that monstrous creation of the blood-sucking philosophy of Enlightenment politics emerging from the French Revolution'.[50] Able to inspire both trust and fear in the hearts of those he met, Sheshkovskii was a sadomasochist who ordered cadets to flog him and personally took on the task of torturing those noblemen and -women arrested by his Secret Bureau. At one point Catherine ordered him to flog two of her ladies-in-waiting for having drawn caricatures of Potemkin. Iadrintsev relates a conversation which supposedly took place between Potemkin and Sheshkovskii, in which the former 'casually' asks the latter how he 'wages war with the knout [*knutoboinchaet*]'. Sheshkovskii replies, 'A little bit at a time [*ponemnozhku*]' – a multi-layered pun on the words 'according to', 'knife' and '(little) foot'. Iadrintsev ends this tale with his own neologism: 'The *knutoboinichan´e* [knout-war] was a constant and natural occurrence during the [eighteenth] century.'[51] Yet Sheshkovskii and his minions could torture only so many malefactors, and so Catherine, like her predecessors, relied on exile to deal with the rest. When in the late 1760s several Horse Guards officers reportedly complained about privileges supposed to be granted the serfs, she charged them with treason and deported them to Siberia. She also exiled the fugitive serf F. I. Bogomolov who, like nine other convicts between the years 1764 and 1772, claimed to be Catherine's deceased husband, Peter III. Bogomolov died on the march to Siberia.[52]

Aleksandr Radishchev is probably the most famous individual Catherine punished with exile. Assigned with his wife and children to Ilimsk, which at the time was a ramshackle village consisting of 46 shacks, Radishchev nonetheless seems to have weathered his banishment well. While there he completed a philosophical treatise entitled *On Man, his Mortality and Immortality*; studied local shamanistic practices; and wrote geographical descriptions which, according to the historian Jesse Clardy, 'contributed considerably to the knowledge of that region'. Anisimov similarly notes that Radishchev 'was able to walk the hills and meadows, and also to collect items for a herbarium, to teach children, and to serve as a physician for local inhabitants. He was even allowed to marry the sister of his deceased wife.'[53] Radishchev returned to European Russia after Catherine's death. In seeing that he and other political exiles from the nobility were treated well Catherine broke with tradition, for prior to her reign exiles from the privileged classes suffered worse than did the unprivileged. This change reflected both her humanitarian sentiments and political adroitness.

Also in Siberia during Catherine's reign was a small group of 'secret prisoners' (*sekretnye arestanty*) about whom little is known. The Soviet historian M. A. Braginskii notes that the term 'secret arrest' first appeared at this time, which may point to the prominence of Sheshkovskii's Secret Bureau. The government certainly viewed its secret prisoners as a threat. According to Braginskii, one of the first was a certain Anton Alekseev assigned to Nerchinsk Zavod in March 1776. His death in 1807 at the ripe old age of 85 suggests he did not so much labor as loll about there.[54] Archival documents concerning seven other secret prisoners held in Siberia suggest they were deemed guilty of either overt political crimes or what was increasingly being called 'political unreliability'. A series of semi-annual reports issued between 1824 and 1835, signed by Irkutsk *guberniia's* governor Ivan B. Tseidler and addressed to Eastern Siberia's governor-general, indicate four of the seven were peasants from the village of Il'dikanskoe in the Nerchinsk Mining District. Of these Osip Anan'in, 89 years old in October 1825, had been in Siberia since April 1788, that is, two years before Radishchev. The other three men, whose ages are unknown, arrived in the district together in November 1797. A fifth man, 55-year-old Nikifor Korokovtsev, had been exiled to Nerchinsk Zavod in October 1821. The final two secret prisoners were under the jurisdiction of Irkutsk's *guberniia* administration. Ninety year-old Vasilii Kalinin, described as an 'exile-laborer [*ssyl'norabochii*] from the Nerchinsk mining *zavody*', had been in exile for 24 years and, as of 1825, was living in Irkutsk, though in what circumstances is unclear. So-called 'foreigner' Fedor Brink had been exiled in 1807 and was now living in Iakutsk in similarly mysterious circumstances. Tseidler's reports on each of these men are perfunctory, providing only their age (if known), location, duration in exile, behavior and mental state. In his October 1825 report he describes all as 'being of sound mind and maintaining themselves well', with the exception of the nonagenarian Kalinin, who was 'not of completely sound mind'. Despite the reports' brevity, each is headlined 'as a matter of high importance'.[55]

As these secret prisoners' existence implies, during Catherine's reign 'political exile' became more broadly defined. As such, it involved large numbers of Poles. Karol Lubicz-Chojecki, exiled following Russia's defeat of the Confederation of Bar in 1772, estimated that 5,000 Poles remained in Siberia even after large numbers were returned home as part of Catherine's temporary abolition of exile. The historian Antoni Kuczynski writes that Polish exiles 'were forced to fight [Pugachev's] insurgents. One party deserted and fought at their side…'[56] During his travels Pallas counted (in addition to Old Believers) 1,534 'Polish colonists' along the Selenga River. Poles also lived along the Lena and Enisei, contributing to the development of agriculture there.[57]

As such, Poles formed part of Siberia's unique ethnic mix, even going so far as to establish their own Catholic monasteries (which Nicholas I would later investigate on suspicion that they were harboring fugitives).[58] In summer 1817 a Polish Catholic priest (*ksendz*) named Mashevskii traveled through Zabaikal´e seeking to minister to believers' spiritual needs. He reported encountering Polish speakers, yet added that many had neither lived in Poland nor were Catholics, all of which suggests they had descended from exiles and converted to Orthodoxy. On 24 July Mashevskii reached Nerchinsk. 'This city is no better than the absolute worst Belorussian cities...,' he complained. 'Here I found nine Catholics. After giving them necessary assistance I visited the Nerchinsk *zavody* where I met more of my co-religionists, bereft of hope.' Despite there being thousands of Poles in Siberia at the time, Mashevskii reported meeting 'only 200 Catholics, of whom 168 made confession'.[59]

Catherine's reign therefore marks the beginning of a long and colorful – though often painful – relationship between Polish nationals and Siberia. Following the 1794 rebellion she exiled the Confederate Iosif Kopets to Kamchatka, where he later managed to attract the favorable attention of Khristofor A. Treiden (or Treident), who briefly served as Siberia's governor-general in 1798. Treiden ignored orders from Petersburg to subject Kopets and other Poles to harsh treatment and so allowed him to relocate to Irkutsk *guberniia*, where he founded a settlement of Polish and Russian exiles called Kir´iuga.[60]

Siberia's most famous exiled revolutionary during this period was the Hungarian count Mauritius Benëvskii, who arrived in Kamchatka in early December 1770 along with another defender of Polish liberty, the Swede Adolf Vinbladt. They and as many as 60 other Confederates were assigned to the local governor, Nilov, who resided with his family at Bol´sheretsk *ostrog*. Located on the peninsula's lower west coast, Bol´sheretsk was Kamchatka's only Russian settlement besides Petropavlovsk, and consisted of 500 izbas occupied by *promyshlenniki* and 700 cossacks and their families and a fort where lived the Nilov family and a 240-man garrison. Benëvskii's memoir is a rollicking tale of intrigue, murder, romance and global travel. How faithful it is to the truth is another matter; but it remains one of few sources on Kamchatka for this period. After the exiles arrived, Nilov gave them three days' provisions and told them they would have to fend for themselves after these ran out. In addition, each Confederate 'receive[d] ... a musket and a lance, with one pound of powder, four pounds of lead, a hatchet, several knives, and other instruments and carpenter's tools, with which we might build cabins,' writes Benëvskii, 'and [Nilov told us] that we were at liberty to choose our situations at a distance of one league from the town'. As part of their punishment the exiles had to spend one day a week laboring for the governorship, as well as provide it with a certain number of furs per year. Benëvskii immediately began conspiring with some other prisoners to escape. Putting into motion what he claims was a master plan, he won Nilov's favor by helping him win a chess game against the local hetman; charmed Nilov's wife and managed to become engaged to the couple's 16-year-old daughter; and bribed an indebted sea captain to secure his brig for leaving Bol'sheretsk. Whatever the truth, Nilov learned of the conspiracy and had Benëvskii arrested in April 1771. This sparked a revolt, and the small group of seasoned revolutionaries proceeded to capture the *ostrog* while much of the garrison was either drunk or off beating the bushes. Benëvskii found himself at one point being choked to death by Nilov, until one of his men 'set me at liberty by splitting [Nilov's] skull' in front of his wife and children. The exiles next foiled a counterattack by herding the cossacks' women and children into the church and threatening to torch it. Two weeks later Benëvskii, Vinbladt and some 100 others, including 29 *promyshlenniki* and nine women, set sail aboard the brig *Saints Peter and Paul*. Despite (or perhaps owing to) her father's murder, Nilov's daughter accompanied them. They undertook a spectacular journey that led them to Formosa (where they fought the natives), Macao (where many, including Nilov's daughter, died from illness), Madagascar and, finally, France. Benëvskii eventually obtained a commission from the French government and in 1784 returned to Madagascar as a colonial administrator.[61]

*   *   *

Catherine depended heavily on exile to remove political opponents and criminals, but its primary function during her reign was as a tool of colonization. She was intent on colonizing not only Siberia, but locations to the south and north of central Russia, particularly Novorossiia and Arkhangel *guberniia*. Prospective colonists were not willing to go to the latter region, but did volunteer for other locations. Many, if not most, were foreigners, including those who came to be known as the Volga Germans. Nonetheless, Petersburg found persuading foreigners to migrate to Siberia difficult. Ukases such as one ordering exile for artisans and laborers discovered intoxicated or gambling suggest the lengths Catherine was prepared to go to advance her agenda. She disingenuously gave landowners the right to exile serfs to Iakutiia 'for a certain length of time', knowing full well that having completed their indeterminate terms these

exiles would lack the means to return home from this proverbial waste-
land. Catherine also continued to offer landowners financial incentives
to turn over serfs as *posel´shchiki*.[62]

Immediately after promulgation of the December 1760 ukase establishing administrative exile, the government had begun gathering
posel´shchiki to build a section of the Great Siberian Road linking Omsk
with the upper Ob region. *Posel´shchiki* were also to be used as coachmen
(*iamshchiki*) to deliver goods and mail along the vast expanse between
Verkhotur´e and the village of Tulun, 320 kilometres west of Irkutsk,
and as colonists in Baraba Steppe. These three interrelated projects
were initiated during the period 1760–5, more or less in the order just
given. First, exiles began building the road; then the Siberian governor
F. I. Soimonov assigned 1,500 *posel´shchiki* to the steppe as coachmen;
and in 1762 assigned the first *posel´shchiki* as settlers. This last phase
reflected Petersburg's desire to secure western Siberia's southern border
and build a social infrastructure that would both produce food and facilitate commerce. During the growing season flooding turns much of this
area into marshland, but this did not deter officials from deporting thousands of *posel´shchiki* there. Petersburg gave each *posel´shchik* family 5
rubles and 54 poods of seed, absolved it of *obrok* payments for three
years and ordered it to farm five *desiatiny* and raise cattle. Denis I. Chicherin, Soimonov's successor as governor in 1763, supervised most of
the colonization project.[63]

Scholars' evaluations of the Baraba operation are mixed. In 1859 an
advocate of exilic colonies named G. Peizen wrote in *The Contemporary*:

> [S]ettlement in Siberia had never been carried out on such a large
> scale as in Baraba Steppe, and there is still no colony derived from
> exiles in Siberia which has been established on such a simple basis
> and brought as much of an actual benefit to the region as that created
> by Governor Chicherin. The blossoming villages and hamlets which
> now exist in the very best condition along the Baraba road constitute
> an indisputable monument to the Siberian administrator's energetic
> efforts.[64]

Peizen's praise for Chicherin should not be dismissed as sycophancy,
for he criticizes other Siberian colonization projects in the same article. Moreover, his use of statistical data suggests he was no dilettante.
The Soviet historian M. M. Gromyko, certainly no Chicherin sympath-
izer, also catalogues the project's accomplishments. As of 1771 a total
of 25 villages, comprising *posel´shchiki* and captured fugitive peasants

and including 2,459 men, 1,399 women, and 634 children, had been founded in western Baraba. One village was composed entirely of serfs originating from the city of Orël (it is not clear if they were fugitives or *posel´shchiki*), while another was made up of convicts originally assigned to the Baltic coast. The largest village consisted of 90 households; the smallest 25. The village of Krepenka, founded in 1764, had the largest adult male population (174).[65] Other scholars maintain that although a road and villages were indeed created, thousands of settlers died trying to graze their cattle in Baraba's marshes. Gromyko himself acknowledges that many of the horses the government gave settlers died and that at least the early harvests were low. Moreover, many of the *posel´shchiki* sent to Baraba were crippled or otherwise infirm. Looking back 140 years later, an official report noted that Baraba's inhabitants were still telling 'gloomy legends' about the thousands who died there.[66]

The model of state support used to settle Baraba was replicated elsewhere in Siberia, insofar as Petersburg typically gave *posel´shchik* families three years' grace from the poll tax and *obrok* until they could better fulfill their responsibilities as state peasants. How many *posel´shchiki* were deported during Catherine's reign is not known, but disparate figures suggest tens of thousands. During the period 1765–7 1,317 *posel´shchiki* arrived in Tara *uezd* in Tobol´sk *guberniia*; and, as of 1782, 3,009 male and 2,730 female *posel´shchiki* were living in 13 villages in the same *uezd*.[67] Gernet writes that the state deported 6,000 peasants (*krest´iane*) to Baraba Steppe in 1771 alone; and that '[p]rior to 1772 the number of peasants exiled by landowners (apparently since 1768) to Tobol´sk *guberniia* [which included Baraba Steppe] and Eniseisk *uezd* reached 20,515'.[68] Despite Gernet's inclusion of Eniseisk *uezd* in this figure, other sources show the autocracy assigned the large majority of *posel´shchiki* to western, not eastern, Siberia. This reflected a *de facto* distinction (made *de jure* in 1859) between eastern Siberia as a location for serious criminals and western Siberia as a location for lesser offenders. The assignment of *posel´shchiki* to western Siberia reflected a policy that more or less separated them from exiled criminals. In 1782 alone, 9,624 *posel´shchiki* were deported to western Siberia. Whether or not this was a typical annual figure is unknown, but only half (4,885) were assigned to Baraba Steppe (specifically, Kainsk *uezd*), while the rest went to other locations. Those sent to Kainsk accounted for over 83 per cent of the peasants there, whereas those sent to other *uezdy* made up less than 10 per cent of the local populations,[69] figures which indicate that in addition to founding exilic colonies, *posel´shchiki*, like peasants deported during the Muscovite era, were used to buttress established villages.

Catherine also assigned malefactors to the Siberian military, though it is difficult to determine if such assignees were exiles (*ssyl'nye*) or not. On 19 April 1778 she ruled that only those accused of 'bad behavior' (*durnoe povedenie* – a phrase typically applied to administrative exiles) could be exiled to colonize Siberia, whereas actual criminals (*prestupniki*) were to be assigned to detachments controlled by the Military College. Serious criminals were sentenced to *katorga*, so it seems the detachments Catherine had in mind were for lesser offenders (*malovazhnye*). The government also forcibly settled retired officers, soldiers and their families near the Chinese border in the Altai. 'The largest military force in Siberia consisted of garrison troops,' writes LeDonne. 'Seven battalions were assigned in 1764, about 5,400 men, three in Tobol´sk, one in Tomsk, another in Irkutsk, and two in Selenginsk, staffed with recruits or retired soldiers and their children.'[70] He adds that the soldiers themselves were probably not living in these cities but were in military settlements and forts along the Siberian Line.

Statistical data and foreign visitors' impressions suggest exile made a significant impact on Siberia during the late eighteenth century, even if it did not appreciably increase the overall population. A. D. Kolesnikov estimates up to 35,000 males were exiled to Siberia between 1761 and 1781. By adding their family members Wood arrives at a figure of 60,000 adults, though he notes that the documents needed to confirm these and similar estimates were destroyed by fire in Tobol´sk in 1788. Two sources nevertheless roughly corroborate Wood's figure. In 1770 Benëvskii, en route to his exile in Kamchatka, learned that 22,000 exiles were living in Tobol´sk *guberniia* alone; and an imperial revision, or census, conducted twelve years later reports 29,108 adult male exiles living throughout Siberia.[71] If just half these men each had a wife and one child who survived into adulthood, then the combined number of adult exiles would have been 45,000. Wood's estimate of 60,000 is therefore plausible. Finally, there are the impressions of the American John Ledyard, who visited Irkutsk and its environs in the late 1780s:

> Not a day passes scarcely but an exile of some sort arrives here[.] There are in this town at present 150. The most of the Inhabitants, and particularly of this remote part of Siberia, are convicts. I find that the worst idea I had formed of the Country, and its Inhabitants does not require correction.[72]

*   *   *

Like exile, *katorga* grew under Catherine, in whose view corporal punishment remained an important component of sentences in this category. A 1781 ukase prescribed 60 knout lashes for males and 25 for females sentenced to *katorga* – enough to maim or kill. Some male convicts still had their nostrils slit, though criminals were increasingly being tattooed instead (women were exempt from this particular scourge). Throughout Catherine's reign ghoulish conglomerations of mutilated, tattooed and welted humanity stumbled in chains across her lands, only to face still greater degradation at Nerchinsk and other sites.

Evidence is scant regarding these sites. A thousand penal laborers are known to have been assigned to Rogervik in 1755; but in 1767 the state began assigning most penal laborers to Nerchinsk. The conflation between *katorga* and exile (*ssylka*) that began under Elizabeth Petrovna continued during Catherine's reign. For example, the use of prisoners to build a canal linking the Tvertsa and Msta rivers seems to have been a case in which convicts were used as laborers without having been sentenced to *katorga*. Besides Nerchinsk, penal laborers were assigned to Siberia's salt works. Salt remained as important as when the Stroganovs panned it at Sol´vychegodsk during the sixteenth century. During the eighteenth century the state established a monopoly, if not completely over production, then certainly over price and distribution. In 1764 it took over the salt works of Turukhansk's powerful Troitskii Monastery in northern Eniseisk *guberniia*, and by the turn of the century this was producing 80,000 poods per annum. Siberia increasingly played a larger role in salt production, though as a percentage of the empire's total output not a particularly large one; moreover, salt production per capita grew only slightly under Catherine. Therefore, although penal laborers comprised the majority of workers in the salt works in Selenginsk, Irkutsk and Okhotsk, relatively few were so assigned. After Rogervik's completion, and because of the absence of peasants and others, most penal laborers ended up in Siberia's metallurgical industries, principally those in Nerchinsk *uezd*. By contrast, sufficient numbers of non-exilic laborers were in Kolyvansk so that Catherine abolished exile there in 1776, perhaps also to protect western Siberia from a large influx of dangerous criminals.

Exiled convicts labored in *zavody*: fortified industrial townships which typically included several factories each. *Zavody* were state-owned cities (*goroda*) and towns consisting of industrial laborers and townspeople. Affiliated peasant villages termed *slobody* supplied foodstuffs. Each *zavod* consisted of a military administration and detachment of soldiers or cossacks charged with keeping penal laborers and others from escaping. In essence these were fortified, militarized, autarkic settlements centered on the production of silver, lead, iron, copper and, later, gold.[73]

Prior to Catherine's reign the number of peasants and laborers assigned to Nerchinsk Zavod would have been small, given that between 1704 and 1750 its smelteries produced only 552 poods silver (valued at 243,708 r.). As of 1756 only 2,123 peasants and an unknown number of laborers were assigned to the *zavod*; but from this date onward their numbers grew throughout the entire Nerchinsk region, as silver and lead production correspondingly increased and remained high until the end of the century. By the end of Catherine's reign nearly 15,000 male peasants were assigned to Nerchinsk *uezd*; and during the 1780s laborers smelted 4,652 poods silver for the crown. Lead was also produced in large quantities: between 1703 and 1800 a total of 2,575,041 poods was smelted.[74]

Unfortunately, figures on the total number of penal laborers in Nerchinsk *uezd* before 1812 are almost nonexistent. As of 1774 the so-called 'Cabinet industries' consisted of 29 mines and five *zavody* (Kutomarsk, Ducharsk, Shilkinsk, Gazimursk and Voskresensk), assigned to which were 504 soldiers, 24 officers, 1,084 miners (*gornorabochie*), 9,938 peasants and 2,833 penal laborers. This last figure, however, only indicates the number assigned. In reality, at the time of this census only 1,090 convicts were actually engaged in labor: another 484 had escaped and 358 had died. Gernet cites Coxe as reporting up to 2,000 convicts being assigned to Nerchinsk *every year*.[75] This seems quite high, but it may have been true for a brief period. Whatever the numbers, conditions at Nerchinsk were soon well enough known to give the very name 'a sinister ring'[76] in the ears of Russians everywhere. Nerchinsk's reputation later stirred Pushkin to imagine himself a penal laborer:

> ... I sighed, groaned, was awestruck,
> Yet, I even laughed,
> Yes, quietly, so that on the path
> To Nerchinsk, I would not give myself up.[77]

In 1739 the government built the Kurynzekaisk Zavod copper works 200 versts southwest of Nerchinsk Zavod. These appear to have been the only *zavody* in the region until the 1760s, when the Nerchinsk District experienced its greatest expansion and the Duchersk, Kutomarsk, Shilkinsk and Kurensel´minsk *zavody* were all built to smelt silver. Other *zavody* were built after the 1760s, most notably Gazimursk (1774), halfway between Nerchinsk and Kurynzekaisk, and the Petrovsk iron-works, built in 1788–90 under the direction of Commandant Barbot de Marni and, despite its location in Verkhneudinsk *uezd* 1,089 versts from Nerchinsk Zavod, operated by the Nerchinsk Mining Command.[78]

The Romanovs acquired private ownership of Nerchinsk's peasants and *zavody* earlier than they did those of Kolyvansk, though the pre-cise date remains unclear. This and the patronage networks identified by LeDonne explain Catherine's decision to appoint as Nerchinsk Dis-trict's commandant her godson, V. V. Naryshkin. Nerchinsk has a history of despotic commandants, but Naryshkin is especially reprehensible. He squandered treasury monies, ordered summary executions and formed his own 'hussar regiment' of hapless convicts. At one point his ongo-ing feud with Irkutsk's governor Fedor G. Nemtsov (or Nemtsev) grew so heated that he decided to invade Irkutsk. Accompanied by pealing bells and the tattoo of drums, Naryshkin marched his ragtag army through Nerchinsk's gates followed by a train of supplies sequestered from local peasants. He eventually reached his destination, albeit in the hands of *guberniia* officials who arrested him in Verkhneudinsk and then forwar-ded him to Petersburg. Learning of the fiasco, Catherine reportedly said her godson had been 'naughty'.[79]

Nerchinsk District operated under what was known as the Dauriia Mining Administration (*Daurskoe gornoe upravlenie*) until 1787, when Petersburg replaced this with the Nerchinsk Mining Bureau (*Nerchinskaia gornaia ekspeditsiia*), whose charter called for the majority of its laborers to be exiles. The bureau consisted of three officials and a *nachal'nik*, or commandant, and also served as executive for the *uezd* (district) admin-istration responsible for production and supervising laborers and exiles. Beginning in 1789 the mining council, which included representatives of the commandant, bureau, *zavod* administrations, mining offices and mining police, would sit from January to mid-April to function as the mining administration's legislative branch. The mining council repor-ted directly to the Imperial Cabinet, established production plans for all factories and mines for the coming year, allocated funds and set labor quotas. The mining and factory offices formed the next administrative tier, with each factory office consisting of a manager (*upravitel*) and assist-ants who oversaw their unit's finances and operations as well as those of the police assigned to them. All mines and mining administrations fell under the control of a single mining office which functioned with assistance from the bureau and the mine commanders (*ober-ofitsery*). The mining office was in charge of all mines and affiliated buildings, stores and supplies, and was responsible for ensuring production, maintaining the mines and issuing instructions to laborers. Several mines together formed a sector (*distantiia*), each of which had its own administration.[80]

Peasants were assigned to each *zavod* in Nerchinsk District and came under *zavod* administrations' complete control. As throughout Russia, they lived in villages organized according to *volosti* (cantons), each of which possessed a local assembly (*skhod*), a headman (*starosta*) and other, usually peasant, authorities. Nerchinsk's peasants functioned as did those assigned to Kolyvansk District, producing food and providing temporary factory labor. Peasants suffered much from their enforced association with Nerchinsk *zavody*: each paid a yearly poll tax of 1 r. 73.5 k., even if laboring for a *zavod* and not working the land. In 1777, for instance, 1,096 'souls' were assigned to the village of Gorodishchensk, 530 of whom were industrial laborers. Of the remaining 566, 113 were elderly; 23 were blind or lame; 360 were children; 18 were listed as 'peasant exiles'; and 52, though deceased, had not been stricken from the books and therefore still owed the poll tax, which of course their still-breathing neighbors had to pay.[81]

The autocracy's exploitation of natural resources in this region conditioned its exploitation of human resources, and so it is no surprise that each year 300–400 convicts fled the Nerchinsk *zavody*, as did an equal number of soldiers and peasants. Reasons for their flight were various. One was disease: smallpox ravaged Zabaikal´e in the 1730s and 1740s and again under Catherine; a typhus epidemic struck in 1786–9; and it can be added here that syphilis was common among Nerchinsk laborers, spread probably more by homosexual than heterosexual sex. The *zavody* were assigned their first doctor in 1741; and in 1767 a pharmacy was established in Nerchinsk *zavod*. But convicts would have benefited little from either. Contrary to claims by Soviet historians, however, starvation does not seem to have been a major cause of flight prior to the 1850s. The economic historian Arcadius Kahan found that prior to 1762 the treasury budgeted 18 r. 85.75 k. per annum per convict, from which each man received 6 kopeks cash plus a 'monthly ration of 1 pood and 32.5 pounds of rye flour'. Such amounts would seem to have been sufficient, and were in any case increased under Catherine.[82] A more likely factor behind escapes was the corporal punishments to which convicts were subject under military justice. Even minor offences earned up to 200 lashes of the birch rod or 25 of the knout, either of which could prove fatal. Dostoevskii details both the physical and psychological effects of corporal punishment in his *Notes from a Dead House*, writing of one convict who died two days after being flogged and another who went insane at the prospect of receiving 2,000 lashes.

That escape was a major problem for Nerchinsk administrators is demonstrated by efforts to curb it. In 1777 the mining administration formed a detachment of 260 Tungus cossacks specifically for the purpose of tracking down fugitives. It tried prophylactic measures in 1783, increasing to 24 rubles and in some cases 30 rubles the yearly amount budgeted for each convict; establishing a twelve-hour workday; and ordering that every two weeks of continuous labor be followed by one full week of rest. These measures coincided with others aimed at improving convicts' and exiles' conditions in general, and suggest Beccaria and Montesquieu's influence on Catherine as well as efforts to systematize labor exploitation. But executioners (*palachi* or those who executed punishments), guards and administrators largely ignored the regulations. For example, at Nerchinsk the week set aside for rest was transformed into a kind of extended proto-*subotnik* (Soviet working holiday), during which convicts were made to repair barracks and other prison buildings. Faced with such interminable labor, convicts continued to flee. Out of desperation, the administration in 1785 offered a bounty of 5 rubles for each captured fugitive; but seven years later Barbot de Marni cancelled it, recognizing as he did the futility of reducing the escape rate.[83]

*   *   *

To her credit, Catherine II seems to have been the first Russian monarch to foresee the problems exile was beginning to cause. Formation of a large, mostly unpoliced population of criminals and political dissidents in a region of increasing geostrategic and economic importance was not a positive development. However, even a ruler as politically willful as she could not remove what was by now a well-entrenched penal institution. It remained simply *too convenient* to dispatch malefactors to Siberia's wide-open spaces where, if they did not behave like Benëvskii, they could be conveniently forgotten about. Summing up exile during the eighteenth century, most Russian scholars agree with Fel'dstein, who writes that the 'practical measures of resettlement' such as those described 'made not the slightest impact in the growth of permanent settlement in Siberia'.[84] Indeed, these practical measures served mainly to release a criminal element that would plague Siberian society for years to come. If exiles did not quickly die they tended to eke out an existence as vagabonds, petty thieves or bandits. During an 1802 inspection of Siberia Major-General Nikolai Osipovich Laba determined that only 10,430 exiles had been successfully established as agriculturalists in Irkutsk, Tomsk and Tobol´sk *gubernii*. 'Such were the beggarly results of exile to Siberia,' Iadrintsev later caustically observed.[85] However, penal laborers and exiles working in Nerchinsk and other locations, and who together probably totaled between 4,000 and 5,000, seem to have been left out of Laba's figure, which, like similar calculations, should be multiplied several times over when estimating the total numbers deported during Catherine's reign. While it is true that many died from the rigors of the march or soon thereafter, an enormous number escaped to create a unique substratum of Siberian society known as the *brodiagi*. In addition, as large as the numbers of exiles were during the seventeenth and eighteenth centuries, they are dwarfed by those which followed. Problems resulting from the mismanagement of the exile system, far from going away, would accordingly expand geometrically.

4
'Whoever's not with us is Against us'

Paul I's brief reign (1796–1801) was characterized by the militarization of government administrations including that of the exile system. Fel´dstein rather approvingly notes that the military came to play a greater role in transporting exiles and overseeing their labor in factories, and that it achieved cooperation with local authorities supervising agricultural exiles. Paul also continued to use exile as a weapon against political opponents and the Poles. Finally, despite his abolition of the workhouses called for by his mother Catherine II, a workhouse did come into existence in Siberia during his reign. Founded in 1799 on the outskirts of Irkutsk by the military governor Boris B. Letstsano, this seems to have been the first workhouse for rehabilitating exiled convicts. The institution allegedly allowed 400 exiles and their families to establish their own hamlet, earn a living and train their offspring in various trades. This bucolic description comes from Shcheglov, on whom one must rely given the absence of any other description with which to compare it.[1] Even if Irkutsk's workhouse was less than admirable (and the discussion of exilic conditions that follows suggests it was), its very existence suggests Letstsano and other Siberian officials may have been effecting modernistic penological notions on their own initiative.

Whether Irkutsk's workhouse reflected humanitarian concerns or was simply designed to better utilize convict labor is difficult to say, but whatever the case it was an exception to the rules regarding exiles under Paul, who more than any autocrat since Peter I embraced the service-state ethos. Aside from his father Peter III's brief time on the throne, Paul's reign marked the first in a series of martial administrations in Russia, each headed by an autocrat who unfailingly dressed in uniform. The military did not control tsarist Russia during its last 120 years, but each emperor spent his youth training to be a soldier and so inevitably a

militaristic approach to administration developed. With regard to exile following the chaotic period of 1725–96, such an approach might at first glance suggest a return to the Petrine era's systematized exploitation of convicts. However, spanners were in the works, one being the declining yield of metals from Nerchinsk that began after Catherine's death and eventuated in decreasing funding for the region and growing disregard for its penal laborers. Other *katorga* sites similarly suffered from a combination of limited funding and what seems to have been increasing embezzlement by local officials. The result was that conditions for penal laborers became simply wretched. Another spanner was administrative exile. Each year this poured into Siberia a number of deportees equal to or greater than those judicially sentenced to exile and led to formation of a huge, impoverished, unproductive diaspora. The state provided some support for administrative exiles, but even so, many resorted to crime simply to survive, and once having committed a serious crime, individuals frequently took to the taiga to join the growing population of *brodiagi* who would come to emblematize Siberia's social disorder. Large numbers of *brodiagi* also originated as penal laborers who, in contrast to administrative exiles, were more likely to be violent and helped render Siberia the empire's most murderous region save the Caucasus.

Paul made his first mark on exile's development in 1797, when he created a new scale of punishments consisting of the following precepts: 1) serious criminals (*ugolovnye prestupniki*), such as murderers, rebels and black marketeers, were, as before, to be assigned to *katorga*, specifically to Nerchinsk; 2) lesser criminals, who under the old system would have been exiled to settlement, were to be sent to the Tel´minsk linen factory outside Irkutsk; 3) those convicted of defaulting on loans or of other minor crimes, and who would have been slated for Catherine's planned series of workhouses, were now assigned to labor in fortresses. A year later the Senate provided for women and those sentenced to brief terms to be assigned to workhouses, though this may have been a provisional ruling since no workhouses appear to have existed at that point. In any case, there were not enough labor sites to absorb Russia's expanding convict population, especially because a significant number of peasants and *masterovye* were now being used as laborers. As a result the goal of colonization soon displaced that of labor in the use of exiles. Such a reversal reflects the bifurcated and inconsistent exilic policies of Peter's successors. The expansion of the police apparatus, along with an increasingly discontent population, meant more people were being convicted and more exiles were being produced, but the state failed to have a clear notion of what their functions should be. For example, in

1798 provisions were made for lesser offenders to be sent not only to the Ekaterinburg gold mines but also to Siberia for resettlement, as had originally been prescribed by regulations established during Elizabeth's reign.[2]

The swinging of the penological pendulum during Paul's reign is most sensationally demonstrated by the profoundly misconceived colonization experiment which highlights this martinet's attitude to his subjects, and which put a final stamp on a century that, as much as it witnessed a growing use of exile, was merely a precursor to what followed. Immediately contradicting his own regulations to use exiles as laborers, Paul uncharacteristically followed in his mother's footsteps with a plan to use exiles to colonize the frontier. Petersburg had decades earlier turned its attention to Zabaikal´e when the Academy of Sciences, responding to recommendations from exiled Swedes, sent researchers to study its geography, population and economic potential. '[B]y the 1770s,' writes Raeff, 'when a great deal of this information had been accumulated and the ideas of the physiocrats digested, the government tried to apply [such ideas] to Siberian circumstances.'[3] As we have seen, Petersburg's efforts to colonize Siberia actually began long before physiocratic ideas were embraced, but with the qualified exception of Chicherin's Baraba Steppe project, all such efforts had been failures as abysmal as Lake Baikal's unfathomable depths. Yet for Paul and his experts, such failures merely demonstrated the need for a stronger hand.

The very size of the Pauline project evidences the emperor's effort to outdo his predecessors, as well as his delusion that he could manoeuvre his subjects across the breadth of Russia like Frederick II directing troops over a Silesian battlefield. On 17 October 1799, following the advice of Prince Gavriil P. Gagarin, who was director of the State Loan Bank and later became president of the Commerce College, Paul set in motion what *Exile to Siberia* later derided as a 'grandiose project' to settle along the Chinese border in Zabaikal´e some 10,000 men consisting of exiles (*ssyl´nye*), fortress peasants and military recruits. To assist in what it hoped would become burgeoning agricultural colonies and an impediment to China's supposed plans to invade the region, the state even intended to assign retired soldiers to these *poseleniia* to serve as landowners (literally, *pomeshchiki*). Each *poselenie* was to comprise no more than 100 domiciles. Ideally, convicts would live in *poseleniia* separate from those of the other settlers, but if they satisfied certain standards of good behavior and hard work for a period of ten years, they would be given the right to transfer to other *poseleniia*. Petersburg was to provide each settler with the funds needed to establish himself, although it expected the first echelon of colonists to build houses for those who followed. Each colonist was allotted 30 *desiatiny* of arable land, 18 months' supply of foodstuffs, as well as cattle, seed and farm tools. Similar to those sent to the Baraba Steppe, these colonists were to receive certain inducements, such as freedom from taxes for ten years, to facilitate their accumulation of capital. The plan even called for agricultural experts to be appointed to advise colonists on the best farming methods *à la* the physiocrats. Paul put Governor Letstsano in charge of the operation; and in 1800 98,156 rubles was allocated for this use from the Siberian treasury. Gagarin, who seems to have originated most of the plan, envisaged that the money to pay for everything would come from landowner contributions in return for the state canceling military recruitment quotas.

Not surprisingly, Paul's government did not possess the wherewithal to carry off the job. For one thing, the emperor had exhausted the patience of his court and been murdered by the time the first group of 1,454 colonists – an unholy mélange of convicts and *posel'shchiki* – staggered into Irkutsk in 1801. Letstsano was supposed to have distributed them to points east, but the corpulent governor lacked both the will and manpower to keep most exiles from escaping back to Russia or fleeing into the countryside, where they formed bandit gangs that terrorized locals for years to come. As a result, only a very small proportion arrived at their designated locations.

In 1802 the Senate dispatched Major-General Nikolai Osipovich Laba to the region to investigate what had gone wrong and how to fix it, since despite this initial debacle the project as a whole was still viable as far as Alexander I was concerned. Laba found problems from start to finish. Landowners had taken the opportunity to rid themselves of less productive serfs, and so many exiles were over the age limit of 45, crippled or otherwise unsuitable for their tasks: 260 were epileptic and 91 mentally retarded or mentally ill (*maloumnye, bezumnye*). During their march into Siberia they had typically not been provided with clothes or foraging money (*kormovye den'gi*) because these were embezzled by officials. This and the physical and mental handicaps many suffered caused a significant number to die before they reached Irkutsk. In addition, officers in Tobol'sk had siphoned off a certain number for military service. In Zabaikal'e, Letstsano's subordinates did practically nothing to prepare for the exiles' arrival. Similar to those charged with delivering the exiles to Irkutsk, these officials sold the tools and provisions stockpiled for their arrival and put the deportees to work on their own pet projects. As for the nearly 100,000 rubles budgeted for the project, this vanished into the pockets of Letstsano and his cronies. In the end, Laba's investigation revealed that this grandiose project had resulted in only 236 exiles being crammed into 35 makeshift huts east of Lake Baikal.[4]

Accounts of Laba's investigation provide the earliest evidence that serf owners were capitalizing on administrative exile to rid themselves of the mentally or physically unfit, but there is little doubt that this began in the 1760s with administrative exile itself. The commodification of individuals within the service-state economy conditioned such use and moreover suggests that peasant communes had similar motives for exiling their members. Exclusion of the 'other' by the hegemonic society was hardly unique to tsarist Russia, as archaeological and sociological studies show;[5] but in the Russian case the deporting of manifestly unfit persons revealed both the weakness of administrative oversight and the power of the nobility. Exiled *posel'shchiki* were to have served statist ends, but nobles were able to leverage their advantage over the state to render deportation serviceable to their private economic goals. Despite state and society being the big losers in this arrangement, and irrespective of the malfeasance uncovered by Laba, Petersburg persisted in its efforts to convert exiles into colonists in Zabaikal'e and elsewhere in Siberia. Prior to Alexander II's reign (1855–81) no sovereign considered her- or himself in a position to dictate terms to the serf-owning nobility. Along with the central government's limited control over the countryside and Siberia, this resulted in thousands of dependants being cast into the wilderness. Administrative exile was a form of social cleansing.

*   *   *

During the first two decades of the nineteenth century Alexander I utilized exile for both colonization and manufacturing purposes along lines similar to those established by his predecessors. Petersburg's reluctance to establish a prison system to replace exile, as well as the devastating impact of Napoleon Bonaparte's invasion and general disorder in the countryside, resulted in a steady rise in the number of exiles. The bureaucratic malfeasance larded on top of this managed to push the exile system into crisis by 1819, at which point Alexander appointed Speranskii to take charge of Siberia. The stop-gap measures Speranskii ordered during his first year in Irkutsk signalled the need for more far-reaching reforms, and so paved the way for the Siberian Committee and its 1822 reforms.

Turning first to issues of administration, it bears repeating that Siberia's Governor Letstsano was a magnificently incompetent and corrupt figure. Almost immediately after taking the throne Alexander therefore dispatched privy councilor and senator Ivan O. Selifontov to investigate the situation. Selifontov had been Tobol´sk's vice-governor during the early 1790s and in 1796 was officially appointed Irkutsk's governor-general, though he never took up this position because Paul I abolished the governor-generalships. Selifontov's investigation actually preceded Laba's, but whereas Laba mostly focused on exile, Selifontov was more generally concerned with administrative affairs. Both men's investigations nonetheless dovetailed to produce recommendations the emperor acted on in 1803–4. *Inter alia*, Laba and Selifontov advised that a new *guberniia* (Tomsk) be carved out of Tobol´sk *guberniia* so as to better administer western Siberia. Under Paul, Tobol´sk *guberniia* had been part of a separate governorship whose jurisdiction included Kolyvansk *guberniia*. Alexander changed this by putting Tobol´sk, Tomsk and Irkutsk *gubernii* under a single governor-generalship. This allowed him to dismiss Letstsano from his now defunct post and name Selifontov governor-general of a reorganized and united Siberia.

Unfortunately for Siberians, Selifontov proved even more corrupt than Letstsano. LeDonne observes that he 'chose to live unabashedly in the world of *kormlenie*, and he sold his offices to the highest bidder'.[6] He even used his position to steal (presumably through agents) prized manuscripts from the Manchu government. Alexander learned of Selifontov's corruption, but characteristically waffled for a long time before acting. In May 1805 the emperor sent a letter to Petersburg's representative in China, Count Iurii A. Golovkin, secretly granting him *de facto* powers as Siberia's governor-general and encouraging him to address the problems emanating from Irkutsk. Golovkin responded by recommending Siberia be uniquely administered as a government fiefdom (*kazennoe pomest´e*), but neither his sub rosa appointment nor recommendation led to any changes. This episode nonetheless demonstrates Alexander's tendency to pass responsibility on to others instead of confronting powerful officials. He finally summoned enough courage to force Selifontov to retire in 1806 and replace him with Ivan B. Pestel, another senator and privy councilor (as well as father of the Decembrist Pavel Pestel). Pestel would remain governor-general until 1819, like his predecessors casually using the powers of his office to enrich himself while allowing his lieutenants to perform most of his duties. Following an investigation he was removed from office and brought to trial, though never punished.[7]

Beginning in 1801 Alexander overhauled Russia's central administrative apparatus, replacing the colleges with ministries. Mikhail M. Speranskii emerges on the political stage at this point, recognized for his organizational skills by Viktor P. Kochubei, who chose the young man to help establish the Ministry of Internal Affairs (MVD). Within the MVD Speranskii became director of the Bureau of State Services (*Eksped-itsiia gosudartsvennogo blagoustroitsva*). The MVD would come to control the exile system more than any other ministry, though not completely, as it had to contend with the Imperial Cabinet and Ministry of Finance as well as other, less consistent, interlopers. This rivalry over exile resulted to a large extent from a document dated 25 August 1810 and circulated among Siberian officials by the Irkutsk *guberniia* administration (IGP). This document distilled Alexander I's manifesto of two months earlier (25 July) defining the ministries' responsibilities according to five broad categories: foreign relations; war; state economy; civil and criminal courts; and domestic security. Alexander assigned to the MVD control over the national economy and outlined its responsibilities as 'the promotion of land-use [*zemledeliia*]; colonies; internal resettlement [*vnutrennyia pereseleniia*]; the various branches of the economy related to these categories; [and]...factories.' The Ministry of Finance was also given responsibilities in this category, including maintenance and operation of state properties, especially those dealing with mining and salt production. The state treasury was also to play a role in administering state properties. To one degree or another, then, exile and *katorga* came to be among the tools necessary for these organizations to fulfil their responsibilities. The emperor assigned the Ministry of Police (which despite its title was a sub-department of the MVD) to the fifth category of domestic security, summarizing its responsibilities as 'fulfillment of court-ordered sentences, collection of arrears, establishment of a domestic police force [*vnutrennaia strazha*]' and administration of 'strait-houses, laborers, Secret Police [*Politsiia temnichnaia*], etc.'.[8] He left undefined this ministry's responsibilities concerning laborers (*rabochiia*), but this group would seem to have included *masterovye*, factory serfs and all convicts (not just penal laborers) assigned to work sites. Hence this arrangement predisposed to competition the ministries, crown, landowners and communes for control of exiles. Landowners and communes already clashed over when and in what cases to use administrative exile, while the ministries would now fight over how to use administrative exiles as well as those exiled by the court. Should they be used as laborers or colonists? Who controlled them after they left the legal system and were en route to Siberia? Finally, and as will become clear below, the crown would, because of this arrangement, become increasingly perplexed at (especially administrative) exile's unabated growth. These problems and the policy debates they provoked remained unresolved as Russia groped towards administrative systematization, such that Speranskii would later try to straighten out the coil of competing claims.

For the historian, Alexander I's reign provides no small satisfaction insofar as it marks the beginning of reasonably accurate statistics on exiles. Originating from the Tobol'sk *guberniia* administration, which processed incoming deportees, these statistics testify to both the government's systematizing efforts and the steady growth of exiles, from an annual average of 1,606 during 1807–13 to 2,476 during 1814–18 and 4,570 during 1819–23.[9] Several factors explain this increase, but the difficult life of the peasantry is perhaps primary. Both *obrok* and *barshchina* demands expanded significantly between 1760 and 1800 and continued to do so through Alexander I's reign. Additional sources of hardship were Russia's wars against Persia, the Ottomans and Sweden. Recruits were drafted into the army for 25-year terms, and so quite understandably '[y]oung males viewed conscription as comparable to a sentence of death'.[10] These wars and the recruits used to fight them created a population of actual and virtual widows in the countryside. For example, during 1812–19 in the serf community of Manuilovsk in Tver *guberniia* one-third of all households included widows, 53 per cent of whom were 39 years old or younger. Rodney Bohac writes that such women faced 'poverty' and 'social isolation',[11] and so it is reasonable to conclude that many turned to crime in order to survive. Economic pressures also led to a growing number of acts directed against authority,[12] and so both civilian and official authorities increasingly relied on exile as a response.

Exacerbating pre-existing difficulties for peasants and townspeople alike was Napoleon's 1812 invasion, which ravaged much of the country's most densely settled areas, left Moscow a smoking ruin and condemned many to survive by whatever means necessary. One was migration. Kabuzan and others have documented a large exodus during 1811–15 from central European Russia to Siberia, whose Russian male population increased as a result by nearly 30 per cent (from 682,597 to 871,850).[13] Another result of the invasion was the nobility's dispersal into the countryside following the destruction of their Moscow residences. Raeff has reasoned that serf owners' closer proximity to serfs prompted 'heavier impositions, greater exactions and exploitation (including such terrible things as the sale of villages or individual peasants to raise cash)'.[14] Still another result of the invasion was a breakdown of local authority. Before hostilities commenced, belief spread among serfs that France's diminutive revolutionary was going to emancipate them, and so they began increasingly disobeying their masters. According to one source, in 1812 there were 'sixty-seven minor peasant revolts in thirty-two different provinces...more than twice the annual aver-age'.[15] Peasants soon realized that Napoleon – what with his horror at the prospect of even an enemy empire dissolving into chaos due to an unrestrained *canaille* – had no such intention. The Grand Army's officers proved even more rapacious than Russian landowners, and so peasants fought back in ways that, even if exaggerated by Soviet propagandists, nonetheless created a sense of personal autonomy, which subsequently led them to square off against landowners in a post-war landscape where survival rewarded criminality. Given the breakdown of law and order which always follows war, exile became a way for authorities to try to restore the *status quo ante bellum*.

Another factor to consider when accounting for the increase in exiles is Russia's demobilization of soldiers after 1815. This would have released into society an element inured to violence and familiar with killing. Like those in different places and times, many former tsarist soldiers brought home a disdain for authority and a greater propensity to engage in crime.[16] Moreover, most of them rejoined a peasantry which gener-ally believed its sacrifices in the 1812 war should be rewarded with serf emancipation and a return of the land. But Alexander I conceptualized quite differently Napoleon's invasion as divine punishment from a God angered by the sins of this same *narod*, and reasoned that peasants were not to be rewarded but rather *instructed* to fear worse punishments in the future if they did not amend their sinful ways.[17] The reactionary nature of Alexander's government after 1815 thus obliterated any hope of eman-cipation and fed peasant anger and resentment towards the regime much in the same way Soviet citizens lost faith in Stalin's government after World War II. 'Intellectual repression, economic hardship, and an acute lack of justice in Russia during the last years of Alexander's reign led to increased dissent,' writes W. Bruce Lincoln,[18] and this in turn led to further reliance on exile as a means of social control.

Lastly, several other uses of exile contributed in varying degrees to the numbers deported. One was the government's use of exile against prisoners-of-war and as a tool to pacify Poland, Central Asia and the newly annexed territories of Finland, Bessarabia and the Caucasus. In 1814 Polish prisoners exiled to Tomsk were discovered to be plotting with other exiles to stage a mass uprising and march on European Russia to foment revolution.[19] Documents circulated among Siberian admin-istrators and authored by foreign minister Karl Nesselrod related the French government's inquiries about persons captured during the Napo-leonic wars.[20] Another small cohort of exiles originated from among the growing number of 'possessional peasants' assigned to factories whose owners acquired exilic authority during this period.[21] Finally, both crown and church were alarmed at the spread of the self-castrating *skoptsy*, the pacifistic Dukhobors and other schismatic sects, and so responded by exiling them and other so-called non-believers (*inovertsy*) to Siberia, the Caucasus and elsewhere on the periphery. An 1820 circular from the IGP relates a Senate resolution ordering female *skoptsy* be exiled to textile mills in Irkutsk.[22] It should be added that many of these measures were in place before Napoleon's invasion, the caesura supposedly dividing Alexander's reign into reformist and reactionary periods.

Administrative exile also expanded, despite Alexander's genuine attempts to curb it. In August 1808 the highly decorated 30 year-old senator Dmitrii P. Runich led an investigation into conditions in Viatka *guberniia* which revealed serious abuses in the use of administrative exile. In particular, Runich found that to avoid military recruitment wealthy peasants were bribing village headmen to offer up their neighbors as *posel´shchiki*, who as such would count against communal recruitment quotas. This led to the convictions of 24 persons who themselves were subsequently deported as *posel´shchiki*. A year later another investigation revealed similar abuses among certain *meshchanstva*. However, neither investigation resulted in cancellation of the right by *meshchanstva* and *obshchestva* to administratively exile their members.[23] The emperor was more concerned about landowners' use of administrative exile, perhaps because he saw it as contributing to disturbances in the countryside or as fomenting resentment towards authority in general. Richard Pipes argues that landowners rarely used administrative exile against their serfs; but the figure he cites in support of this claim is erroneous and superseded by those in E. N. Anuchin's 1873 study of the exile population.[24] First, it is clear that landowners resorted to administrative exile more often than did communes; second, Alexander's efforts to abolish administrative exile indicate it was prolific enough to cause Petersburg to challenge the nobility on this matter.

Early in her reign Catherine II had given landowners the right to punish serfs by 'sentencing' them to so-called 'navy *katorga*'. This punishment appears to have been rarely invoked, however, with landowners instead typically turning over serfs as *posel´shchiki*. But in 1809 a certain landowner sentenced several serfs to a particularly egregious punishment of 20 years' navy *katorga* 'in order to moderate the impudence of their behavior'. Alexander responded by withdrawing landowners' right to use *katorga* to punish their serfs.[25] A year later a Tver landowner named Vorob´eva appealed to local officials for permission to exile to settlement

several domestic serfs who had attempted to escape. Tver officials consen-
ted to the request, but the *guberniia's* newly appointed governor-general,
Prince Georgii P. Ol´denburgskii, used the case to make an appeal to the
emperor for a definitive ruling concerning landowners' exilic rights.

The answer came in the form of an imperial ukase dated 5 July 1811, in
which Alexander wrote that he disagreed with the Tver officials' decision
and that, in any case, they had no authority to rule on Vorob´eva's
request. He then went on to consider the overall legality of administrative exile. He divided criminal acts and corresponding punishments into
three tiers: 1) those guilty of the most serious (*vazhnye*) crimes including 'murder, robbery, commission of an outrage [*vozmushchenie*, which
in this context probably meant rape], and bribery' were to be sentenced
to *katorga*; 2) those guilty of less serious crimes, such as 'the theft of no
more than 100 silver rubles, repeated thefts, black marketeering, and vagabondage', were to be exiled to settlement or, if able-bodied, assigned to
the military; and 3) those guilty of petty theft or disobedience were to be
remanded to their homes and placed under police surveillance or held in
strait- or workhouses.[26] (This introduces once again the rather mysterious
workhouses, for whose existence during Alexander's reign no concrete
evidence has been found.)

Of major significance in this ukase was the emperor's decision that
peasants charged with second-tier crimes no longer be administratively
exiled on a serf owner's say-so, but only judicially, that is, by court
order. He further limited serf owners' punitive rights to an ability to
remit to strait- and workhouses only those serfs guilty of third-tier (petty)
crimes, so that in effect these peasants were to be punished for just a brief
period before being allowed to return home. Most importantly, the ukase
abolished landowners' right to remit serfs to the state as *posel´shchiki*
to satisfy recruitment quotas. Through sleight-of-hand Alexander had
managed to revoke the privilege enjoyed by landowners since Elizabeth
to unilaterally exile their serfs. By reasserting state control over exile he
signaled it would henceforth be used solely to deal with judicially convicted criminals. But this legislation contained a crucial weakness, for
silence over the right of landowners to punish serfs by 'exiling' them to
military service left a loophole through which they could still remove
undesirables.[27]

Although this same ukase made no mention of communes' rights concerning exile, Alexander's emphasis on exile as a judicial rather than
administrative procedure made clear his intentions, as he later clarified
in an ukase dated 31 June 1812. This ordered that all those 'sentenced'
by communes to the military for 'bad behavior' would as before serve as

recruits, but if unfit for service they were *not*, as earlier, to be exiled to settlement, but would instead receive corporal punishment commensurate with the severity of their offences (and perhaps be fined as well), and *in all cases* be left in their places of residence. That Alexander promulgated this ukase soon after Napoleon crossed the Niemen River was probably no coincidence, for he did not need peasant communes banishing their own while the enemy bore down on Moscow. This legislation's provisional quality is further made clear by the fact that within three months of issuing it Alexander retreated so as to allow at least village bailiffs to exile crown serfs guilty of bad behavior. The ukase specifying this concession also problematized the earlier legislation, since it stipulated that *all serfs* (crown, state and private) deemed both guilty of bad behavior and unfit for military service should be exiled to settlement after all! In other words, and possibly owing to his loss of authority over much of central Russia as a result of the invasion, Alexander reversed his position and restored to communes their exilic authority. As for his ban on landowners' use of administrative exile, this remained in force until the early 1820s, when a series of piecemeal decisions culminated to restore this as well: on 29 February 1824 the Senate finally ordered imperial governors to accept 'without limitation' serfs presented to them for exile by landowners. This capped the complete renunciation of the 1811–12 ukases.[28]

Clearly, the exigencies of war influenced the growth of exile during Alexander's reign, yet this growth also reflected the government's anaemic presence in the countryside. The police apparatus had expanded to a considerable extent with establishment of the Ministry of Police and MVD, but surveillance and police protection remained virtually nonexistent outside urban areas. The countryside, the peasants' world, was literally a lawless place, and the state depended on those self-policing powers granted to landowners and peasants and which included administrative exile, to maintain some semblance of order. But this was a fraught dependency, for civilian authorities had neither the state's nor society's larger interests in mind when they banished people; nor could they have had such interests, given their lack of the general perspective the systematizing central bureaucracy was only beginning to develop. The investigative commissions and Alexander's efforts to limit exile together show officials knew of the problems exile was creating, but that this knowledge did not translate into coherent policy-making. The persistence of human bondage combined with the absence of any public debate on penology meant that only the state could resolve the developing crisis, but to supersede civilian authorities' exilic powers it would have needed much more widespread policing abilities, and at the time this was a practical impossibility in a country as large as Russia. A disjuncture therefore became acute from the beginning of the nineteenth century, wherein production of deportees resulting from a combination of state and societal factors quickly began outpacing construction of a penal apparatus with which to punish or rehabilitate them. Tsarism was falling apart at the very time it began creating a modern bureaucratic government.

*   *   *

We now turn to a doleful period in Siberia's history when nothing short of despotism characterized the regional administration. Siberians were, as we have seen, no strangers to corrupt and tyrannical officials; but as the nineteenth century dawned and Petersburg increasingly tried to systematize the ruling apparatus, such officials became increasingly anachronistic and detrimental to national interests. That said, 'Siberian leaders at this time persuaded the government that all disorder in Siberia stemmed from the slandering and scandal-mongering of local inhabitants and not from shortcomings of the administration,' explains Iadrintsev,[29] and Petersburg's ability to deal with such officials was anyway limited by enormous logistical and communication problems that arose when dealing with the Siberian territories. Hence the crooks who served as the tsar's regional executives continued to pursue their activities with aplomb. This period, however, came to a close with Alexander I's appointment of Speranskii as governor of Siberia, an event which marked the beginning of an era in Siberian and exilic history qualifiedly different from the one discussed so far, and is mentioned here to emphasize the significance of the events preceding it and to which we now turn.

Ivan B. Pestel's assumption of the Siberian governor-generalship in 1806 inaugurated a 13-year period remarkable for both its corruption and cruelty. Pestel lived in the Siberian capital Irkutsk during only the first year of his tenure; in 1809 he retreated to Petersburg where he enjoyed the privileges of his office while avoiding most of the responsibilities associated with it. He never returned to Siberia. Soon after taking office Pestel shuffled Siberia's top administrators so as to establish a coterie willing to participate in, or at least to condone, his soon to be legendary greed. He began by transferring A. M. Kornilov from the governorship of Irkutsk to that of Tobol´sk and naming Nikolai I. Treskin to replace him. In 1808 he removed Tomsk governor V. S. Khvostov on the pretext that he was 'slow in following orders' and replaced him with his in-law (*ziatia*) Frants A. von Brin. The following year Brin also took over from Kornilov as governor of Tobol´sk, though at some point Vasilii R. Marchenko assumed Brin's duties as Tomsk governor. Possibly because Marchenko failed to tolerate his associates' activities or wanted to fight the French, he was replaced in 1812 by Damian V. Illichevskii, who, like Pestel, would later stand trial for corruption. Ensconced in Petersburg, Pestel bent most of his efforts towards enriching himself through bribery and extortion schemes he operated with his lieutenants in the field: von Brin of Tobol´sk, Illichevskii of Tomsk and Treskin of Irkutsk. LeDonne surmises that Pestel was able to continue as long as he did because he gained the 'full confidence' of Alexander, who was preoccupied by for-eign affairs. Whatever allowed Pestel full rein, his absence from Siberia gave these lieutenants considerable autonomy, though it was Treskin on whom Pestel primarily depended to rule on his behalf.[30]

Both a petty martinet and economic visionary of boundless energy, Treskin actually did much in his own ruthless way to advance regional development. He was rare among Siberia's governors for having been born there, and was like Speranskii the son of a priest and a self-made man. But his rule over eastern Siberia from 1806 to 1819 was marked by such corruption, abuse and terror that eventually even Alexander, dis-tracted as he was, concluded a change was necessary and sent Speranskii to exterminate the rats' nest. V. I. Shteingeil, who before becoming a Decembrist worked in the Treskin administration, recalled 'that Pestel and Treskin held the strict belief: "Whoever's not with us is against us"; and whoever was opposed, whoever thought differently... thought his way to the grave, as they say.'[31]

Prior to Speranskii's arrival Treskin operated unhindered, but let us first consider some of his beneficial accomplishments. Of significance was his improvement of the road along the south shore of Lake Baikal terminating in Kiakhta, Russia's commercial gateway to China. Before improvement the Baikal Circle-Road (*Krugobaikal´skii trakt*) was little more than a pair of ruts snaking through the taiga, where marauding gangs of fugitive exiles threatened those few traders and merchants who dared venture. Treskin increased the number of troops patrolling the road and scared off the bandits, which alone stimulated trade. Another accomplishment, in a manner of speaking, was his reconfiguring of street matrices in Irkutsk and other locations, though the demolition of entire neighborhoods which this process necessitated angered many residents. Also, he so improved production at the Tel´minsk linen factory that it became the sole supplier for the Siberian military; and he took the remarkably humane step of convincing the Committee of Ministers to facilitate issuance of passports to crippled and otherwise incapacitated exiles so they could live anywhere in the region, rather than having to rot in their assigned prisons or settlements.

Of all Treskin's accomplishments, however, the most beneficial concerned agriculture. During a period of just three years he oversaw a nearly one-third increase in the amount of land brought under cultivation, and expanded the number of state granaries to create an emergency food supply and prevent speculators from cornering the grain market. 'In a word,' writes Shteingeil, 'there was not a single area that escaped his attention, and he strongly held the reins of authority in his *guberniia*.'[32] Treskin's very enthusiasm explains in part why he earned powerful enemies in Petersburg. Preferring not to await an official response to his request to take control of the Finance Ministry's regional distilleries, he seized them outright. The ensuing long-distance political wrangle between him and the ministry lasted almost ten years and culminated in the Committee of Ministers censuring Treskin. However, Alexander I was so pleased with the governor's successes (and was apparently so blind to his corruption at this stage), that he refused to take action against him.[33]

But it is his corruption rather than accomplishments which has secured the governor a place in history. Treskin ruled with an iron will, in the words of one Irkutsk historian, 'becoming a despot and demanding mute subordination'.[34] Shteingeil recalled: 'Neither Pestel nor Treskin failed to identify people's vices. They apparently believed the advice that thrashing good-for-nothings, evil-doers, and sneaks was "for the good of the entire region".'[35] Collaboration by many 'little Treskins' turned the IGP into a despotism. Treskin 'gave free rein to his subordinates,' writes Raeff in his inimitable way,

> who often abused this confidence or acted with much greater ruthlessness than was perhaps necessary. They clung to the principles of paternalistic despotism; they believed in prescribing the actions of their subjects down to the last detail, and they also felt that obedience and fulfilment of duties should be exacted not by kind words lost on an illiterate and crude people but by harsh, repressive punishments. *Qui aime bien, châtie bien* could have been their motto.[36]

For instance, Treskin issued a deadline by which Irkutsk residents should shift and square their houses commensurate with his plans for straightening the city's winding streets, then dispatched soldiers to literally saw off the offending sections of those buildings still blocking planned thoroughfares. 'It is said he prosecuted the consumption of tea,' writes Iadrintsev, 'forbade the planting of tobacco in kitchen-gardens, forced Buriats into agricultural work, and, finally, flooded the courthouse while trying to divert the river.'[37] Less dramatically, but more persistently noxious, Treskin's thuggish police force regularly raided homes and conducted interrogations. Both he and Pestel dispensed favors to merchants on a per bribe basis. The Englishman John Dundas Cochrane, who happened to be ambling across Eurasia at the time, recounts in his memoir how supplicants would deliver tributary gifts to Treskin's wife who, perched upon a sofa, occasionally deigned to acknowledge their presence by allowing them to kiss her hand. She and Treskin's secretary would then sell the gifts in a shop they maintained for that very purpose.[38]

Another example of Treskin's tyrannical nature was his treatment of notables who dared oppose him. These included the wealthy merchant and mayor of Irkutsk, Mikhail Ivanovich Sibiriakov. Seeking to defend the rights of the much-abused local merchants, Sibiriakov sent a formal complaint to Pestel about Treskin's conduct. Pestel forwarded the letter to Treskin, who responded by exiling one of Sibiriakov's brothers to Nerchinsk, another to Zhigansk 750 kilometers north of Iakutsk, and fellow merchant and co-founder of the Russian-American Company Nikolai Prokop´evich Myl´nikov to Barguzin, a mountainous settlement 600 kilometers northeast of Selenginsk. Despite intervention from the justice minister Gavriil Derzhavin and other prominent figures, each of these men perished in exile. Treskin pursued his subjugation of the merchantry by imprisoning in an asylum a certain Kiselev – described by Shteingeil as an 'intelligent and passionate man' – who eventually went insane. When the wife of disgraced former councilor Peredovshchikov, exiled to the region in the 1790s for murder, tried to intercede on Kiselev's behalf, Treskin had her arrested, interrogated for an entire night and put on trial. An Irkutsk court fined her 600,000 rubles. After she signed a promissory note Treskin's senatorial confederates added another 400,000 rubles to her fine. Despite Peredovshchikov's connections, Pestel's proved more powerful, and so Alexander I confirmed the fine.[39] Facing such formidable opponents, Irkutsk's merchants nonetheless got a petition through to the emperor detailing Pestel and Treskin's excesses. The charges were serious enough and signatories so renowned that it sparked the fateful investigation into both men's activities.

Owing to his persecution of merchants, who were never popular in Russia but were especially reviled by Siberian peasants, Treskin may actually have enjoyed some popular support in the countryside. Indeed, in his own mind and as envisaged by Petersburg, Treskin's main task was to promote Siberian agriculture, in line with the leadership's physiocratic goals and desire to secure the region against the Chinese. Moreover, the Siberian-born Treskin was acutely aware of the need to ensure bountiful harvests and to build up grain surpluses to feed the population after poor harvests.

The disaster surrounding Paul I's efforts to create an exilic colony in Zabaikal´e has been discussed, and so it need only be added that in 1804 a similar attempt was begun to settle some 7,000 exiles in Tomsk *guberniia*. Petersburg is known to have budgeted 383,000 ruble assignats for this purpose. Unfortunately, sources reveal nothing more about this project and so it is doubtful, given what we know of the annual number of exiles during this period, that more than a fraction of the 7,000 proposed exiles was ever sent there.[40] Alexander nonetheless remained committed to realizing his father's grandiose plan, albeit with some modifications. In addition to the administrative reorganization discussed earlier, the emperor ordered that governors Marchenko and Treskin, rather than governor-general Pestel, be primarily responsible for settling the exiles, and that each should establish bureaus specifically for this purpose. This followed a suggestion from Laba, who moreover recommended that Petersburg send its own overseers (*smotriteli*) to assist in managing the *poseleniia* to be established. Whether a naïve faith in these *guberniia* governors or simply a desire to limit Pestel's interference led the emperor to issue these instructions is unknown, though the center's dispatching of its own deputies to manage *poseleniia* indicates a growing recognition that a more systematic approach to exilic affairs was needed.

On 29 June 1806 Petersburg acted on Laba's and others' recommendations by modifying procedures for establishing state *poseleniia*. Such was the grandiosity still animating these plans that this ukase was intended to serve as a blueprint for the eventual colonization of all Siberia, chiefly by convicts. For the most part, the government followed Laba's recommendations while also ordering him to remain in Irkutsk to oversee this next phase of the operation. The ukase hinted at plans to construct *poseleniia* in all three Siberian *gubernii*: the first were to be established in Irkutsk *guberniia*, whereas those designated for Tomsk and Tobol´sk *gubernii* were to be established later and reserved solely for *posel´shchiki*, as opposed to convicts. It nevertheless appears that no one was ever sent to Tomsk *guberniia* as a result of this particular ukase and that Tobol´sk *guberniia* came to be regarded merely as a reserve for possible future relocations.

With western Siberia therefore not of immediate concern, Petersburg designated Nizhneudinsk, Verkhneudinsk and Nerchinsk *uezdy* – each within Treskin's jurisdiction – as loci for the revivified operation. Zabaikal´e still possessed a couple of hundred exiles left over from the 1801 disaster, and there may have been as many as 700 others living in Nizhneudinsk *uezd*; but the total number of exiles actually settled and living in Irkutsk *guberniia* seems to have been very small given the IGP's reluctance to provide for them or keep them in their assigned locations. The new batch of exiles was for this reason to be handled differently: Petersburg would send the overseers Laba had suggested to make sure they were provided with sufficient tools, food and cattle, as well as tax relief.[41]

Yet none of the *uezdy* in which planners hoped exiles would thrive was particularly well suited for agriculture. Verkhneudinsk and Nerchinsk *uezdy* were in Zabaikal´e, the former centered on the Selenga River immediately southeast of Lake Baikal, the latter further east, straddling the Argun and Shilka rivers. This entire region is heavily forested and mountainous, with dry soil and little annual rainfall. The rural population consisted at the time primarily of Buriats, descendants of the Golden Horde who raised cattle and practiced shamanism or lamaistic Buddhism (as they still do). Also living in the region were small groups of Tungus and, as noted, communities of Poles and Old Believers. Like the Buriats the Old Believers abjured agriculture in favor of cattle-raising, hunting, trapping and fishing. There were also the so-called *sibiriaki*, descendants of cossacks, fugitive serfs and exiles who had intermarried with natives and dressed and generally lived like them. As for Nizhneudinsk *uezd*, this was a similarly mountainous and heavily forested region halfway between Krasnoiarsk and Irkutsk northwest of Lake Baikal. Inhabited by Buriats as well as smaller groups of Tungus and Karagasy, it had a long-established though probably small population of Russian peasants, referred to in sources as either *sibiriaki* or *starozhily* (long-time residents). Poles and Old Believers do not appear to have settled in Nizhneudinsk *uezd* prior to Nicholas I's reign. Despite *starozhil* peasants' relative success in Nizhneudinsk, both this and the Zabaikal´e *uezdy* presented a formidable challenge to Petersburg's dreams of agricultural plenitude, especially since they were destinations for criminals and other social outcasts rather than *bona fide* farmers. Moreover, despite indigenes' and other groups' presence, these regions were largely uninhabited, untamed wilderness. Nonetheless, officials in the capital managed to convince themselves that criminals and other deportees, after having marched over 3,000 kilometers, would blithely proceed to clear-cut fields from the taiga and sow seed. Clear-cutting required tremendous physical effort and could not be accomplished by the faint-hearted; but such obstacles only imbued Treskin and his little Treskins with a greater sense of mission. The emperor personally entrusted the governor with the project's success and this son-of-a-priest responded with enthusiasm, ordering that exiles be forced to transform the wilderness into a 'plantation culture' (*nasazhdenaia kul´tura*).[42]

In 1806, the first year of the operation, the government deported to Irkutsk 2,769 exiles with all necessary household items plus 10 rubles each. The fact that the ukase ordering this deportation was not issued until late June suggests they could not have reached Irkutsk before 1807, which further indicates they had to travel through the depth of a Siberian winter. Archival documents covering the period 1807–20 variously refer to these and succeeding batches of deportees as 'exile-settlers' (*poselentsy*), 'resettled exiles' and '*posel´shchiki*', all of which indicates that, at least prior to Alexander's 1811 ban on landowners' use of administrative exile, some (i.e. the *posel´shchiki*) were privately owned serfs. Little other information exists concerning these deportees' origins; however, judging from the names of many for whom arrest warrants would soon be issued, a disproportionate number came from the Caucasus or Central Asia and may have been victims of military pacification.[43]

The material success of the Treskin colonies is, like that of the Baraba Steppe colonies, difficult to gauge. Dizhur later concluded that all of Alexander I's exilic colonial experiments had been 'completely without success'. Fel´dstein as well as the authors of *Exile to Siberia* conceded that Treskin was successful for a brief time, but that the colonies he founded ultimately failed. Raeff believes they became sufficiently productive to cover the government's outlay for tools, surveying and other associated costs, and quotes an IGP official, M. M. Gedenshtrom, to the effect that even the most recalcitrant exiles were compelled to serve the state's interests. Of all writers on this topic Peizen judged the operation most favorably: 'The naming of Treskin as Irkutsk civilian governor was all to the good for the establishment of *poseleniia* in Irkutsk *guberniia*.'[44] Peizen and Raeff alone provide empirical evidence. Their data show that within a year of arriving in Irkutsk *guberniia* fewer than half the 2,769 exiles dispatched in 1806 were settled in their assigned locations. The rest had either escaped or died. This first echelon was followed by another 1,267 exiles in 1807; 2,375 in 1808; and 2,000 in 1809. A comparison with the average annual number (1,606) of convicts and administrative exiles known to have been deported during the period 1807–13 suggests these latter groups contained a large majority of criminals and *posel´shchiki*, with at most a couple hundred *perevedentsy*.[45]

During the period of the Treskin colonies' existence a higher percentage of these latter groups, in comparison to the first, appear to have remained in their assigned locations. Positive factors influencing this retention rate turned primarily on Treskin's ability to provision exiles with locally sourced goods. This negated a dependence on imported supplies and reflected his earlier steps to promote agriculture, improve the Baikal Circle-Road, and stimulate trade with China. The absence of a ferry lane across Lake Baikal resulted in two discrete supply networks in eastern Siberia, each fairly self-sufficient and indicative of Petersburg's efforts to coordinate agricultural and industrial sectors. In the network east of the lake, in Zabaikal´e, exiles obtained cattle from Buriats and Old Believers and iron tools from the Petrovsk ironworks in Verkhneudinsk *uezd*. West of the lake, Nizhneudinsk *uezd's* exiles obtained cattle from herdsmen along the Enisei River and tools from the Kolyvansk *zavody* and other industries in Tomsk *guberniia*. Despite a crop failure in 1809, the IGP was able to report in June 1812 that from an original base of 8,597 head of cattle, Zabaikal´e *poseleniia* now possessed 14,242 head – a 66 per cent increase. Nizhneudinsk *poseleniia* had 7,683 head in 1812, though what they began with is not known. Another crop failure occurred in 1817; however, by that point exiles in Nizhneudinsk *uezd* had constructed 18 *poseleniia* comprising 936 izbas, eight chapels, 19 forges, 29 stores, eleven mills and five tanneries. In both Verkhneudinsk and Nerchinsk *uezdy* exiles had established a total of 34 *poseleniia* comprising 1,359 izbas, 19 chapels, 36 forges, 45 stores, ten mills and one tannery. According to Peizen, each *poselenie* consisted of a single main street lined with exiles' izbas; each izba housed two 'families', which initially each consisted of a woman and two bachelors, such was the government's desire to foster procreation. Based on these figures and others showing the total number of people exiled to Siberia during this period, as many as 14,000 exiles were living in these colonies, though the actual population constantly fluctuated because of the arrival of new exiles and the flight of others. Nonetheless, the existence of chapels, forges, mills and other structures indicates that many exiles were making lives for themselves and intended to remain there. The nearly 45,000 square *arshiny* of canvas produced by mills in Nizhneudinsk's *poseleniia* during the first half of 1816 is further evidence that exiles were becoming the productive peasants the government had long hoped for.[46]

Yet a different picture emerges when we shift attention away from the colonies' material success, for this abundance was accompanied by imposition of a terror regime. Not because life in the *poseleniia* was so good but because they were concentration camps did more exiles not escape. Treskin regimented *poselenie* life along strict military lines and his overseers dispensed corporal punishment for the slightest infractions. '[O]nly birch blows maintained order' in what Fel'dstein characterizes as a 'huge prison'.[47] Torture may even have been used to cow exiles into submission. Whereas all Treskin's henchmen abused their authority to one degree or another, the most notorious was Fedor Borisovich Loskutov, a constable in Nizhneudinsk *uezd* who had previously worked there as a government overseer in charge of exile-settlers. 'Pitiless and unrelenting severity transformed even the most depraved convicts into peaceful peasants,' Gedenshtrom later recalled of Loskutov's methods. 'The clearing of fields and pastures . . . was done at the price of unthinkable efforts, but it was finally accomplished by means of unrelenting compulsion and supervision.'[48] Loskutov personally threatened to beat to death exiles who did not work hard enough, yet at the same time told others that if they could not succeed as farmers they should contribute to their *poselenie* by robbing local peasants and natives. One source reports that under Loskutov the Nizhneudinsk *poseleniia* amassed a capital fund of as much as 100,000 rubles, while another notes that when Speranskii eventually dismissed him in 1819 Loskutov was found to have embezzled up to 150,000 rubles worth of furs and other items. Perhaps the two figures refer to the same monies, but ascribe them to different owners. There is an anecdote that when Speranskii publicly announced the overlord's removal and arrest, a startled local gawked at the Petersburg emissary and said, '*Batiushka* [little father], what are you doing? Don't you know this is Loskutov?' According to *Exile to Siberia*, long after Speranskii left Irkutsk 'there remained only the notorious memory of Loskutov, whose name has since been recalled by Siberians with terror'.[49]

Archival documents support an interpretation of the Treskin colonies as open-air carcerals. Escapes occurred regularly, not just from *poseleniia* but every other place exiles were assigned in Irkutsk *guberniia*. Given the nature of the documentation it is sometimes difficult to tell whether certain wanted fugitives were exiles or not. Half or more during this period appear to have been factory serfs or soldiers, though as we have seen, many could be classified as exiles. Nevertheless, a sufficient number of circulars definitively ordering capture of 'exile-settlers', '*posel'shchiki*' or 'penal laborers' shows that exilic fugitives were indeed a growing problem.

Exiles ran away from Loskutov's *poseleniia* in especially large numbers. For example, in June 1810 the IGP issued a circular relaying a report from Loskutov that 19 exiles had just escaped his command. The following month the IGP warned officials that exile-settlers from Nizhneudinsk *uezd* were crossing the Chinese border and heading toward Bukhara (which seems to have been a metonym for Central Asia in general; in any case, the destination further suggests many fugitives were Kirghiz or Kazakhs exiled as part of Russia's pacification of their homelands). The total numbers of *poseleniia* and exiles controlled by Loskutov are unknown, but there was a constant haemorrhaging of fugitives from such *poseleniia* under his control as Algashetsk, Reshetinsk, Verkhneingashevsk and Cheremshansk. Loskutov was the harshest constable in this new, more efficient slave administration, but exiles and penal laborers fled all sites in Treskin's fiefdom. For example, in September 1807 an overseer in Zabaikal´e named Baklanov reported that 'over various months [*v raznyia mesiatsy*] a total of 32 persons have escaped from state *poseleniia*'. A roster (*spisok*) indicates many of these escapes occurred between May and August, though many others are not dated.[50]

Exiles also routinely escaped from those Bashkirs unfortunate enough to have been impressed into convoy duty.[51] In 1810 the Nerchinsk Land Court, outraged by the escape of eleven exiles from 'Bashkir cossacks', asked the IGP to launch 'an investigation into the inadequacies of the Bashkirs' deportation of criminals . . . with the recognition that they not rarely, but almost always . . . allow criminals to escape'.[52] Aside from a few subsequent ukases in which the IGP took the unusual step of identifying by name those who let their charges escape,[53] the court's request produced little result. Such requests were probably frequent, but probably just as often ignored. Speranskii would later devote an entire regulation (*ustav*) to improving the deportation of exiles.

Exiles and factory serfs also escaped from the region's salt works, mines, smelteries and textile mills. In June 1807 the IGP called for

> the capture of exiles Ivan Korobeinikov of Selenginsk and Petr Gondaburenok, Abram Gaidukov, Ivan Kukhtin, Nikita Alekseev, *Zhenka* [the Woman] Aksin´ia Agapitova, Kozma Berdenikov, Osip Mikhailov, and Grigor Ekimov, who escaped from the Irkutsk salt works. Upon capture, punish by dispatching to said salt works.[54]

That same month a total of 31 exiles were reported to have recently fled the Irkutsk and Selenginsk salt works. A few days later Pestel, momentarily roused from his customary sloth, ordered that all individuals in

Siberia detained without passports, whether or not identified as fugitives from factories or *poseleniia*, be sent directly to *zavody* or factories provided they had committed no further crimes. He ordered officials to effect these assignations as administrative procedures to obviate the need for time-consuming trials in local courts. The order was designed not only to return fugitive laborers to factories but also to shanghai new laborers for Siberia's expanding industries, and so Pestel cited as legal precedent a series of imperial rulings during the period 1760–99 that allowed impressment of Russia's dwindling class of freemen into industrial labor.[55]

Despite Pestel's and the IGP's orders to return fugitives to factories there was no consistent policy. The day after Korobeinikov and the other exiles listed above were ordered returned to the Irkutsk salt works, the IGP instructed officials that if they captured the *posel´shchik* Zasilii Sarkil´deev he was to be remanded to the Nizhneudinsk court. Similar instructions were later issued regarding one Mikhail Matyiasevich, who reportedly escaped from the Cheremkhovsk *poselenie*.[56] Remanding captured fugitives to court rather than returning them to their assigned workplaces suggests conflict between different authorities. Treskin's primary goal was to make the *poseleniia* a success, and so it would have been in his interest to have fugitives sent to local courts, which he controlled and from whence they could be assigned as he wished. Pestel, residing in Petersburg, was more answerable to the ministries, particularly the Ministry of Finance from whose works most of these penal laborers were fleeing, and therefore seems to have favored returning them to their workplaces without the rigmarole of a trial. Hence officials were told in 1810 that if they captured 33 year-old Ivan Nikitin he was to be returned to the Aleksandrovsk distillery.[57] IGP officials therefore served two masters.

With regard to the overall escape rate, Speranskii's arrival in Irkutsk in 1819 did nothing to reduce it. In July 1820, during their monthly roll call, Ilginsk distillery officials discovered 31 workers missing, ranging from a youth named Fedot Ivanov to the septuagenarian Ivan Beznosov ('Without-a-Nose' – probably a seasoned veteran of *katorga* who had had his nostrils slit). The following month another 14 laborers went missing from Ilginsk.[58] Indeed, between 20 May and 22 August 1820 a total of 154 escapes were reported from Irkutsk *guberniia*'s state industries. The Aleksandrovsk distillery outside Irkutsk lost 82 workers during this brief period.[59] Laborers naturally escaped more often during the summer than at any other time, and so these figures do not characterize winter months; but they also do not include escapes from the Nerchinsk Mining District and other *katorga* sites such as the Okhotsk salt works. Moreover, reporting was always incomplete and haphazard at best, and officials had an interest in covering up the numbers at their particular sites.

After Speranskii became governor-general escapes may actually have increased, at least in Irkutsk *guberniia*. This was in part a reflection of the larger population of exiles in the *guberniia* at the end of Treskin's governorship than at the beginning. There was also a growth in local industry during this period, and so more laborers would have been assigned to the region, and these people too were fleeing in large numbers despite not being exiles *per se*. Speranskii's dismantling of the local administration created a power vacuum in the region, his dismissal of Loskutov and the other constables prompting an exodus from the hated *poseleniia*. Many fugitives escaped Siberia altogether: in August 1820 the IGP reported that in addition to fleeing south to Bukhara large numbers of *brodiagi* and other passport-less individuals were showing up in Perm *guberniia*, just west of the Urals. 'Due to its location,' the IGP quoted from a Senate report issued one month earlier, 'the number of fugitives and *brodiagi* escaping along the Great Siberian Road through Perm *Guberniia* is steadily growing.'[60] Perm was a popular destination because the law subjected *brodiagi* captured there to lesser punishments than if caught in Siberia.

Nonetheless, a significant proportion of fugitives remained in Siberia and as such demand closer attention so as to determine their social impact. Fel´dstein, Iadrintsev and others write that escape by numerous exiles released a criminal element that contaminated Siberian society. But whereas fugitive exiles and factory serfs probably committed most of the crimes in the region, it is difficult to know if the majority of those fugitives who committed crimes were criminals beforehand – as these same historians would have us believe – or became so as a result of circumstance. As discussed, beginning in the 1760s many arrived in Siberia as a result of administrative procedures. Given the abusive use of administrative exile it would be mistaken to categorize those so deported as criminals; and in any case, an administrative exile was not a felon. Also, a number of escapees originated in factories where labor forces consisted mostly of factory serfs with a minority of penal laborers and other criminal exiles (i.e. both *katorzhnye* and *ssyl´nye*). All of which suggests less than half of Siberia's fugitives were in fact criminal convicts. Many fugitives had no criminal intentions but simply wanted to return to their homes in European Russia or elsewhere, or to fade anonymously into local society. In at least one case the motive for escape seems to have been love, when a pair of married exiles ran away with their respective lovers.[61]

Despite such considerations, it is clear that as a group, these fugitives – even if certain individuals were neither classifiable as criminals nor guilty of the crimes for which they were exiled – committed violent crimes in numbers large enough to render eastern Siberia a killing field. Furthermore, it has to be acknowledged that many fugitives were not immune to a life of crime before they arrived in Siberia: many were originally sentenced to *katorga*, and so at least this cohort comprised dangerous individuals. That penal laborers were among fugitives is evidenced by the physical descriptions given in circulars ordering their capture. For instance, a July 1807 circular describes the nostrils of half a group of 13 fugitives from the Aleksandrovsk distillery as having been slit.[62] Many others were reported as identifiable by their lash scars – evidence of the knouting which nearly every convict sentenced to *katorga* received (though any exile could be knouted or lashed after arriving in exile).

IGP circulars' description of crimes suggests both that a population of habitual criminals was introduced to the region and that this Hobbesian world transformed others into killers and thieves. In May 1807, in woods near the Aleksandrovsk distillery, five thieves armed with firearms and cudgels robbed the merchant Pashchenikov and two coachmen of bricks of tea worth 700 rubles. Officials were told to be on the lookout for anyone trying to offload the booty.[63] Several years later the Irkutsk court reported that Savelei Mikhailov was wanted for stealing the peasant Malygin's money and Ivan Orlov '[f]or robbing cossacks of two rifles, two swords, and one sabre, and for stealing during his escape local supplies and cows'. Around the same time three exiles were wanted for assaulting the elder (*starshina*) Kazakov in Oëk, a village 30 kilometers northeast of Irkutsk to which many exiles were assigned.[64]

Prior to 1807 Irkutsk officials routinely ignored inhabitants' complaints about the crime wave spreading throughout their region. But that year Irkutsk *uezd*'s constable Alad´in (or Olad´in) announced regulations which suggest how serious the situation already was, as these established pickets at checkpoints to corral fugitives and check passports; relocated exiles living in such distant locations as mills and encampments to villages for surveillance; conscripted armed watchmen from the peasantry to patrol villages at night; ordered all those 'with *katorga* marks' (i.e. slit nostrils and tattoos) to turn over their 'firearms, ammunition, and gunpowder'; and prescribed fines for those failing to report crimes.[65] Similar measures chart the development of the Treskin despotism, for while it was reasonable that convicted murderers and rapists not possess firearms, authorities capitalized on residents' fears to impose less justifiable measures. After Alad´in the IGP 'exiled suspicious *posel´shchiki* and *propitannye* from their locations to distant villages and, in case of incorrigibility or insubordination, subjected them to punishment by the village assembly'. The reader may recall that *propitannye* were those exiles aged, crippled or otherwise unfit for work assigned to villages to eke out a meager existence at the behest of *starozhily*. The IGP also banished non-Orthodox religionists to distant locations 'to maintain the safety of village institutions'. Several years later Treskin added to these regulations by giving peasants the right to shoot fugitives on sight – something previously directed only at state criminals who had escaped.[66] How persons were to be identified as fugitives is not explained in the ukase, and so it amounted to a license to kill in an East that was getting ever wilder rather than tamer. A generation later Iadrintsev would describe this conflict between Siberian peasants and fugitive exiles as a guerrilla war.[67] Records show it had begun by 1807.

Whereas crime reports from 1810 suggest the police measures introduced three years earlier were accomplishing little in the way of public safety, an absence of legible documentation renders the effectiveness of these measures during the decade 1810–20 impossible to gauge.[68] Nonetheless, it seems Treskin's police were fighting a losing battle, given that Petersburg continued deporting criminals to Irkutsk throughout this period. Between 1807 and 1818 more than 23,000 exiles arrived in Siberia, the majority almost certainly assigned to Irkutsk *guberniia*. The fact that in 1816 the *guberniia*'s non-native male population numbered just 110,000 suggests the extent of these exiles' impact on local society.[69] It is therefore not surprising to learn that even after Speranskii's arrival regional administrators believed a crime wave to be in progress.

In September 1820 the IGP confided in a circular that Speranskii was well aware of

> endless reports . . . from City and Land Courts and other locations noting the increase since a certain time [*s nekotorogo vremian*] of various crimes such as robbery, murder, theft, and other mischief occurring not only in the cities but also in the *uezdy* and villages, on the roads, and in various places where the majority are exiles and *posel´shchiki*, and where fugitives from *zavody* and factories are staying in villages, spreading their immorality . . . [70]

Impressionistic evidence suggests that both the number and severity of crimes in 1820 were greater than previous years. The only statistical evidence found concerns cases investigated by a single district court, but the numbers are striking. On 9 November 1820 the IGP reported: 'according to the Irkutsk Land Court . . . from 1 January to the present it has reviewed 480 cases involving robbery, theft, and similar crimes caused for the most part by exiles and *posel´shchiki* in the *Uezd* . . .'[71] Because no comparable figure for an earlier period was found, there is no statistical proof that this or other eastern Siberian courts were adjudicating larger numbers of cases. One is nevertheless struck by reports of the beating to death of an Alarsk Monastery lama named Bakunov near the village of Ust´kut, a known location of many exiles; the robbery of 6,000 rubles from Kalmyk chief (*Taita*) Chechurin and the mutilation of two of his wives by three fugitives who escaped from a nearby *zavod* thanks to what reports say was 'a Yid from among the *posel´shchiki*'; and the separate robberies and murders of two peasant woman householders in Oëk *volost* near Irkutsk. Each of these crimes happened during summer 1820 amid a series of other crimes ranging from simple escape to armed robbery. While Speranskii was still plumbing the depths of the cesspool of corruption in the city of Irkutsk, bandits were visiting their own noxiousness on the surrounding countryside. In April 1820 a gang large enough to subdue a group of 16 peasants robbed them of property and four muskets not far from Tel´minsk; a month later, between 10 and 15 raiders broke into the home of the peasant Matveev, bound him and stole his belongings. Meanwhile, *brodiagi* were swarming throughout the region stealing from and accosting peasants and townspeople alike. Like those of wanted criminals, their numbers were so great that officials appear to have resisted arresting them for fear of losing their lives.[72]

*   *   *

On 24 May 1819 Speranskii arrived in Tobol´sk, where three days later he was ceremoniously recognized as Siberia's new governor-general. Not counting Russia's heads-of-state he was the last individual to govern the whole of Siberia. On 4 September he arrived in the capital of Irkutsk to begin the enormous task of righting the many wrongs that Pestel, Treskin and their predecessors had inflicted on the population. It was a task at which he would be only be partly successful.[73]

Speranskii's rise, disgrace, redemption and later pathetic humiliation under Nicholas I constitutes one of the more remarkable stories in Russian history. Between 1802, when Kochubei chose him to help establish the MVD, and 1812 Speranskii rose to the rank of privy councilor and became Alexander I's personal assistant. The emperor entrusted him with reorganizing Russia's financial and bureaucratic administrations and even approved his work on a constitution, though Alexander may never have taken it seriously. Speranskii's career came to a screeching halt with his disgrace and exile the year Napoleon invaded. A cabal led by Moscow commandant Fedor V. Rostopchin and historian Nikolai M. Karamzin succeeded in tarring Speranskii, already a known franco-phile, with treason. Speranskii may indeed have been guilty of some injudicious correspondence with the French foreign minister Talleyrand, but as Raeff suggests, the clincher could simply have been Alexander's bruised ego at learning of Speranskii's snide remarks about him. Whatever the reason, in March 1812 the emperor summoned Speranskii to a personal interview during which he informed him he was being exiled to Nizhnii Novgorod. Speranskii was neither formally charged nor sentenced, nor was he relieved of his titles or councillorship. This was a good thing in more ways than one, for during the carriage ride into exile Speranskii's convoy officer had to invoke his prisoner's rank to procure fresh horses and supplies.

In Nizhnii Novgorod police surveilled Speranskii as they did all polit-ical exiles before and after. Their interpretations of his activities, along with Rostopchin's continuing machinations and war hysteria about fifth columnists, soon led Nizhegorod's governor Petr A. Tolstoi to send Sper-anskii further east to Perm. In this small city on the Kama River, in what had once been the Stroganovs' mercantile empire, Speranskii, far from suffering the lot of the average exile, even the average exiled aristocrat, was nevertheless contemned and shunned by local officials and public alike. A loner by nature, he nevertheless smarted from this treatment and said so in letters to Petersburg confidants. Soon enough, his situation changed overnight following the Perm governor's receipt of a letter from the emperor. Despite winning a standing invitation to join what passed for high society in Perm, Speranskii continued his lonely existence, made all the more so when in late 1813 he dis-patched to Petersburg his beloved daughter and mother-in-law, who until then had been living with him. Perm's recluse now turned his attention to learning the German language and philosophy, which to some extent informed his 1822 regulations. After his daughter arrived home she gave the emperor a letter from her father in which he implored him to review his case. This and another letter shortly thereafter con-vinced Alexander to allow Speranskii to retire to his country estate in Novgorod *guberniia* in 1814, where Speranskii maintained his isolation partly to avoid those locals ordered to spy on him. In 1816, in response to another personal appeal, Alexander named him governor of Penza *guberniia*.

To some extent, the emperor considered Speranskii's governance of Penza and, later, Siberia as redemptive assignments that would allow him back into the fold. Yet by 1816 Napoleon was securely ensconced on St Helena and Speranskii's identity as an *agent provocateur* no longer taken seriously. For this reason, concludes Raeff, Speranskii's appointments to Penza and Siberia suggest the emperor sincerely wanted him to reform these regions' administrations. This seems to have been the case, especially when considering the administrative and personnel changes made by the emperor prior to assigning Speranskii to Siberia. While Speranskii was still in Penza Alexander received the Irkutsk merchants' petition concerning Pestel and Treskin, but for some time he had been dissatisfied with the situation there. For example, in 1813 he authorized Kochubei to establish a Committee on Siberian Affairs (*Komitet po delam sibirskogo kraia*),[74] but the resumption of war appears to have rendered this committee ineffective. Vladimir Tomsinov writes that Alexander first broached the idea of dismissing Pestel in April 1817, and was planning to force him and Illichevskii to retire and to name the commander of the Siberian Corps, Lieutenant-General Grigorii I. Glazenap, as Siberia's new governor-general. But if Alexander was really serious about this, then the 67-year-old Glazenap was hardly an inspired choice, and moreover one which makes all the more interesting the fact that the conservative Arakcheev dissuaded the emperor from it.

In spring 1818 a letter from Stepan A. Gornovskii, a Siberian official removed for opposing Treskin, managed to reach Alexander. After detailing Treskin's crimes, Gornovskii recommended convening an investigatory commission to be headed by the historian P. A. Slovtsov, director of Irkutsk's *gimnaziia*. According to Tomsinov, Gornovskii's letter decided Alexander to begin soliciting recommendations as to how to reconfigure the Siberian administration. Prince Petr V. Lopukhin, who sat on both the Committee of Ministers and the State Council, accordingly recommended that two senators be locally assigned to administer Siberia and that two corresponding departments, dealing with criminal and civilian affairs, be established in the Senate. His intention seems to have been to do away with the governor-generalship and civilian governors and to tie Siberia much more directly to the central government, albeit to the Senate rather than the ministries. His recommendation suggests a lack of faith not only in regional administrators but in the governing hierarchy that culminated in the tsar, though of course the tsar would have retained final word on any decisions. Another recommendation was sent on 24 October 1818 to Arakcheev by interior minister Osip P. Kozodavlev, who called for the creation of a high council (*verkhovnyi sovet*) for Siberia that would consist of bureaucrats assigned by Petersburg as well as representatives of Siberia's various estates (*sosloviia*). In his scheme, this council would possess supreme authority over a governor-general assigned merely an executive role. Kozodavlev also asked that greater powers over trade, industry and education be given to the cities. His plan was more radical than Lopukhin's, insofar as it called for and gave precedence to an at least partially popular representative council.

Had either of these recommendations been effected the subsequent history of Siberia, and even of Russia, might have been drastically different. As it was, the Committee of Ministers refused even to consider them. Instead of recommending reform the ministers, in meetings held 14 and 16 November 1818, denounced the Siberian administration and agreed (as Kozodavlev had also urged) to force Pestel to retire. Such limited measures indicate the government remained divided between a conviction that Siberia's problems could be solved by replacing personnel and a call for systemic change. Finally, in late November, the committee formally recommended that Pestel be replaced; but more importantly, called for the administration to be reorganized.

Alexander characteristically hesitated until 22 March 1819 before removing Pestel, but that same day wrote Speranskii a letter worth quoting at length, since it reveals much about his knowledge of his eastern territories:

> For some time I have been receiving the most dispiriting news about the Siberian territory's [*krai*] administration. I have received various reports about the *Guberniia* administrations [*Gubernskie nachal´stva*] and cronyism relating to the Governor-General himself. The Committee of Ministers, having read and deemed them of great importance, recommended I send a Senate delegation to reorganize the Siberian *gubernii*. Having already repeatedly experienced the failure of several similar revisions in so distant and enormous a territory, one finds it impossible to expect greater success. This is why I find it more efficacious to appoint you Governor-General and empower you to carry out an inspection of the Siberian *gubernii* and, with all the rights and authority attached to the position of Governor-General, to be Commandant [*Nachal´nik*] of a unified administration until a certain time. By being given this authority you should be most empowered to expose the persons engaged in embezzlement and judge them as need be according to the law; to put in place a more efficacious system

and administration for this distant territory; and, upon conclusion of your important assignment, to describe this in a report that you will personally deliver to Me in Petersburg, so that I have an oral account from you about the actual situation in this important territory...[75]

As this demonstrates, Alexander felt he had not been told the truth about Siberia for some time. Moreover, he had no faith in the Senate's ability to correct the situation, and so was arranging to bypass the administrative and legislative apparatus by appointing his most trusted (albeit still technically disgraced) adviser as plenipotentiary to the region. His emphasis that Speranskii personally deliver an 'oral account' is particularly telling in this regard, since he trusted no one – not even a scribe – to come between them. Yet Alexander's faith in even Speranskii was not total, for he wrote to Kochubei around this time telling him that Speranskii should remain in Irkutsk no longer than two years to prevent his succumbing to corruption.[76] As for Kochubei, who had himself chaired the first committee on Siberia, he was pleased to learn of Speranskii's nomination, and wrote him on 22 April: 'I cannot believe there have not been enormous abuses in Siberia.'[77]

On 5 May Speranskii's replacement as governor of Penza, F. P. Lubianovskii, arrived. Speranskii wasted no time and left next day for Siberia. Believing his Irkutsk investigation would be the final hoop through which he had to jump to regain sovereign favor, Speranskii wrote his daughter shortly beforehand: 'Confidentially, I will tell you that I will be in Siberia for no longer than a year or possibly a year and a half in order to fulfil the important mission there and, with this, return to Petersburg.'[78] This and the emperor's letter to Kochubei suggest everyone involved assumed Speranskii's was to be no long-term assignment. Raeff believes that once in Siberia the allure of a return to both the center of power and his daughter Elizabeta impelled Speranskii to work too quickly, and as a result he failed to appreciate the full extent of the problems there. It is true he did not fully grapple with the challenges involved before returning to the capital, but in light of the restrictions on his time there, he did what was possible.[79] Speranskii's supporters certainly showed faith in him, extolling his virtues in letters redolent of the sycophancy of court politics. 'Having for a long time not mentioned Siberia,' wrote Sergei S. Uvarov on 1 December 1819, 'I realize that the history of Siberia is divided into two epochs: the first from Ermak to Pestel, the second from Speranskii to xx...'[80] Speranskii became enamoured of this comparison, as a subsequent letter to his daughter attests.

Speranskii arrived in Tobol´sk in late May to begin addressing two broad categories: official corruption and exile administration. His letters show him dismayed by the corruption he found in the Tobol´sk and Tomsk administrations. Speranskii already possessed the authority to remove lower administrators; but as early as 31 July he wrote to the tsar for permission to remove Illichevskii and, as necessary, the other governors. Problems in western Siberia were serious, but as Tomsinov writes, in Irkutsk *guberniia* he found a *bona fide* 'criminal organization, in which [Treskin's] secretary Beliavskii and three *uezd* constables played the leading roles'.[81] Loskutov, the most egregious offender, despite seizing all the ink, quills and paper in Nizhneudinsk *uezd*, could not prevent petitions reaching Speranskii, and so he was quickly arrested and taken to Petersburg for trial.

After dealing with Nizhneudinsk, Speranskii took up residence in the governor's mansion in Irkutsk in late August. Here he formed an investigatory commission which succeeded in removing Irkutsk *uezd's* constable Voloshin and eventually brought charges against 681 officials. Erazm Stogov, who served under Speranskii, years later recalled that he 'brutally punished these robbers without mercy – he *exiled them to Russia!* The wretches relocated, some to Moscow, some to Petersburg.'[82] In fact, fewer than half were punished in any way, and only a very few were harshly punished. Finally, on 20 October, Speranskii received permission to remove the governors. He immediately dethroned Treskin, who, along with Illichevskii and Pestel, was later tried in Petersburg. What happened to Illichevskii is not clear, but Pestel's and Treskin's trials dragged on for years until both men's political connections resulted in their receiving little more than reprimands. In addition to relying on the compromised judicial system, Speranskii authorized Siberia's police to surveil local officials at a time when elsewhere in Russia police were being subordinated to regional administrators.[83] But replacing and policing officials was not a solution to Siberia's problems, as Speranskii soon realized. While travelling he had found 'complaints and abuses are nearly quotidian throughout all [of Tobol´sk] *guberniia*'; and after some time in Irkutsk he concluded: 'The problem is not within the second- or third-tier of officialdom...but...within the entire structure of the Siberian administration.'[84]

The major challenge facing administrative reform anywhere in Russia was the economic reality of rank-and-file civil servants. During the first half of the nineteenth century the civil service did become more egalitarian, better educated and, on a per capita basis, dealt with fewer citizens,[85] but most civil servants continued to be paid very little and 'therefore, corruption of public servants was not an aberration', as Pipes has written, adding that 'bribery in Russia developed an elaborate etiquette'.[86] Moreover, the improvements just listed were slow to reach the provinces, where this etiquette was far more developed than that found in Petersburg or Moscow thanks to the persistence of *kormlenie*. What drove clerks and other petty bureaucrats in Siberia to befoul their reputations is illustrated by Raeff's description of conditions facing those in Penza *guberniia*:

> The salaries were so low that the poor devils had barely enough to eat and could not afford adequate clothing; on days of bad weather, only half of an office staff might show up for work, as there was but one pair of boots for every two clerks. Unmarried copyists slept in the rooms in which they worked, for they could not afford regular lodgings.[87]

Knowing the treasury might approve only a slight increase in wages for these peons, Speranskii seems to have believed that bureaucratic corruption could be made to evaporate by exemplary moral leadership alone, that an *esprit de corps* would unite all officialdom towards a higher goal. But this pipe-dream would not carry him far when he came to rely on these same civil servants to effect the changes called for by his reforms.

However, this realization only came later. For the time being he addressed his second category of immediate concern, exile administration, by ordering, in his September 1820 ukase acknowledging 'endless reports . . . of various crimes', several stop-gap measures to keep the region from sliding further into chaos. In this document he cites the weakness of cossack units assigned to locations such as Tel´minsk as one reason for the large number of escapes, and orders police to incarcerate in city jails all captured *brodiagi* and fugitives. Speranskii faced a significant challenge in trying to reform Treskin's corrupt apparatus, and the mere fact that he felt obliged to order police to do their jobs speaks to this.[88] At the same time, his ukase ignored the fact that even the Treskin regime had not created a police force large enough to contend with the army of bandits and fugitives besieging the region, and so his injunctions had little effect. Looking back on the Treskin era Stogov wrote, 'I noticed a huge change in less than one generation in the population's moral behavior – and people knew they were misbehaving! There was little protection in the city, frequent murders, thefts, robberies, and two bandit gangs in the hills not far from Irkutsk . . . ' But even Stogov felt that little changed with Speranskii's arrival:

It appeared that with the destruction of the police's despotic power and deliverance from the constables' illegal extortions the peasants' life should have improved, but the opposite resulted. Old people who had begrudged the Treskin administration now often recalled it had been peaceful, whereas these days ...[89]

The troubles besetting these peasants surely made the past seem better than it really had been, just as Russians today sometimes look back on the Soviet era through rose-tinted glasses. But it does appear that Speranskii's curtailing of even a corrupt police force may have emboldened criminals, at least in the short term.

Certain of Speranskii's other measures issued at this time show that he saw the need both to keep better account of exiles' locations and to prevent them from congregating in cities and towns, which he believed were nexuses where criminals acquired accomplices and information prior to launching sorties into the countryside. Stogov and other sources suggest that urban crime rates were as high as those in the countryside, which explains why Speranskii prevented officials from releasing exiles and *propitannye* to the cities except in rare instances, and then only with passes specifying their destinations. The release to cities of exiles on work permits was a practice common even at this early date. In addition to serving as an incentive to promote good work habits it may have functioned to relieve industries of those who were difficult to monitor or incapable of work, and from having to feed and house surplus workers when production slowed down. A report of workers assigned as of December 1810 to Irkutsk's state textile mill lists 889 laborers, all of whom were 'owned' as either factory serfs or exiles; however, 150 of them were working elsewhere that month, mostly in the Nerchinsk Mining District, and a smaller number had been sent to locations in Irkutsk, where many worked for the merchant Myl´nikov or at the state salt works.[90] Regarding the *propitannye*, it will be recalled that Treskin had secured permission for them to live anywhere in the region, not just their assigned locations. Speranskii's 1820 ukase seems to have limited this concession. Speranskii also announced immediate measures to deal with the distribution of exiles. His dissolution of *poseleniia* in Nizhneudinsk *uezd* prevented officials from assigning there those exiles gathered in Irkutsk, and so one by-product of this was Irkutsk *uezd* assuming the highest crime rate in the *guberniia*. Speranskii did order the Nizhneudinsk court to accept Irkutsk's exiles, but to distribute them not to *poseleniia* but to peasant villages, for he had abandoned any hope of maintaining the Treskin colonies. In addition, he ordered the transfer of 'up to 500 young and healthy persons no older than 40' from Irkutsk *uezd* to Verkhneudinsk *uezd* to establish agriculture there, since people were already 'abundant' in the former.[91] Such language indicates little had changed regarding the government's utilitarian view of exiles.

Finally, Speranskii's 1820 ukase addressed the issue of the numerous cripples and others incapable of labor. Defending Irkutsk *guberniia's* wish not to receive such dependants, Speranskii enjoined

> the Tomsk Administration to limit the sending here [Irkutsk] of those exile-settlers who are old and sickened with paroxysms [*boleznennym pripadkam*].[92] In the future they will not be designated for a *poselenie*, not only because it is difficult for them to earn a living, but [because] they demand support from local residents there.[93]

According to Speranskii's arrangement, such individuals were to remain in western Siberia, where a social infrastructure had developed sufficient to render conditions less onerous than in eastern Siberia. Nonetheless, with an eye towards the need to populate eastern Siberia, Speranskii exempted female exiles from this provision and ordered them assigned to either Zabaikal´e or, if too weak to withstand the rigors of life there, Nizhneudinsk *uezd*.

When Speranskii closed the door of his carriage to begin his long-anticipated return to St Petersburg in February 1821 he carried with him two things: a report to Alexander detailing Siberia's many problems and the need for wholesale reforms, and a collection of experiences gained during his sojourn which would inform the regulations he and the Siberian Committee soon developed. His September 1820 measures had been meant merely to keep the patient breathing; now he was poised to revive Siberia entirely and give it a new lease on life. He did not foresee that he would in fact be prolonging its agony at the hands of the mother country.

5
'Only Ermak can Compete with Me'

Speranskii's opinion of the petty bureaucracy as a servile class in need of leadership correlated with his view of the peasantry as a child-like, dependent people. Extrapolating on both ideas, Speranskii believed that beyond administrative restructuring Siberian society needed to be socially engineered. He envisaged the government in a paternal role, guiding the population towards a higher moral and educational level. Treskin had previously assumed a similar role, though it was more particularly that of a stern and punishing father; Speranskii wanted to replace such individuals and their arbitrary rule with executors whose predictable actions stemmed from systematized, codified policies. At the same time, the governing institutions he planned were not only to represent a system of greater and fairer efficiency, but would embody the spiritual benevolence redolent of Alexander I's reign, during which manifestos and monuments alike expressed a view at once didactic and sanctimonious. Speranskii was no Alexander when it came to mysticism, but nevertheless was, in addition to being a creature of the rational and organizational precepts of the Enlightenment, strongly influenced by the German Romantic philosophy he read while in Perm and elsewhere, and despite believing in some ways that his Irkutsk assignment was an extension of his banishment from Petersburg, he came to envisage while there a glorious future for Siberia and its inhabitants, one that recognized the land's great natural and geopolitical potential and promised that *starozhily* and natives could be made to conform to a *narodnost* ('nationality-ness') for the betterment of all Russia. The only thing separating his vision from reality was a structure, a *Gebilde*, that would allow his idea, or more precisely the conceptual spirit animating his idea, to be manifested. In February 1820 Speranskii wrote to his daughter: 'I have discovered the true political problem of Siberia. Only Ermak can compete with me in this respect.'[1] This discovery, coming as it did less than six months into his stay in Irkutsk, would seem to confirm Speranskii the visionary rather than the administrator; but faced with the inherent limitations of the system as it then was, he likely preferred to embrace an ideal rather than lock horns with the recalcitrant officials who remained in office, especially since he knew that complete execution of his plans would have to await his return to Petersburg and what he optimistically believed would be the emperor's full support.

Speranskii returned to Petersburg on 8 February 1821. On 28 July, Alexander I established the Siberian Committee to consider Speranskii's plans and assist in reforming Siberia's administration. In producing the first administrative regulations specific to Siberia the committee recognized on the one hand the need for a more systematized approach and, on the other, the region's uniqueness. Besides Speranskii, the committee consisted of Aleksei A. Arakcheev (later replaced as chairman by Viktor Kochubei), Prince Aleksandr N. Golitsyn, Baron Baltazar B. Kampengauzen (Kampenhausen) and Dmitrii A. Gur'ev – senior officials all, whose ranks indicate the importance the emperor attached to this issue. Speranskii's personal secretary, F. I. Tseier, initially handled the committee's paperwork; but the eventual Decembrist Gavriil S. Baten'kov soon replaced him.[2] The committee would meet regularly until 1838 to monitor implementation of the reforms.

The reforms' many contradictions and lack of clarity indicate Speranskii's vision did not emerge from the collective decision-making process unscathed. Indeed, it may be more correct to describe the committee's work as a combative process distilling overarching ideological battles about Russian society and methods of governance. Of these battles, that most relevant to exile concerned the prison reform movement which emerged shortly before the Siberian Committee convened. In 1819 the Quaker Walter Venning succeeded in gaining the emperor's approval to establish in Petersburg the country's first Prison Aid Society (*Obshchestvo popechitel'nago o tiur'makh*; hereafter, OPT). The intermediary for these negotiations was Golitsyn, a close friend of Alexander I, who appointed him OPT's first president. 'According to Prince Golitsyn,' writes Bruce Adams,

> the state's only responsibility was to provide justice, which it did by putting criminals in prison. The society, he hoped, could do more; its members would show mercy and thereby win sinners for Christ. Such were corrections in the early part of the century. [3]

During the two decades leading up to the Siberian Committee's establishment penological treatises by Jeremy Bentham, John Howard and other reformers were translated into other languages and digested by Golitsyn and like-minded statesmen.[4] But the group Golitsyn represented – and of which Alexander only partially approval – faced opposition. Kampengauzen, who replaced Golitsyn as OPT's president in 1822, complained to fellow committee member and arch-reactionary Arakcheev in September of that year:

> it is difficult to reach agreement with this colorful assemblage of grandiloquent philosophers, sensitive philanthropists, enlightened ladies and ingenuous people. Sometimes you agree, if only to avoid falling out altogether, and wind up signing something horrible.[5]

Like Golitsyn, many of those sympathetic to prison reform were Freemasons. Douglas Smith's observation that Masons 'claimed both to possess the secret knowledge required to attain virtue and to be the personification of virtue' helps explain why Kampengauzen found his contemporaries so insufferable.[6]

Competing and virtually irreconcilable factions were therefore represented on the Siberian Committee. But while Speranskii's biographers as well as historians of exile admit that the extent of his authorship of the reforms is indeterminable, they nevertheless agree it was Speranskii who bore primary responsibility for their content. It is therefore reasonable to refer to them as 'Speranskii's reforms', though in the analysis that follows I highlight problem areas by emphasizing the Siberian Committee's collective authorship over that of Speranskii. There is admittedly some guesswork in this; but at the same time a coherent organizational theory bearing Speranskii's imprint emerges from a close reading of the reforms, and the exceptions to it betray little coherence when looked at comparatively, and as such, almost certainly did not originate with Speranskii but were alterations he was forced to accept.

Issued by decree from the imperial palace of Peterhof on 22 July 1822, the Siberian Reforms[7] made a lasting impact on the history of Siberia and exile, though it should be noted from the outset that they were not fully implemented. Speranskii detailed the structure he had designed for realizing his ideas as well as the conceptual spirit behind them, and so the pages of this document reveal the dreams of a man about to be torn between the world of thought and the realities of statecraft. The reforms include several regulations (*ustavy*), but we are concerned here only with those that transformed the general organizational and administrative structure of Siberia, most especially the 'Regulation on Exiles' (*Ustav o ssyl´nykh*) and the 'Regulation on Exile Transfer within Siberian *Gubernii*' (*Ustav ob etapakh v sibirskikh guberniiakh*). Because discussion of the reforms draws attention to their application, certain of their provisions will be more fully examined by noting subsequent relevant legislation and examples from the post-1822 period.

Speranskii wanted to better integrate Siberia into the Russian state, but also to take account of its regional peculiarities and the difficulties which distance and natural conditions imposed on governance. While serving in Irkutsk he traveled extensively and came to appreciate that life in Siberia was unique, different from that in Russia, and moreover that Siberia possessed distinct geographies and resources. This appreciation led not only to establishment of a set of regulations specific to Siberia, but caused him to divide it administratively in half along the topographical boundary of the Enisei River. These halves corresponded to what are in fact two separate geological zones, the Western Siberian Plate and the Siberian Platform, though it is unlikely he knew this at the time. What officially became Western and Eastern Siberia each comprised *gubernii* as well as an *oblast* (in tsarist usage, an *oblast* signified a less populated territorial unit), and within each of these larger regions *uezdy* were re-designated *okruga* (sing., *okrug*).[8] In order that Western and Eastern Siberia each be able to function as a self-sustaining economic region, Speranskii assigned the Kolyvansk Mining District to the former and the Nerchinsk Mining District to the latter. These districts were similarly administratively organized, though remained under the Imperial Cabinet's ultimate control.[9] (See Table 5.1.)

Table 5.1   Administrative reorganization of Siberia, 1822*

	Western Siberia		**Eastern Siberia**
Gubernii:	Tobol´sk		Irkutsk
		Okrug cities:	
	Tobol´sk		Irkutsk
	Tiumen´		Nizhneudinsk
	Ialutorovsk		Verkhneudinsk
	Kurgan		Nerchinsk
	Ishim		Kirensk
	Tiukalinsk		
	Tara		
	Turinsk		
	Berezov		

Gubernii:	**Tomsk**		**Eniseisk**
		Okrug cities:	
	Tomsk		Krasnoiarsk
	Kolyvan´		Eniseisk
	Kainsk		Achinsk
	Kuznetsk		Minusinsk
	Barnaul		Kansk
	Charyshsk		
Oblasti:	**Omsk**		**Iakutsk**
		Okrug cities:	
	Omsk		Iakutsk
	Petropavlovsk		Olekminsk
	Semipalatinsk		Viliuisk
	Ust´kamenogorsk		Verkhoiansk
			Srednekolymsk
Naval Port Jurisdictions:			**Okhotsk Maritime Administration**
			Okrug cities:
			Okhotsk
			Gizhiginsk
			Kamchatka Maritime Administration
Mining Bureaus:	**Kolyvansk Mine Bureau**		**Nerchinsk Mine Bureau**
		Zavody:	
	Barnaul´sk		Nerchinsk
	Pavlovsk		Ducharsk
	Loktevsk		Kutomarsk
	Zmeevsk		Ekaterinsk
	Gavrilovsk		Gazimursk
	Gur´evsk		Shilkinsk
	Suzunsk (copper)		Petrovsk (iron)
	Tomsk (iron)		(7 *distantsii*)
	(18 major mines)		

* 'Nachertanie Geograficheskago i Statisticheskago pisaniia Sibiri i eia ostrovov', *Sibirskii vestnik* 17 (15 September 1823): 138–42. The first *okrug* city listed in any *guberniia* or *oblast'* is that region's administrative center. The names of *okruga* correspond to the list of *okrug* cities. For example, Tiukalinsk and Kirensk were the administrative centers *(goroda)* of Tiukalinsk *okrug* and Kirensk *okrug*. In 1822 all *zavody* principally engaged in the production of silver, with exceptions as noted. Each of *Nerchinsk's* seven *distantsii* designated a series of individual mines.

To improve the government of Siberia, Speranskii created two new administrations of equal standing: the Main Administration of Western Siberia (*Glavnoe upravlenie Zapadnoi Sibiri*; hereafter, GUZS), headquartered in Tobol´sk (after 1839, in Omsk); and the Main Administration of Eastern Siberia (*Glavnoe upravlenie Vostochnoi Sibiri*; hereafter,

GUVS), headquartered in Irkutsk. Each was placed under a governor-general possessing both military and civilian authority.[10] Speranskii deliberately gave the governors-general broad control over economic, administrative and judicial matters. Assisting each governor-general was a Council (*Sovet*) of six high-ranking officials. The governor-general was to defer in certain matters to this council, though in practice it merely functioned as an advisory body. One bit of confusion inherent in this structure, and which may reflect Alexander I's interference in the Siberian Committee's activities, is that whereas the sovereign continued to appoint governors-general personally, the councils the governors-general chaired reported directly to the Senate. Moreover, the governors-general held positions within separate administrative hierarchies that culminated in the MVD, Ministry of War and Imperial Chancery. Despite the fact that GUZS and GUVS were supposed to operate executively rather than legislatively, the governors-general did not have to clear all decisions with Petersburg in advance. For this reason, and like the *voevody* of old, a governor-general's personality could powerfully shape policies in his region. Siberian governors-general after Speranskii certainly did not possess the nearly unbridled control their predecessors had enjoyed; nevertheless, their autonomy remained unmatched by governors elsewhere in the empire. 'All this created an enormous space for "legalized illegality," opened up possibilities for conflicts and malfeasance, and strengthened . . . the significance of personal relations with governors-general and governors,' writes N. P. Matkhanova in her study of the mid-nineteenth-century Eastern Siberian administration.[11]

It is important to note that whereas the governor-generalships were eliminated in 1837 in all interior *gubernii* except those of Petersburg and Moscow, they remained in Siberia until 1917. The Romanovs always considered Siberia distinct from Russia and approved of its governance by officials possessing an unusual degree of autonomy. In many ways, the governor-generalships were antithetical to the ministerial structure introduced under Alexander I, and the authority bestowed on them, despite the well-established tradition of bureaucratic malfeasance in Siberia, suggests a majority on the Siberian Committee had little faith in the ministries' ability to control the region effectively. As for Speranskii, it is difficult to say whether or not he approved of this. On the one hand, during his time in Siberia he recognized that Petersburg really had no idea what was going on there, and for this reason may have thought it preferable for Siberian administrators to be able to operate with minimal interference from the center. Yet on the other, this lack of interference had largely been what allowed Pestel and his predecessors' abuses in the first place. Whatever Speranskii's view on the matter, the committee's decision suggests a realization of the logistical limitations at that time on ministries' control over local bureaus, not just in Siberia but throughout most of the empire. The abolition of almost all governor-generalships in 1837 represented the ministries' growing power; but like so many other changes, ministerial dominance was slow to reach Siberia, not least because its governors-general actively resisted it. 'You are neither my predecessor, my chief, nor my judge,' Yaney quotes one Siberian governor-general writing the interior minister in 1839. 'My rank is higher than yours, and therefore whenever you have occasion to pass judgment on my work, I request that you communicate it directly to His Imperial Highness.'[12] Distance therefore continued to work in Siberian leaders' favor after the 1822 Reforms.

Subordinate to GUZS and GUVS were the *guberniia* administrations, each of which comprised a local (*chastnoe*) and a general (*obshchee*) division. The local *guberniia* administration (*chastnoe gubernskoe upravlenie*) was a tripartite structure consisting of a police department (*pravlenie*), treasury (*kazennaia palata*) and court (*sud*). Supervision of exiles who passed through and were assigned to their *guberniia* numbered among the police's responsibilities. The treasury was to some degree involved with exile, in that it determined land availability and assigned exiles to parcels of land or factories and *zavody*. The court oversaw both civil and criminal cases, either of which might involve exiles. The police, treasury and court served as regional bureaus for the Ministries of the Interior, Finance and Justice, respectively. Given the autonomy of the governors-general, this ministerial subordination led to confusion and jurisdictional conflicts. Moreover, the Siberian Committee's decision to allow *guberniia* governors and ministries to share authority over these bodies suggests its members failed to agree on a more coherent organizational structure. As with the irresolvable conundrum over whether governors-general took their orders from the ministers or the sovereign, Speranskii must have been fully aware of the operational problems this arrangement would present; but the fact that he was working within a committee of powerful decision-makers who were, moreover, reporting to the same emperor who had recently exiled him, renders such arrangements understandable. The circular command structures they created nonetheless testify to the autocracy's systemic inability to right itself. As for the general *guberniia* administration (*obshchee gubernskoe upravlenie*), it consisted of a civil governor and council on which sat representatives of individual *guberniia* settlements (*mesta*), the *guberniia* procurator and such other officials as the postmaster and director of education. General administrations received orders from GUVS and GUZS and executed them via local administrative functionaries, and were involved with exilic affairs on a daily basis.

Siberia's two *oblast* administrations operated in different ways from each other. Iakutsk *oblast* continued to be administered for the time being by Irkutsk's *guberniia* administration. Omsk *oblast* was controlled by the divisional military commander (*nachal'nik*) in charge of the Siberian Corps headquartered in Omsk. Because this *oblast*'s population consisted primarily of soldiers and nomads, the commander's duties were simpler than those of other territorial leaders, though like them he was responsible for exiles assigned either to Omsk fortress (to which Dostoevskii would be sent) or as soldiers to the Siberian Corps. Like Iakutsk, Omsk *oblast*'s administration was subordinate to its respective main administration, GUZS.

The maritime administrations (*primorskie upravleniia*) of Kamchatka and Okhotsk were subordinate to the Irkutsk administration, though the so-called port commander of each exerted direct control over his region's police, treasury and court bureaus. Exile to Kamchatka appears to have ended in the eighteenth century, though penal laborers continued to be sent to the Okhotsk salt works. The mining bureaus (*gornye vedomstva*) in charge of the Kolyvansk and Nerchinsk *zavody* were military administrations at first subordinate to the Imperial Cabinet and later transferred to the main Siberian administrations' direct control.

Siberia's *okruga* were divided into three categories based on the size of their Russian populations. The most populous each had its own police, treasury and court as well as a general *okrug* administration composed of a commander (*nachal'nik*) and council. The council included representatives from the *okrug*'s settlements, administrative offices and a solicitor (*striapchii*). Secondary *okruga* each had a smaller administration comprising a circuit (*okruzhnii*) court, land (*zemskii*) court and treasury (*kazennoe okruzhnoe upravlenie*). Tertiary *okruga* were regions mostly inhabited by indigenes essentially left to administer themselves, albeit overseen by constables (*ispravniki*) who handled extraneous police and economic affairs. Each *okrug* had a central *okrug* city (*gorod*) that was administered separately. Like the *okruga*, these cities were ranked according to population. Primary cities each possessed a legislature (*duma*), local and general police departments, and a city court or magistrate. Secondary cities had only a local police, and their economic and legal matters were handled by a city panel (*riatuta*). Tertiary cities had no police and appear to have been administered in much the same way *volosti* were. Officially, the *volost* represented the lowest level in the new Siberian administrative system: its government consisted of a mayor (*volostnoi golova*), headman (*starosta*) and clerk (*pisar*). The first two were village residents chosen by electors who each represented 100 souls.

For some reason, Raeff concludes that villages in Siberia were not regulated by those peasant assemblies (*skhoda*) which administered villages elsewhere in Russia. 'The township [*volost*],' he writes, 'had only dependent, subordinate functions, and, although its administration was made up of elected representatives from the peasantry, it remained at the mercy of the bureaucracy, whose obedient executive tool it was.'[13] Raeff is incorrect about the absence of *skhoda* in Siberia, whose existence is well documented and, pursuant to our subject, notable for their frequent refusal to cede land to incoming exiles.[14] For example, Iadrintsev quotes from an 1806 petition from 'peasants of the upper Lena communes' (*krest'iane verkholenskikh obshchin*) to Irkutsk constable Alad'in opposing his plan to assign exile-settlers to their land: '[T]he commune [*obshchestvo*] of Lena peasants is completely unable to agree with the honorable constable regarding acceptance of exile-settlers and giving to each two *desiatiny* of cleared, available land . . .'[15] Iadrintsev goes on to quote similar petitions by communes that could only have expressed their collective will by convening *skhoda*. Even if peasants allowed exiles onto their land, *skhoda* frequently denied them acceptance into the *krugovaia poruka* – the body of rights and responsibilities shared by those in the commune. Moreover, *skhoda* often forced exiles to perform a disproportionate amount of the obligations (*povinnosti*) demanded by officials. More dramatically, *skhoda* would prioritize and purge via *samosud* (peasant justice) the most offensive *brodiagi* hanging around their villages. Iadrintsev, a native-born Siberian, recounts in detail peasants' use of 'lynch law' ('*zakon Lincha*', he writes, apparently assuming it was named after a person) to rid their *volosti* of pilfering *brodiagi*; he also mentions an instance in 1838 when peasants organized a posse to hunt and kill some bandits who had just robbed them.[16] These examples indicate that Siberian peasants decided and acted collectively, and were not as mute and obedient as Raeff suggests.

This then was Siberia's new (and not so new) administrative structure, and it would, with some territorial and terminological modifications, remain largely unchanged until 1917. Governing bodies from the main administrations down to *volosti* and villages were more or less involved in managing exiles and the exile system. For this reason, it is impossible to understand the history of Siberia without understanding both how exile worked and the nature of its impact on society.

The 'Regulation on Exiles'

The 'Regulation on Exiles' contains 35 articles (*glavy*) comprising 435 clauses, and forms the third section of the 1822 Siberian reforms. It is most significant for its establishment of new categories of exile and an exile administration, the Tobol´sk Exile Office (*Tobol´skii Prikaz o ssyl´nykh*; hereafter, TobPS), which later relocated to Tiumen. Regardless of Elizabeth Petrovna's abolition of the death penalty 70 years earlier, the regulation begins by specifying that execution and exile are the only two types of sentences which criminal courts may deliver.[17] Since capital punishment was in fact extremely rare by 1822, used only to punish crimes considered treasonous, this regulation essentially maintained that anyone convicted in criminal court was to be exiled. There is no clearer indication that the Siberian Committee regarded Siberia as Russia's multi-purpose prison. Although the regulation deals only with exile to Siberia, it should be noted here that Siberia was, as earlier, not the sole destination for exiles: offenders were also sent to Finland, Arkhangel *guberniia*, the Caucasus and the far corners of European Russia. However, Siberia was far and away exiles' principal destination.

The section entitled 'Preliminary Principles' states that there are only two possible forms of exile: *katorga* and exile to settlement (*ssylka na poselenie*). It is significant that Speranskii classifies *katorga* as a form of exile (*ssylka*), since this indicates his intention to integrate these two penal apparatuses. At the same time, by excluding from the regulation any mention of administrative exile and exile to residence (*ssylka na zhit´ë*),[18] Speranskii seems to have been trying to will out of existence the extra-judicial procedures introduced under Elizabeth. Yet, despite their absence in the text, official and civilian authorities continued to use both procedures after 1822. Ten years later the Collection of Laws (*Svod zakonov*) officially sanctioned continued use of exile to residence; but as a result of terminological inexactitude and the phrase's frequent appearance in orders concerning the use of administrative exile, a great deal of confusion among both courts and administrators persisted as to what exactly 'exile to residence' meant.[19] Curiously, in this same section of the regulation there is a brief provision that convicts who complete their terms of exile are to be allowed to return home to European Russia or elsewhere,[20] whereas subsequent and more precise clauses in the same regulation contradict this provision, particularly as far as penal laborers (*katorzhnye*) are concerned. The contradiction meant little in practice, for according to Foinitskii a rule allowing former exiles to apply to live anywhere in Siberia (albeit nowhere else) superseded this provision.[21]

By creating a series of standardized forms supposed to cover every eventuality, Speranskii also designed a rather complex procedure for documenting exiles' whereabouts. There is perhaps no greater indication of both the benefits and drawbacks of administrative systematization than the standardized form. One group of forms literally ran from A to Z (albeit in Cyrillic: A to Я), and were to be used to establish the origins, status and to some extent destinations of individual exiles, as well as to notify officials if exiles left the march route due to sickness, death, escape or other reason.[22] For example, form 'Я' was used if an exile died during the march. A most important form was the 'sentence notification' (*uvedom-lenie*), supposed to accompany each exile and bearing a letter-stamp (not to be confused with the lettered forms just mentioned) indicating which court had convicted the exile concerned: lower courts[23] were signified by 'A'; *guberniia* or *oblast* criminal courts by 'Б'; and military courts by 'B'. TobPS was to assign exiles to their locations based in part on these stamps. If an exile arrived in Tobol´sk without a sentence notification, then TobPS was to wait for his paperwork before assigning him.[24]

After sentencing by a court the exile came under the jurisdiction of the *guberniia* in which he was sentenced. This *guberniia*'s administration was responsible for organizing deportation parties, supplying them with food and clothing, and its police for convoying them along specified march routes in the direction of Siberia until they reached the border of the next *guberniia*, whence that *guberniia*'s administration would similarly take over. In this way, exile parties would pass through European Russia to arrive at Tobol´sk *guberniia*'s western border and become TobPS's responsibility. *Guberniia* administrations were also responsible for organizing much of the documentation mentioned above and forwarding sentence notifications to TobPS so it could begin determining which locations to assign individuals. Yet the regulation called for these same *gubernii* to generate still more documents. For example, a record was to be made of each exile assigned to a deportation party giving his name, sentence and city of origin (i.e. the closest relevant city [*gorod*]); one copy was to be given to the convoy officer, another forwarded to TobPS. Another required document was a roster listing all exiles in a party, copies of which were to be kept by the officer and sent to TobPS as well as those administrations through whose *gubernii* the party would be passing, with the aim that these administrations would use the rosters as a basis for preparing necessary supplies and convoy guards.[25]

Although deportation parties undoubtedly carried some rations with them, march routes were designed to pass through villages so exiles could purchase food from peasants, similar to Trans-Siberian trains' present-day practice of stopping at stations to allow passengers to purchase boiled eggs, vodka and roast chickens from local *babushki*. The arrangement begun during tsarist times allowed convoys to travel lighter and faster and, as the frequency of deportation parties increased and parties grew much larger over the years, gave a considerable boost to local economies, though it is true peasants often simply donated food to exiles.[26] The money given exiles to buy food was called *kormovye den´gi* ('foraging money'). In 1824 the government also began providing *kormovye den´gi* to those who voluntarily accompanied exiles (so-called *dobrovol´nye*). Adults received the same amount as exiles; children half as much. In 1840 Nicholas I ordered that children's *kormovye den´gi* equal that of adults.[27] *Kormovye den´gi* rates varied greatly according to *guberniia*, though how they were determined is unclear. As of early 1827 the per diem across the empire's 53 governorships ranged between 3 and 17 kopeks.[28] The MVD sent *guberniia* administrations periodic revisions of these rates, which suggests that despite the 1822 reforms' assertion that *gubernii* be solely responsible for provisioning exiles, Petersburg eventually provided compensation. (See Table 5.2.)

The 'Regulation on Exiles' called for TobPS to issue *kormovye den´gi* in the form of scrip, so that deportees would not be carrying cash.[29] This seems to have been intended more to prevent embezzlement by convoy guards than exiles misusing funds, since Speranskii must have realized convicts could gamble or trade scrip just as easily as they could hard currency. Given the necessary involvement of credit, this scrip system depended heavily on coordination by several administrative bodies as well as the post's efficiency and safety. As a result, it seems to have been abandoned almost immediately, if indeed it was ever used at all. In practice, the convoy officer would issue each exile a lump sum in cash just as the party began its march through a given *guberniia*. Evidence for this are the frequent references in the literature to exiles who gambled away their *kormovye den´gi* or had it stolen before they reached the next disbursement point. To survive, such exiles depended on peasants' and fellow exiles' charity, or resorted to robbery. In many instances they offered themselves as servants to those hardened criminals who comprised the core of most deportation parties. The resultant master–servant relationships replicated those within prison society, where such paupers were derisively called *zhigany* (from *zhiganut*, 'to lash'). *Zhigany* cleaned the wards of way-stations and prisons alike, emptied slop buckets and performed other menial tasks.[30]

Table 5.2 Kormovye den'gi Rates in Selected Districts (in kopeks)

Guberniia or other administrative unit	1825–27	1827–29
Arkhangel'	12	11
Astrakhan	6	6
Vil'no	13	20
Grodno	6	11
Estliand	15	15
Irkutsk	6	11
Kazan'	8	7
Kiev	5	6
Moscow	9	12
Nizhegorod	10	9
Orel	6	7
Penza	6	7
Perm'	9	9
Podol'ia	7	12
St. Petersburg	15	18
Sloboda-Ukraine	7	5
Tver'	13	14
Tobol'sk	9	7
Tomsk	7	7
Kherson	9	11
Caucasus oblast'	9	7
Bessarabia oblast'	3 (silver)	5 (silver)
Georgia	5 (silver)	7 (silver)
Iakutsk oblast'	na	10
Omsk oblast'	na	6
Eniseisk	na	5

Source: GAIO, f. 435, op. 1, d. 146, ll. 58–59; d. 155, ll. 198–199.

Deportation parties were to depart *guberniia* capitals once a week. Despite being sequentially convoyed by individual *gubernii*'s police, exiles were from the moment of departure considered to be under TobPS's jurisdiction, perhaps to ensure their rapid forwarding and to prevent regional officials from siphoning off convicts for their own ends. Speranskii doubtless recalled Laba's discovery that Tobol'sk officials had impressed exiles into the military. It was important that parties stay on schedule, since any delay had a domino effect along the entire march route. For this reason, convoy officers pushed both guards and exiles forward no matter the conditions. Convoys were allowed to halt for only two reasons: serious illness or the commission of new crimes. In the first instance, parties were to wait only long enough for medical help to arrive; in the second, long enough for 'police punishment', that is, floggings, to be administered. If an exile committed a serious crime such as murder or stealing more than 100 rubles, two guards were to deliver him to the nearest local court then catch up with the party later, after which the convoy officer would report the incident to TobPS. If a sick exile remained in a site along the march route longer than three months, a medical official was to send a report to the *guberniia* administration, whence the latter was to fill out the appropriate lettered form and forward it to TobPS. Convoy officers also had to report exiles who fled and were not captured within two weeks.[31]

As soon as parties entered the first city (*gorod*) of the next *guberniia* they became the responsibility of that *guberniia's* administration, though, as when marching through previous *gubernii*, TobPS still maintained ultimate jurisdiction. The regulation allows these cities' administrations some flexibility in the time needed to organize and outfit deportation parties; however, barring special circumstances such as illness or missing documentation, exiles were to be held no longer than six days.[32] In practice, officials routinely violated this for a number of reasons, not least of which were their own ineptitude and callousness, often forgetting or ignoring for months or even years on end certain exiles idling in transit prisons. The time these convicts spent waiting to be forwarded to their final destinations did not count against their sentences.

Speranskii designated that Kazan replace Orenburg as the primary collection and distribution point for exiles originating in almost all locations west of the Urals. He established within its *guberniia* administration a new agency called the Kazan Exile Bureau (*Kazanskaia Ekspeditsiia o ssyl'nykh*), charged with organizing new parties and driving them eastward via Perm to Tobol'sk. *Gubernii* closer to Siberia – specifically, those of Perm, Orenburg, Viatka and *okruga* in eastern Vologda – had no reason to send their exiles west or south to Kazan. Instead, within the first two *gubernii* the cities of Perm, Kungur, Ekaterinburg, Kamyshlov and Orenburg were to send parties directly to Tobol'sk.[33] The regulation parenthetically adds that an unspecified number of exiles were to remain in Perm *guberniia* for use in the distilleries there. Exiles who originated in Viatka *guberniia* and one of the Vologda *okruga* were to be herded into parties in the cities of Malmyzh, Debesy and Okhansk, then sent via Perm to Tobol'sk.[34] In sum, this article of the regulation indicates that *most* of the empire's exiles passed through the collection point of Kazan, but that *all* exiles (with the minor exception of those originating east of Perm and the numerically more significant exception of those coming from Orenburg in the south) marched through Perm to reach the Siberian border. Eddying pools fed by great streams of wretches pouring out of every corner of the empire west of the Urals, Kazan and Perm therefore served as the exile system's principal non-Siberian cities.

At the end of each year *guberniia* cities' police departments were to tally on form 'H' (Cyrillic) the total number of exiles convoyed during the preceding year and send this figure to TobPS, which would collate and total the various reports before submitting a general report to Petersburg.[35] As a result of this provision reasonably accurate figures exist on the annual number of exiles deported to Siberia from 1823 until nearly the end of tsarism.

The Tobol´sk Exile Office

Following its description of *guberniia* administrations' responsibilities for deporting exiles the regulation details the new administration that was to be concerned solely with exile. One must bear in mind that TobPS was not the only administrative apparatus with jurisdiction over exile: individual *guberniia* administrations, not to mention government ministries, played significant roles as well. But TobPS was unique in being the first administration in Russian history specifically designed to manage exile. Speranskii had recognized the need for such an apparatus while in Siberia. Despite its designated function, TobPS was not a discrete entity with direct links to the MVD or Imperial Chancery, as it probably should have been. Instead, it functioned as a branch of Tobol´sk's *guberniia* administration,[36] subordination to which may have stemmed from a belief among Siberian Committee members that exile would be better managed by a local organ, though the power struggle between ministries and governors-general was just as likely a factor in this decision. In either case, Tobol´sk's civil governor ended up exercising considerable authority over an office which ought to have served the interests of the entire empire, and so the quality of his leadership was extremely important.

A similar overlapping of hierarchical authority involved the exile bureaus (*ekspeditsii o ssyl´nykh*) Speranskii created to assist TobPS. Although they had the same name as the bureau established in Kazan, this city's bureau did not report to TobPS at all, but took its orders from an independent assessor. By contrast, the exile bureaus established in Tobol´sk, Tomsk, Eniseisk and Irkutsk were to some extent TobPS's subordinate, regional branches, with responsibility to distribute and supervise exiles. Yet they were also subordinate to their respective *guberniia* administrations and police departments and as such, each bureau was headed by a *guberniia* councillor (*sovetnik*) and staffed by *guberniia* chancery officials.[37] One result of this was that bureaus did not possess sufficient legal authority to fulfill their mission. 'The Bureaus were unable, for example, without exceeding their authority, to impose disciplinary punishment on exile-settlers, to compel them to carry out work, to launch necessary incentives... etc.,' writes Fel´dstein, who therefore concludes they did little to foster exiles' 'productivity'.[38] Another result was a conflict of interest that erupted between Tobol´sk's *guberniia* governor in his capacity as chief of TobPS and the other *guberniia* governors in their capacity as chiefs over their respective bureaus. These conflicts frequently manifested themselves over where to assign exiles after they arrived in designated locations. TobPS was nominally in charge of making these assignments (within certain court-imposed restrictions), but in reality regional bureaus often ignored its instructions and assigned exiles to conform to their civilian governors' wishes. In addition, the Imperial Cabinet, military, MVD and Finance Ministry continually interfered in assigning exiles.

Six categories of exile

Speranskii used the 'Regulation on Exiles' to designate six categories for classifying and utilizing convicts sentenced to exile to settlement. These categories, as well as his designated uses for penal laborers to be discussed below, demonstrate, on the one hand, Speranskii's attempt to accommodate ministries' competing interests and, on the other, his emphasis on exile's utilitarian function. That he designed a taxonomy to wring the utmost benefit out of an institution he himself did not favor is ironic, for his abolition of the Treskin colonies as well as his conclusion, reported to his daughter, that exiles had contributed virtually nothing to the growth of Siberia's population, show he did not support forced settlement in Siberia. Indeed, he urged Petersburg to allow state peasants to migrate there instead. Treadgold claims that Speranskii's efforts led to an ukase being issued the same year as his reforms that to some degree permitted voluntary emigration, though he is silent about its results. Neither Raeff nor any other historian mentions such an ukase,[39] all of which suggests that if indeed such permission was given, it was either quickly annulled or encumbered by so many qualifications as to be useless.

Whatever the case, provisions in the 'Regulation on Exiles' for eventual assignment to the land of almost all exiles do not reveal a colonizing initiative on Speranskii's part, but rather a capitulation to committee members who refused to buck a penological tradition that was by then two centuries old. Speranskii could make this concession because he had convinced himself exiles' numbers were small. 'Do not believe and don't allow yourself to think that Siberia has been populated by exiles and criminals,' he wrote his daughter on 6 September 1819, shortly after settling in Irkutsk:

> Their numbers are like droplets in the sea; they're almost invisible, except in certain [industrial] works. Incredibly, their numbers are very small. According to the most accurate information, they make up barely 2 t[housand] a year and among that number never more than a tenth are women. The point of this letter will seem strange to you: but it is necessary, because I shared in all respects your sincere understanding about our Fatherland. In due time I will provide statistical tables which will amaze educated Europe. They will show hardly a single criminal can be found among 20,000 of us, and that he's but a petty thief; of those more serious, there's not more than one in a hundred thousand. I myself could not at first believe this and consider it a great ethical discovery.[40]

This understatement of exiles' impact suggests why Speranskii's regulatory schema proved unable to cope with later developments: not only did he fail to foresee a growth in the number of exiles sent to Siberia, but his faith in the fatherland and what he imagined to be the essential goodness of the Russian people prevented him from probing into the region's past to arrive at a better understanding. For all that, neither can Speranskii be said to have been a liberal regarding penality. Influenced to some extent by Beccaria and other theorists, Speranskii nonetheless considered harsh punishment a necessity; most important for him was that any and all punishments be codified and consistently applied according to specific standards. His ultimate goal was to systematize Russian penality.

Let us now turn to these six categories of exilic punishment. The regulation states that with the exception of penal laborers, the most serious criminals ('namely, those flogged with the *plet*', since by now the knout was prohibited) were to be assigned as temporary workers to replenish industrial labor forces. The number of exiles assigned to this first category would depend on requests furnished by the Ministry of Finance's regional treasury chambers (*kazennye palaty*), which administered all Siberia's state industries except those in the Kolyvansk and Nerchinsk mining districts.[41] Such temporary workers were not to be kept at an industrial site longer than one year (during which there was no practicable difference between them and penal laborers [*katorzhnye*]). If these exiles served their labor terms without committing any new crimes or infractions necessitating punishment, they would be assigned by the local exile bureau to another of the six categories. If, however, an exile committed violations during that year, he could be kept at the site for up to two more years. A clause vaguely stipulates that if, during this extended term, he commits another crime or proves incorrigible, he may be sentenced to *katorga* or to remain in the factory 'for as long as the law requires'.[42] During their first year exiles in this category were to receive double the pay penal laborers received, and upon expiry this year would count as two years towards the lengths of their terms in the category to which they were next assigned. However, if an exile attempted to escape or committed further crimes, then this melioration was withdrawn.[43]

The next category for exiles was that of 'road workers' (*dorozhnye rabotniki*) in the service of the Department of Overland Communications (*Vedomstvo sukhoputnykh soobshchenii*), which among other things maintained march routes into Siberia. This category required that exiles constantly be outside, and so the regulation stipulates only the 'healthiest, strongest and youngest' be so assigned. Also, specialists with relevant skills were to join road crews. Whereas exiles in almost all other categories came under the jurisdiction of the exile bureaus, those in the Department of Overland Communications were to reside in villages or settlements (*seleniia*) administered by regional treasury chambers. Road workers possessed rights similar to those of state peasants, and were to receive pay from regional administrations via their labor teams (*arteli*). If because of persistent violations an exile in this category was permanently deprived of such rights or became disabled or otherwise unfit to work, he was to be reassigned to another of the six categories.[44]

The most skilled of those exiles not assigned to the preceding category were to be assigned as artisans to crafts houses (*remeslennye doma*) in what comprised the third category. Each crafts house was to be composed of separate departments (*otdeleniia*) consisting of 15–30 persons each. The regulation lists a total of seven departments, one each for carpenters and woodworkers; masons; smiths and other metalworkers; copper- and silversmiths; tanners and saddlers; painters; and common laborers (*chernorabochie*). Each department was to be headed by a master of the associated trade in cooperation with a headman nominated from among the exile-artisans. Although the regulation associates this category with skilled workers, it orders a distinction be made between those skilled enough to belong to the craftsman *soslovie* (i.e. the *masterstvo* who made all necessary workplace decisions) and those whose comparative lack of skill required them to function as assistants. Administrators were to retain 2 kopeks from every 2 rubles an exile-artisan earned to send to the local exile bureau for the exiles' economic fund (explained below).[45] Tiumen, Eniseisk, Verkhneudinsk and Kiakhta are identified as principal locations for these crafts houses. Although the regulation states that crafts houses were not to be limited to these four cities, it is unclear why the Siberian Committee chose these in particular, especially since the regulation also gives *guberniia* governors the right to determine both crafts houses' locations and the number of exiles assigned to them. Governors were also allowed to assign exile-artisans to locations without crafts houses if there were an appropriate purpose for which they could be used, such as constructing buildings, mills, dams, etc. However, exile-artisans were not to be employed at any one job away from a crafts house for longer than six months, and there could be no fewer than five and no more than 50 artisans per assignment.[46]

Speranskii possibly envisaged the artisan category as a sort of engineer corps to be made readily available for certain projects; but contradictions concerning their planned use appear to have resulted from the competing jurisdictional interests already mentioned. The regulation is similarly vague as to this category's establishment. If one assumes the committee intended each crafts house in the four principal locations to include all seven of the departments listed above, then based on the numbers just given this meant only 420–840 exile-artisans would be living and working in Siberia at any one time. Such a small figure suggests the four crafts houses called for by the regulation bore some resemblance to the strait- and workhouses legislated during Catherine II's reign, insofar as they may have been planned as merely the first in a series of reformatories intended to replace exile to settlement. We have already seen the intimate relationship that existed between the Prison Aid Society and the Siberian Committee, and this relationship is further evidenced by the latter's progressive (in a manner of speaking) notion of these crafts houses: *guberniia* administrations were to be responsible for housing exile-artisans in buildings supervised by special wardens (*smotriteli*); and each warden was to collaborate with a bookkeeper to present regular reports to a supervisory office (*kontora*).[47] Such an arrangement, akin to today's halfway houses for convicted felons, not only indicates OPT's influence but also Speranskii's organizational ingenuity and idealism. Yet the notion behind the crafts houses also evokes the insidiousness of Bentham's Panopticon and the modern prisons then appearing in Britain and the United States. Foucault has seen in the Panopticon the perfection of the use of power, whether as an idea ('panopticism') or as physically manifested in 'the psychiatric asylum, the penitentiary, the reformatory, the approved school and, to some extent, the hospital,' because its 'major effect . . . [is] to induce in the inmate a state of conscious and permanent visibility that assures the automatic functioning of power'.[48] The crafts houses called for by the Siberian Committee seem to have been similarly intended to facilitate the execution of state authority over societal deviants for the purpose of rendering them serviceable subjects.

The Siberian Committee reserved its fourth category of exile for 'house serfs, Jews and people little capable of work' and called it 'exile to the servant guild [*v tsekh slug*]'. Because these exiles were to work as personal servants for high officials and notables in Siberia, GUZS and GUVS were each responsible for determining how many exiles would be needed in this category. Unmarried women could be assigned to the servant guild, but an apparent compromise within the committee produced the lukewarm qualification that their 'numbers should not be too great'. Nevertheless, this category obviously presented an opportunity for these women's sexual exploitation. The exile bureaus were to maintain administrative control over such exiles, while those employing them were to pay each no more than 25 and no less than 5 rubles per month. The government was to retain 5 kopeks from every ruble paid for the exiles' economic fund. Exiles in this category were to serve eight years, after which they would be allowed to join the *meshchane* with general, though limited, rights.[49] Whereas this category of house serfs and those little capable of work suggests Speranskii's sympathy for underlings who led relatively privileged lives of little physical labor, the inclusion of Jews suggests the committee's hardliners hoped to segregate this religious minority from the general population.

It will be recalled that the Elizabethan ukases of 1753–4 created the category of exile to settlement. In his regulations Speranskii takes note of the four subdivisions of this category (only one of which actually assigned exiles to specific settlements) and expressly abolishes them. Yet because these categories had been more or less in use through to 1822, he orders that exiles assigned to *poseleniia* prior to 1806 should, as of 1 January 1823, be granted all the rights and obligations of state peasants. Exiles assigned to *poseleniia* after 1806 were to remain in them until the end of their sentences, whence they would transfer to *starozhil* settlements. This latter provision would seem to account for the Treskin colonies, as these appear to have been the only *poseleniia* established during Alexander I's reign; however, the evidence given in chapter 4 indicates that these *poseleniia* collapsed after Treskin's fall, and so this clause suggests cognitive dissonance among policy-makers as to the realities on the ground. Speranskii further prescribes that exiles already assigned to workhouses remain there (though the existence of these workhouses has proved impossible to establish); and that *propitannye* – now identified by the no less demeaning term 'incapables' (*nesposobnye*) – likewise remain in their present locations.[50] With abolition of the Elizabethan categories of exile to settlement, Speranskii's fifth category of exile to settlement actually did assign to settlements those exiles deemed capable of living as agriculturalists. Moreover, among all convicts now sentenced to exile to settlement, only those in this fifth category were officially termed *poselentsy* (exile-settlers), so as to distinguish them from exiles in all other categories. As should now be clear, the distinction was by no means merely semantic.[51]

The regulation further defines two types of settlements to which exile-settlers might be assigned: a newly established state *poselenie* or a previously established village (*derevnia*). Turning to the first, one of the *poseleniia's* express functions was to settle under-populated regions (*maloliudnye mesta*). This and another clause ordering that all unmarried female exiles capable of labor automatically enter *poseleniia*[52] suggest a colonialist intent behind the creation of this subcategory, which as such renders it an anomaly within the Speranskii system. Such an anomaly almost certainly points to interference by conservative committee members or possibly the emperor. As it turned out, after 1822 Petersburg relied far more on existing villages as destinations for exile-settlers than on state *poseleniia* built from scratch. But whatever type of settlement exile-settlers were to be sent to, this category represented for some decision-makers at the time a realistic way to deal with convicts whose crimes did not warrant a sentence to *katorga* or a factory and who were not artisans.

GUZS and GUVS were to determine the sites for *poseleniia* and the number of exiles placed in them. Following approval by 'the Ministry' (apparently the MVD), regional exile bureaus were to send exile-artisans to complete the groundwork necessary for constructing a *poselenie*. Exile-settlers were to arrive in spring to help with this preparatory work, which would have included the clearing of trees and the building of izbas, and to begin sowing immediately. Labor was expected to be intensive, as exile-settlers worked to prepare communal living quarters and crops before winter's onset. 'During this time they are held under strict military discipline,' the regulation states, 'and all workers produce jointly for everyone in the village.' The government was to provide foodstuffs to the exiles until their first harvest. At the beginning of the second year, each exile was to be assigned his own izba, plot, tools and household items; and over the course of the following two years all necessary final constructions in the settlement were to be completed. Overseers were to supervise exile-settlers' activities during their first two years in a *poselenie*, after which these convicts were to have their rights incrementally returned, culminating in the option to move to another settlement. If an exile-settler chose to leave, his place in the *poselenie* – his izba, land – was to be taken by a new arrival, but only during the first three years of the *poselenie*'s existence, since the goal was for the settlement eventually to evolve into a community of ex-convicts, each of whom had regained his full rights. Once a settlement's community reached this stage – that is, when there were no more exiles still completing 'terms-without-rights' (*l´gotnye let*) – the overseer was to be sent to a new location and 'the exile-settlers [were to] enter the jurisdiction of land [*zemskii*] police and become comparable to State peasants'.[53]

If *guberniia* administrations determined certain exiles designated for *poseleniia* would, on arrival, face difficulties establishing themselves, such exiles were to be redirected to established villages to serve as peasants' helpers. In such capacity, they were to be free from taxes for three years and from military recruitment for 20, and were to occupy their positions as helpers no longer than five years. The regulation optimistically speculates that within that time they would be accepted into the commune to which they had been assigned. However, if an exile were not accepted, he was to be returned to the place where he lived before being exiled.

It is uncertain what the committee intended by this provision, since it contravened the entire intention behind exile to settlement. More importantly, the lack of realism girding this entire article suggests it did not originate with Speranskii but was insisted upon by the conservatives. Further evidence for this is the extent to which the article relies upon the Siberian peasantry to provide a welfare net for the state's convicted criminals. Unfortunately for peasants and exiles alike, this anomalous category came to characterize more than any other the nature of exile during the nineteenth century, and proved the source of many of Siberia's most profound social ills.

If at any time an exile became incapacitated, he was to be assigned to the 'incapables' category – the sixth and final category of exile to settlement. At certain points the regulation refers to this group as 'infirm exiles' (*ssyl´nye driakhly*), though it is clear that Speranskii intended the incapables category to account for all exiles with physical or mental disabilities. The delineation of an entire category of incapables indicates how senility, old age, insanity, retardation, physical handicaps and other impediments exposed peasants and others to administrative exile. Incapables were to be assigned to specific *volosti*, whence they were to receive sustenance from the exiles' economic fund. The regulation states that if an exile in this category had been exiled for vagabondage (which was quite likely, because this charge was often leveled at those who could not work because of their conditions),[54] he was to assist peasants according to rules covering the servant guild category. This rather odd concession creating what were in effect personal servants for the Siberian peasantry is however not elaborated upon.[55]

It will be recalled that in his September 1820 ukase issued from Irkutsk, Speranskii announced his intention to prevent what were then called *propitannye* from becoming a burden on the peasantry. However, that ukase merely shifted this burden from the shoulders of peasants living in Irkutsk *guberniia* to those in Tomsk *guberniia*. The 1822 regulation deals more substantively with the problem, establishing a series of exiles' economic funds to be administered by the exile bureaus and supported, as noted above, by deductions from the wages paid exiles. In addition to this source of support, provisions were made so that if exiles died leaving no family members, their personal property would pass to the exile fund in the *guberniia* to which they had been assigned. Even if family members did survive the deceased, they could exercise ownership over his property only if they remained in Siberia. This seemingly conservative-sponsored proviso was plainly designed to bind these people to the land. Speranskii designated the funds themselves to be applied primarily to that subcategory of incapables who, because of age, illness or handicap, could not maintain even a subsistence existence in the villages. Such people were instead to be assigned to sick wards and asylums supposed to be established by local administrations and supported by the exile funds. Speranskii imagined the funds would also assist non-*katorga* exiles who suffered fires, floods, crop failures or other natural disasters, in which cases the main administrations would be responsible for dispensing these monies.[56]

Speranskii's provision reflects Treskin's earlier establishment of emergency grain reserves and uncharacteristic support for the *propitannye*. Speranskii's position in the central government allowed such progressive moves to be expanded upon, but his mistake was to place too much faith in those bureaucrats eventually responsible for collecting and administering the exile funds. During the years following the reforms exile bureau officials routinely embezzled the monies to such an extent that the funds can be said to have never existed. Instead of being supported by special institutions set up for the purpose, most incapables were, as before 1822, simply dumped in villages to burden resentful peasants. Even a provision later introduced in the 1845 'Regulation on Exiles' to establish a similar fund proved futile. Mikhail N. Galkin-Vraskoi, director of the Main Prison Administration (*Glavnoe Tiur'emnoe Upravlenie*) eventually established in 1879, disgustedly wrote in 1886 that 'forty years' worth of exile to settlement has been carried out contrary to the requirements of the law'.[57] He could just as easily have dated this period back to 1822.

These then were the six categories of exile to settlement as outlined by the 'Regulation on Exiles'. TobPS was to assign exiles to locations based on category and *guberniia*, all the time keeping track of how many were entering both. Because Tomsk and Eniseisk *gubernii* were the largest grain-producing regions, the majority of exile-settlers (those in the fifth category) were to be sent there. If there were insufficient numbers to fill all six categories, the most labor-oriented of them – the categories of temporary workers and road workers – were to be filled first, while the rest received smaller quotas.[58] Transfers between the six categories were possible on instructions from *guberniia* administrations, and it was the responsibility of the exile bureaus to execute such transfers. For example, if exiles assigned to 'road work' proved supernumerary for the tasks at hand, they might be assigned to join the exile-artisans for up to four months, after which, if they were still not needed for road work, they were to be assigned to *poseleniia*. Road workers and exile-artisans who became incapacitated were to be transferred to either *poseleniia* or the servant guild, possibly as a reward for these exiles' 'skilled' labor. Upon completion of their temporary labor terms in *zavody* or factories, exiles in the first category were to be transferred to either the exile-artisans or *poseleniia*. Finally, all those exiles who served out their full sentences in whatever capacity were to be allowed to settle anywhere they wished, though they could never leave Siberia. They were to present formal requests specifying desired locations to TobPS, which would then make arrangements to formally enrol them in communities (*obshchestva*) in these areas.[59]

This complicated and largely self-contradictory transfer and reassignment scheme once again indicates the ideological split within the Siberian Committee between Speranskii and (probably) Golitsyn on one side, both of whom more or less believed convicts could be reformed through labor, and conservatives like Arakcheev and Kampengauzen on the other, who believed criminals were essentially irredeemable but nonetheless useful for colonizing Siberia. Actually, for many of those in the conservative camp, colonization was merely a pretext for banishing Russia's criminal element far away, to where it was mistakenly believed they could be forgotten.

Katorga

In contrast to the provisions outlining exile to settlement, which completely replaced the Elizabethan penal categories, Speranskii's provisions concerning *katorga* generally codified existing practices. This suggests the influence of the Ministry of Finance and Imperial Cabinet, both of which had vested interests in *katorga*. Speranskii nevertheless succeeded in reducing the maximum sentence from life to a term of 20 years.[60] He may have done so because he either ascribed to a belief in rehabilitation or wanted to limit the state's responsibility for maintaining elderly convicts.

According to the 'Regulation on Exiles' penal laborers were to be assigned to either *zavody* or factories based on requests submitted by treasury chambers at these sites. In no instance was TobPS allowed to reassign penal laborers unilaterally: its job *vis-à-vis katorga* was restricted to convoying penal laborers to their assigned locations and to maintaining situational rosters (*spiski*). Speranskii ordered that if more penal laborers were available than requested by the treasury chambers, then supernumeraries were to be evenly divided among the factories of all Siberia's *gubernii* except that of Irkutsk, which exception existed to limit superimposition on this *guberniia* of a larger number of exiles than it could absorb and because the other *gubernii* had more industrial sites. The regulation calls for a rather odd division of supervisory responsibilities over penal laborers: while the Finance Ministry and Imperial Cabinet were respectively to administer those factories and *zavody* to which penal laborers were assigned, and could therefore employ them as they saw fit, the exile bureaus were responsible for maintaining *katorga* rosters and overseeing local civilian administrations responsible for policing these exiles. Although the bureaus were nominally subordinate to the administrations of those *gubernii* in which they operated, there were, as we have seen, competing superiors in the chain(s) of command to which they were linked. *Ipso facto*, no fewer than three agencies exerted authority over penal laborers – the Ministry of Finance or Imperial Cabinet (depending on whether convicts were in a factory or one of the Nerchinsk *zavody*); the local exile bureau; and the police (who themselves were beholden to both the MVD and the *guberniia* administration). It should come as no surprise that penal laborers were routinely lost or forgotten.[61]

The regulation states almost in passing that at the expiry of the new maximum sentences of 20 years penal laborers, if they have committed no new crimes, will be allowed to settle under police supervision within the jurisdiction of the same institution (*zavedenie*) in which they have served their labor terms. If they do not possess the 'means to resettle, they live on charity [*na vol'noe propitanie*] in the *volost* of the nearest state *zavod*' – though in what capacity is not clear from the wording.[62] Despite now being limited to 20 years, maximum sentences were still termed 'indeterminate' (*bezsrochnaia*) or, in other instances, 'permanent' (*vechnaia*) – the lack of a standard lexicon being yet one more curse on tsarist officials and historians alike. The purpose behind retention of these terms was similar to that behind formulae expressed in the 1649 *Ulozhenie* to convey that the sovereign was pardoning convicts from harsher sentences. Penal laborers who completed less severe, so-called 'fixed' (*srochnaia*) sentences were either assigned like those who completed indeterminate terms or placed in settlements alongside exile-settlers, or, if they had been in the military at the time of their convictions, were returned to their units.[63]

The regulation specifies that officials are to deduct 2 kopeks from every eight days' pay for individual penal laborers and put this into a fund to maintain the sick who, because unable to work, would not be paid.[64] (This measure seems to have been designed to prevent 'fakers' from seeking a few days' rest in the sick wards. If so, this was not well communicated to penal laborers, who probably never knew how the finances concerning them were handled and who often took respite in sick wards to recover their health.) These funds were to be kept separate from the exile funds already discussed, and unlike them did in fact come into existence, though how efficacious they were is difficult to tell. In comparison to the exiles' economic funds, *katorga* funds were handled by fewer officials, with individual factory and *zavod* administrations immediately responsible for assessing taxes and disbursing monies via the prisoners' headmen. Moreover, these administrations had an economic incentive to maintain the collective health of their labor forces and so were probably more likely to apply the funds as intended. Nonetheless, misappropriations and embezzlement certainly occurred.

The 'Regulation on Exile Transfer within Siberian *Gubernii*'

Section 4 of the reforms, the 'Regulation on Exile Transfer within Siberian *Gubernii*', immediately follows the 'Regulation on Exiles' and comprises 13 articles containing 199 clauses. This regulation replaced the old march route from Orenburg *guberniia* into Siberia with a more logical one corresponding to a rigidly prescribed transfer schedule; and replaced the impressment of Meshcheriak and Bashkir tribesmen with a contiguous series of convoy commands staffed by regular military units. The march route into Siberia was designed as a succession of stages (*etapy*), each of which generally involved a one-day march from a way-station (also called an *etap*) to a semi-station (*polu-etap*), and a one-day trek from there to another way-station. After arriving on Tobol´sk *guberniia*'s western border or in Tobol´sk itself, parties were convoyed to Irkutsk by individual commands assigned to each march route stage.

'First of all – what is this way-station trail like?' P. F. Iakubovich rhetorically asks in his 1912 memoir of exile to Nerchinsk:

> Imagine that the entire length of this endless Siberian trail, which stretches from Tomsk to Sretensk (focusing on Nerchinsk *katorga*) – that is, extends three thousand versts – is divided into twenty forty-verst segments culminating in huge, gloomy buildings with barred windows – for the most part tumbled-down, withered, and battered by cold – standing alone beside the road somewhere in a field or on a village outskirts. These are the so called way-stations – roadside prisons in which exhausted parties rest and spend the night. Speaking more precisely, of two such prisons the smaller one is called a semi-station, and only the other, larger and better, is the way-station. In the latter there are barracks for the local military unit that convoys prisoners, and an apartment for the officer – unbridled master over an expanse of two or even four such prisons. A party spends only a night at a semi-station, starting again the next morning along the road; arriving at a way-station, it stays a day to rest, which is therefore called a 'day off.'[65]

George Kennan further describes the standard semi-station as being composed of a low stockade enclosing a yard measuring some 100×75 feet. Inside were usually three one-storey log buildings painted a regulation ocher, one housing the convoy commander and the other two serving as barracks for soldiers and exiles. Inside the exiles' barracks were three or four large wards (*kamery*), each of which contained a Russian stove and, running along their walls, usually an upper and a lower row of wide plank shelving called *nary*. Sometimes a pair of *nary* ran down the center of a ward as well. The *nara* served as a place to sit, sleep and keep one's belongings, though because of its contiguous nature provided little in the way of privacy. Each barracks was designed to accommodate 100–150 people, yet during the 1870s and 1880s, when deportations peaked, more than 400 were regularly crammed inside. Full-size stations were similarly organized, but slightly larger than semi-stations, usually with an extra ward or two in the prison barracks and a barn and storehouse for the *etap*-command.[66]

Dostoevskii's casual comments throughout *Notes from a Dead House* convey the *nary's* importance in providing exiles their only personal space. Although his description is of a *katorga* prison, in which exiles might occupy their *nara*-positions for years, every social unit comprising exiles, whether in transit or sedentary, had at its core a pecking order which minutely dictated who slept where. Those most feared career criminals and murderers took spaces nearest the stove in winter and closest the windows in summer, while everyone else found spaces as best they could. As growing volumes of exiles increasingly tested these wards' capacities, sometimes as many as half the deportation party would have to lie on the muck-encrusted floors beneath the *nary*, gagging as did everyone on the fumes pouring from the stove and open latrine vats (*parashi*).[67]

Stations called for by the 1822 regulation presumably necessitated construction of many from scratch, though the new march route seems to have taken advantage of some existing ones. But even if many stations were in acceptable working order at first, they very quickly dilapidated due to weather, the thousands passing through them every year and the fact that they were rarely, if ever, cleaned or otherwise maintained. Kennan quotes a letter from Dmitrii G. Anuchin, Eastern Siberia's governor-general from 1879 to 1885, to Alexander III: 'The etapes ... with the most insignificant exceptions, are tumble-down buildings, in bad sanitary condition, cold in winter, saturated with miasm [*sic*], and, to crown all, affording very little security against escapes.'[68] Kennan opined that despite Anuchin's appropriation of 250,000 rubles to repair these facilities, many remained untouched because of 'corrupt and incapable administration, and ... the inherent defects of a bureaucratic system of government.'[69]

In addition to enduring the filth inside these accommodations, women and children who followed deportees into Siberia had to bed down among the sweating or shivering mass of human flesh beside convicts whose morality had long before succumbed to libido. Rapes and molestations occurred with such regularity they became a matter of course among deportation parties. D. A. Dril, a human rights advocate and Justice Ministry official who investigated conditions in Siberia, wrote in his 1898 report to the Senate:

> There is nothing to say about morality. In the words of one closely familiar with the effect of the conditions of deportation, younger and older women, and not just the penal laborers but the ones voluntarily accompanying their husbands, are often corrupted to the core in deportation parties, and arrive in *katorga* already turned into prostitutes.[70]

Children especially suffered horrors both in the stations and during the march itself. Iadrintsev claimed as many as half died before completing the journey.[71] He may not have been exaggerating. During his 1871 inspection of *katorga*, V. I. Vlasov, an MVD official, learned that children witnessed couples having sex and were being raped by convicts in the stations.[72] Later in the century the ethnographer V. I. Semevskii accompanied a party of 500 exiles and family members to the Lena goldfields. Most of the men were unaccompanied, though the party did include some women with children and nursing infants. Entering a ward in which many were lying on the floor rather than on *nary*, Semevskii, aided by a convoy officer's expert analysis, observed that '[s]ince the men were far cleverer than the women, morals were very loose: among them were eleven-year-old boys who drank, played cards, and were interested in women; there was also a twelve-year-old girl who was considered common property by the convict party.'[73] Not until 1883 did the government order unaccompanied male exiles kept separate from exiles with families during the march and in the stations.[74]

Problems in using indigenes to convoy exiles had largely resulted from their being little more than exiles themselves. Despite estimates that as many as three out of four exiles prior to 1822 may have died during the march into Siberia,[75] anecdotal sources are all that remain to indicate these indigenous guards' efficiency at transferring their charges.[76] Kazarian seems to suggest cossacks were used for convoy duty within Iakutiia throughout that region's entire exilic history, and asserts that a so-called internal guard was created in October 1816 to convoy exiles along the march route into Siberia at that time. 'Stations [*etapy*] were organized in 1818–1820 for the forwarding of exiles,' he writes,[77] without providing information as to who was responsible for establishing either the guard or stations, or about those who made up this guard. Nonetheless, he concludes that Petersburg's importunities to Siberia's governors to provide guards and supplies for the forwarding of exiles were frequently ignored or only partly complied with, and it would seem that march route conditions, poor as they were after 1822, were absolutely horrifying before.

Speranskii took care to indicate precisely both the *etap*-sequence and composition of the *etap* commands, each of which was to consist of one officer, two junior officers, one drummer (who may have been used to set the pace of the march), and 25 foot soldiers from the Siberian Corps' Selenginsk Garrison Regiment. Each command had at its service four horse cossacks for capturing fugitives, as well as carts and horses for carrying supplies, children and the sick.[78] (See Table 5.3.)

Table 5.3 *Etap* Commands, 1822

	# of *etap* commands	Senior officers	Junior officers	Musicians	Soldiers	Medics	Station attendants	Cossacks	Horse Cossacks	Carts
Tobol'sk *gub.*	19	19	38	19	475	2	19	76	152	76
Tomsk *gub.*	21	21	42	21	525	2	21	84	168	84
Total in W. Siberia	40	40	80	40	1,000	4	40	160	320	160
Irkutsk *gub.*	13	13	26	13	325	2	13	52	104	52
Eniseisk *gub.*	8	8	16	8	200	2	8	32	64	32
Total in E. Siberia	21	21	42	21	525	4	21	84	168	84
Grand Total	61	61	122	61	1,525	8	61	244	488	244

Source: Ustav ob etapakh v sibirskikh guberniiakh, table, pp. 36–7.

Despite the fact that regular soldiers now began convoying exiles, they should not be imagined to have been professionals in the modern sense. For one thing, they were peasants first and foremost; in addition, assignment to the Siberian Corps tended to be a form of punishment, with those assigned to convoy duty representing the army's ugly underbelly. Convoy soldiers led what one exile euphemistically observed was a 'monotonous life', pinioned as they were for years on end within a world whose eastern horizon was no further than a two-day march from its western, and saddled with the task of convoying the suffering and dying across this bleak stretch only to return to their stockaded existence to await the arrival of the next group of wretches. The political exile I. P. Belokonskii later observed that 'the majority of them', numbed by this Sisyphean task, 'are bitter drunks or people who are somber and silent'.[79] Not surprisingly, exiles became the focus of these soldiers' enmity. For example, *Siberia*, Irkutsk's daily newspaper, reported in 1885 that cossacks on convoy duty in Zabaikal´e often beat their charges for no reason; and Iakubovich details a savage beating he witnessed on the march to Nerchinsk.[80] But the dismal treatment of exiles turned into concentrated fury when one tried to escape, because the guards themselves faced criminal charges if he was successful. As if foreseeing the problems to come, Speranskii ordered that only those soldiers who had served two or more years in a border battalion be assigned to convoy duty, presumably to ensure they were conditioned to military discipline. Nonetheless, he implicitly admitted the possibility that, like exiles, convoy soldiers might themselves try to escape, and so he subjected them to the same corporal punishments.[81]

'As many years' experience has shown that exiles in Siberia effect their escapes in the summer,' runs article 2 of the regulation, each party organized during summer months was to contain no more than 60 exiles. For similar reasons, large groups of penal laborers were not to be convoyed together; and if a party totaled ten or more exiles, then penal laborers were to be in the minority. If, as a result of these limits, exiles had to be left behind in *guberniia* cities, then local governors were allowed to temporarily employ them as laborers. The regulation further orders that no more than one party a week may embark on the march route from the collection point on Tobol´sk's western border – a decision indicative of Speranskii's mistaken belief that exile rates would remain manageable.[82]

The clause limiting the size of parties and the (largely unelaborated) exceptions to it later resulted in confusion among officials attempting to convoy exiles yet still adhere to regulations. Because the number of exiles increased 64 per cent in 1824 over the previous year, from 8,764 to 14,345,[83] there immediately arose a problem as to how to keep parties within their quantitative maximums while at the same time conform to the weekly departure schedule, for the regulation's vague reference to assigning surplus exiles to temporary labor positions only muddied the waters. Even if Kazarian and N. P. Eroshkin are correct in asserting that 100 became the maximum number allowed in a party,[84] it remains clear that Speranskii did not anticipate an exile rate significantly greater than when he drafted the reforms. The reasons for such a phenomenal increase are beyond the scope of this study; but the issue here is that if either the size of individual parties or the rate of parties per week increased (which they both did), then it follows that the size of the *etap* commands should have increased as well. However, they did not; or at best, they increased only slightly. For example, it was observed in 1863 that parties were averaging between 300 and 400 persons each; and in August 1880 just 25 soldiers – the number supposed to convoy parties of 60 and certainly no more than 150 – convoyed Belokonskii's party of 300 (itself five times the size permitted). Similarly, Kennan describes parties of this size being convoyed by 'about forty soldiers'.[85]

Speranskii appended a chart to the regulation proper which details *etap* commands, stations, distances and days of march for the entire distance between Tobol´sk's western border and the city of Irkutsk. For some reason, he did not specify a march route beyond Irkutsk, though exiles had for centuries been sent to points east of the city (indeed, all the way to Anadyrsk and Kamchatka). In any case, by 1823 at the latest the IGP designated three separate march routes originating in Irkutsk and concluding at Ilginsk and the Nerchinsk and Petrovsk *zavody*, and also issued provisions for exiles' further removal to Iakutsk, Okhotsk and Kamchatka. In 1827 the IGP reissued these march routes with the warning that *etap* commands were not properly following them.[86] Judging from Kazarian's discussion of the march route through Iakutiia, maintenance of the three march routes radiating from Irkutsk was problematic due to the sparse population in these areas and the fact that the responsibilities of the Department of Overland Communication, as defined by the 1822 regulation, did not extend that far.[87]

Another addendum to the 1822 regulation shows the number of halting-places, which totaled 135, and in addition to stations and semi-stations included the cities of Tiumen, Tobol´sk, Kainsk, Tomsk, Achinsk, Krasnoiarsk, Nizhneudinsk and Irkutsk.[88] At Tyguloe, a small village on Tobol´sk's border, Perm officials were to pool together the various parties originating in Perm and Orenburg and, based on the paperwork supposed to accompany each exile, organize new parties for weekly departures. Tyguloe must therefore have possessed a station with several wards for holding deportees awaiting further removal; however, little information about this site has been found.

After exiles were organized, each party elected from its ranks a head-man who would liaise with the convoy commander.[89] Also prior to the march exiles would form themselves into *arteli* (cooperative cells), each of which had its own headman subordinate to that of the party as a whole. These *arteli* were typically formed along class lines or accord-ing to exilic category.[90] It was the headman's job to distribute rations and *kormovye den´gi* and to adjudicate minor disputes. As throughout Russian society in general, these headmen were respected and obeyed to a remarkable degree by those under them, though they could be usurped under certain conditions; yet it was especially on the march route that both exiles and convoy soldiers relied on headmen to main-tain order, and so not only tolerated, but actually expected them to engage in the graft and embezzlement that served as their compensation. As such, Speranskii's modern system incorporated Muscovy's *kormlenie* tradition.

After these preliminaries were complete, Perm officials were to release parties so that each station and semi-station in Western Siberia, as well as the cities of Tobol´sk, Tomsk and Krasnoiarsk, would be visited once a week and on a specific day. Scheduling was crucial and had to ensure that at the conclusion of each marching day a party would reach a station or semi-station, otherwise catastrophe could ensue, especially in winter. The regulation stipulates that parties were to march five days a week and rest the other two. When they entered cities (*goroda*) exiles were to be housed in the barracks of local invalid regiments which, like those garrisons in Tobol´sk, Tomsk and Irkutsk, assumed the role otherwise specified for *etap* commands.[91] In every case the march was to be con-ducted according to strict military procedures, with all soldiers armed and all exiles in iron shackles. Penal laborers were to be kept separate from other exiles, though this was usually ignored in practice. The con-voy commander could corporally punish exiles; and if he uncovered a plan to mutiny was allowed to punish every exile in the party. If an exile fled the convoy the commander was to detail no more than one foot soldier and two cossack horsemen to capture him, while the party itself would proceed. Each exile was allowed to bring only 30 *funty* (equivalent to 27 lb or just over 12 kg) of baggage, which was piled into the four *telegi* (one-horse spring-less carts) assigned to each convoy. If sufficient space was left in the *telegi* then women and children could ride too.[92]

Telegi were also used to transport the sick until they could be left in those cities with medical services. Because of the distances between such locations, many of the sick had to travel for hundreds of kilometers before obtaining care. For instance, as late as 1880 only three hospitals were to be encountered during the month-long march between Tomsk and Krasnoiarsk. The time spent waiting for medical help was brutal, as Kennan observed:

> [W]hen a prisoner is suffering from one of the diseases of the respiratory organs that are so common in *etape* life it is simply torture to sit in a cramped position for six or eight hours in an open *telega*, breathing the dust raised by the feet of 350 men marching in close column.[93]

Such exiles suffered miserably before often expiring. 'Here come those with typhus, diphtheria, dragged in *telegi*, covered with government cassocks, soaked by the rain, coated with grime or snow, who are as yet not being taken to hospital,' Belokonskii vividly recalled.[94]

Let us now consider the journey of a party of exiles as imagined by Speranskii. Headquartered at Tyguloe station, the First *Etap* Command (one of 19 such commands in Tobol´sk *guberniia* alone) began on Wednesday to convoy its party in a one-day march 35 versts to the semi-station at Uspenskoe. (The further into Siberia the fewer were the stations situated in actual villages. For example, many of the stations identified by the IGP march route were not in villages, and two were seasonal, occupying locations on Lake Baikal's frozen surface.[95]) On Thursday, these exiles had only 15 versts to march before the command turned them over to the Second *Etap* Command at Perevlova, a full-size station. Here, exiles received what the regulation terms a *rastakh* and later became known as a *dnevka*, or 'day off', during which they could use the bath house. After their first *dnevka*, these exiles marched on Saturday over 21 versts to Tiumen, their first Siberian city (*gorod*), where the Second *Etap* Command turned them over to the Tiumen Invalid Command. Tiumen was unique in that it gave exiles their only two-day rest before having to march 262 versts to Tobol´sk.[96]

Tobol´sk was important for several reasons. As headquarters of TobPS, it was where exiles were enrolled and their documents evaluated and tabulated. Following these procedures officials assigned exiles to their locations. This requirement, plus the arrival of deportation parties which had originated in locations between Tyguloe and Tobol´sk and, as a result, marched directly to the latter, made it necessary to organize entirely new parties for further removal. The regulation's schedule shows that

Speranskii intended for exiles to remain in Tobol'sk no longer than four days,[97] but in practice they were kept in the transit prison for weeks, months and, if forgotten through bureaucratic oversight, sometimes years. Another reason exiles might remain in Tobol'sk, or for that matter any other place along the march route, was the flooding of the rivers during the spring thaw. This was a perennial problem in a land where most rivers empty to the north and the ice lingering at their mouths causes them to overflow in the south, particularly in the flood plains west of the Enisei. For this reason, observed the regulation, many rivers along the march route were impassable for up to three weeks after 10 April. Speranskii's regulation precisely notes that beginning on 17 April, in locations between Tiumen and Tobol'sk, parties might have to wait up to two weeks to resume moving. In a recommendation which seems at odds with the precision otherwise called for in the scheduling, the Siberian Committee ruled that Siberian governors could, when rivers became impassable, distribute exiles to various locations.[98] Like other vagaries in the reforms, what exactly the committee had in mind here is unclear, and as such, this provision seems an interpolation in an arrangement otherwise wholly devised by Speranskii.

After leaving Tobol'sk the exiles marched an astounding 1,470 versts until they reached Tomsk, where their time in its transit prison was again dictated by the (in)efficiency of officials, this time of the Tomsk Exile Bureau. By this point the exiles had marched for twelve weeks with no more than one full day of continuous rest, the average distance covered on marching days being just under 30 versts. They faced similar demands over the next 550 versts to Krasnoiarsk, though it appears they were to receive there a full week's rest. Some five months after crossing the Siberian border, they must have needed it. Another 350 versts brought them to the border of Irkutsk *guberniia*; and 640 versts further, never having had a rest of more than one full day since leaving Krasnoiarsk, the exiles at last dragged themselves into Irkutsk.[99] Yet Irkutsk was still not the end of the line, though it might offer a period of rest comparable to those given, intentionally or not, in Tobol'sk, Tomsk or Krasnoiarsk: those exiles assigned, for example, to Nerchinsk *zavod* still had another 1,000 versts to march![100]

To summarize Speranskii's schedule along his planned march route: a hypothetical exile who began in Tyguloe, adhered precisely to the schedule as it was laid out and received only the minimum rest days therein specified, would, on reaching Irkutsk, have walked 3,342.5 versts in 29½ weeks. The average distance this exile covered on a marching day would have been nearly 25 versts. Once he left the holding prison at Irkutsk and finally reached, say, the Petrovsk ironworks to which his *katorga* sentence had assigned him, then and only then would the clock begin ticking on his 20-year term. A hypothetical exile is necessary because very few real ones accomplished this journey as planned, not only because of their physical limitations, but also because of the myriad natural and bureaucratic obstacles to be encountered along the way.

In 1863, following the introduction of river barges that reduced much of the time spent traveling on foot, an anonymous contributor to *The Contemporary* could nevertheless write:

> The majority of prisoners come from distant Russian *gubernii*, and to get to assigned locations takes them two years, but in case of illness and convalescence in hospital, [maybe] all of three years. There are examples of some prisoners taking four or five years, and I know one example where a prisoner came to Irkutsk only after eight years, and when he entered the *zavod* this marked the first minute of his [*katorga* sentence of] eight years.[101]

Based on this and other aspects of the march route, this same author reasoned that the journey into exile was more onerous than *katorga* itself.

Not every exile had to march all the way to Irkutsk, of course; many were assigned to Western Siberia and so ended the march much sooner than their comrades. Nevertheless, the challenges of the odyssey which every exile shared to a greater or lesser extent should not be underestimated. 'At first glance it may not seem difficult to make 30 versts [a day],' writes Belokonskii of the route between Tomsk and Krasnoiarsk,

> but it is necessary to keep in mind the following hindrances: in the party marched a people [*narod*] not only exhausted by prison, but being forced to go in the first place; in the second, such a trip continued for an entire month ([moreover,] for the majority it was necessary to go not a hundred, but a thousand versts [further], e.g., to *katorga* at Kara, or to settlement in Iakutsk *oblast*); thirdly, the financial circumstances for prisoners and the poorly-constructed stations resulted in not being able to relax on a day off; finally, the climate was difficult.[102]

Only a Russian could write that during a Siberian winter 'the climate was difficult', and Belokonskii does not even mention the iron fetters most deportees wore, or how they cut into the ankles causing wounds that could become gangrenous. Perhaps it took a more incensed foreigner such as Kennan to measure the full extent of this tragedy:

Only a moment's reflection is needed to satisfy one that, even under the most favorable circumstances, [every year] six or eight thousand men, women, and children cannot march two thousand miles across such a country as Eastern Siberia without suffering terrible hardships. The physical exposure alone is enough to break down the health and strength of all except the most hardy, and when to such inevitable exposure are added insufficient clothing, bad food, the polluted air of overcrowded stations, and the almost complete absence of medical care and attention, one is surprised, not that so many die, but that so many get through alive.[103]

*   *   *

The 1822 reforms are most significant not for having meliorated an inhuman penal system, but rather for attempting to systematically exploit deportees through an administrative infrastructure and set of regulations that, if followed, and as at least Speranskii seemed to believe, would ensure clock-like efficiency. For all the liberal sympathies historians credit him with, Speranskii actually presaged those twentieth-century technocrats who imagined people as machines serving the high purposes of the Fatherland, the Motherland – in other words, the state.

Conclusion: 'Siberian Exile and Biopolitics'

Statist goals consistently conditioned Russian penality during the period 1590–1822. This fact does not distinguish Russia from other European polities striving at the time to make use of their convict populations in one way or another. The concept of rehabilitating prisoners emerged only during the late eighteenth and early nineteenth centuries, as reflected in the establishment of the penitentiary, or modern prison, and for this reason one should be wary of passing judgment based on anachronistic norms. Nonetheless, and as the Muscovite administration's actions especially indicate, there was from Siberian exile's very beginnings a notion that by assigning offenders to various functions and roles, they might be reformed insofar as they would be more useful to the autocracy. Muscovy's employment of exiles further indicates a confluence between bureaucratic systematizing processes and penological development. Due to the weakening of this connection after 1725, and as particularly demonstrated by the Treskin colonies of 1806–19, exile and *katorga* became increasingly chaotic and probably more lethal for convicts and deportees. The 1822 Siberian reforms renewed systematizing efforts that necessarily involved exile and *katorga*.

Whether exiles fared better under the Muscovite or Petersburg system is difficult to say, however, especially since different standards of measurement will yield different answers. The former incorporated exiles into existing *sosloviia* and treated them for the most part like non-exiles; yet it is also true that because Siberia's infrastructure was underdeveloped, conditions were especially difficult and threatening. By the same token, although penal laborers and others were assigned to what amounted to concentration camps during Alexander I's reign, escape frequently proved possible and, given Siberia's sparse population and absence of landlords and serfdom, fugitives could more easily than before take up vagabondage or simply adopt new identities and merge into rural or urban communities. Beyond dispute is that convicts and deportees were increasingly commodified throughout this period. Even if the efficacy of the system utilizing these commodities wavered, the sheer determinacy of an expanding bureaucracy and state-based economy meant that the dehumanization of convicts and other subjects proceeded inexorably. As I have shown, this process was not the result of any conspiracy among society's elites but rather corresponded with other modernizing and technological processes which greatly accelerated after 1822, in Russia and elsewhere. As the primary beneficiary of dehumanization and commodification, the state facilitates and exacerbates various agents associated with these processes, though does not necessarily generate them.

During the early nineteenth century Paul I and Alexander I perpetuated Elizabeth Petrovna's and Catherine II's state-building and colonization in eastern Siberia, because they believed a stronger state could augment and improve on their predecessors' agenda. To the extent that the Treskin colonies were even created, they were therefore a measure of success, but one that came only through imposition of a terror regime which brutalized all involved – perhaps most especially the authorities. Recognizing this, Speranskii, the bureaucratic rationalist *par excellence*, convinced himself that a thorough systematic reform would help to condition human behavior for the better. This led to an early experiment in large-scale social engineering in Russia.

The examples given here of state-building and reform efforts between 1590 and 1822 highlight the enormous problems that surrounded state–society relations in tsarist Russia. The Romanovs' adherence to the servitor-state ideal proved a driving force behind Russia's unique development, and so the examples given here help to contextualize later developments during the nineteenth and early twentieth centuries when the autocracy, given the opportunity to reform itself by adjusting its penal policy and hence its overall approach towards its subjects, preferred to retain the traditional model and even defend it by force. Despite arguments that the regime was reforming during the final years before 1917, a *longue durée* approach suggests it was too burdened by historical baggage to accept the compromises necessary to fundamentally alter state–society relations and perhaps allow it to survive. Then again, because exploitation was key to tsarism's very method of governance, it failed to honor even the limited compromises it did make and so, by persisting in using commodified subjects as cannon fodder during the First World War, condemned itself to oblivion.

Studies such as this one concerning the commodification of subaltern groups should provoke consideration of commodifying trends more generally. In a 1976 lecture on the war that he argued continually rages between state and society, Michel Foucault said:

> after a first seizure of power over the body in an individualizing mode, we have a second seizure of power that is not individualizing but, if you like, massifying, that is directed not at man-as-body but at man-as-species. After the anatomo-politics of the human body established in the course of the eighteenth century, we have, at the end of that century, the emergence of something that is no longer an anatomo-politics of the human body, but what I would call a 'biopolitics' of the human race.[1]

Having considered the biopolitics of the early period of Siberian exile, this study supports critical analysis of our own bodies and others' relationships to them – that is, an investigation into who owns these bodies and what functions they do or are expected to serve. A simple qualitative evaluation of the past based on quaint standards of happiness and self-fulfillment must be replaced by a critique which is admittedly unsettling but of utmost importance, and to which the study of disfranchised and subaltern groups is germane. The furthering of inquiry itself demonstrates the constancy of change.

Notes

Introduction

1. W. G. Aston, trans., *Nihongi: Chronicles of Japan from the Earliest Times to A.D. 607, Transactions and Proceedings of The Japan Society, Supplement I* (London: Kegan, Paul, Trench, Trubner & Co., 1896), excerpted in *The Global Experience: Readings in World History to 1550, Volume I*, 4th edn., ed. Philip F. Riley et al. (Upper Saddle River, NJ: Prentice Hall, 2002), 9–10.
2. Robert Fitzgerald, trans., 'Oedipus at Colonus', in *Sophocles I*, ed. David Grene and Richmond Lattimore (1954; rpt. New York: Washington Square Press, 1967), 101.
3. John Milton, *Paradise Lost*, book I, ll. 34–9.
4. Genesis 3: 23–4, King James Version.
5. Genesis 4: 12–14.
6. Muhammad Taqî-ud-Dîn Al-Hilâlî and Muhammad Muhsin Khân, *Translation of the Meanings of the Noble Qur'an in the English Language* (Madinah, K. S. A.: King Fahd Complex for the Printing of the Holy Qur'an, n.d.), Sûrah 59: 1–3.
7. Erin Mooney, 'The Concept of Internal Displacement and the Case for Internally Displaced Persons as a Category of Concern', *Refugee Survey Quarterly* 24, no. 3 (2005): 9–26; Wendy Everett and Peter Wagstaff, eds., *Cultures of Exile: Images of Displacement* (New York: Berghahn Books, 2004); Mahnaz Afkhami, *Women in Exile* (Charlottesville, VA: University Press of Virginia, 1994); Ingrid E. Fey and Karen Racine, eds., *Strange Pilgrimages: Exile, Travel, and National Identity in Latin America, 1800–1990s* (Wilmington, DE.: Scholarly Resources, 2000); Hamid Naficy, *The Making of Exile Cultures: Iranian Television in Los Angeles* (Minneapolis: University of Minnesota Press, 1993); Bülent Diken and Carsten Bagge Laustsen, *The Culture of Exception: Sociology Facing the Camp* (London: Routledge, 2005); Roelof Hortulanus et al., *Social Isolation in Modern Society* (London: Routledge, 2006); Ronaldo Munck, *Globalization and Social Exclusion: A Transformationalist Perspective* (Bloomfield, CT: Kumarian, 2005); Joel S. Kahn, *Modernity and Exclusion* (London: Sage, 2001).
8. Edward Said, 'Reflections on Exile', *Granta* 13 (1984): 157–72 [here, p. 165].
9. For example, Robert H. Johnston, *New Mecca, New Babylon: Paris and the Russian Exiles, 1920–1945* (Kingston, Ontario: McGill-Queen's University Press, 1988).
10. George Kennan, *Siberia and the Exile System*, 2 vols. (New York: Century Co., 1891).
11. Gabriele Griffin, 'Exile and the Body', in *Cultures of Exile*, 111–24 [here, p. 111].
12. See Philip D. Morgan, 'Work and Culture: The Task System and the World of Lowcountry Blacks, 1700 to 1880', in *Colonial America: Essays in Politics and Social Development*, 4th edn., ed. Stanley N. Katz et al. (New York: McGraw-Hill, 1993), 486–523; Christine Hünefeldt, *Paying the Price of Freedom: Family*

and Labor among Lima's Slaves, 1800–1854 (Berkeley, CA: University of California Press, 1994); Eugene D. Genovese, *Roll, Jordan, Roll: The World the Slaves Made* (New York: Vintage, 1976); Judith R. Walkowitz, *Prostitution and Victorian Society: Women, Class, and the State* (New York: Cambridge University Press, 1980); Donna J. Guy, *Sex and Danger in Buenos Aires: Prostitution, Family, and Nation in Argentina* (Lincoln, NB: University of Nebraska Press, 1991); Detlev J. K. Peukert, *Inside Nazi Germany: Conformity, Opposition, and Racism in Everyday Life* (New Haven, CT: Yale University Press, 1987).

13. Griffin, 'Exile and the Body', 111.
14. Immanuel Wallerstein, *Capitalist Agriculture and the Origins of the European World-Economy in the Sixteenth Century* (New York: Academic Press, 1974); idem, *The Modern World System II: Capitalist Agriculture, Mercantilism and the Consolidation of the European World-Economy, 1600–1750* (New York: Academic Press, 1980); Robert L. Reynolds, *Europe Emerges: Transition toward an Industrial World-Wide Society, 600–1750* (Madison, WI: University of Wisconsin Press, 1967); Iain Wallace, *The Global Economic System* (Boston, MA: Unwin Hyman, 1990).
15. Michael Roberts, *The Military Revolution 1560–1660: An Inaugural Lecture Delivered before the Queen's University of Belfast* (Belfast: M. Boyd, 1956); Martin L. Van Creveld, *Technology and War: From 2000 B.C. to the Present* (New York: Free Press, 1989); Jared Diamond, *Guns, Germs, and Steel: The Fates of Human Societies* (New York: W. W. Norton, 1997).
16. Cf. P. C. Emmer and M. Mörner, eds., *European Expansion and Migration: Essays on the Intercontinental Migration from Africa, Asia, and Europe* (New York: Berg, 1992); Paul Kennedy, *The Rise and Fall of the Great Powers: Economic Change and Military Conflict from 1500 to 2000* (New York: Vintage, 1987).
17. Wendy Everett and Peter Wagstaff, 'Introduction', in *Cultures of Exile*, ix–xix [here, p. x].
18. Vitorino Magalhães Godinho, 'Portuguese Emigration from the Fifteenth to the Twentieth Century: Constants and Changes', in *European Expansion and Migration*, 19.
19. Michel Foucault, *Discipline and Punish: The Birth of the Prison* (New York: Vintage, 1977), 29 *et passim*.
20. Marshall T. Poe, *'A People Born to Slavery': Russia in Early Modern Ethnography, 1476–1748* (Ithaca, NY: Cornell University Press, 2000), 196–226.
21. This quotation comes from Paperno's description of Kantorowicz's ideas. Irina Paperno, *Suicide as a Cultural Institution in Dostoevsky's Russia* (Ithaca, NY: Cornell University Press, 1997), 27; Ernst Hartwig Kantorowicz, *The King's Two Bodies: A Study of Mediaeval Political Theology* (Princeton, NJ: Princeton University Press, 1957).
   On developments in cartography, etc., see Valerie A. Kivelson, ' "The Souls of the Righteous in a Bright Place": Landscape and Orthodoxy in Seventeenth-Century Russian Maps', *Russian Review* 58, no. 1 (1999): 1–25 [esp. p. 4]; idem, 'Cartography, Autocracy and State Powerlessness: The Uses of Maps in Early Modern Russia', *Imago Mundi* 51 (1999): 83–105; J. B. Harley, 'Maps, Knowledge, and Power', in *The Iconography of Landscape: Essays on the Symbolic Representation, Design and Use of Past Environments*, ed. Denis Cosgrove and Stephen Daniels (Cambridge: Cambridge University Press, 1988), 277–312; Richard S. Wortman, *Scenarios of Power: Myth and Ceremony in Russian Monarchy*, Vol. 1 (Princeton, NJ: Princeton University Press, 1995), 3–41.

22. See Foucault, *Discipline*, esp. 3–31; idem, *Power/Knowledge: Selected Interviews and Other Writings, 1972–1977* (New York: Pantheon, 1980), 56–8, 94–7 *et passim*; idem, *Society Must Be Defended* (London: Penguin Books, 2003), 43–64 *et passim*. Concerning forms of torture and execution, see Evgenii Anisimov, *Dyba i knut: politicheskii sysk i russkoe obshchestvo v XVIII veke* (Moskva: Novoe literaturnoe obozrenie, 1999), ch. 10.

23. See also Kathleen Canning, 'The Body as Method? Reflections on the Place of the Body in Gender History', *Gender & History* 11, no. 3 (1999): 499–513; Emily Michael and Fred S. Michael, 'Corporeal Ideas in Seventeenth-Century Psychology', *Journal of the History of Ideas* 50, no. 1 (1989): 31–48.

24. George L. Yaney, *The Systematization of Russian Government: Social Evolution in the Domestic Administration of Imperial Russia, 1711–1905* (Urbana, IL: University of Illinois Press, 1973), 136.

25. In the Siberian context 'cossack' most often meant an irregular soldier rather than a member of a distinct ethnic group. I make a distinction in this book between 'cossack' and 'Cossack' by using the latter to refer to, e.g., Don Cossacks. See Lantzeff, *Siberia*, 67–9; I. R. Sokolovskii, *Sluzhilye 'inozemtsy' v Sibiri XVII veka (Tomsk, Eniseisk, Krasnoiarsk)* (Novosibirsk: 'Sova,' 2004), passim; N. E. Bekmakhanova, *Kazach´i voiska Aziatskoi Rossii v XVIII-nachale XX veka (Astrakhanskoe, Orenburgskoe, Sibirskoe, Semirechenskoe, Ural´skoe): Sbornik dokumentov* (Moskva: Insitut possiskoi istorii RAN, 2000), 42 *et passim*.

26. John J. Stephan, *The Russian Far East: A History* (Stanford, CA: Stanford University Press, 1994), 25.

27. For example, Galina Mihailovna Ivanova, *Labor Camp Socialism: The Gulag in the Soviet Totalitarian System*, trans. Carol Flath (Armonk, NY: M. E. Sharpe, 2000); Michael Jakobson, *Origins of the GULAG: The Soviet Prison Camp System, 1917–1934* (Lexington, KY: University Press of Kentucky, 1993); Anne Applebaum, *Gulag: A History* (New York: Doubleday, 2003).

28. *Sibir´ i katorga*, 3 vols. (S.-Peterburg: Tip. A. Transhelia, 1871); *Sibir´ i katorga*, 3rd edn. (S.-Peterburg: Izdanie V. I. Gubinskago, 1900).

29. *Russkaia obshchina v tiur´ me i ssylke* (S.-Peterburg: Tip. A. Morigerovskago, 1872); *Sibir´ kak koloniia: k iubileiu trekhsotletiia. Sovremennoe polozhenie Sibiri. Eia nuzhdy i potrebnosti. Eia proshloe i budushchee* (Sanktpeterburg: Tipografiia M. M. Stasiulevicha, 1882); *Sibir´ kak koloniia v geograficheskom, etnograficheskom i dopolnennoe* (S.-Peterburg: Tip. I. M. Sibiriakova, 1892); *Sibir´ kak koloniia v geograficheskom, etnograficheskom i dopolnennoe*, ed. L. M. Goriushkin et al. (Novosibirsk: Sibirskii khronograf, 2003).

30. *Uchenie o nakazanii v sviazi s tiur´ movedeniem* (S.-Peterburg: Tipografiia Ministerstva putei soobshcheniia [A. Benke], 1889).

31. *Ssylka: eia genezisa, znacheniia, istorii i sovremennogo sostoianiia* (Moskva: T-vo skoropechatni A. A. Levenson, 1893).

32. *Ssylka v Sibir´: ocherk eia istorii i sovremennago polozheniia* (S.-Peterburg: Tipografiia S.-Peterburgskoi Tiur´my, 1900).

33. *Katorga i ssylka*, published by Vsesoiuznoe obshchestvo politiches kikh katorzhan i ssyl´noposelentsev.

34. *Russkie krest´ iane v Iakutii (XVII-nachalo XX vv.)* (Iakutsk: Knizhnoe izd-vo, 1961); *Ssylka v vostochnuiu Sibir´ v XVII veke* (Iakutsk: Iakutsk knizh. izd-vo, 1967).

35. *Ssylka i katorga v Sibiri (XVIII-nachalo XX v.)* (Novosibirsk: Nauka, 1975); *Politicheskie ssyl´nye v Sibiri: XVIII—nachalo XX v.* (Novosibirsk: Nauka, 1983).

36. For example, P. L. Kazarian, *Olekminskaia politicheskaia ssylka, 1826–1917 gg.* 2nd edn. (Iakutsk: GP NIPK 'Sakhapoligrafizdat,' 1996); G. V. Shebaldina, *Shvedskie voennoplennye v Sibiri: Pervaia chetvert´ XVIII veka* (Moskva: Rossiiskii gosudarstvennyi gumanitarnyi universitet, 2005).

37. Basil Dmytryshyn et al., eds. and trans., *Russia's Conquest of Siberia, 1558–1700: A Documentary Record*, vol. 1 (Portland, OH: OHS Press, 1985).

38. G. F. Miller [Müller], *Istoriia Sibiri*, 3 vols., ed. E. P. Bat´ianova et al. (Moskva: Vostochnaia literatura, 1999–2005).

39. *Khronologicheskii perechen´ vazhneishikh dannykh iz istorii Sibiri: 1032–1882 gg.* (1883; rpt. Surgut: Severnyi dom, 1993).

40. *Istoriia tsarskoi tiur´my*, 3rd edn., 5 vols. (Moskva: Gosudarstvennoe izdatel´stvo iuridicheskoi literatury, 1960–63).

41. A. P. Okladnikov et al., eds., *Istoriia Sibiri s drevneishikh vremen do nashikh dnei*, 5 vols. (Leningrad: Nauka, 1968–9).

42. *Pervoe stoletie sibiriskikh gorodov. XVII vek* (Novosibirsk: Sibirskii khronograf, 1996).

43. R. R. Sullivan, 'The Birth of the Prison: Discipline or Punish?' *Journal of Criminal Justice* 24, no. 5 (1996): 449–58; K. von Schriltz, 'Foucault on the Prison: Torturing History to Punish Capitalism', *Critical Review* 13, nos. 3–4 (1999): 391–411.

44. For example, C. F. Alford, 'What Would it Matter if Everything Foucault Said about Prison were Wrong?: *Discipline and Punish* after Twenty Years', *Theory and Society* 29 (2000): 125–46.

45. Hayden V. White, 'Foucault Decoded: Notes from Underground', *History and Theory* 12 (1973): 23–54; Louis A. Sass, *Madness and Modernism: Insanity in the Light of Modern Art, Literature, and Thought* (New York: Basic Books, 1992), 251–4 *et passim*.

46. Jan Plamper, 'Foucault's Gulag', *Kritika: Explorations in Russian and Eurasian History* 3, no. 2 (2002): 255–80.

47. N. D. Sergeevskii, *Rech´ v godovom SPB Iuridicheskago Obshchestva, 8 Marta 1887 goda, O ssylke v drevnei Rossii* (S.-Peterburg: Tipografiia Ministerstva putei soobshcheniia [A. Benke], 1887), 15.

48. George G. Weickhardt, 'Pre-Petrine Law and Western Law: The Influence of Roman and Canon Law', *Harvard Ukrainian Studies* 19 (1995): 756–83.

49. Peter H. Solomon, Jr., 'Courts and Their Reform in Russian History', in *Reforming Justice in Russia, 1864–1996: Power, Culture, and the Limits of Legal Order*, ed. idem (Armonk, NY: M. E. Sharpe, 1997), 6.

50. Foinitskii, *Uchenie*, 266.

51. George V. Lantzeff and Richard A. Pierce, *Eastward to Empire: Exploration and Conquest on the Russian Open Frontier, to 1750* (Montreal: McGill-Queen's University Press, 1973), 113.

52. Isabel de Madariaga, *Russia in the Age of Catherine the Great* (New Haven, CT: Yale University Press, 1981), 155.

53. Cf. John P. LeDonne, *Ruling Russia: Politics and Administration in the Age of Absolutism, 1762–1796* (Princeton, NJ: Princeton University Press, 1984), 187, 189–92; Evgeny V. Anisimov, *Empress Elizabeth: Her Reign and Her Russia,*

1741–1761, ed. and trans. John T. Alexander (Gulf Breeze, FL: Academic International Press, 1995), 49ff.; A. B. Kamenskii, *Ot Petra I do Pavla I: Reformy v Rossii XVIII veka* (Moskva: Rossiiskii gosudarstvennyi gumanutarnyi universitet, 1999), ch. 4; idem, *The Russian Empire in the Eighteenth Century: Searching for a Place in the World* (Armonk, NY: M. E. Sharpe, 1997), 177–88; W. Bruce Lincoln, *The Romanovs: Autocrats of All the Russias* (New York: Doubleday, 1981), 280–3; Cyril Bryner, 'The Issue of Capital Punishment in the Reign of Elizabeth Petrovna', *Russian Review* 49, no. 4 (1990): 389–416. Bryner credits Elizabeth Petrovna's decision to abolish capital punishment to three main factors: 1) her religiosity; 2) her father's reformist legacy; and 3) her fondness for French novels. This last factor, I would argue, represented just one way in which the Enlightenment came to influence the empress.

54. Marc Raeff, *Siberia and the Reforms of 1822* (Seattle: University of Washington Press, 1956), 16.

55. David J. Rothman, *The Discovery of the Asylum: Social Order and Disorder in the New Republic* (Boston, MA: Little, Brown, 1971).

1 'To where the Sovereign chooses...'

1. James Forsyth, *A History of the Peoples of Siberia: Russia's North Asian Colony, 1581–1990* (Cambridge: Cambridge University Press, 1994), 10; Donald W. Treadgold, *The Great Siberian Migration: Government and Peasant Resettlement from Emancipation to the First World War* (Princeton, NJ: Princeton University Press, 1957), table 1, p. 32; Victor L. Mote, *Siberia: Worlds Apart* (Boulder, CO: Westview Press, 1998), 39; Yuri Slezkine, *Arctic Mirrors: Russia and the Small Peoples of the North* (Ithaca, NY: Cornell University Press, 1994), 2 and maps, pp. xv, xvi.

2. Forsyth, *History*, 26.

3. Treadgold, *Migration*, 16–17. The difference between *iasak* and *dan´*, also translatable as 'tribute', is that, at least initially, the former specified a payment in furs whereas *dan´* did not dictate the type of tribute to be handed over. Moreover, under the Russians there were two types of *iasak*: *okladnoi*, which required a fixed number of pelts, usually between five and ten per male native, and *neokladnoi*, which allowed the collector to extort or cajole from natives as many pelts as possible. *Iasak* was designated as tribute and not a tax; but later, when the Russians did begin taxing indigenes, they allowed *iasak* to be paid in cash rather than in pelts, thus blurring the distinction between tribute and taxes. In some areas of Siberia *iasak* (so called) persisted until 1917. Terence Armstrong, *Russian Settlement in the North* (Cambridge: Cambridge University Press, 1965), 196–7; George V. Lantzeff, *Siberia in the Seventeenth Century: A Study of the Colonial Administration* (New York: Octagon Books, 1972), 123–32.

4. *Polnoe sobranie russkikh letopisei*, vol. XIII (Moskva: Izd-vo vostochnoi lit-ry, 1965), 276.

5. G. F. Miller [Müller], *Istoriia Sibiri*, 5 vols., ed. E. P. Bat´ianova et al. (Moskva: Vostochnaia literatura, 1999–2005) 1: 204–5; Forsyth, *History*, 26; G. Patrick March, *Eastern Destiny: Russia in Asia and the North Pacific* (Westport, CT: Praeger, 1996), 27–8.

6. M. G. Levin and L. P. Potapov, eds., *The Peoples of Siberia* (Chicago: University of Chicago, 1964), *passim*. (This is a translation of *Narody Sibiri* [Moskva: AN SSSR, 1956].) Slezkine gives a narrower definition for 'Iugriians'. Cf. Slezkine, *Arctic*, index. On Russians' early views of Iugriians and other indigenes, see Andrei I. Pliguzov, 'Skazanie "O chelovetsekh neznaemykh v vostochnei strane"', *Russian History* 19, nos. 1–4 (1992): 401–32.

7. Treadgold, *Migration*, 17. See also Armstrong, *Russian*, 13–14, 46; Terence Armstrong, ed., *Yermak's Campaign in Siberia* (London: Haklyut Society, 1975), 1; Mote, *Siberia*, 39–40; Janet Martin, *Treasure of the Land of Darkness: The Fur Trade and its Significance for Medieval Russia* (New York: Cambridge University Press, 1986), 95ff.

8. Forsyth, *History*, 38.

9. Quoted in Janet Martin, 'The Fur Trade and the Conquest of Sibir´', in *Sibérie II: Questions sibériennes*, ed. Boris Chichlo (Paris: Insitut d'études slaves, 1999), 69. See also idem, *Treasure*, passim; Slezkine, *Arctic*, 11, 12.

10. Janet L. Abu-Lughod, *Before European Hegemony: The World System A.D. 1250–1350* (New York: Oxford University Press, 1989), 154 *et passim*; Immanuel Wallerstein, *The Modern World System: Capitalist Agriculture and the Origins of the European World-Economy in the Sixteenth Century* (New York: Academic Press, 1974), 302–3, 315–19 *et passim*; Thomas R. Shannon, *An Introduction to the World-System Perspective*, 2nd edn. (Boulder, CO: Westview Press, 1996), 62 *et passim*.

11. Martin, *Treasure*, 166.

12. Cf. Wallerstein, *Modern* (1974), 306–7.

13. Giles Fletcher, *Of the Russe Commonwealth by Giles Fletcher, 1591: Facsimile Edition with Variants*, intro. Richard Pipes (Cambridge, MA: Harvard University Press, 1966), 40–1v.

14. Forsyth, *History*, 40.

15. Robert J. Kerner, *The Urge to the Sea. The Course of Russian History. The Role of Rivers, Portages, Ostrogs, Monasteries, and Furs* (New York: Russell & Russell, 1970), 86. See also W. Bruce Lincoln, *The Conquest of a Continent: Siberia and the Russians* (New York: Random House, 1994), 43; Martin, *Treasure*, 163–6; P. N. Pavlov, 'Vyvoz pushniny iz Sibiri v XVII v.', in *Sibir´ perioda feodalizma, vypusk 1*, ed. V. I. Shunkov et al. (Novosibirsk: Izdatel´stvo Sibirskogo otdeleniia AN SSSR, 1962), 121–38; Lantzeff, *Siberia*, 153–4.

16. Armstrong, *Russian*, 61.

17. Martin, *Treasure*, 145; Forsyth, *History*, 40.

18. Martin, *Sibérie*, 71.

19. The 1558 and 1568 charters are reproduced in Miller, *Istoriia* 1: 325–31. See his commentary in ibid., 206. On the Nogai, see Michael Khodarkovsky, *Russia's Steppe Frontier: The Making of a Colonial Empire, 1500–1800* (Bloomington, IN: Indiana University Press, 2002), 120–4. See also Armstrong, *Yermak's Campaign*, 3ff.

20. *Polnoe sobranie russkikh letopisei*, vol. XIV, 33. The quote comes from a chronicle (*Novyi letopis´*) begun in 1584 to record the reign of Fedor Ivanovich.

21. (This Orël is not to be confused with today's Orël in western Russia.) Armstrong, *Yermak's Campaign*, 5–6, 13; Miller, *Istoriia* 1: 207–10. Sources disagree as to the size of Ermak's host at this time. Müller makes a convincing argument that the figures given in the Remezov Chronicle are the most

accurate. As for Ermak's origins, they are extremely vague. For an entertaining discussion, see Valentin Rasputin, *Siberia, Siberia*, trans. and intro. Margaret Winchell and Gerald Mikkelson (Evanston, IL: Northwestern University Press, 1996), 37ff *et passim*.

22. Imperatorskaia Arkheograficheskaia Kommissiia [*sic*], *Sibirskiia avtopisi* (S-Peterburg: Tipografiia I. N. Skorokhodova, 1907), 10. This reproduces various manuscript copies (*spiski*) of the three chronicles – the Stroganov, Esipov and Remezov – detailing the history of the Russians in Siberia during the late sixteenth century. Due to confusion in the chronicles some historians date the invasion in 1581. However, this does not accord with an edict Ivan sent the Stroganovs in November 1582 (see below). The chronicles are translated into English in Armstrong, *Yermak's Campaign*.

23. Instruction reproduced in Miller, *Istoriia* 1: 335–6; and translated in Basil Dmytryshyn et al., eds., *Russia's Conquest of Siberia, 1558–1700: A Documentary Record*, vol. 1 (Portland, OR: Oregon Historical Society Press, 1985), doc. no. 6.

24. Miller, *Istoriia* 1: 233.

25. Martin, *Sibérie*, 68, 77 *et passim*.

26. Isabel de Madariaga, *Ivan the Terrible: First Tsar of Russia* (New Haven, CT: Yale University Press, 2005), 335.

27. Quoted in Treadgold, *Migration*, 17.

28. Khodarkovsky, *Russia's Steppe Frontier*, 2.

29. Sources sometimes refer to *strel'tsy* as 'musketeers'. However, these soldiers were initially armed with arquebuses. See Thomas Esper, 'Military Self-Sufficiency and Weapons Technology in Muscovite Russia', *Slavic Review* 28, no. 2 (1969): 185–208 [here, p. 193]; Michael C. Paul, 'The Military Revolution in Russia, 1550–1682', *The Journal of Military History* 68, no. 1 (2004): 9–45 [here, p. 20].

30. Ivan V. Shcheglov, *Khronologicheskii perechen´ vazhneishikh dannykh iz istorii Sibiri: 1032–1882 gg.* (1883; rpt. Surgut: Severnyi dom, 1993), 44; Kerner, *Urge*, 185–90 *et passim*.

31. Document quoted in Richard Hellie, *Enserfment and Military Change in Muscovy* (Chicago: University of Chicago Press, 1971), 134.

32. Eva-Maria Stolberg, 'The Genre of Frontiers and Borderlands: Siberia as a Case Study', in *The Siberian Saga: A History of Russia's Wild East*, ed. Stolberg (Frankfurt-am-Main: Lang, 2005), 14.

33. See the distinction made in Jerome Blum, *Lord and Peasant in Russia: From the Ninth to the Nineteenth Century* (Princeton, NJ: Princeton University Press, 1961), 6–9, 93, 419, 475–7.

34. Dmytryshyn, *Russia's Conquest*, doc. no. 37; A. P. Okladnikov et al., eds., *Istoriia Sibiri s drevneishikh vremen do nashikh dnei*, 5 vols. (Leningrad: Nauka, 1968–9) 2: 66; M. M. Gromyko, 'Tserkovnye votchiny Zapadnoi Sibiri nakanune sekuliarizatsii', in *Sibir´ perioda feodalizma, vypusk 1*, table, p. 162; idem, *Zapadnaia Sibir´ v XVIII veke: Russkoe naselenie i zemledel´cheskoe osvoenie* (Novosibirsk: Nauka, 1965), 224; Kerner, *Urge*, 182–4 *et passim*. On the powerful Troitskii Monastery in Turukhansk, see K. I. Protopopov, 'Eniseiskaia politicheskaia ssylka ot dekabristov do 1917 goda', in *Eniseiskaia ssylka: Sbornik eniseiskogo zemliachestva*, ed. V. N. Sokolov (Moskva: Politkatorzhan, 1934), 5–16.

35. Instruction reproduced in Miller, *Istoriia* 2: 576.

36. A title which incidentally points to the absence of an independent judiciary and the bureaucracy's performance of judicial functions.

37. Miller, *Istoriia* 2: 103–4; Lantzeff, *Siberia*, 4–5; Okladnikov, *Istoriia Sibiri* 2: 124; Shcheglov, *Khronologicheskii perechen´*, 70; Dmytryshyn, *Siberica*: 10; idem, 'Introduction', *Russia's Conquest*, xlv. *Sibirskii prikaz*'s authority was temporarily suspended under Empress Anna. However, even then it does not appear to have been abolished.

    Dvorianov asserts: 'The *Razboinyi prikaz* [Crime Department], which dealt with runaway peasants and utilized exile to Siberia as one of its punitive measures, was established in Tobol´sk in 1586.' (V. N. Dvorianov, *V sibirskoi dal´nei storone . . . (ocherki istorii politicheskoi katorgi i ssylki. 60-e gody XVIII v.-1917 g.)* [Minsk: Nauka i tekhnika, 1985], 23.) But Dvorianov's date of 1586 is earlier than both the founding of Tobol´sk and the first case of exile to Siberia. Further undermining his assertion is his date of 1595 for *Sibirskii prikaz*'s establishment, a date supported by no other source.

38. Miller, *Istoriia* 2: 104; Okladnikov, *Istoriia Sibiri* 2: 125; Lantzeff, *Siberia*, 6; Dmytryshyn, 'Introduction', *Russia's Conquest*, xlv; V. O. Kliuchevskii, *Sochineniia*, 8 vols. (Moskva: Izd-vo. sotsial´no-ekonomicheskoi literatury, 1956–9) 3: 46, 60–2, 72–3, 77, 131, 225, 322, 325–36; 4: 19, 41, 149, 154, 166, 181, 386. Streshnev was originally an *okol´nichii* (second in rank to a boyar) but was promoted to boyar in 1676. See Lantzeff, *Siberia*, 6 n. 20.

39. Robert O. Crummey, *Aristocrats and Servitors: The Boyar Elite in Russia, 1613–1689* (Princeton, NJ: Princeton University Press, 1983), 51.

40. Dmytryshyn, 'Introduction', *Russia's Conquest*, xlviii–ix.

41. J. Michael Hittle, *The Service City: State and Townsmen in Russia, 1600–1800* (Cambridge, MA: Harvard University Press, 1979), 52.

42. Crummey, *Aristocrats*, 51.

43. Ibid., 19–24, 32, 54, 61; Dmytryshyn, *Siberica*: 10; idem, 'Introduction', *Russia's Conquest*, xlviii; G. S. Fel´dstein, *Ssylka: eia genezisa, znacheniia, istorii i sovremennogo sostoianiia* (Moskva: T-vo skoropechatni A. A. Levenson, 1893), 150; Forsyth, *History*, 34.

44. F. G. Safronov, *Russkie krest´iane v Iakutii (XVII – nachalo XX vv.)* (Iakutsk: Knizhnoe izd-vo, 1961), 384.

45. Borivoj Plavsic, 'Seventeenth-Century Chanceries and their Staffs', in *Russian Officialdom: The Bureaucratization of Russian Society from the Seventeenth to the Twentieth Century*, ed. Walter McKenzie Pintner and Don Karl Rowney (London: Macmillan, 1980), 19–45. See also Lantzeff, *Siberia*, 13, 205.

46. Dmytryshyn, *Russia's Conquest*, doc. no. 26, p. 70.

47. Cf. Stephen Kotkin, 'Introduction: Rediscovering Russia in Asia', in *Rediscovering Russia in Asia: Siberia and the Russian Far East*, ed. Kotkin and David Wolff (Armonk, NY: M. E. Sharpe, 1995), 3.

48. Dmytryshyn, *Siberia's Conquest*, doc. no. 41, p. 121.

49. Shcheglov, *Khronologicheskii perechen´*, 46, 70. Shcheglov's use of the word *devka* also implies 'tart' or 'whore', but there is no indication that these women were being punished for prostitution or similar behavior. (See also Forsyth, *History*, 67.)

    Vologda, Sol´vychegodsk, Tot´ma, and Zheleznyi Ustiug were early on associated with industry and trade. Vologda is one of Russia's oldest cities, founded in 1147, 500 km northwest of Moscow. During the fifteenth and sixteenth centuries it developed into a major center of industry and trade. In 1565 its inhabitants began constructing a stone fortification, but this remained uncompleted, and in 1612 it suffered grievously at the hands of Swedish and Polish forces. Sol'vychegodsk, 830 km southeast of Arkhangel' on the Vychegda River, was (as already noted) the base of the Stroganov empire. The Stroganovs 'contributed significant means to the cultural life of the city, built a church, a collection of rare books and icons, and founded an arts industry' so that by the late seventeenth century it was a 'major center of Russian artistry'. Tot'ma, 217 km southwest of Vologda, had like Sol'vychegodsk begun as a salt works (albeit under the ownership of Feodosii Sumorin), producing by the sixteenth and seventeenth centuries 50–170 poods of salt per annum, more even than the Stroganov salt works. It became a major trade center along the route to the White Sea, and '[b]y 1623, there were 199 homes, 20 cathedrals, and 8 salt works in Tot'ma'. The ancient city of Zhelcznyi Uotiug (today called Ustiuzhna) is located 191 km south of Vologda. By the second half of the 1500s it was a vast trade center. False Dmitrii II laid siege to it in 1609, but it rebounded soon afterwards to become a metallurgical center and home to Russia's second largest armory after that in Tula. G. M. Lappo, ed., *Goroda Rossii* (Moskva: Nauchnoe izdatel'stvo, 1994), 87, 432, 475, 497.

50. N. N. Pokrovskii, ed., *Pervoe stoletie sibiriskikh gorodov. XVII vek* (Novosibirsk: Sibirskii khronograf, 1996), doc. no. 26. XI, p. 84.

51. Officials at first tried to make the conquered indigenes serve as food producers but they proved stubbornly nomadic, and then smallpox and alcoholism began reducing their numbers. James Forsyth, 'Native Peoples before and after the Russian Conquest', in *The History of Siberia: From Russian Conquest to Revolution*, ed. Alan Wood (London: Routledge, 1991), 82–3; idem, *History*, 161 *et passim*; Slezkine, *Arctic*, 26–7.

52. Petition dated 1616. Dmytryshyn, *Russia's Conquest*, doc. no. 27, p. 74.

53. Ibid., doc. nos. 27 and 30, pp. 71, 80. Litva was the name given to all Polish, Swedish and Lithuanian prisoners-of-war at that time.

54. *Gramota* dated no earlier than 24 November 1624, reproduced in Miller, *Istoriia* 2: 370.

55. Dmytryshyn, *Russia's Conquest*, doc. no. 43, p. 127.

56. V. I. Shunkov, *Ocherki po istorii kolonizatsii Sibiri v XVII-nachale XVIII vekov* (Moskva: AN SSSR, 1946), 14.

57. F. G. Safronov, *Ssylka v vostochnuiu Sibir' v XVII veke* (Iakutsk: Iakutskoe knizhnoe izdatel'stvo, 1967), 38.

58. Okladnikov, *Istoriia Sibiri* 2: 120.

59. See, e.g., the discussion in de Madariaga, *Ivan*, 35.

60. Dmytryshyn, *Russia's Conquest*, doc. no. 88, p. 335.

61. *Ssylka v Sibir': ocherk eia istorii i sovremennago polozheniia* (S.-Peterburg: Tipografiia S.-Peterburgskoi Tiur'my, 1900), 1; A. D. Margolis, *Tiur'ma i ssylka v imperatorskoi Rossii: issledovaniia i arkhivnye nakhodki* (Moskva: Lanterna, 1995), 7; Safronov, *Ssylka*, 6, 10.

62. Ivan nevertheless had Vorotynskii executed in 1573. Safronov, *Ssylka*, 10–11, 17–18; Roy R. Robson, *Solovki: The Story of Russia Told Through Its Most Remarkable Islands* (New Haven, CT: Yale University Press, 2004), 42–3;

Kliuchevskii, *Sochineniia* 2: 188; Andrei Pavlov and Maureen Perrie, *Ivan the Terrible* (London: Pearson Longman, 2003), 98–101.

63. Maureen Perrie, *Pretenders and Popular Monarchism in Early Modern Russia: The False Tsars of the Time of Trubles* (Cambridge: Cambridge University Press, 1995), 17–20; S. F. Platonov, *Boris Godunov: Tsar of Russia*, trans. L. Rex Pyles (Gulf Breeze, FL: Academic International Press, 1973), 125–52; Shcheglov, *Khronologicheskii perechen´*, 47; Safronov, *Ssylka*, 12, 19; N. M. Iadrintsev, *Sibir´ kak koloniia v geograficheskom, etnograficheskom i dopolnennoe* (S.-Peterburg: Tip. I. M. Sibiriakova, 1892), 245 n. 2. Some sources mistakenly attribute the Uglichians with founding Pelym, which was in fact established by Prince Petr Gorchakov in 1592. See *gramota* dated December 1592, reproduced in Miller, *Istoriia* 1: 339 (also see p. 271). Lantzeff and Pierce write 'that the builders of the fort had instructions to bring to Pelym the first Russian exiles to Siberia, the family of Ignatii Khripunove from Rzhev'. They cite Müller as their source. However, all other accounts (including the Müller edition used here) reference Pelym's exiles as originating in Uglich. Cf. George V. Lantzeff, and Richard A. Pierce, *Eastward to Empire: Exploration and Conquest on the Russian Open Frontier, to 1750* (Montreal: McGill-Queen's University Press, 1973), 120.

64. *Gramota* dated 27 February 1603, reproduced in Miller, *Istoriia* 2: 208.

65. P. A. Slovtsov, *Istoricheskoe obozrenie Sibiri. Stikhotvoreniia. Propovedi*, ed. and intro. V. A. Kreshchik (Novosibirsk: Ven-mir, 1995), 149.

66. Ibid.

67. Shcheglov, *Khronologicheskii perechen´*, 51; Safronov, *Ssylka*, 24; Miller, *Istoriia Sibiri* 2: 18, 22; V. I. Shunkov, *Ocherki po istorii zemledeliia Sibiri (XVII vek)* (Moskva: AN SSSR, 1956), 64.

68. P. L. Kazarian, *Iakutiia v sisteme politicheskoi ssylki Rossii, 1826–1917 gg.* (Iakutsk: GP NIPK 'Sakhapoligrafizdat,' 1998), 113.

69. Pokrovskii, *Pervoe stoletie*, doc. no. 18, p. 58.

70. S. Maksimov, 'Gosudartsvennye prestupniki. Piataia chast´', *Otechestvennyia zapiski* 9 (September 1869): 229–72 [here, pp. 238–9 *et passim*].

71. *Gramota* dated 30 January 1645, reproduced in Miller, *Istoriia Sibiri* 3: 302.

72. *Gramota* dated 5 March 1649, reproduced in Miller, *Istoriia Sibiri* 2: 616.

73. Pokrovskii, *Pervoe stoletie*, doc. no. 31. III, p. 105.

74. Quoted in Kazarian, *Iakutiia*, 119.

75. Safronov, *Ssylka*, 23–4. At the time of M. N. Romanov's imprisonment Perm´ was administered as part of Siberia.

76. The charge of *nevezhlivye slova* appears to have been similar to *nepristoinye slova* ('indecent words'), which Shunkov notes was a rhetorical formula signifying treason. Shunkov, *Ocherki* (1956), 16.

77. Ibid., 17; Shcheglov, *Khronologicheskii perechen´*, 81, 88, 95; Perrie, *Pretenders*, 235.

78. Miller, *Istoriia* 2: 41.

79. Shunkov, *Ocherki* (1946), 18–19.

80. Kazarian, *Iakutiia*, 126–7.

81. P. L. Kazarian, 'Zadachi rossiiskoi i pol´skoi istoricheskoi nauki v izuchenii ssylka Poliakov v Iakutiiu', in *Rossiia i Polsha: Istoriko-kul´turnye kontakty (Sibirskii fenomen)*, ed. V. N. Ivanov et al. (Novosibirsk: Nauka, 2001), 43.

82. Pokrovskii, *Pervoe stoletie*, doc. no. 43. Kuznetsk is today called Novok-uznetsk, located west of the Altai; Uzhum is just west of the Urals. Both regions were at the time administratively part of Siberia.
83. Ibid., doc. no. 45, p. 119.
84. I. R. Sokolovskii, *Sluzhilye 'inozemtsy' v Sibiri XVII veka (Tomsk, Eniseisk, Krasnoiarsk)* (Novosibirsk: 'Sova,' 2004), 86ff.
85. V. A. Aleksandrov and N. N. Pokrovskii, 'Mirskie organizatsii i adminis-trativnaia vlast´ v Sibiri v XVII veke', *Istoriia SSSR* 1 (1986): 47–68 [here, p. 53].
86. S. V. Maksimov, *Sibir´ i katorga*, 3rd edn. (S.-Peterburg: Izdanie V. I. Gub-inskago, 1900), 326–7. Cf. John J. Stephan, *The Russian Far East: A History* (Stanford, CA: Stanford University Press, 1994), 29–31. Stephan contradicts the claim that rebels paid *iasak* to Nerchinsk.
87. Shcheglov, *Khronologicheskii perechen´*, 55; Paul Avrich, *Russian Rebels 1600–1800* (1972; rpt. New York: W. W. Norton, 1976), 37–8; Shunkov, *Ocherki* (1956), 116, 216–17, table, p. 115.
88. Pokrovksii, *Pervoe stoletie*, doc. no. 99, p. 224.
89. Paul Bushkovitch, *Religion and Society in Russia: The Sixteenth and Seventeenth Centuries* (New York: Oxford University Press, 1992), 135.
90. N. N. Pokrovskii and E. K. Romodanovskaia, eds., *Tobol´skii arkhiereiskii dom v XVII veke* (Novosibirsk: Sibirskii khronograf, 1994), doc. no. 60, p. 189.
91. Valerie A. Kivelson, email to author, 18 August 2003; idem, 'Through the Prism of Witchcraft: Gender and Social Change in Seventeenth-Century Muscovy', in *Russia's Women: Accommodation, Resistance, Transformation*, ed. Barbara Evan Clements et al. (Berkeley, CA: University of California Press, 1991), 74–94; idem, 'Patrolling the Boundaries: Witchcraft Accusations and Household Strife in Seventeenth-Century Muscovy', *Harvard Ukrainian Studies* 19 (1995): 302–23; Evgenii Anisimov, *Dyba i knut: politicheskii sysk i russkoe obshchestvo v XVIII veke* (Moskva: Novoe literaturnoe obozrenie, 1999), 25–9; Christine D. Worobec, *Possessed: Women, Witches, and Demons in Imperial Russia* (DeKalb, IL: Northern Illinois University Press, 2001), 24–9 *et passim*; Georg Bernhard Michels, *At War with the Church: Religious Dissent in Seventeenth-Century Russia* (Stanford, CA: Stanford University Press, 1999), 149, 180.
92. Cited in Kazarian, *Iakutiia*, 121–2.
93. Ibid., *passim*; Michels, *At War*, 99–100; idem, 'The Violent Old Belief: An Examination of Religious Dissent on the Karelian Frontier', *Russian History* 19, nos. 1–4 (1992): 203–29; Bushkovitch, *Religion and Society*, 66. The conditions for prisoners at Pustozersk nearly defy comprehension. See Sergei Zen´kovskii, *Russkoe staroobriadchestvo: Dukhovnye dvizheniia semnadtsatogo veka* (Moskva: Tserkov´, 1995), 280, 313.
94. See Michels, *At War*, *passim*; Alan Wood, 'Avvakum's Siberian Exile, 1653–64', in *The Development of Siberia: People and Resources*, ed. Wood and R. A. French (Basingstoke: Macmillan, 1989), 11–34; Bruce T. Holl, 'Avvakum and the Genesis of Siberian Literature', in *Between Heaven and Hell: The Myth of Siberia in Russian Culture*, ed. Galya Diment and Yuri Slezkine (New York: St. Martin's Press, 1993), 33–46.

95. [Avvakum,] *Zhitie protopopa Avvakuma, im samim napisannoe i drugie ego sochineniia*, ed. N. K. Gudziia et al. (Moskva: Gos. izd-vo Khudozh. lit-ry, 1960), 82.

96. Ibid., 72. It is something of a miracle Avvakum did not die from his wounds. Alan Wood suggests a medical explanation rather than divine intervention. Wood, 'Avvakum's Siberian Exile': 33 n. 57.

97. *Zhitie protopopa Avvakuma*, 82.

98. Michels, 'Violent Old Belief': *passim*; idem, *At War*, 206; Shcheglov, *Khronologicheskii perechen'*, 91 and n.; Bushkovitch, *Religion and Society*, 71–2; Zen'kovskii, *Russkoe staroobriadchestvo*, 395.

99. Basil Dmytryshyn, 'The Confinement of Juraj Križaníc in and his Thoughts on Siberia, 1661–1676', in *Sibérie II*, 184–5, 188; Shcheglov, *Khronologicheskii perechen'*, 84 and n.; Paul Kevin Meagher et al., eds., *Encyclopedic Dictionary of Religion*, vol. F–N (Washington, DC: Corpus Publications, 1979), 2007.

100. Butsinkii's figures are cited in Safronov, *Ssylka*, 19; and in Shunkov, *Ocherki* (1946), 15 (see also pp. 17–18, 20); idem, *Ocherki* (1956), 64.

101. Valerie A. Kivelson, *Autocracy in the Provinces: The Muscovite Gentry and Political Culture in the Seventeenth Century* (Stanford, CA: Stanford University Press, 1996), 220, 229. On the 1648 uprising, see idem, 'The Devil Stole His Mind: The Tsar and the 1648 Moscow Uprising', *American Historical Review* 98, no. 3 (1993): 733–56.

102. Avrich, *Russian Rebels*, 55.

103. Anisimov, *Dyba*, 16, 25–9. Accusations of witchcraft and sorcery were also generated by non-authorities. See Kivelson, 'Patrolling the Boundaries': *passim*.

104. Michel Foucault, *Power/Knowledge: Selected Interviews and Other Writings, 1972–1977*, ed. Colin Gordon (New York: Pantheon, 1980), 94–5.

105. K. A. Sofronenko, ed., *Sobornoe ulozhenie tsaria Alekseia Mikhailovicha, 1649 goda* (Moskva: Iuridicheskaia literatura, 1957).

106. Weickhardt writes that the *Ulozhenie* reflected Western influences insofar as it 'provided for adversarial procedure in civil litigation' and substantiated what he argues was the recently introduced use of torture as an inquisitorial method. Both might safely be termed 'modernistic' without contradicting what I have written above, since inquisitorial torture served a different function from retributive corporal punishment. See George G. Weickhardt, 'Probable Western Origins of Muscovite Criminal Procedure', *Russian Review* 66 (January 2007): 55–72.

107. Quoted in Safronov, *Ssylka*, 15 (ellipsis in source). 'Lower cities' typically referred to those in the Kazan' region.

108. Ibid., 14, 15, 17, 24; *Ssylka v Sibir'*, 4-5 n. 2; Fel'dstein, *Ssylka*, 130–1; Shcheglov, *Khronologicheskii perechen'*, 85, 90, 96; N. D. Sergeevskii, *Rech' v godovom SPB Iuridicheskago Obshchestva, 8 Marta 1887 goda, O ssylke v drevnei Rossii* (S.-Peterburg: Tipografiia Ministerstva putei soobshcheniia [A. Benke], 1887), 3–8; N. M. Iadrintsev, *Russkaia obshchina v tiur'me i ssylke* (S.-Peterburg: Tipografiia A. Morigerovskago, 1872), 504–5; F. G. Safronov, 'Ssylka v vostochnuiu Sibir' v pervoi polovine XVIII v.', in *Ssylka i katorga v Sibiri (XVIII-nachalo XX v.)*, ed. L. M. Goriushkin et al. (Novosibirsk: Nauka, 1975), 15.

109. Quoted in Iadrintsev, *Russkaia obshchina*, 504; *Ssylka v Sibir´*, 4 n. 2.
110. Safronov, *Ssylka*, 32–3, 38–41; A. P. Kopylov, 'Gosudarevy pashennye krest´iane Eniseiskogo uezda v XVII v.', in *Sibir´ perioda feodalizma, vypusk 1*, 34; Shunkov, *Ocherki* (1956), table, p. 115.
111. Quoted in Shunkov, *Ocherki* (1946), 16.
112. Safronov, *Ssylka*, table, p. 28.
113. Fel´dstein, *Ssylka*, 148–9.
114. Ibid., 150; Safronov, *Russkie krest´iane*, 381; idem, *Ssylka*, 34. Paraskov´ia Romodanovskaia (*née* Saltykova) was Prince Fedor Iur´evich Romodanovskii's wife. See *O proekte Oglavelenie Rossiia Portrety Gerby Zvuki Disk Avtory*. http://kolibry.astroguru.com/01170369.htm [accessed 3 October 2003].
115. Safronov, *Ssylka*, 21–2, 32–3, 38–41.
116. Except where noted, what follows is from Safronov, *Ssylka*, 71-5. See also Kazarian, *Iakutiia*, 114ff.
117. Dated 6 August 1638. Dmytryshyn, *Russia's Conquest*, doc. no. 53, quote on p. 173.
118. Safronov notes 'several dozen' of the original 188 people who arrived in Eniseisk in 1642 never left the *ostrog*, though does not explain why. If they did not die, it is likely they found a niche within the servitor or *posadskie liudi* estates.
119. Shcheglov, *Khronologicheskii perechen´*, 99.

2   'Exile to the service in which he will be useful'

1. V. I. Shunkov, *Ocherki po istorii zemledeliia Sibiri (XVII vek)* (Moskva: AN SSSR, 1956), table, p. 115.
2. *Ssylka v Sibir´: ocherk eia istorii i sovremennago polozheniia* (S.-Peterburg: Tipografiia S.-Peterburgskoi Tiur´my, 1900), 5.
3. J. Michael Hittle, *The Service City: State and Townsmen in Russia, 1600–1800* (Cambridge, MA: Harvard University Press, 1979), 26–7 *et passim*.
4. V. I. Shunkov, *Ocherki po istorii kolonizatsii Sibiri v XVII–nachale XVIII vekov* (Moskva: AN SSSR, 1946), 17.
5. *Ssylka v Sibir´*, 4–5 and n. 1.
6. Michel Foucault, *Power/Knowledge: Selected Interviews and Other Writings, 1972–1977* (New York: Pantheon, 1980), 125.
7. Ibid., 119.
8. *Gramota* dated 30 November 1614, reproduced in G. F. Miller, *Istoriia Sibiri*, 3 vols., ed. E. P. Bat´ianova et al. (Moskva: Vostochnaia literatura, 1999–2005) 2: 268.
9. *Gramota* dated 1650, reproduced in Miller, *Istoriia* 3: 342.
10. Shunkov, *Ocherki* (1956), 62, 64–5, 91 *et passim*. See also idem, *Ocherki* (1946), 13, 20.
11. Miller, *Istoriia* 2: 20; notes dated 1653–4 and reproduced in ibid., 626–7.
12. Shunkov, *Ocherki* (1956), table 9, p. 131.
13. A. P. Kopylov, 'Gosudarevy pashennye krest´iane Eniseiskogo uezda v XVII v.', in *Sibir´ perioda feodalizma, vypusk 1*, ed. V.I. Shunkov et al. (Novosibirsk: Izdatel´stvo Sibirskogo otdeleniia AN SSSR 1962), tables, pp. 33–5. Figures are based on the number of taxpaying individuals (*tiagletsy*), i.e. heads of household.

14. Shunkov, *Ocherki* (1956), 114, 120–1, 198, 216–18, table 21, p. 218; P. A. Slovtsov, *Istoricheskoe obozrenie Sibiri. Stikhotvoreniia. Propovedi*, ed. and intro. V. A. Kreshchik (Novosibirsk: Ven-mir, 1995), 221. See also James Forsyth, *A History of the Peoples of Siberia: Russia's North Asian Colony, 1581–1990* (Cambridge: Cambridge University Press, 1994), ch. 4; G. Patrick March, *Eastern Destiny: Russia in Asia and the North Pacific* (Westport, CT: Praeger, 1996), ch. 5.

15. Quoted in F. G. Safronov, *Russkie krest´iane v Iakutii (XVII–nachalo XX vv.)* (Iakutsk: Knizhnoe izd-vo, 1961), 13, 231 (ellipsis in original). The inclusion of '*obrok* peasants' appears odd here and may refer to house serfs in debt servitude (*kabala*) rather than to agricultural peasants.

16. Ibid., 14–15; F. G. Safronov, *Ssylka v vostochnuiu Sibir´ v XVII veke* (Iakutsk: Iakutskoe knizhnoe izdatel´stvo, 1967), 42–3; Shunkov, *Ocherki* (1956), table, p. 174.

17. Safronov, *Russkie krest´iane*, 231, 246; idem, *Ssylka*, table, p. 30. The foregoing undercuts Levin and Potapov's contention that eastern Siberia's economic fortunes at this early date rested more in agriculture than the fur industry. Cf. M. G. Levin and L. P. Potapov, eds., *The Peoples of Siberia* (Chicago: University of Chicago, 1964), 125.

18. Miller, *Istoriia* 2: 72.

19. As demonstrated by a *gramota* dated no earlier than 20 November 1653, reproduced in Miller, *Istoriia* 3: 380.

20. Kopylov, 'Gosudarevy', 31–2, 33, 36.

21. Safronov, *Russkie krest´iane*, 154–5.

22. Leonid M. Goryushkin, 'Late Nineteenth- and Early Twentieth-Century Siberian Regionalists' Views on the Economic Independence of Siberia', trans. Alan Wood, *Siberica* 1, no. 2 (1990–1): 152–68 [here, p. 158].

23. Safronov, *Russkie krest´iane*, 231–2; G. S. Fel´dstein, *Ssylka: eia genezisa, znacheniia, istorii i sovremennogo sostoianiia* (Moskva: T-vo skoropechatni A. A. Levenson, 1893), 128–9; *Ssylka v Sibir´: ocherk eia istorii i sovremennago polozheniia* (S.-Peterburg: Tipografiia S.-Peterburgskoi Tiur´my, 1900), 6.

24. Goryushkin, *Siberica*: 157–8.

25. These were provided non-exilic peasants in Siberia, though it is uncertain if exiles received them. Cf. A. P. Okladnikov et al., eds., *Istoriia Sibiri s drevneishikh vremen do nashikh dnei*, 5 vols. (Leningrad: Nauka, 1968–9) 2: 65; Safronov, *Russkie krest´iane*, 154–5.

26. V. A. Aleksandrov and N. N. Pokrovskii, 'Mirskie organizatsii i administrativnaia vlast´ v Sibiri v XVII veke', *Istoriia SSSR* 1 (1986): 47–68 [here, p. 53].

27. This account is derived from slightly different versions in different MSS of the Stroganov and Esipov chronicles, as reproduced in Imperatorskaia Arkheograficheskaia Kommissiia [*sic*], *Sibirskiia avtopisi* (S-Peterburg: Tipografiia I. N. Skorokhodova, 1907), 39–40, 85–6, 102–3, 151–3, 223–5, 256–7, 268–9, 290–1. Ostiaki were also known as Khanty. Obskii *gorodok* was technically the first Russian settlement (*russkii naselennyi punkt*) in Siberia, established one year before Tiumen´, but it proved ephemeral. See Safronov, *Ssylka*, 19.

28. Gregory L. Freeze, 'The *Soslovie* (Estate) Paradigm and Russian Social History', *The American Historical Review* 91, no. 1 (February 1986): 11–36 [here, pp. 14–16].

29. J. Michael Hittle, *The Service City: State and Townsmen in Russia, 1600–1800* (Cambridge, MA: Harvard University Press, 1979), 15.
30. Fel´dstein, *Ssylka*, 128
31. Dmytryshyn, 'Glossary', in Dmytryshyn et al., eds., *Russia's Conquest of Siberia, 1558–1700: A Documentary Record*. Vol. 1 (Portland, OR: Oregon Historical Society Press, 1985), lxxxiv–xv. Cf. George V. Lantzeff, *Siberia in the Seventeenth Century: A Study of the Colonial Administration* (New York: Octagon Books, 1972), 60.
32. Dmytryshyn, *Russia's Conquest*, doc. no. 68, p. 219.
33. Lantzeff, *Siberia*, 67.
34. Literally 'Tobol´sk *razriad*.' N. I. Nikitin, *Sluzhilie liudi v Zapadnoi Sibiri XVII veka* (Novosibirsk: Nauka, 1988), table 1, p. 29.
35. Safronov, *Ssylka*, 44–8.
36. Okladnikov, *Istoriia Sibiri* 2: 76.
37. Nikitin, *Sluzhilye liudi*, 27. See also Lantzeff, *Siberia*, 74.
38. Nikitin, *Sluzhilye liudi*, table 3, p. 33.
39. D. Ia. Rezun, *Russkie v srednem Prichulym´e v XVII–XIX vv. (Problemy sotsial´no-ekonomicheskogo razvitiia malykh gorodov Sibiri)* (Novosibirsk: Nauka, 1984), 90.
40. N. I. Nikitin, 'Pervyi vek kazachestva Sibiri', *Voenno-istoricheskii zhurnal* 1 (1994): 77–83 [here, pp. 78–9]. See also O. N. Vilkov, 'Promyshlennost´ nerusskikh narodov Tobol´skogo uezd v XVII v.', in *Sibir´ perioda feodalizma, vypusk 1*, 84ff; Safronov, *Ssylka*, 43–4.
41. Shunkov, *Ocherki* (1946), 17. A total of 124 known exiles passed through Tobol´sk during this period: one was put in prison in Krasnoiarsk; 28 were assigned 'to the land'; the fate of the remaining 15 is unknown.
42. Safronov, *Ssylka*, 48. The text reads '1780s' rather than '1680s', but this is clearly a typographical error.
43. Ibid., 46–7.
44. P. N. Pavlov, 'Vyvoz pushniny iz Sibiri v XVII v.', in *Sibir´ perioda feodalizma, vypusk 1*, tables 1, 2, and 3, pp. 126, 128, 130.
45. Dmytryshyn, *Russia's Conquest*, doc. nos. 76, 85, 97 (quotations on pp. 242, 243, 313, 356).
46. Nikitin, *Sluzhilye liudi*, table, pp. 110–13.
47. Nikitin, 'Pervyi vek kazachestva Sibiri': 82.
48. Nikitin, *Sluzhilye liudi*, table, pp. 110–13.
49. Dmytryshyn, *Russia's Conquest*, doc. no. 47, pp. 152–7.
50. *Gramota* dated 1651–2, reproduced in Miller, *Istoriia* 3: 366–9.
51. Dmytryshyn, *Russia's Conquest*, doc. no. 88 (quote on p. 335).
52. *Gramota* dated 29 November 1648, reproduced in Miller, *Istoriia* 3: 323.
53. Fel´dstein, *Ssylka*, 128.
54. S. V. Maksimov, *Sibir´ i katorga*, 3rd edn. (S.-Peterburg: Izdanie V. I. Gubinskago, 1900), 218.
55. Nikitin, *Sluzhilye liudi*, tables 24–7, pp. 168–71.
56. Okladnikov, *Istoriia Sibiri* 2: 67.
57. '*Posad*' designated either that part of a city located between the kremlin and the outer wall, or a settlement just outside city walls and subordinate to the urban administration. To avoid the confusion that would be caused by 'town', 'city' (both of which are too restrictive), or 'settlement' (which will

refer to a later developed exile category), *posad* is translated here as 'suburb'. Cf. Hittle, *Service City*, 26ff; Dmytryshyn, 'Glossary', in *Russia's Conquest*, lxxxiii; V. I. Dal´, *Tolkovyi slovar´ zhivogo velikorusskogo iazyka*, 4 vols. (1882; rpt. Moskva: Izdatel´stvo 'Russkii iazyk', 1999) 3: 328.

58. N. N. Pokrovskii, ed., *Pervoe stoletie sibiriskikh gorodov. XVII vek* (Novosibirsk: Sibirskii khronograf, 1996), doc. no. 51, p. 136.

59. Ibid., pp. 136–61.

60. *Gramota* dated no earlier than 31 January 1623, reproduced in Miller, *Istoriia* 2: 342–7. Sections are translated in Dmytryshyn, *Russia's Conquest*, doc. no. 38, p. 107.

61. O. I. Vilkov, 'Tobol´skii posad XVII v.', in *Sibir´ perioda feodalizma, vypusk 3*, ed. V. I. Shunkov et al. (Novosibirsk: Nauka, 1968), 42.

62. *Gramota* dated 23 May 1625, reproduced in Pokrovskii, *Pervoe stoletie*, doc. no. 12, pp. 46–7.

63. Safronov, *Ssylka*, 49–51; idem, *Russkie krest´iane*, 18. See also Shunkov, *Ocherki* (1956), table 8, p. 126.

64. Okladnikov, *Istoriia Sibiri* 2: 67.

65. Fel´dstein, *Ssylka*, 151–2; N. M. Iadrintsev, *Sibir´ kak koloniia v geograficheskom, etnograficheskom i dopolnennoe* (S.-Peterburg: Tip. I. M. Sibiriakova, 1892), 13 *et passim*; Wood, *Siberica*: 43–4; Basil Dmytryshyn, 'Russian Expansion to the Pacific, 1580–1700: A Historiographical Review', *Siberica* 1, no. 1 (1990): 4–37 [here, p. 8].

66. Slovtsov, *Istoricheskoe*, 220–1.

67. Peter Wilson Coldham, *Emigrants in Chains: A Social History of Forced Emigration to the Americas of Felons, Destitute Children, Political and Religious Non-Conformists, Vagabonds, Beggars and other Undesirables, 1607–1776* (Baltimore, MD: Genealogical Publications, 1992), 1; Clare Anderson, *Convicts in the Indian Ocean: Transportation from South Asia to Mauritius, 1815–53* (Basingstoke: Macmillan, 2000), 2; L. L. Robson, *The Convict Settlers of Australia*, 2nd edn. (Carlton: Melbourne University Press, 1994), 3.

68. *Ssylka v Sibir´*, 7–8.

69. Quoted in ibid., 8–9 [emphasis added].

70. Established roughly in chronological order, these were the Tobol´sk, Tomsk, Eniseisk, Irkutsk and Verkhotur´e *razriady*. There were also some regions near the southern borders of Muscovy organized into *razriady* during the late seventeenth century, but neither these nor Siberian *razriady* appear to have been administered by *Razriadnyi prikaz* which, during the sixteenth and seventeenth centuries, was assigned to oversee 'the administration of military servitors, the military system and the southern ("fortified") sectors of the state'. Founded in the mid-1500s, this *prikaz* soon lost much of its authority, and so any influence it may have had on the development of Siberia or exile was ephemeral at best. See Okladnikov, *Istoriia Sibiri* 2: 126.

71. These cities were as follows: Tobol´sk, Eniseisk, Ilimsk, Tara, Berezov, Surgut, Tiumen´, Tomsk, Mangazeia, Irkutsk, Kuznetsk, Turinsk, Narym, Verkhotur´e, Iakutsk, Nerchinsk, Krasnyi Iar, Pelym, Ketsk, Kungur, Perm´ Velikaia, Cherdyn, Sol´kamsk, Kai-gorodok, Iarensk and Viatka. I. V. Shcheglov, *Khronologicheskii perechen´ vazhneishikh dannykh iz istorii Sibiri: 1032–1882 gg.* (1883; rpt. Surgut: severnyi dom, 1993), 108.

72. Vasili Klyuchevsky, *Peter the Great*, trans. Liliana Archibald (New York: Random, 1958), 198.
73. Philip Johann Tabbert von Stralenberg [*sic*], *An histori-geographical description of the north and eastern part of Europe and Asia...* (London: W. Innys and R. Manby, 1736), 246.
74. The first complete geographical atlas of Siberia, dated 1745, schematizes the following distribution of *uezd* cities in Siberia after detachment of Viatka and Sol´kamsk provinces:

   A) Tobol´sk province: 1) Tobol´sk, 2) Tiumen´, 3) Turinsk, 4) Verkhotur´e, 5) Pelym, 6) Tara, 7) Berezov, 8) Surgut, 9) Narym, 10) Tomsk, 11) Kuznetsk, 12) the fortresses of Omsk, Zhelezinsk, Iamyshevsk, Semipalatinsk, and Ust-Kamenogorsk.
   B) Eniseisk province: 1) Eniseisk, 2) Mangazeia (renamed Turukhansk), 3) Krasnoiarsk.
   C) Irkutsk province: 1) Irkutsk, 2) Balagansk, 3) Verkholensk, 4) Selenginsk, 5) Nerchinsk, 6) Ilimsk, 7) Iakutsk, 8) Okhotsk, 9) Kamchatka and the cities of Nizhne- and Verkhne-Kamchatsk, Bol´sheretsk, and Petropavlovsk gavan´.

   Atlas cited in Shcheglov, *Khronologicheskii perechen´*, 156.
75. See James Cracraft, *The Petrine Revolution in Russian Culture* (Cambridge, MA: Harvard University Press, 2004).
76. Quoted in P. L. Kazarian, *Iakutiia v sisteme politicheskoi ssylki Rossii, 1826–1917 gg.* (Iakutsk: GP NIPK 'Sakhapoligrafizdat', 1998), 69.
77. John P. LeDonne, *Ruling Russia: Politics and Administration in the Age of Absolutism, 1762–1796* (Princeton, N J: Princeton University Press, 1984), 277–90; idem, 'Frontier Governors General 1772–1825. III. The Eastern Frontier', *Jahrbücher für Geschichte Osteuropas* 48 (2000): 321–40.
78. Marc Raeff, *Siberia and the Reforms of 1822* (Seattle: University of Washington Press, 1956), 6.
79. LeDonne, 'Eastern Frontier': 338. Orenburg served as a location of exile until the mid-nineteenth century and during Catherine II's reign was administered as part of Siberia.
80. Ibid., 335–9.
81. Brenda Meehan-Waters, 'Social and Career Characteristics of the Administrative Elite, 1689–1761', in *Russian Officialdom: The Bureaucratization of Russian Society from the Seventeenth to the Twentieth Century*, ed. Walter McKenzie Pintner and Don Karl Rowney (London: Macmillan, 1980), 91.
82. Robert D. Givens, 'Eighteenth-Century Nobiliary Career Patterns and Provincial Government', in *Russian Officialdom*, 123–4, 129.
83. Letter dated 29 January 1764, quoted in M. O. Akishin, 'Sibirskii gubernator D. I. Chicherin: Raport ober-shter-krigs-komissara G. M. Osipova imperatritse Ekaterine II. 1779 g.', *Istoricheskii arkhiv*, no. 3 (1996): 193–210 [here, p. 193].
84. See V. M. Kabuzan and S. M. Troitskii, 'Dvizhenie naseleniia Sibiri v XVIII v.', in *Sibir´ perioda feodalizma, vypusk 1*, tables 1 and 3, pp. 144, 146; Okladnikov, *Istoriia Sibiri* 2: table, p. 184.
85. The 14,000 male serfs owned by Siberian monasteries in 1762 were converted to state peasants as a result of the state's confiscation of ecclesiastical

lands that year. See V. M. Kabuzan, *Izmeneniia v razmeshchenii naseleniia Rossii v XVIII–pervoi polovine XIX v. (Po materialam revizii)* (Moskva: Nauka, 1971), appendix 2, tables, pp. 63, 111, 113. Kabuzan's total figure for Siberia's peasantry as given on p. 63 is erroneous, as is the corresponding percentage. Cf. Okladnikov, *Istoriia Sibiri* 2: table, p. 183; Shcheglov, *Khronologicheskii perechen'*, table, p. 209.

86. Kabuzan, *Izmeneniia*, appendix 2, tables, p. 78 *et passim*; Kabuzan and Troitskii, 'Dvizhenie', table 3, p. 146.

87. *Novaia perepis' Sibirskago naseleniia* (6th ed.), reproduced in Shcheglov, *Khronologicheskii perechen'*, table, pp. 208–9.

88. George L. Yaney, *The Systematization of Russian Government: Social Evolution in the Domestic Administration of Imperial Russia, 1711–1905* (Urbana, IL: University of Illinois Press, 1973), 68.

89. See Helju Aulik Bennett, '*Chiny, Ordena*, and Officialdom', in *Russian Officialdom*, 187.

90. I. Ia. Foinitskii, *Uchenie o nakazanii v sviazi s tiur'movedeniem* (S.-Peterburg: Tipografiia Ministerstva putei soobshcheniia [A. Benke], 1889), 274–5.

91. Akishin, 'Sibirskii gubernator': 195.

92. Raeff, *Siberia*, 9–10.

93. Evgenii V. Anisimov, *The Reforms of Peter the Great: Progress through Coercion in Russia*, trans. John T. Alexander (Armonk, NY: M. E. Sharpe, 1993), 296.

94. Fel'dstein, *Ssylka*, 131–2, 135.

95. See Michael Roberts, *The Military Revolution, 1560–1660: An Inaugural Lecture Delivered before the Queen's University of Belfast* (Belfast: M. Boyd, 1956); Geoffrey Parker, *The Military Revolution and the Rise of the West, 1500–1800* (Cambridge: Cambridge University Press, 1996); John P. LeDonne, *The Grand Strategy of the Russian Empire: 1650–1831* (New York: Oxford University Press, 2003); idem, *The Russian Empire and the World, 1700–1917: The Geopolitics of Expansion and Containment* (New York: Oxford University Press, 1997); Immanuel Wallerstein, *The Modern World System: Capitalist Agriculture and the Origins of the European World-Economy in the Sixteenth Century* (New York: Academic Press, 1974); idem, *The Modern World-System II: Mercantilism and the Consolidation of the European World-Economy, 1600–1750* (New York: Academic Press, 1980); Robert L. Reynolds, *Europe Emerges: Transition toward an Industrial World-Wide Society, 600–1750* (Madison, WI: University of Wisconsin Press, 1967); Iain Wallace, *The Global Economic System* (Boston: Unwin Hyman, 1990).

96. Anisimov, *Reforms*, 229.

97. Adele Lindenmeyr, *Poverty Is Not a Vice: Charity, Society, and the State in Imperial Russia* (Princeton, NJ: Princeton University Press, 1996), 36ff.

98. A. L. Beier, *Masterless Men: The Vagrancy Problem in England, 1560–1640* (New York: Methuen, 1985).

99. G. V. Shebaldina, *Shvedskie voennoplennye v Sibiri: Pervaia chetvert' XVIII veka* (Moskva: Rossiiskii gosudarstvennyi gumanitarnyi universitet, 2005), 33.

100. Ibid., 41–9.

101. Ibid., 174.

102. Ibid., 60–1.

103. C. H. Van Schooneveld, ed., *Pamiatniki sibirskoi istorii XVIII veka. Kniga vtoraia, 1713–1724* (1885; rpt. The Hague: Mouton, 1969), doc. no. 42, p. 167.

104. Stralenberg, *An histori-geographical description*, 246n. See also Gunnar Jar-ring, 'Swedish Relations with Central Asia and Swedish Central Asian Research', *Asian Affairs* 61, Part III (October 1974): 257–66 [here, pp. 258–60].

105. S. Maksimov, 'Gosudartsvennye prestupniki. Piataia chast'', *Otechestvennyia zapiski* 9 (September 1869): 229–72 [here, pp. 241–2]. Udsk, Anadyrsk and Kolymsk were located in northeastern Siberia; Bratsk, Ilimsk and Balagansk in Zabaikal'e. Tunkinsk seems to have been the pre-revolutionary name of a town in Buriatiia.

106. James R. Gibson, *Feeding the Russian Fur Trade: Provisionment of the Okhotsk Seaboard and the Kamchatka Peninsular, 1639–1856* (Madison, WI: University of Wisconsin Press, 1969), 12.

107. Dmytryshyn, *Russia's Conquest*, doc. no. 132, p. 496.

108. Edward J. Phillips, *The Founding of Russia's Navy: Peter the Great and the Azov Fleet, 1688–1714* (Westport, CT: Greenwood Press, 1995), 40. See also table 2, p. 133.

109. Letter dated 1709 and reproduced in I. I. Kirievskii, ed., *Bulavinskoe vosstanie (1707–1708 gg.)* (Moskva: Izdatel'stvo Vsesoiuznago obshchestva politkat-orzhan i ssyl'no-poselentsev, 1935), 119. See also pp. 124, 360.

110. Quoted in Evgenii Anisimov, *Dyba i knut: politicheskii sysk i russkoe obshchestvo v XVIII veke* (Moskva: Novoe literaturnoe obozrenie, 1999), 650.

111. Stralenberg, *An histori-geographical description*, 310.

112. Okladnikov, *Istoriia Sibiri* 2: 147–51.

113. Richard Hellie, *Slavery in Russia, 1450–1725* (Chicago: University of Chicago Press, 1982).

114. Lucia Zedner, 'Wayward Sisters: The Prison for Women', in *The Oxford History of the Prison: The Practice of Punishment in Western Society*, ed. Norval Morris and David J. Rothman (New York: Oxford University Press, 1995), 295. Zedner gives a date of 1645 for the opening of the *spinhuis*. This is contradicted by Spierenburg, whose date is used here. Cf. Pieter Spierenburg, *The Prison Experience: Disciplinary Institutions and Their Inmates in Early Modern Europe* (New Brunswick: Rutgers University Press, 1991), 51.

115. Anisimov, *Dyba*, 656–7. Anisimov cites letters in which directors explicitly refused to accept old or sickly 'dames' (*baby*).

116. 'Izvlechenie iz otcheta po Upravleniiu Irkutskoiu Guberniiu, za 1839 god. (Okanchanie)', *Zhurnal Ministerstva vnutrennykh del* 38 (October 1840): 25–7.

117. David J. Rothman, *The Discovery of the Asylum: Social Order and Disorder in the New Republic* (Boston, MA: Little, Brown, 1971), xix.

118. Cf. E. J. Simmons, 'The Trial Begins for Soviet Literature', *The Massachusetts Review* 7, no. 4 (1966): 714–24; M. Grayson L. Taylor, 'Prison Psychosis', *Social Justice* 27, no. 3 (2000): 50–5; J. L. Miller et al., 'Perceptions of Justice: Race and Gender Differences in Judgments of Appropriate Prison Sentences', *Law and Society Review* 20, no. 3 (1986): 312–34.

119. Michel Foucault, *Discipline and Punish: The Birth of the Prison* (New York: Vintage, 1977), 25–6.

3   'Punishment for insignificant crimes'

1. Alan Wood, 'Siberian Exile in the Eighteenth Century', *Siberica* 1, no. 1 (1990): 38–63.

2. F. G. Safronov, 'Ssylka v vostochnuiu Sibir´ v pervoi polovine XVIII v.', in *Ssylka i katorga v Sibiri (XVIII–nachalo XXV.)*, ed. L. M. Goriushkin et al. (Novosibirsk: Nauka, 1975), 19–21; Wood, *Siberica*: 47–8. Despite having been abolished by Peter, *voevody* briefly reappeared during Anna's reign.

3. I. V. Shcheglov, *Khronologicheskii perechen´ vazhneishikh dannykh iz istorii Sibiri: 1032–1882 gg.* (1883; rpt. Surgut: Severnyi dom, 1993), 129–30; Wood, *Siberica*: 49; S. Maksimov, 'Gosudartsvennye prestupniki. Piataia chast´, *Otechestvennyia zapiski* 9 (September 1869): 229–72 [here, p. 245].

4. N. M. Iadrintsev, *Russkaia obshchina v tiur´me i ssylke* (S.-Peterburg: Tipografiia A. Morigerovskago, 1872), 514. Cf. Evgenii Anisimov, *Dyba i knut: politicheskii sysk i russkoe obshchestvo v XVIII veke* (Moskva: Novoe literaturnoe obozrenie, 1999), 655; Aleksandr B. Kamenskii, *The Russian Empire in the Eighteenth Century: Searching for a Place in the World*, trans. David Griffiths (Armonk, NY: M. E. Sharpe, 1997), 148.

5. V. A. Il´in, 'Fedor Ivanovich Soimonov', *Voenno-istoricheskii zhurnal* (1988): 94–6; Shcheglov, *Khronologicheskii perechen´*, 148 and n.

6. Maksimov, 'Gosudartsvennye prestupniki': 247. Maksimov cites the Tobol´sk chronicle as the source for this figure.

7. Safronov, 'Ssylka', 34–5; Anisimov, *Dyba*, 649; *Russkii biograficheskii slovar´ v dvadtsati tomakh*, 20 vols. (Moskva: Terra-Knizhnyi klub, 2001) 10: 200.

8. Anisimov, *Dyba*, 653. Although the chancery was established to pursue state criminals, this category expanded to include a number of non-political acts. On the chancery's activities, see ibid., 112ff *et passim*.

9. Iadrintsev, *Russkaia obshchina*, 518, 546. The figure for Siberia's Russian population includes both sexes and is based on those provided in *Tabeli gubernii, provintsii i uezdov s oznacheniem ikh narodonasaleniia v 1766 godu*, as reproduced in Shcheglov, *Khronologicheskii perechen´*, 180. See also A. P. Okladnikov et al., eds., *Istoriia Sibiri s drevneishikh vremen do nashikh dnei*, 5 vols. (Leningrad: Nauka, 1968–9) 2: tables, pp. 183–4.

10. G. Peizen, 'Istoricheskii ocherk kolonizatsii Sibiri', *Sovremennik* 77, no. 9 (1859): 9–46 [here, pp. 22–4]; I. Ia. Foinitskii, *Uchenie o nakazanii v sviazi s tiur´movedeniem* (S.-Peterburg: Tipografiia Ministerstva putei soobshcheniia [A. Benke], 1889), 267; *Ssylka v Sibir´: ocherk eia istorii i sovremennago polozheniia* (S.-Peterburg: Tipografiia S.-Peterburgskoi Tiur´my, 1900), 14–15; Shcheglov, *Khronologicheskii perechen´*, 132; G. S. Fel´dstein, *Ssylka: eia genezisa, znacheniia, istorii i sovremennogo sostoianiia* (Moskva: T-vo skoropechatni A. A. Levenson, 1893), 152, 156; G. M. Lappo, ed., *Goroda Rossii* (Moskva: Nauchnoe izdatel´stvo, 1994), 547. Not all sources agree on the year the Okhotsk colony was attempted.

11. M. M. Gromyko, *Zapadnaia Sibir´ v XVIII v.: Russkoe naselenoe i zemledel´cheskoe osvoenie* (Novosibirsk: 'Nauka' Sibirskoe Otdelenie, 1965), table, p. 55, and p. 94.

12. Iu. I. Smirnov, *Orenburgskaia ekspedistiia (komissiia) i prisoedinenie Zavolzh´ia k Rossii v 30–40-e gg. XVIII veka* (Samara: Samarskii universitet, 1997), 41, table 1, pp. 56–7, table 9, p. 142. For more on the expedition, see Willard Sunderland, *Taming the Wild Field: Colonization and Empire on the Russian Steppe* (Ithaca, NY: Cornell University Press, 2004), 46–9.

13. Sergei Dizhur, 'Russkaia ssylka. Eia istoriia i ozhidaemaia reforma', *Russkoe bogatstvo* 4 (April, 1900): 45–64 [here, pp. 48–9].

14. On the whole, rather than accurately describing the disposition of the exiles in question, 'exile to settlement' became an anachronistic signifier for a penal category whose members continued to be called *ssyl´no-poselentsy* (exile-settlers). Although some receiving this sentence did enter the settlements described, over time the government abandoned the vast majority to existing peasant villages. Also, many so-called exile-settlers lived in *zavody* (see below).

15. Smirnov, *Orenburgskaia ekspeditsiia*, 47. The local commander reported that it was God's will these criminals died.

16. K. I. Protopopov, 'Eniseiskaia politicheskaia ssylka ot dekabristov do 1917 goda', in *Eniseiskaia ssylka: Sbornik eniseiskogo zemliachestva*, ed. V. N. Sokolov (Moskva: Politkatorzhan, 1934), 7.

17. Fel´dstein, *Ssylka*, 156–7. See also Shcheglov, *Khronologicheskii perechen´*, 166–7.

18. The *plet´* was similar to the knout in construction. Harry De Windt, who toured Siberia in 1894, describes it as a heavy whip weighing 8 lb, with a handle 1 foot long and a solid leather lash 2½ feet long tapering into three circular thongs the size of a man's little finger. Harry De Windt, *The New Siberia* (London: Chapman and Hall, 1896), 92.

19. Iadrintsev, *Russkaia obshchina*, 507–8.

20. Tamginsk's workforce totalled 75 laborers. Tel´minsk was originally designed as a state ironworks but its output was unsatisfactory and it was sold to a partnership headed by Iakov Bobrovskii, who transformed it into a textile mill in 1736. Ibid., 518–19; Fel´dstein, *Ssylka*, 140–1; Shcheglov, *Khronologicheskii perechen´*, 160–1; Foinitskii, *Uchenie*, 270; I.I. Komogortsev, 'Iz istorii chernoi metallurgii Vostochnoi Sibiri v XVII–XVIII vv.,' in *Sibir´ perioda feodalizma, vypusk 1*, ed. V. I. Shunkov et al. (Novosibirsk: Izdatel´stvo Sibirskogo otdeleniia AN SSSR), 109–11.

21. M. A. Braginskii, ed., *Nerchinskaia katorga: Sbornik nerchinskogo zemliachestva* (Moskva: Politkatorzhan, 1933), 8; I. Bogoliubskii, *Istoriko-statisticheskii ocherk proizvoditel´nosti Nerchinskago Gornago Okruga s 1703 po 1871 god* (S.-Peterburg: V Tip. V. Demakova, 1872), 1–3; Anon., 'Vzgliad na Dauriiu i v osobennosti na Nerchinskie gornye zavody' [part of a series], *Sibirskii vestnik* 9 (15 May 1823): 107–20 [here, p. 108]; Komogortsev, 'Iz istorii chernoi metallurgii', 100–3; Arcadius Kahan, *The Plow, the Hammer, and the Knout: An Economic History of Eighteenth-Century Russia* (Chicago: University of Chicago Press, 1985), 81, table 3.7, and pp. 84–5. In the 1710s Peter sponsored expeditions to Central Asia and the Irtysh region to search for gold. Although small amounts were mined in Siberia during the eighteenth century, gold mining would not become a significant industry there until the middle of the nineteenth century. Kahan estimates that during the eighteenth century gold production 'was never more than one-third of the [empire's] total value of silver and gold output'. *The Plow*, 81. See also Z. G. Karpenko, *Gornaia i metallurgicheskaia*

promyshlennost' Zapadnoi Sibiri v 1700–1860 godakh (Novosibirsk: Izdatel'stvo Sibirskogo otdeleniia AN SSSR, 1963), 37.

22. W. Bruce Lincoln, *The Conquest of a Continent: Siberia and the Russians* (New York: Random House, 1994), 97.

23. V. I. Semevskii, *Rabochie na sibirskikh zolotykh promyslakh: istoricheskoe izsledovanie*, 2 vols. (S.-Peterburg: Tipografiia M. Stasiulevicha, 1898) 1: xxxi–xii, 296–7; ibid. 2: 565; Shcheglov, *Khronologicheskii perechen'*, 103; Lappo, *Goroda Rossii*, 293; 'Vzgliad na Dauriiu,' *Sibirskii vestnik* 3 (15 February 1823): 27–48 [here, pp. 28–9, 37].

24. Vasilii Otemirov, 'Gramota o pervonachal'nom Gornom proizvodstve v Sibiri', *Sibirskii vestnik* 10 (October 1822): 120–4. Shcheglov writes that Levandian was sent to the Tomsk region in 1696; but if his date is correct, it must have been after Levandian sent his letter to Peter, the date Otemirov provides. Cf. Shcheglov, *Khronologicheskii perechen'*, 98 and n.

25. Anisimov, *Dyba*, 654; Shcheglov, *Khronologicheskii perechen'*, 103, 110, 120, 121; Iadrintsev, *Russkaia obshchina*, 510–11; Safronov, 'Ssylka', 15. Foinitskii claims the government began exiling Old Believers (literally, 'certain *raskol'niki*') to the Caucasus in 1719, but provides no further details. Foinitskii, *Uchenie*, 267.

26. Shcheglov, *Khronologicheskii perechen'*, 167, 168; Foinitskii, *Uchenie*, 268. Figures on silver production in Bogoliubskii, *Istoriko-statisticheskii*, table, p. 8. Cf. Kahan, *The Plow*, table 3.7, pp. 84–5. On the series of ukases relating to Nerchinsk's development during this time, see Shcheglov, *Khronologicheskii perechen'*, 132, 138, 143, 148, 159, 164, 172.

27. Cyril Bryner, 'The Issue of Capital Punishment in the Reign of Elizabeth Petrovna', *Russian Review* 49, no. 4 (1990): 389–416.

28. William Coxe, *Travels in Poland and Russia: Three Volumes in One* (New York: Arno Press, 1970) 3: 116–17.

29. Iadrintsev, *Russkaia obshchina*, 507-8; Shcheglov, *Khronologicheskii perechen'*, 132, 138, 143, 148, 159, 164, 167, 168, 172.

30. John P. LeDonne, *Ruling Russia: Politics and Administration in the Age of Absolutism, 1762–1796* (Princeton, NJ: Princeton University Press, 1984), 188 and see discussion beginning on p. 186.

31. Sidney Monas, *The Third Section: Police and Society in Russia under Nicholas I* (Cambridge, MA: Harvard University Press, 1961), 58–9.

32. Jonathan W. Daly, 'Criminal Punishment and Europeanization in Late Imperial Russia', *Jahrbücher für Geschichte Osteuropas* 47 (2000): 341–62 [here, table 3, p. 348].

33. Dostoevskii, who served time during the 1850s, remarks on fellow prisoners' tattooed faces in *Notes from a Dead House*; and a photograph from the period shows a convict with a 'K' tattooed on his forehead and letters on each cheek. Photo reproduced in Lincoln, *Conquest*; Benson Bobrick, *East of the Sun: The Epic Conquest and Tragic History of Siberia* (New York: Poseiden Press, 1992). Frequent references to fugitive exiles being identifiable by tattoos appear in early nineteenth century documents from Irkutsk *guberniia*. See GAIO, f. 435, op. 1.

34. Foinitskii, *Uchenie*, 273–4. See also Shcheglov, *Khronologicheskii perechen'*, 160–1.

35. *Ssylka v Sibir´*, 46–7; V. M. Kabuzan and S. M. Troitskii, 'Dvizhenie naseleniia Sibiri v XVIII v.,' in *Sibir´ perioda feodalizma, vypusk 1*, 149.

36. Alan Wood, 'Crime and Punishment in the House of the Dead', in *Civil Rights in Imperial Russia*, ed. Olga Crisp and Linda Edmondson (Oxford: Clarendon Press, 1989), 221; idem, *Siberica*: 55; idem, 'Administrative Exile and the Criminals' Commune in Siberia', in *Land Commune and Peasant Community in Russia: Communal Forms in Imperial and Early Soviet Society*, ed. Roger Bartlett (New York: St. Martin's Press, 1990), 396–7; V. N. Dvorianov, *V sibirskoi dal´nei storone . . . (ocherki istorii politicheskoi katorgi i ssylki. 60-e gody XVIII v.–1917 g.)* (Minsk: Nauka i tekhnika, 1985), 26–8.

37. Jerome Blum, *Lord and Peasant in Russia: From the Ninth to the Nineteenth Century* (Princeton, NJ: Princeton University Press, 1961), 430.

38. Kabuzan and Troitskii, 'Dvizhenie', 149.

39. Quoted in W. Bruce Lincoln, *The Romanovs: Autocrats of All the Russias* (New York: Doubleday, 1981), 301.

40. Coxe, *Travels* 1: 112–13.

41. Shcheglov, *Khronologicheskii perechen´*, 183, 197, 199 and cf. 266–7; Fel´dstein, *Ssylka*, 154–6; Anisimov, *Dyba*, 652-3; Iadrintsev, *Russkaia obshchina*, 507–8.

42. Reproduced in *Ssylka v Sibir´*, 13–14 [ellipsis in original].

43. Foinitskii, *Uchenie*, 270–2.

44. *Ssylka v Sibir´*, 12. Anisimov writes that, during a flood in 1777, 300 prisoners perished in the jail on Vasil´evskii Island. However, this seems to have been a different structure from the one later built there. Anisimov, *Dyba*, 658.

45. M. N. Gernet, *Istoriia tsarskoi tiur´my*, 5 vols., 3rd edn. (Moskva: Gosudarstvennoe izdatel´stvo iuridicheskoi literatury, 1960–63) 1: 238, 354 *et passim*, and ch. 6.

46. Shcheglov, *Khronologicheskii perechen´*, 183; Laura Engelstein, *Castration and the Heavenly Kingdom: A Russian Folktale* (Ithaca, NY: Cornell University Press, 1999); Isabel de Madariaga, *Russia in the Age of Catherine the Great* (New Haven, CT: Yale University Press, 1981), 239ff.

47. Cf. Marc Raeff, *Siberia and the Reforms of 1822* (Seattle: University of Washington Press, 1956), 17.

48. Shcheglov, *Khronologicheskii perechen´*, 83–4n., 91.

49. A. M. Selishchev, *Zabaikal´skie staroobriadtsy. Semeiskie* (Irkutsk: Izdanie Gosudarstvennago Irkutskago Universiteta, 1920), 71–2, 74; 'O sostoianii novykh poselenii v iuzhnoi Sibiri, i o tamoshchnem pchelovodstve. (Iz *Nordisches Archiv. juni* 1803. Sochinenie G. Berensa.) (Soobshcheno.),' *Sibirskii vestnik* 2 (1820): 293–305; N. A. Minenko, 'Ssyl´nye krest´iane – 'poliaki' na Altae v XVIII–pervoi polovine XIX v.', in *Politicheskie ssyl´nye v Sibiri (XVIII–nachalo XX v.)*, ed. L. M. Goriushkin (Novosibirsk: Nauka, 1983), 199, 201–2; 'Zapiski o Sibiri. (Prolozhenie.) Kratkoe opisanie Zabaikal´skago kraia,' *Zhurnal Ministerstva Vnutrennykh Del* 3 (1830): 165–82 [here, pp. 173–4]; Jeanne Haskett, 'Decembrist N. A. Bestuzhev in Siberian Exile, 1826–55', *Studies in Romanticism* 4, no. 4 (1965): 185–205 [here, p. 193].

50. Quoted in Anisimov, *Dyba*, 132. See also 124–37.

51. Iadrintsev, *Russkaia obshchina*, 522–3. See also LeDonne, *Ruling Russia*, 86–8, 105 *et passim*. Cf. Madariaga, *Catherine* (1981), 559ff.

52. Madariaga, *Catherine* (1981), 240–1, 258.

53. Jesse Clardy, 'Radishchev's Notes on the Geography of Siberia', *Russian Review* 21, no. 4 (1962): 362–9 [here, p. 369]; Anisimov, *Dyba*, 635. See also David Marshall Lang, *The First Russian Radical: Alexander Radishchev, 1749–1802* (London: Allen & Unwin, 1959), 216 *et passim*; Susi K. Frank, 'Aleksandr Radishchev's Interpretation of Shamanism in the Russian and European Context of the Late Eighteenth Century', in *The Siberian Saga: A History of Russia's Wild East*, ed. Eva-Maria Stolberg (Frankfurt-am-Main: Lang, 2005), 43–61.

54. Braginskii, *Nerchinskaia katorga*, 31.

55. These reports are contained in GAIO, f. 24, op. 3, k. 1, d. 11. One dated 8 October 1825 is reproduced, along with some additional information on later reports, in L. M. Goriushkin, ed., *Politicheskaia ssylka v Sibiri: Nerchinskaia katorga* (Novosibirsk: Sibirskii khronograf, 1993), doc. no. 2.

56. Antoni Kuczynski, 'La contribution des Polonais au processus de civilisation de la Sibérie au début de la colonisation russe', in *Sibérie II: Questions sibériennes*, ed. Boris Chichlo (Paris: Insitut d'études slaves, 1999), 241. Concerning those Poles allowed to return home, it appears many obtained this right almost immediately after arriving in Siberia due to the Pugachev rebellion. Recall that in her manifesto abolishing exile, Catherine wrote of 'not an insignificant number of Poles... awaiting resettlement to their homelands'.

57. Ibid., 243; Selishchev, *Zabaikal'skie staroobriadtsy*, 74.

58. As reported in an Irkutsk Guberniia Administration circular dated 6 June 1829. GAIO, f. 435, op. 1, d. 155, l. 308.

59. V. Anastevich, trans., 'Puteshestvie ks[endza] Fadeia Mashevskago iz Irkutska v Nerchinsk (1817 g.) (*Miesiecznih Polocki*[,] N[o.] VIII, 1818 g.[,] str. 298–306)', *Sibirskii vestnik* 14 (1821): 219-34; Minenko, 'Ssyl'nye krest'iane,' 200–2.

60. S. V. Maksimov, *Sibir' i katorga*, 3rd edn. (S.-Peterburg: Izdanie V. I. Gubinskago, 1900), 337. See also Boleslav Shostakovich, 'Irkutskie stranitsy "Dnevnika" ssyl'nogo kostiushkovtsa Iuzef Koptsa (k 200-letiiu pol'skogo vostaniia 1794g.)', *Zemlia irkutskaia* 2 (1994): 46–51; ibid., 3 (1995): 60–2.

61. Oliver Pasfield, ed., *The Memoirs of Mauritius Augustus Count de Benyowsky in Siberia, Kamchatka, Japan, the Liukiu Islands and Formosa*, trans. William Nicholson (New York: Macmillan, 1893), *passim*. See also Maksimov, *Sibir'* (1900), 331–6; Marina Vasilenko, '"Bunt ot soslannykh zlodeev ..."', *Zemlia irkutskaia* 3 (1995): 27–9; G. Patrick March, *Eastern Destiny: Russia in Asia and the North Pacific* (Westport, CT: Praeger, 1996), 77; Edward Kajdanski, 'The Authenticity of Maurice Benyowsky's Account of His Voyage through the Bering Sea: The Earliest Description and the Earliest Drawings of St. Lawrence Island', *Terrae Incognitae* 23 (1991): 51–80.

62. Shcheglov, *Khronologicheskii perechen'*, 192; Iadrintsev, *Russkaia obshchina*, 507–8, 515.

63. Gromyko, *Zapadnaia Sibir'*, 101; Okladnikov, *Istoriia Sibiri* 2: 191. See also LeDonne, *Ruling Russia*, 278ff.

64. Peizen, *Sovremennik*: 25.

65. Gromyko, *Zapadnaia Sibir'*, 101–2 and table 29, p. 103.

66. Gernet, *Istoriia* 1: 65; *Ssylka v Sibir'*, 15. See also Shcheglov, *Khronologicheskii perechen'*, 132; Fel'dstein, *Ssylka*, 156.

67. Okladnikov, *Istoriia Sibiri* 2: 190.

68. Gernet, *Istoriia* 1: 65.

69. Okladnikov, *Istoriia Sibiri* 1: table, p. 190.

70. LeDonne, *Ruling Russia*, 280. See also Kabuzan and Troitskii, 'Dvizhenie naselenie', table 4, p. 150; Robert D. Givens, 'Eighteenth-Century Nobiliary Career Patterns and Provincial Government', in *Russian Officialdom: The Bureaucratization of Russian Society from the Seventeenth to the Twentieth Century*, ed. Walter McKenzie Pintner and Don Karl Rowney (London: Macmillan, 1980), 117 *et passim*; Walter M. Pintner, 'The Evolution of Civil Officialdom, 1755–1855,' in ibid., 209; Richard E. Pipes, 'The Russian Military Colonies, 1810–1831,' *Journal of Modern History* 22, no. 3 (September 1950): 205–19 [here, p. 207]; T. N. Kandaurova and B. B. Davydov, 'Voennye poseleniia v otsenke', *Vestnik Moskovskogo Universiteta. Seriia VIII: Istoriia* 2 (1992): 44–55.

71. A. D. Kolesnikov, 'Ssylka i zaselenie Sibiri', in *Ssylka i katorga v Sibiri (XVIII–nachalo XX v.)*, ed. L. M. Goriushkin et al. (Novosibirsk: Nauka, 1975), 51; Wood, *Siberica*: 56, 59; *Memoirs of...Benyowsky*, 95. Revision cited in Dvorianov, *V sibirskoi storone*, 29.

72. Stephen D. Watrous, ed., *John Ledyard's Journey through Russia and Siberia, 1787–1788: The Journal and Selected Letters* (Madison, WI: University of Wisconsin Press, 1966), 152–3.

73. N. V. Sushkov, 'O Sibirskikh solianykh promyslakh,' *Sibirskii vestnik* 14 (1821): 225–74, 315–26 [here, p. 271 and n.]; S. Maksimov, 'Sibirskaia sol´', in *Zhivopisnaia Rossiia. Otechestvo nashe v ego zemel´nom, istoricheskom, plemennom, ekonomicheskom i bytovom znachenii*, ed. P. P Semenov (S.-Peterburg: Izdanie Tovarishchestva M. O. Vol´f, 1895), 319. See also related chapters in V. B. Borodaev et al., eds., *Guliaevskie chteniia. Vyp. 1: Materialy pervoi, vtoroi i tret´ei istoriko-arkhivnykh konferentsii* (Barnaul: Upravlenie arkhivnogo dela administratsii Altaiskogo kraia and Laboratoriia istoricheskogo kraevedeniia Barnaul´skogo gosudarstvennogo pedagogicheskogo universiteta, 1998).

74. 'Vzgliad na Dauriiu', *Sibirskii vestnik* 3 (15 February 1823): 28–9; Bogoliubskii, *Istoriko-statisticheskii ocherk*, 3 and tables, pp. 4, 8, 16–17.

75. Braginskii, *Nerchinskaia katorga*, 20; Gernet, *Istoriia* 1: 305.

76. Madariaga, *Catherine* (1981), 469.

77. Quoted in Anisimov, *Dyba*, 655.

78. Okladnikov, *Istoriia Sibiri* 2: 252; 'Vzgliad na Dauriiu', *Sibirskii vestnik* 9 (15 May 1823): 110–19; Komogortsev, 'Iz istorii chernoi metallurgii', 117.

79. Okladnikov, *Istoriia Sibiri* 2: 311. Prior to Naryshkin Vasilii Suvorov, cousin of the famous marshal, was commandant from 1763 to 1774. He vastly increased the district's output. Information on commandants during the remainder of the eighteenth century is scarce. It is not clear when Naryshkin was appointed, but he seems to have been removed in the mid-1770s judging by Nemtsov's dates. A Commandant Bekkel´man is cited as being in charge in 1785; and LeDonne writes that a Major-General Karl Handtwig (Gantvig) was appointed to the post in 1786. Barbot de Marni was commandant during at least the years 1788–92, if not longer. Cf. LeDonne, *Ruling Russia*, 283; Bogoliubskii, *Istoriko-statisticheskii ocherk*, 5; Braginskii, *Nerchinskaia katorga*, 14; 'Vzgliad na Dauriiu,' *Sibirskii vestnik* 9 (15 March 1823): 107–20 [here, pp. 118–19].

80. Braginskii, *Nerchinskaia katorga*, 9–10, 14–15; 'Vzgliad na Dauriiu,' *Sibirskii vestnik* 5 (15 March 1823): 49–54.

81. Braginskii, *Nerchinskaia katorga*, 16.

82. Braginskii argues, 'Chronic starvation was one of the causes of massive flight by exiles from *katorga* sites.' Ibid., 9; see also 9–11, 14. Cf. Kahan, *The Plow*, 372 n. 14. See also Okladnikov, *Istoriia Sibiri* 2: 339–40.

83. Okladnikov, *Istoriia Sibiri* 2: 339–40; Braginskii, *Nerchinskaia*, 9–11, 14.

84. Fel'dstein, *Ssylka*, 159–60.

85. Quote and Laba figure in ibid; also in Peizen, 'Istoricheskii ocherk': 30.

4 'Whoever's not with us is against us'

1. I. V. Shcheglov, *Khronologicheskii perechen´ vazhneishikh dannykh iz istorii Sibiri: 1032–1882 gg.* (1883; rpt. Surgut: Severnyi dom, 1993), 213. The workhouse (*rabochii dom*), also referred to in various sources as a crafts house (*remeslennyi dom*), is briefly noted in Nadezhda Bubis, 'Irkutskii tiuremnyi zamok', *Zemlia irkutskaia* 10 (1998): 51–6 [here, p. 52].

2. N. M. Iadrintsev, *Russkaia obshchina v tiur´me i ssylke* (S.-Peterburg: Tipografiia A. Morigerovskago, 1872), 520; I. Ia. Foinitskii, *Uchenie o nakazanii v sviazi s tiur´movedeniem* (S.-Peterburg: Tipografiia Ministerstva putei soobshcheniia [A. Benke], 1889), 271–4; Shcheglov, *Khronologicheskii perechen´*, 208, 210, 211.

3. Marc Raeff, *Siberia and the Reforms of 1822* (Seattle: University of Washington Press, 1956), 12.

4. G. Peizen, 'Istoricheskii ocherk kolonizatsii Sibiri', *Sovremennik* 77, no. 9 (1859): 9–46 [here, pp. 28–30]; *Ssylka v Sibir´: ocherk eia istorii i sovremennago polozheniia* (S.-Peterburg: Tipografiia S.-Peterburgskoi Tiur´my, 1900), 15; G. S. Fel'dstein, *Ssylka: eia genezisa, znacheniia, istorii i sovremennogo sostoianiia* (Moskva: T-vo skoropechatni A. A. Levenson, 1893), 157–8; Foinitskii, *Uchenie*, 276–7 and n.; Raeff, *Siberia*, 18–19.

5. Jane Hubert, ed., *Madness, Disability and Social Exclusion: The Archaeology and Anthropology of 'Difference'* (New York: Routledge, 2000).

6. John P. LeDonne, 'Frontier Governors General 1772–1825. III. The Eastern Frontier', *Jahrbücher für Geschichte Osteuropas* 48 (2000): 321–40 [here, p. 330].

7. Vladimir A. Tomsinov, *Speranskii* (Moskva: Molodaia gvardiia, 2006), 310; Foinitskii, *Uchenie*, 277–8; Raeff, *Siberia*, 21; Stanislav Arkhipovich Chibiriaev, *Velikii russkii reformator: Zhizn´, deiatel´nost´, politicheskie vzgliady M. M. Speranskogo* (Moskva: Nauka, 1989), 113; LeDonne, 'Eastern Frontier': 330–1; Anatolii Viktorovich Remnev, 'Prokonsul Sibiri Ivan Borisovich Pestel´', *Voprosy istorii*, no. 2 (1997): 141–9.

8. GAIO, f. 435, op. 1, d. 94, ll. 264–5.

9. *Ssylka v Sibir´*, appendices, table, pp. 1–2.

10. Steven L. Hoch, *Serfdom and Social Control in Russia: Petrovskoe, a Village in Tambov* (Chicago: University of Chicago, 1986), 151.

11. Rodney D. Bohac, 'Widows and the Russian Serf Community', in *Russia's Women: Accommodation, Resistance, Transformation*, ed. Barbara Evan Clements et al. (Berkeley, CA: University of California Press, 1991), tables 1 and 3, pp. 98, 100 *et passim*.

12. See figures in Jerome Blum, *Lord and Peasant in Russia: From the Ninth to the Nineteenth Century* (Princeton, NJ: Princeton University Press, 1961), 557–8. See also Rodney Bohac, 'Everyday Forms of Resistance: Serf Opposition to Gentry Exactions, 1800–1861', in *Peasant Economy, Culture, and Politics of*

European Russia, 1800–1921, ed. Esther Kingston-Mann and Timothy Mixter (Princeton, NJ: Princeton University Press, 1991), 236–60. Marxist scholars characterize these peasant disturbances as representative of the revolutionary class struggle which brought about the end of Russia's feudal period of development. See e.g. A. S. Nagaev, *Omskoe delo, 1832–1833* (Krasnoiarsk: Krasnoiarskii universitet, 1991), 23–5; S. V. Kodan, 'Osvoboditel´noe dvizhenie i sibirskaia ssylka (1825–1861 gg.)', in *Politicheskie ssyl´nye v Sibiri (XVIII–nachalo XX v.)*. ed. L. M. Goriushkin (Novosibirsk: Nauka, 1983), 152–67.

13. A. P. Okladnikov et al., eds., *Istoriia Sibiri s drevneishikh vremen do nashikh dnei*, 5 vols. (Leningrad: Nauka, 1968-9) 2: 455; V. M. Kabuzan, *Narodonaselenie Rossii v XVIII–pervoi polovine XIX v.* (Moskva: AN SSSR, 1963), table 17, p. 161.

14. Marc Raeff, *Imperial Russia, 1682–1825: The Coming of Age in Modern Russia* (New York: Knopf, 1971), 111.

15. Adam Zamoyski, *1812: Napoleon's Fatal March on Moscow* (London: Harper Perennial, 2004), 201. See also Avrahm Yarmolinsky, *Road to Revolution: A Century of Russian Radicalism* (Princeton, NJ: Princeton University Press, 1957), 16–17.

16. Cf. Douglas Hay, 'War, Dearth and Theft in the Eighteenth Century: The Record of the English Courts', *Past & Present* 95 (1982): 117–60 [esp. pp. 124–6]; Vadim Volkov, 'The Political Economy of Protection Rackets in the Past and the Present', *Social Research* 67, n. 3 (2000): 706–42; Karen Elizabeth Myers, 'The Relationship of Post-Traumatic Stress Disorder and the Incarcerated Vietnam Veteran' (PhD dissertation, United States International University, 1983).

17. Alexander's understanding of the invasion is exemplified by a manifesto he issued in December 1812 proclaiming construction of a monument-cathedral to commemorate Russia's deliverance from evil. See Andrew Gentes, 'The Life, Death and Resurrection of the Cathedral of Christ the Saviour, Moscow', *History Workshop Journal* 46 (Autumn 1998): 63–95. On his mysticism, see Allen McConnell, *Tsar Alexander I: Paternalistic Reformer* (New York: Thomas Y. Crowell, 1970), 134–5; Alan Palmer, *Alexander I: Tsar of War and Peace* (New York: Harper & Row, 1974), 318–20, 318 n, 325–7, 334–5; Madame la Comtesse de Choiseul-Gouffier, *Historical Memoirs of the Emperor Alexander I and the Court of Russia*, trans. Mary Berenice Patterson (Chicago: A. C. McClurg & Co., 1900), 152–3 n.

18. W. Bruce Lincoln, *The Romanovs: Autocrats of All the Russias* (New York: Doubleday, 1981), 557.

19. Okladnikov, *Istoriia Sibiri* 2: 455. Documents on Caucasian tribesmen and Poles exiled during Alexander's reign are in GARF, f. 1183, op. 1, d. 55; ibid., d. 137.

20. GAIO, f. 435, op. 1, d. 147, ll. 200, 203.

21. Blum, *Lord*, 314–15.

22. GAIO f. 435, op. 1, d. 133, l. 251. For examples of other *skoptsy* exiled before and after 1822, see GAIO, f. 24, op. 3, k. 36, d. 50, ll. 3–10. For information and figures on religious groups exiled during this period, see T. S. Mamsik, 'Ssyl´nye religioznye protestanty v Sibiri v pervoi chetverti XIX v. (pravitel´stvennaia politika)', in *Politicheskie ssyl´nye v Sibiri*, 177–97.

23. *Ssylka v Sibir´*, 49–50.
24. Cf. Richard Pipes, *Russia Under the Old Regime* (New York: Charles Scribner's Sons, 1974), 152; E. N. Anuchin, *Izsledovaniia o protsente soslannykh v Sibir´ v period 1827–1846 godov: materialy dlia ugolovnoi statistiki Rossii* (S.-Peterburg: Tipografiia Maikova, 1873), tables, pp. 18, 22, 23.
25. Blum, *Lord*, 431.
26. *Ssylka v Sibir´*, 50–1; Iadrintsev, *Russkaia obshchina*, 524–5.
27. *Ssylka v Sibir´*, 49–54.
28. Ibid.
29. N. M. Iadrintsev, *Sibir´ kak koloniia v geograficheskom, etnograficheskom i dopolnennoe*, ed. L. M. Goriushkin et al. (Novosibirsk: Sibirskii khronograf, 2003), 350.
30. LeDonne, 'Eastern Frontier': 330–1; Raeff, *Siberia*, 21ff; Tomsinov, *Speranskii*, 312; V. I. Shteingeil´, *Sochineniia i pis´ma*, 2 vols. (Irkutsk: Vostochno-Sibirskoe knizhnoe izdatel´stvo, 1985, 1992) 2: 193.
31. Shteingeil´, *Sochineniia* 2: 197 [original ellipsis].
32. Ibid., 199. See also Liudmila Elizarova, 'Istoriia Krugobaikal´skogo trakta', *Zemlia irkutskaia* 4 (1995): 22–7.
33. Raeff, *Siberia*, 28–33.
34. Irina Dameshek, 'Mikhail Speranskii', *Zemlia irkutskaia* 8 (1997): 2–9 [here, p. 4].
35. Shteingel´, *Sochineniia* 2: 198.
36. Raeff, *Siberia*, 34–5.
37. Iadrintsev, *Sibir´ kak koloniia* (2003), 353.
38. John Dundas Cochrane, *A Pedestrian Journey through Russia and Siberian Tartary to the Frontiers of China, the Frozen Sea and Kamchatka*, ed. and intro. Mervyn Horder (1823; rpt. London: Folio Society, 1983), 119.
39. Shteingel´, *Sochineniia* 2: 194–5, 380 n. 47 and n. 50; Iadrintsev, *Sibir´ kak koloniia* (2003), 353.
40. The only reference to this project was found in Shcheglov, *Khronologicheskii perechen´*, 221.
41. Ibid., 224–5; Sergei Dizhur, 'Russkaia ssylka. Eia istoriia i ozhidaemaia reforma', *Russkoe bogatstvo* 4 (April 1900): 45–64 [here, pp. 48–9]; Foinitskii, *Uchenie*, 277.
42. Fel´dstein, *Ssylka*, 159.
43. See GAIO, f. 435, op. 1, d. 87; d. 94; d. 133.
44. Dizhur, 'Russkaia ssylka': 48–9; Fel´dstein, *Ssylka*, 159; *Ssylka v Sibir´*, 16.; Raeff, *Siberia*, 25–6, 162 n. 43; Peizen, 'Istoricheskii ocherk': 33.
45. Raeff, *Siberia*, 18–19; Peizen, 'Istoricheskii ocherk': 34–5. Figures on the average number of exiles per annum in *Ssylka v Sibir´*, appendices, table, pp. 1–2; P. I. Liublinskii, 'Glavneishie momenty razvitiia ugolovnogo prava i suda v dorevoliutsionnoi R[ossii]', in *Entsiklopedicheskii slovar´ Russkogo Bibliograficheskago Instituta Granata*, 7th edn., vol. 36, part V (Moskva: Russkii Bibliograficheskii Institut Granat, n.d.), table, p. 643; S. S. Ostroumov, *Prestupnost´ i ee prichiny v dorevoliutsionnoi Rossii* (Moskva: Izdatel´stvo universiteta, 1980), table 22, p. 53.
46. Peizen, 'Istoricheskii ocherk': 34, 35; Raeff, *Siberia*, 18–19; *Ssylka v Sibir´*, appendices, table, pp. 1–2.
47. Fel´dstein, *Ssylka*, 159.

48. Quoted in Raeff, *Siberia*, 162 n.43. See also Shteingel´, *Sochineniia* 2: 381 n. 63.
49. *Ssylka v Sibir´*, 16. The anecdote is quoted in Marc Raeff, *Michael Speransky: Statesman of Imperial Russia, 1772–1839* (The Hague: Martinus Nijhoff, 1957), 253–4; Shcheglov, *Khronologicheskii perechen´*, 246; Chibiriaev, *Velikii russkii reformator*, 116.
50. GAIO, f. 435, op. 1, d. 87, l. 50; d. 94, ll. 21-2, 174, 351.
51. Ibid., l. 446; d. 94, ll. 19, 243–5.
52. Ibid., d. 94, l. 237.
53. E.g., ibid., ll. 243–4.
54. Ibid., d. 87, l. 48.
55. Ibid., d. 87, ll. 48, 72, 123.
56. Ibid., d. 87, ll. 87, 267. For numerous other examples see ibid., d. 94, *passim*.
57. Ibid., d. 94, l. 85. For a similar instruction see ibid., l. 130.
58. Ibid., d. 133, ll. 27–8, 62.
59. Ibid., ll. 252–6.
60. Ibid., l. 108.
61. Ibid., d. 94, ll. 104–5.
62. Ibid., d. 87, ll. 118–19.
63. Ibid., l. 68.
64. Ibid., d. 94, l. 326.
65. Ibid., d. 133, ll. 166, 171–3 [interpolated single document]. This is an IGP circular dated 20 September 1820 concerning contemporary crime issues and tracing the history of the previous measures taken.
66. Ibid.
67. Iadrintsev, *Russkaia obshchina*, 488ff.
68. Relevant GAIO *fondy* covering this period were unavailable because of mold contamination.
69. Exile figure is in *Ssylka v Sibir´*, appendices, table, pp. 1–2. Figure on *guberniia* population is in G. Spasskii, 'Nechto o Russkikh v Sibiri starozhilakh', *Sibirskii vestnik* 1 (1818): 122–7 [here, table appended to the review on pp. 206–12]. The *guberniia's* total male population was 268,102. Kabuzan gives a somewhat higher figure of 291,772, but makes no distinction between indigenes and others. Cf. Kabuzan, *Narodonaselenie*, table 17, p. 161.
70. GAIO, f. 435, op. 1, d. 133, l. 166.
71. Ibid., l. 266.
72. Ibid., ll. 166, 171–3.
73. What follows is based on Raeff, *Speransky*; Chibiriaev, *Velikii russkii reformator*; Tomsinov, *Speranskii*.
74. This should not be confused with the Siberian Committee convened in 1821 (see chapter 5).
75. Quoted in Tomsinov, *Speranskii*, 296.
76. Alexander quoted in Raeff, *Speransky*, 252–3; his opinion concerning Speranskii's stay in Irkutsk is cited in idem, *Siberia*, 40. See also Dameshek, 'Mikhail Speranskii': 2-9; LeDonne, 'Eastern Frontier': 331–2.
77. Quoted in Tomsinov, *Speranskii*, 304.
78. Letter dated 5 April 1819 quoted in Chibiriaev, *Velikii russkii reformator*, 113.
79. Cf. Raeff, *Siberia*, 38–40.
80. Quoted in Tomsinov, *Speranskii*, 319.
81. Ibid., 322.

82. Quoted in ibid., 324.
83. Sidney Monas, *The Third Section: Police and Society in Russia under Nicholas I* (Cambridge, MA: Harvard University Press, 1961), 47. Later, under Nicholas I, the police acquired significant authority to surveil all levels of officialdom throughout the entire empire. See ibid., *passim*; Jonathan W. Daly, *Autocracy under Siege: Security Police and Opposition in Russia, 1866–1905* (DeKalb, IL: Northern Illinois University Press, 1998), *passim*.
84. Quoted in Dameshek, 'Mikhail Speranskii': 5, 6 [ellipses in source].
85. Trend demonstrated by the following three articles, all in *Russian Officialdom*, comprising pp. 130–249: Bruce W. Menning, 'The Emergence of a Military-Administrative Elite in the Don Cossack Land, 1708–1836'; Bennett, '*Chiny, Ordena*, and Officialdom'; Pintner, 'Evolution'.
86. Pipes, *Old Regime*, 284.
87. Raeff, *Speransky*, 235.
88. GAIO, f. 435, op. 1, d. 133, l. 166.
89. Quoted in Tomsinov, *Speranskii*, 325.
90. GAIO, d. 435, op. 1, d. 94, ll. 553–63.
91. Ibid., d. 133, ll. 166, 171–3.
92. This term probably signifies epilepsy and its presence here suggests this was a common reason for deportation.
93. Ibid.

5   'Only Ermak can compete with me'

1. Quoted in Marc Raeff, *Michael Speransky: Statesman of Imperial Russia, 1772–1839* (The Hague: Martinus Nijhoff, 1957), 267.
2. Irina Dameshek, 'Mikhail Speranskii', *Zemlia irkutskaia* 8 (1997): 2–9 [here, p. 6]; I. V. Shcheglov, *Khronologicheskii perechen´ vazhneishikh dannykh iz istorii Sibiri: 1032–1882 gg.* (1883; rpt. Surgut: Severnyi dom, 1993), 251.
3. Bruce F. Adams, *The Politics of Punishment: Prison Reform in Russia, 1863–1917* (DeKalb, IL: Northern Illinois University Press, 1996), 40–5 *et passim*. Adams gives the name of the society as *Popechitel´noe Obshchesvto o Tiur´makh*, for which he creates the acronym POoT. In the archival documents I found the society's name appears as above. Hence the different acronym. See also V. N. Nikitin, *Tiur´ma i ssylka: Istoricheskoe, zakonodatel´noe, administrativnoe i bytovoe polozhenie zakliuchennykh, peresyl´nykh, ikh detei i osvobozhnennykh iz pod strazhi, so vremeni vozniknoveniia russkoi tiur´my, do nashikh dnei, 1560–1880 g.* (S.-Peterburg: Tipografiia G. Shparvart, 1880), chs. 2–5 (despite this work's title it contains almost no discussion of exile and less than ten pages devoted to the period before 1822); Judith C. Zacek, 'A Case Study in Russian Philanthropy: The Prison Reform Movement in the Reign of Alexander I', *Canadian Slavic Studies/Revue canadienne d'études slaves* 1, no. 2 (1967): 196–211. John Venning continued the work of his brother Walter after the latter's death in 1821. See Thulia S. Henderson, ed., *Memorials of John Venning, Esq., with Numerous Notices from His Manuscripts Relative to the Imperial Family of Russia* (1862; rpt. Cambridge: Oriental Research Partners, 1975); Barry Hollingsworth, 'John Venning and Prison Reform in Russia, 1819–1830', *Slavonic and East European Review* 48, no. 113 (1970): 537–56.

4. M. N. Gernet, *Istoriia tsarskoi tiur'my*, 5 vols. 3rd edn. (Moskva: Gosudarstven-noe izdatel'stvo iuridicheskoi literatury, 1960–63) 2: 17–35.

5. Quoted in Adams, *Politics*, 43.

6. Douglas Smith, 'Freemasonry and the Public in Eighteenth-Century Russia', in *Imperial Russia: New Histories for the Empire*, ed. Jane Burbank and David L. Ransel (Bloomington and Indianapolis: Indiana University Press, 1998), 293.

7. Originally published as *Uchrezhdenie dlia upravleniia Sibirskikh gubernii* (Sankt-peterburg: Pechatano v Senatskoi Tipografii, 1822). This text, and not that in *Pol'noe Sobranie Zakonov*, is analysed here since it better reflects the Siberian Committee's intentions as well as its foibles.

8. These units were originally termed *okrugi* (sing., *okruga*); however, *okrug* (sing.) soon replaced *okruga* (sing.) in official usage (note, however, the use of *okruga* [sing.] in the early years of Priamur *krai*), with no apparent change in meaning or function. For purposes of simplification, *okrug* (*okruga*, pl.) is used here throughout.

9. Cf. A. G. Pshenichnyi, 'Upravlenie Kolyvano-Voskresenskogo gornogo okruga v kontse 20-kh godov XIX veka', in *Guliaevskie chteniia. Vyp. 1: Materialy pervoi, vtoroi i tret'ei istoriko-arkhivnykh konferentsii*, ed. V. B. Borodaev et al. (Barnaul: Upravlenie arkhivnogo dela administratsii Altaiskogo kraia and Laboratoriia istoricheskogo kraevedeniia Barnaul'skogo gosudarstvennogo pedagogicheskogo universiteta, 1998), 257–62.

10. This and most of what follows is from [Anon.], 'O novykh postanovleniiakh dlia upravleniia Sibiri', *Sibirskii vestnik* 9 (September 1822): 1–28; Marc Raeff, *Siberia and the Reforms of 1822* (Seattle: University of Washington Press, 1956), 73ff.; N. P. Eroshkin, *Ocherki istorii gosudarstvennykh uchrezhdenii dorevoliutsion-noi Rossii* (Moskva: Gosudarstvennoe Uchebno-Pedagogicheskoe Izdatel'stvo Ministerstva Prosveshcheniia RSFSR, 1960), 240ff.

11. N. P. Matkhanova, *Vysshaia administratsiia Vostochnoi Sibiri v Seredine XIX veka: Problemy Sotsial'noi stratifikatsii* (Novosibirsk: sibirskii khronograf, 2002), 37.

12. George L. Yaney, *The Systematization of Russian Government: Social Evolution in the Domestic Administration of Imperial Russia, 1711–1905* (Urbana, IL: University of Illinois Press, 1973), 218. On the relationship of governor-generalships to the ministries, see ibid., 215ff. The writer to whom Yaney refers would have been either Western Siberia's governor-general P. D. Gorchakov or his Eastern Siberian counterpart, V. I. Rupert. A. G. Stroganov replaced D. N. Bludov as interior minister sometime during 1839.

13. Raeff, *Siberia*, 82–3.

14. N. A. Minenko, 'Obshchinnyi skhod v Zapadnoi Sibiri XVIII – pervoi poloviny XIX v.', in *Obshchestvennyi byt i kul'tura russkogo naseleniia Sibiri (XVIII–nachalo XX v.)*, ed. L. M. Rusakova (Novosibirsk: Nauka, 1983), 3–19; *Ssylka v Sibir': ocherk eia istorii i sovremennago polozheniia* (S.-Peterburg: Tipografiia S.-Peterburgskoi Tiur'my, 1900), 21, 57, 108, 144, 149–50.

15. N. M. Iadrintsev, *Sibir' kak koloniia v geograficheskom, etnograficheskom i dopolnennoe* (S.-Peterburg: Izdanie I.M. Sibiriakova, 1892), 294–5. Iadrintsev gives further examples on the following pages using the variant spelling 'Olad'in'.

16. On *skhoda's* refusal of *krugovaia poruka* see *Ssylka v Sibir'*, 157–8, 157n. For examples of their extortion of obligations from exiles, see Iadrintsev, *Sibir' kak*

koloniia (1892), 258. Examples of peasant justice (which Iadrintsev explicitly terms *samosud*) were found in N. M. Iadrintsev, *Russkaia obshchina v tiur´me i ssylke* (S.-Peterburg: Tipografiia A. Morigerovskago, 1872), 493–4, 499. On *samosud* generally, see Stephen Frank, *Crime, Cultural Conflict, and Justice in Rural Russia, 1856–1914* (Berkeley, CA: University of California, 1999).

17. Ustav o ssyl´nykh, g. 1. References are to regulation and *glava* (article).
18. I. Ia. Foinitskii, *Uchenie o nakazanii v sviazi s tiur´movedeniem* (S.-Peterburg: Tipografiia Ministerstva putei soobshcheniia [A. Benke], 1889), 282.
19. This confusion renders distinguishing exile to residence as a judicial or administrative punishment difficult. Cf. P. L. Kazarian, *Iakutiia v sisteme politicheskoi ssylki Rossii, 1826–1917 gg.* (Iakutsk: GP NIPK 'Sakhapoligrafizdat,' 1998), 155; *Ssylka v Sibir´*, 109n.
20. Ustav o ssyl´nykh, g. 1.
21. Foinitskii, *Uchenie*, 280–2.
22. These forms are mentioned throughout the regulation and sample copies are appended to it.
23. Literally, *sudebnye mesta*. As used in the regulations, these seem to refer to the various courts created below the *guberniia* level by the Catherinian reforms. Cf. John P. LeDonne, *Ruling Russia: Politics and Administration in the Age of Absolutism, 1762–1796* (Princeton, NJ: Princeton University Press, 1984), 146–65, esp. 158–9.
24. Ustav o ssyl´nykh, g. 1.
25. Ibid., g. 1–2.
26. Both Tolstoi and Kennan note the peasants' 'business of furnishing [food]'. George Kennan, *Siberia and the Exile System*, 2 vols. (New York: The Century Co., 1891) 1: 370; Leo Tolstoi, *Resurrection*, trans. Rosemary Edmonds (New York: Penguin Books, 1966), 466–7.
27. The 1824 ruling is cited in Shcheglov, *Khronologicheskii perechen´*, 278; the latter in [Anon.], 'Rasporiazheniia: 12-go Iiunia. O proizvodstve nakhodiashchimsia pri peresyl´nykh arestantakh maloliutnim detiam kormovykh deneg narovne s vzroslymi arestantami', *Zhurnal Ministerstva vnutrennykh del* 36, no. 4 (April 1840): cxxi–ii.
28. GAIO, f. 435, op. 1, d. 146, ll. 58–9.
29. Ustav o ssyl´nykh, g. 1-2.
30. See I. P. Belokonskii (Petrovich), *Po tiur´mam i etapam: ocherki tiuremnoi zhizni i putevyia zametki ot Moskvy do Krasnoiarska* (Orel: Izdanie N. A. Semenovoi, 1887), 157–8, 159.
31. Ustav o ssyl´nykh, g. 4–5, 9–10.
32. Ibid., g. 6.
33. For some reason the regulation includes the city of Tiumen´ in this list, implying it belonged to either Perm´ or Orenburg *guberniia*; but this was a *gorod*-city in Tobol´sk *guberniia*. (See the taxonomy in V. M. Kabuzan, *Narodonaselenie Rossii v XVIII–pervoi polovine XIX v.* [Moskva: AN SSSR, 1963], appendix, table, pp. 208, 210, 221.) Although the 'Regulation on Exiles' does not include Orenburg in the list of cities in the section referred to, common sense, geography and an article of the 'Regulation on Exile Transfer within Siberian *Gubernii*' (specifically, g. 2) strongly suggest the Siberian Committee intended that exiles from Orenburg *guberniia* also march to Tobol´sk, and not westward to

Kazan´. Because exiles from Orenburg *guberniia* would have been organized
into parties in the capital city Orenburg, I have inserted it into the list above.
34. Ustav o ssyl´nykh, g. 11.
35. Ibid., g. 13.
36. Ibid., g. 14.
37. Ibid., g. 11, 14. In Omsk *oblast´*, which was governed by a military administration, there was no exile bureau. Instead, exilic responsibilities were handled by a so-called executive bureau (*ispol´nitelnaia ekspeditsiia*). The Irkutsk Exile Bureau also had responsibility over Iakutsk *oblast´*. But see Kazarian, *Iakutiia*, 208ff.
38. G. S. Fel´dstein, *Ssylka: eia genezisa, znacheniia, istorii i sovremennogo sostoianiia* (Moskva: T-vo skoropechatni A. A. Levenson, 1893), 166.
39. Donald W. Treadgold, *The Great Siberian Migration: Government and Peasant Resettlement from Emancipation to the First World War* (Princeton, NJ: Princeton University Press, 1957), 27. Cf. *Ssylka v Sibir´*, 17; Raeff, *Siberia*, 58–9.
40. Quoted in Vladimir A. Tomsinov, *Speranskii* (Moskva: Molodaia gvardiia, 2006), 326.
41. Prior to absorption by the finance ministry in 1821, whence it was renamed a department (*departament*), the State Treasury was in charge of the *kazennye palaty*. See Eroshkin, *Ocherki*, 206–7, 234–5.
42. Ustav o ssyl´nykh, g. 17, 25.
43. Ibid., g. 25.
44. Ibid., g. 17, 25. See also Kazarian, *Iakutiia*, 210.
45. Ustav o ssyl´nykh, g. 17, 26.
46. Ibid., g. 26.
47. Ibid.
48. Michel Foucault, *Discipline and Punish: The Birth of the Prison*, trans. Alan Sheridan (New York: Vintage, 1977), 199, 201 and 195–228.
49. Ustav o ssyl´nykh, g. 17, 27.
50. Ibid., g. 35.
51. Ibid., g. 17.
52. Ibid., g. 29.
53. Ibid.
54. Andrew A. Gentes, 'Vagabondage and Exile to Tsarist Siberia', in *Cast Out: A History of Vagrancy in Global Perspective*, ed. Lee Beier and Paul Ocobock (Athens, OH: University of Ohio Press, 2008), 165–87.
55. Ustav o ssyl´nykh, g. 17, 28, 29.
56. Ibid., g. 34. See also Foinitskii, *Uchenie*, 280–2.
57. Nachal´nik Glavnago tiuremnago upravleniia [M. Galkin-Vraskoi], *O ssylke*, 28 December 1886, p. 6. [Report addressed to the MVD, filed in Rossiskaia gosudarstvennaia biblioteka (Moscow) rare books division under catalog number W 15/63.]
58. Ustav o ssyl´nykh, g. 19.
59. Ibid., g. 30.
60. *Ssylka v Sibir´*, 16–17, 17n.1.
61. Ustav o ssyl´nykh, g. 17, 19, 23.
62. Ibid., g. 23. Concerning the disposition of incapacitated penal laborers, the regulation is somewhat contradictory. It states in one section that those who grow too old or become disabled are to be entered into a settlement overseen

by TobPS, albeit located in the same *volost'* in which such penal laborers' *zavod* is situated. Given the fact that '*zavod*' is specified here, this stipulation would seem to have applied only to penal laborers in the cabinet industries – that is, in the Nerchinsk Mining District. Elsewhere, the regulation states that TobPS is to reassign all incapacitated penal laborers to the incapables category and relocate them to any site in Siberia except Irkutsk *guberniia* (a restriction which probably reflected that many incapables were already there). Yet, at the time, Nerchinsk would have been a part of this excluded area, since it was still part of Irkutsk *guberniia*, thus nullifying the rule of disposing of penal laborers assigned to the cabinet industries. Cf. ibid., g. 17, 19, 23.

63. *Ssylka v Sibir'*, 16–17, 17 n. 1. See also Foinitskii, *Uchenie*, 280–2. This disparity between a titular sentence and its actual length was consistently maintained down the scale of *katorga* sentences. For example, a fixed sentence of 20 years actually meant 15, a sentence of 15 meant ten, and so on. This regularly confused Siberian officials and so the MVD and superiors were constantly issuing circulars reminding officials of the schedule. For example, see the list of Decembrists' *katorga* sentences in an IGP ukase dated 24 January 1827 in GAIO, f. 435, op. 1, d. 147, l. 80; and the equivalencies given in article 24 of the first of the three ukases of the 1845 'Ulozhenie o Nakazaniiakh Ugolovnykh i Ispravitel'nykh', reproduced in *Dopolnitel'nyia postanovleniia o praspredelenii i upotreblenii osuzhdennykh v katorzhnyia raboty. Polozhenie o ispravitel'nykh arestantskikh rotakh grazhdanskago vedomstva. Dopolnitel'nyia pravila k ustavu o soderzhashchikhsia pod strazheiu* ([n. l.: n.p.], 1845).

64. Ustav o ssyl'nykh, g. 23.

65. P. F. Iakubovich, *V mire otverzhennykh: zapiski byvshego katorzhnika*, 2 vols. (Moskva: Khudozhestvennaia literatura, 1964) 1: 81–2.

66. Kennan, *Siberia* 1: 382–3, 387–8. See also Belokonskii, *Po tiur'mam i etapam*, 101-2, 175; Tolstoy, *Resurrection*, 488.

67. See also Kennan, *Siberia* 1: 384, 386, 389; Tolstoy, *Resurrection*, 493ff. John Venning describes a similar scene in Moscow's transit prison in the early 1820s. Henderson, *Memorials*, 53–6.

68. Translated and reproduced in Kennan, *Siberia* 2: appendix G, p. 546. (Kennan refers to and quotes from this letter, interpolating it with an earlier, similar letter Anuchin sent to Alexander II [ibid. 1: 388] but the footnote on this same page mistakenly refers to its full reproduction in a non-existent 'appendix H'.)

69. Kennan, *Siberia* 1: 388–9.

70. D. A. Dril', *Ssylka i katorga v Rossii (Iz lichnykh nabliudenii vo vremia poezdki v Priamurskii krai i Sibir')* (S.-Peterburg: Tipografiia Pravitel'stvuiushchago Senata, 1898), 6–7.

71. Iadrintsev, *Sibir' kak koloniia* (1892), 254.

72. [V. I.] Vlasov, 'Kratkii ocherk neustroistv, sushchestvuiushchikh na katorge,' 31 January 1873, p. 38, Biblioteka Irkutskogo gosudarstvennogo universiteta, Irkutsk, Rare Books and Manuscripts Division, 'Sakhalin' *delo* RUK. 345.

73. V. I. Semevskii, *Rabochie na sibirskikh zolotykh promyslakh: istoricheskoe izsledovanie*, 2 vols. (S.-Peterburg: Tipografiia M. Stasiulevicha, 1898) 1: xvii–iii. See also Tolstoi's characterization of Nekhliudov's perception of a young boy sleeping on a convict's lap. *Resurrection*, 523–4.

74. Kennan, *Siberia* 1: 370.

75. Cited (ambiguously) in Jerome Blum, *Lord and Peasant in Russia: From the Ninth to the Nineteenth Century* (Princeton, NJ: Princeton University Press, 1961), 430.
76. For example, GAIO, f. 435, op. 1, d. 94, l. 237.
77. Kazarian, *Iakutiia*, 206–7.
78. Ustav ob etapakh v sibirskikh guberniiakh, g. 1.
79. Belokonskii, *Po tiur'mam i etapam*, 175–6.
80. *Sibir'*, 23 June 1885; Iakubovich 1: 58–61.
81. Ustav ob etapakh v sibirskikh guberniiakh, g. 1, 5.
82. Ibid., g. 2.
83. G. Peizen, 'Istoricheskii ocherk kolonizatsii Sibiri', *Sovremennik* 77, no. 9 (1859): 9–46 [here, table, pp. 42–3].
84. Eroshkin, *Ocherki*, 241; Kazarian, *Iakutiia*, 209. Eroshkin and Kazarian claim party sizes of 60–100 or more were permitted in winter. I was unable to find in the regulation any instructions concerning the size of deportation parties during non-summer months, and so it appears these figures are based on later practices.
85. Kennan, *Siberia* 1: 369. See also [Anon.], 'Arestanty v Sibiri', *Sovremennik* 11, no. 99 (November 1863): 133–75 [here, p. 147]; Belokonskii, *Po tiur'mam i etapam*, 167–8. Writing in 1892, Iadrintsev stated there were 20 convoy commands comprising 1,386 soldiers assigned to the primary march route. In terms of the number of soldiers, this corresponds quite closely to the figures already given but is far below the number of *etap*-commands specified by the regulation. The discrepancy may be accounted for by the fact that as of 1892, much of the journey into Siberia was completed by barge along major river systems, and so many of these stations became unnecessary. Nevertheless, Iadrintsev somewhat confusingly adds that besides the soldiers assigned to the march route, a total of 14,867 soldiers (*nizhnie chiny*) were involved in 'convoying not only exiles, but also those transferring between exile locations'. Iadrintsev, *Sibir' kak koloniia* (1892), 290.
86. GAIO, f. 435, op. 1, d. 147, ll. 531–5.
87. Kazarian, *Iakutiia*, 208–12.
88. Ustav ob etapakh v sibirskikh guberniiakh, table, pp. 26–33.
89. Ibid., g. 2. Such headmen are specified in Ustav o ssyl'nykh, g. 20.
90. Kennan, *Siberia* 1: 390ff.; Belokonskii, *Po tiur'mam i etapam*, 154ff.
91. Ustav ob etapakh v sibirskikh guberniiakh, g. 3.
92. Ibid., g. 3, 5, 8, 12.
93. Kennan, *Siberia* 1: 378.
94. Belokonskii, *Po tiur'mam i etapam*, 173.
95. Seasonal fishing stations are today built on the ice there. I was told by my guide that when a car plummets through the ice it signals the end of ice-fishing season (usually late March–early April).
96. Ustav ob etapakh v sibirskikh guberniiakh, g. 3, and table, pp. 26–33. The regulation specifies the following rules concerning the use of the bath house (*bania*). Following opportunities to buy soap from locals, separate groups of no more than ten exile-settlers or two penal laborers each may leave the ward to enter the bath house. Exile-settlers are to be kept under watch; penal laborers under armed guard. Belokonskii describes exiles' use of the bath house at the transit prison in Moscow before his party was moved east, noting that the men used it first, then the women. During the men's turn Russians entered first,

followed by Jews, probably to allow the former to secure the best positions on the top shelves and leaving the latter to sit on the lower shelves or floor. Belokonskii, *Po tiur´mam i etapam*, 56–7.

97. Ustav ob etapakh v sibirskikh guberniiakh, table, pp. 26–33.
98. Ibid., g. 2.
99. Ibid., table, pp. 26–33.
100. Distance based on figures in GAIO, f. 435, op. 1, d. 147, ll. 531–5.
101. 'Arestanty v Sibiri': 146.
102. Belokonskii, *Po tiur´mam i etapam*, 170.
103. Kennan, *Siberia* 1: 398–9. Note that Kennan's figure is for the number of exiles who went as far as Eastern Siberia; the total number exiled in 1885, the year Kennan visited, was 13,281. *Ssylka v Sibir´*, appendices, table, pp. 3–5.

Conclusion: 'Siberian Exile and Biopolitics'

1. Michel Foucault, *Society Must Be Defended* (London: Penguin Books, 2003), 243.

Selected Bibliography

Archival sources

GAIO – Irkutsk District State Archive (*Gosudarstvennyi arkhiv Irkutstkoi oblasti*), Irkutsk: Fond 24: Main Administration of Eastern Siberia (*Glavnoe upravlenie Vostochnoi Sibiri*) 1822–87; Fond 435: Kirensk City Government (*Kirenskaia gorodskaia uprava*) 1784–1867.

GARF – Russian Federation State Archive (*Gosudarstvennyi arkhiv Rossiiskoi Federatsii*), Moscow: Fond 1183: Tobol´sk Exile Office (*Tobol´skii prikaz o ssyl´nykh*) 1822–90.

Abbreviations: f. = *fond* (collection); op. = *opis´* (listing); k. = *karton* (carton); d. = *delo* (sheaf); l. = *list* (sheet)

Documents and document collections

Akishin, M. O. 'Sibirskii gubernator D. I. Chicherin: Raport ober-shter-krigs-komissara G. M. Osipova imperatritse Ekaterine II. 1779 g.', *Istoricheskii arkhiv* 3 (1996): 193–210.

Armstrong, Terence, ed. *Yermak's Campaign in Siberia*. London: Haklyut Society, 1975.

Dmytryshyn, Basil et al., eds. and trans. *Russia's Conquest of Siberia, 1558–1700: A Documentary Record*. Vol. 1. Portland, OR: Oregon Historical Society Press, 1985.

Goriushkin, L. M., ed. *Politicheskaia ssylka v Sibiri: Nerchinskaia katorga*. Vol. 1. Novosibirsk: Sibirskii khronograf, 1993.

Imperatorskaia Arkheograficheskaia Kommissiia [*sic*], *Sibirskiia avtopisi*. S-Peterburg: Tipografiia I. N. Skorokhodova, 1907.

Kirievskii, I. I., ed. *Bulavinskoe vosstanie (1707–1708 gg.)*. Moskva: Izdatel´stvo Vsesoiuznago obshchestva politkatorzhan i ssyl´no-poselentsev, 1935.

Miller [Müller], G. F. *Istoriia Sibiri*. 3 vols. Ed. E. P. Bat´ianova et al. Moskva: Vostochnaia literatura, 1999–2005.

Pokrovskii, N. N. and E. K. Romodanovskaia, eds. *Tobol´skii arkhiereiskii dom v XVII veke*. Novosibirsk: Sibirskii khronograf, 1994.

Pokrovskii, N. N., ed. *Pervoe stoletie sibiriskikh gorodov. XVII vek*. Novosibirsk: Sibirskii khronograf, 1996.

Polnoe sobranie russkikh letopisei. Vol. XIII. Moskva: Izd-vo vostochnoi lit-ry, 1965.

Sofronenko, K. A., ed. *Sobornoe ulozhenie tsaria Alekseia Mikhailovicha, 1649 goda*. Moskva: Iuridicheskaia literatura, 1957.

Uchrezhdenie dlia upravleniia Sibirskikh gubernii. Sanktpeterburg: Pechatano v Senatskoi Tipografii, 1822.

Van Schooneveld, C. H., ed. *Pamiatniki sibirskoi istorii XVIII veka. Kniga vtoraia, 1713–1724*. 1885; rpt. The Hague: Mouton, 1969.

Zol'nikova, N. D. "'Chto svoemu bratu uchinesh', takozhde i sam priimesh'":
Gramotki i chelobitnye krasnoiarskomu voevode S. I. Durnovo. 1696–1698 gg.',
Istoricheskii arkhiv 5 (1993): 190–7.

Nineteenth-century Russian periodicals

Aziatskii vestnik
Otechestvennyia zapiski
Russkaia starina
Russkoe bogatstvo
Sibir'
Sibirskii vestnik
Sovremennik
Zhurnal grazhdanskago i ugolovnago prava
Zhurnal Ministerstva iustitsii
Zhurnal Ministerstva vnutrennykh del

Memoirs

Anastevich, V., trans. 'Puteshestvie ks[endza] Fadeia Mashevskago iz Irkutska v
Nerchinsk (1817 g.) (Miesiecznih Polocki[,] N[o.] VIII, 1818 g.[,] str. 298–306)',
Sibirskii vestnik 14 (1821): 219–34.
Anon. 'Arestanty v Sibiri', *Sovremennik* 11, no. 99 (November 1863): 133–75.
[Avvakum.] *Zhitie protopopa Avvakuma, im samim napisannoe i drugie ego sochineniia.*
Ed. N. K. Gudziia et al. Moskva: Gos. izd-vo Khudozh. lit-ry, 1960.
Belokonskii (Petrovich), I. P. *Po tiur'mam i etapam: ocherki tiuremnoi zhizni i
putevyia zametki ot Moskvy do Krasnoiarska.* Orel: Izdanie N. A. Semenovoi,
1887.
Cochrane, John Dundas. *A Pedestrian Journey through Russia and Siberian Tartary
to the Frontiers of China, the Frozen Sea and Kamchatka.* Ed. and intro. Mervyn
Horder. 1823; rpt. London: Folio Society, 1983.
Coxe, William. *Travels in Poland and Russia: Three Volumes in One.* New York: Arno
Press, 1970.
Fletcher, Giles. *Of the Russe Commonwealth by Giles Fletcher, 1591: Facsimile Edition
with Variants.* Intro. Richard Pipes. Cambridge, MA: Harvard University Press,
1966.
Henderson, Thulia S., ed. *Memorials of John Venning, Esq., with Numerous Notices
from His Manuscripts Relative to the Imperial Family of Russia.* 1862; rpt. Cam-
bridge: Oriental Research Partners, 1975.
Iakubovich, P. F. *V mire otverzhennykh: zapiski byvshego katorzhnika,* 2 vols. Moskva:
Khudozhestvennaia literature, 1964.
Pasfield, Oliver, ed. *The Memoirs of Mauritius Augustus Count de Benyowsky in Siberia,
Kamchatka, Japan, the Liukiu Islands and Formosa.* Trans. William Nicholson.
New York: Macmillan, 1893.
Shteingeil', V. I. *Sochineniia i pis'ma.* 2 vols. Irkutsk: Vostochno-Sibirskoe knizhnoe
izdatel'stvo, 1985–92.
Von Stralenberg [*sic*], Philip Johann Tabbert. *An histori-geographical description of
the north and eastern part of Europe and Asia: but more particularly of Russia, Siberia,*

and Great Tartary; both in their ancient and modern state: together with an entire new polyglottable of the dialects of 32 Tartarian nations: and a vocabulary of the Kalmuck-Mungalian tongue: as also, a large and accurate map of those countries; and variety of cuts, representing Asiatick-Scythian antiquities/written originally in High German by Philip John von Strahlenberg; now faithfully translated into English. London: W. Innys and R. Manby, 1736.

Watrous, Stephen D., ed. *John Ledyard's Journey through Russia and Siberia, 1787–1788: The Journal and Selected Letters*. Madison and Milwaukee: University of Wisconsin Press, 1966.

Secondary sources

Abu-Lughod, Janet L. *Before European Hegemony: The World System A.D. 1250–1350*. New York: Oxford University Press, 1989.

Adams, Bruce F. *The Politics of Punishment: Prison Reform in Russia, 1863–1917*. DeKalb, IL: Northern Illinois University Press, 1996.

Aleksandrov, V. A. and N. N. Pokrovskii. 'Mirskie organizatsii i administrativnaia vlast´ v Sibiri v XVII veke', *Istoriia SSSR* 1 (1986): 47–68.

Anisimov, Evgenii V. *The Reforms of Peter the Great: Progress through Coercion in Russia*. Trans. John T. Alexander. Armonk, NY: M. E. Sharpe, 1993.

Anisimov, Evgenii. *Dyba i knut: politicheskii sysk i russkoe obshchestvo v XVIII veke*. Moskva: Novoe Literaturnoe Obozrenie, 1999.

Anisimov, Evgeny V. *Empress Elizabeth: Her Reign and Her Russia, 1741–1761*. Ed. and trans. John T. Alexander. Gulf Breeze, FL: Academic International Press, 1995.

Anuchin, E. N. *Izsledovaniia o protsente soslannykh v Sibir´ v period 1827–1846 godov: materialy dlia ugolovnoi statistiki Rossii*. S.-Peterburg: Tipografiia Maikova, 1873.

Armstrong, John A. 'Old-Regime Governors: Bureaucratic and Patrimonial Attributes', *Comparative Studies in Society and History* 14, no. 1 (1972): 2–29.

Armstrong, Terence. *Russian Settlement in the North*. Cambridge: Cambridge University Press, 1965.

Avrich, Paul. *Russian Rebels 1600–1800*. 1972; rpt. New York: W. W. Norton, 1976.

Bakhrushin, S. V. *Ocherki po istorii kolonozatsii Sibiri v XVI i XVII vv*. Moskva: Izdanie M.S. Sabashnikovykh, 1928.

Beier, A. L. *Masterless Men: The Vagrancy Problem in England, 1560–1640*. New York: Methuen, 1985.

Bekmakhanova, N. E. *Kazach´i voiska Aziatskoi Rossii v XVIII–nachale XX veka (Astrakhanskoe, Orenburgskoe, Sibirskoe, Semirechenskoe, Ural´skoe): Sbornik dokumentov*. Moskva: Institut rossiiskoi istorii RAN, 2000.

Blondel, Jean and Nick Manning. 'Do Ministers Do What They Say? Ministerial Unreliability, Collegial and Hierarchical Governments', *Political Studies* 50 (2002): 455–76.

Blum, Jerome. *Lord and Peasant in Russia: From the Ninth to the Nineteenth Century*. Princeton, NJ: Princeton University Press, 1961.

Bogoliubskii, I. *Istoriko-statisticheskii ocherk proizvoditel´nosti Nerchinskago Gornago Okruga s 1703 po 1871 god*. S.-Peterburg: V. Tip. V. Demakova, 1872.

Borodaev, V. B. et al., eds. *Guliaevskie chteniia. Vyp. 1: Materialy pervoi, vtoroi i tret´ei istoriko-arkhivnykh konferentsii*. Barnaul: Upravlenie arkhivnogo dela administratsii Altaiskogo kraia and Laboratoriia istoricheskogo kraevedeniia Barnaul'skogo gosudarstvennogo pedagogicheskogo universiteta, 1998.

Braginskii, M. A. *Nerchinskaia katorga: Sbornik nerchinskogo zemliachestva*. Moskva: Politkatorzhan, 1933.

Bryner, Cyril. 'The Issue of Capital Punishment in the Reign of Elizabeth Petrovna', *Russian Review* 49, no. 4 (1990): 389–416.

Bubis, Nadezhda. 'Irkutskii tiuremnyi zamok', *Zemlia irkutskaia* 10 (1998): 51–6.

Bushkovitch, Paul. *Religion and Society in Russia: The Sixteenth and Seventeenth Centuries*. New York: Oxford University Press, 1992.

Canning, Kathleen. 'The Body as Method? Reflections on the Place of the Body in Gender History', *Gender & History* 11, no. 3 (1999): 499–513.

Chibiriaev, S. A. *Velikii russkii reformator: Zhizn´, deiatel´nost´, politicheskie vzgliady M. M. Speranskogo*. Moskva: Nauka, 1989.

Chichlo, Boris, ed. *Sibérie II: Questions sibériennes*. Paris: Insitut d'études slaves, 1999.

Cizova, Tatiana. 'Beccaria in Russia', *Slavonic and East European Review* 40, no. 95 (1962): 384–408.

Clardy, Jesse. 'Radishchev's Notes on the Geography of Siberia', *Russian Review* 21, no. 4 (1962): 362–9.

Cracraft, James. *The Petrine Revolution in Russian Culture*. Cambridge, MA: Harvard University Press, 2004.

Crummey, Robert O. *Aristocrats and Servitors: The Boyar Elite in Russia, 1613–1689*. Princeton, NJ: Princeton University Press, 1983.

Crummey, Robert O. *The Old Believers & the World of Antichrist: The Vyg Community and the Russian State, 1694–1855*. Madison, WI: University of Wisconsin Press, 1970.

Dal´, V. I. *Tolkovyi slovar´ zhivogo velikorusskogo iazyka*. 4 vols. Moskva: 'Russkii iazyk', 1999.

Dameshek, Irina. 'Mikhail Speranskii', *Zemlia irkutskaia* 8 (1997): 2–9.

De Madariaga, Isabel. *Ivan the Terrible: First Tsar of Russia*. New Haven, CT: Yale University Press, 2005.

De Madariaga, Isabel. *Russia in the Age of Catherine the Great*. New Haven, CT: Yale University Press, 1981.

Diment, Galya and Yuri Slezkine, eds. *Between Heaven and Hell: The Myth of Siberia in Russian Culture*. New York: St. Martin's Press, 1993.

Dizhur, Sergei. 'Russkaia ssylka. Eia istoriia i ozhidaemaia reforma', *Russkoe bogatstvo* 4 (April 1900): 45–64.

Dmytryshyn, Basil. 'Russian Expansion to the Pacific, 1580–1700: A Historiographical Review', *Siberica* 1, no. 1 (1990): 4–37.

Dvorianov, V. N. *V Sibirskoi dal´nei storone ... (ocherki istorii politicheskoi katorgi i ssylki. 60-e gody XVIII v.–1917 g.)*. Minsk: Nauka i tekhnika, 1985.

Eisenstadt, S. N., ed. *Max Weber on Charisma and Institution Building*. Chicago: University of Chicago Press, 1968.

Elizarova, Liudmila. 'Istoriia Krugobaikal'skogo trakta', *Zemlia irkutskaia* 4 (1995): 22–7.

Emel´ianova, I. A. *Vysshie organy gosudarstvennoi vlasti i upravleniia Rossii v doreformennyi period*. Kazan´: Izd-vo Kazanskogo universiteta, 1962.

Emmer, P. C. and M. Mörner. *European Expansion and Migration: Essays on the Intercontinental Migration from Africa, Asia, and Europe*. New York: Berg, 1992.

Eroshkin, N. P. *Ocherki istorii gosudarstvennykh uchrezhdenii dorevoliutsionnoi Rossii.* Moskva: Gosudarstvennoe Uchebno-Pedagogicheskoe Izdatel´stvo Ministerstva Prosveshcheniia RSFSR, 1960.

Everett, Wendy and Peter Wagstaff, eds. *Cultures of Exile: Images of Displacement.* New York: Berghahn Books, 2004.

Fel´dstein, G. S. *Ssylka: eia genezisa, znacheniia, istorii i sovremennogo sostoianiia.* Moskva: T-vo skoropechatni A. A. Levenson, 1893.

Foinitskii, I. Ia. *Uchenie o nakazanii v sviazi s tiur´movedeniem.* S.-Peterburg: Tipografiia Ministerstva putei soobshcheniia (A. Benke), 1889.

Forsyth, James. *A History of the Peoples of Siberia: Russia's North Asian Colony, 1581–1990.* Cambridge: Cambridge University Press, 1994.

Foucault, Michel. *Discipline and Punish: The Birth of the Prison.* New York: Vintage, 1977.

Foucault, Michel. *The History of Sexuality: An Introduction.* Vol. 1. New York: Vintage, 1990.

Foucault, Michel. *Power/Knowledge: Selected Interviews and Other Writings, 1972–1977.* New York: Pantheon, 1980.

Foucault, Michel. *Society Must Be Defended.* London: Penguin Books, 2003.

Garland, David. *Punishment and Modern Society: A Study in Social Theory.* Oxford: Oxford University Press, 1991.

Gentes, Andrew A. ' "Licentious Girls" and Frontier Domesticators: Women and Siberian Exile from the Late 16th to the Early 19th Century', *Sibirica* 3, no. 1 (2003): 3–20.

Gentes, Andrew A. '*Katorga*: Penal Labor and Tsarist Siberia', in *The Siberian Saga: A History of Russia's Wild East.* Ed. Eva-Maria Stolberg. Frankfurt am Main: Lang, 2005, pp. 73–85.

Gentes, Andrew A. 'Towards a Demography of Children in the Tsarist Siberian Exile System', *Sibirica* 5, no. 1 (2006): 1–23.

Gentes, Andrew A. 'Vagabondage and Exile to Tsarist Siberia', in *Cast Out: A History of Vagrancy in Global Perspective.* Ed. Lee Beier and Paul Ocobock. Athens, OH: University of Ohio Press, 2008, pp. 165–87.

Gernet, M. N. *Istoriia tsarskoi tiur´my.* 5 vols. 3rd edn. Moskva: Gosudarstvennoe izdatel´stvo iuridicheskoi literatury, 1960–63.

Gibson, James R. *Feeding the Russian Fur Trade: Provisionment of the Okhotsk Seaboard and the Kamchatka Peninsular, 1639–1856.* Madison, WI: University of Wisconsin Press, 1969.

Goriushkin, L. M., ed. *Politicheskaia ssylka v Sibiri XIX–nachalo XX v.: Istoriografiia i istochniki.* Novosibirsk: Nauka, 1987.

Goriushkin, L. M., ed. *Politicheskie ssyl´nye v Sibiri (XVIII–nachalo XX v.).* Novosibirsk: Nauka, 1983.

Goriushkin, L. M., ed. *Ssylka i obshchestvenno-politicheskaia zhizn´ v Sibiri (XVIII–nachalo XX v.).* Novosibirsk: Nauka, 1978.

Goriushkin, L. M. et al., eds. *Ssylka i katorga v Sibiri (XVIII–nachalo XX v.).* Novosibirsk: Nauka, 1975.

Gromyko, M. M. *Zapadnaia Sibir´ v XVIII v.: Russkoe naselenoe i zemledel´cheskoe osvoenie.* Novosibirsk: Nauka, 1965.

Harley, J. B. 'Maps, Knowledge, and Power', in *The Iconography of Landscape: Essays on the Symbolic Representation, Design and Use of Past Environments.* Ed. Denis Cosgrove and Stephen Daniels. Cambridge: University of Cambridge Press 1988, pp. 277–312.

Hellie, Richard. *Enserfment and Military Change in Muscovy*. Chicago: University of Chicago Press, 1971.

Hittle, J. Michael. 'The Service City in the Eighteenth Century', in *The City in Russian History*. Ed. Michael F. Hamm. Lexington, KY: University Press of Kentucky, 1976, pp. 53–68.

Hittle, J. Michael. *The Service City: State and Townsmen in Russia, 1600–1800*. Cambridge, MA: Harvard University Press, 1979.

Holl, Bruce T. 'Avvakum and the Genesis of Siberian Literature', in *Between Heaven and Hell: The Myth of Siberia in Russian Culture*. Ed. Galya Diment and Yuri Slezkine. New York: St. Martin's Press, 1993, pp. 33–46.

Hollingsworth, Barry. 'John Venning and Prison Reform in Russia, 1819–1830', in *Slavonic and East European Review* 48, no. 113 (1970): 537–56.

Hughes, Robert. *The Fatal Shore*. New York: Knopf, 1987.

Humphreys, Robert. *No Fixed Abode: A History of Responses to the Roofless and the Rootless in Britain*. Basingstoke: Macmillan, 1999.

Huttenbach, Henry R. 'Muscovy's Penetration of Siberia: The Colonization Process, 1555–1689', in *Russian Colonial Expansion to 1917*. Ed. Michael Rywkin. New York: Mansell, 1988, pp. 70–102.

Iadrintsev, N. M. *Russkaia obshchina v tiur´me i ssylke*. S.-Peterburg: Tipografiia A. Morigerovskago, 1872.

Iadrintsev, N. M. *Sibir´ kak koloniia v geograficheskom, etnograficheskom i dopolnennoe*. Ed. L. M. Goriushkin et al. Novosibirsk: Sibirskii khronograf, 2003.

Iadrintsev, N. M. *Sibir´ kak koloniia v geograficheskom, etnograficheskom i dopolnennoe*. S.-Peterburg: Tip. I. M. Sibiriakova, 1892.

Iadrintsev, N. M. *Sibir´ kak koloniia: k iubileiu trekhsotletiia. Sovremennoe polozhenie Sibiri. Eia nuzhdy i potrebnosti. Eia proshloe i budushchee*. Sanktpeterburg: Tipografiia M. M. Stasiulevicha, 1882.

Ivanova, Galina Mihailovna. *Labor Camp Socialism: The Gulag in the Soviet Totalitarian System*. Trans. Carol Flath. Armonk, NY and London: M. E. Sharpe, 2000.

Jakobson, Michael. *Origins of the GULAG: The Soviet Prison Camp System, 1917–1934*. Lexington, KY: University Press of Kentucky, 1993.

Jarring, Gunnar. 'Swedish Relations with Central Asia and Swedish Central Asian Research', *Asian Affairs* 61, Part III (1974): 257–66.

Kabuzan, V. M. *Izmeneniia v razmeshchenii naseleniia Rossii v XVIII–pervoi polovine XIX v. (Po materialam revizii)*. Moskva: Nauka, 1971.

Kabuzan, V. M. *Narodonaselenie Rossii v XVIII–pervoi polovine XIX v.* Moskva: AN SSSR, 1963.

Kahan, Arcadius. *The Plow, the Hammer, and the Knout: An Economic History of Eighteenth-Century Russia*. Chicago: University of Chicago Press, 1985.

Kamenskii, A. B. *Ot Petra I do Pavla I: Reformy v Rossii XVIII veka*. Moskva: Rossiiskii Gosudarstvennyi Gumanitarnyi Universitet, 1999.

Kamenskii, Aleksandr B. *The Russian Empire in the Eighteenth Century: Searching for a Place in the World*. Trans. David Griffiths. Armonk, NY: M. E. Sharpe, 1997.

Kandaurova, T. N. and B. B. Davydov, 'Voennye poseleniia v otsenke', *Vestnik Moskovskogo Universiteta. Seriia VIII: Istoriia* 2 (1992): 44–55.

Kantorowicz, Ernst Hartwig. *The King's Two Bodies: A Study of Mediaeval Political Theology*. Princeton, NJ: Princeton University Press, 1957.

Karpenko, Z. G. *Gornaia i metallurgicheskaia promyshlennost' Zapadnoi Sibiri v 1700–1860 godakh*. Novosibirsk: AN SSSR, 1963.

Kazarian, P. L. 'Zadachi rossiiskoi i pol'skoi istoricheskoi nauki v izuchenii ssylka Poliakov v Iakutiiu', in *Rossiia i Polsha: Istoriko-kul'turnye kontakty (Sibirskii fenomen)*. Ed. V. N. Ivanov et al. Novosibirsk: Nauka, 2001, pp. 42–6.

Kazarian, P. L. *Iakutiia v sisteme politicheskoi ssylki Rossii, 1826–1917 gg*. Iakutsk: GP NIPK 'Sakhapoligrafizdat', 1998.

Kennan, George. *Siberia and the Exile System*. 2 vols. New York: The Century Co., 1891.

Kerner, Robert J. *The Urge to the Sea. The Course of Russian History. The Role of Rivers, Portages, Ostrogs, Monasteries, and Furs*. 1942; rpt. New York: Russell & Russell, 1970.

Khodarkovsky, Michael. *Russia's Steppe Frontier: The Making of a Colonial Empire, 1500–1800*. Bloomington, IN: Indiana University Press, 2002.

Kivelson, Valerie A. ' "The Souls of the Righteous in a Bright Place": Landscape and Orthodoxy in Seventeenth-Century Russian Maps', *Russian Review* 58 (1999): 1–25.

Kivelson, Valerie A. 'Cartography, Autocracy and State Powerlessness: The Uses of Maps in Early Modern Russia', *Imago Mundi* 51 (1999): 83–105.

Kivelson, Valerie A. 'Patrolling the Boundaries: Witchcraft Accusations and House-hold Strife in Seventeenth-Century Muscovy', *Harvard Ukrainian Studies* 19 (1995): 302–23.

Kivelson, Valerie A. 'The Devil Stole His Mind: The Tsar and the 1648 Moscow Uprising', *American Historical Review* 98, no. 3 (1993): 733–56.

Kivelson, Valerie A. 'Through the Prism of Witchcraft: Gender and Social Change in Seventeenth-Century Muscovy', in *Russia's Women: Accommodation, Resistance, Transformation*. Ed. Barbara Evan Clements et al. Berkeley, CA: University of California Press, 1991, pp. 74–94.

Kivelson, Valerie A. *Autocracy in the Provinces: The Muscovite Gentry and Political Culture in the Seventeenth Century*. Stanford, CA: Stanford University Press, 1996.

Kliuchevskii, V. O. *Sochineniia*, 8 vols. Moskva: Izd-vo. Sotsial'no-ekonomicheskoi literatury, 1956–59.

Kotkin, Stephen and David Wolff, eds. *Rediscovering Russia in Asia: Siberia and the Russian Far East*. Armonk, NY: M. E. Sharpe, 1995.

Lang, David Marshall. *The First Russian Radical: Alexander Radishchev, 1749–1802*. London: Allen & Unwin, 1959.

Lantzeff, George V. and Richard A. Pierce, *Eastward to Empire: Exploration and Conquest on the Russian Open Frontier, to 1750*. Montreal: McGill-Queen's University Press, 1973.

Lantzeff, George V. *Siberia in the Seventeenth Century: A Study of the Colonial Administration*. 1943; rpt. New York: Octagon Books, 1972.

Lappo, G. M., ed. *Goroda Rossii*. Moskva: Nauchnoe izdatel'stvo, 1994.

LeDonne, John P. 'Frontier Governors General 1772–1825. III. The Eastern Frontier', *Jahrbücher für Geschichte Osteuropas* 48 (2000): 321–40.

LeDonne, John P. *Ruling Russia: Politics and Administration in the Age of Absolutism, 1762–1796*. Princeton, NJ: Princeton University Press, 1984.

LeDonne, John P. *The Grand Strategy of the Russian Empire: 1650–1831*. New York: Oxford University Press, 2003.

LeDonne, John P. *The Russian Empire and the World, 1700–1917: The Geopolitics of Expansion and Containment*. New York: Oxford University Press, 1997.

Levin, M. G. and L. P. Potapov, eds. *The Peoples of Siberia*. Chicago: University of Chicago, 1964.

Lincoln, W. Bruce. *The Conquest of a Continent: Siberia and the Russians*. New York: Random House, 1994.

Lincoln, W. Bruce. *The Romanovs: Autocrats of All the Russias* New York: Doubleday, 1981.

Lindenmeyr, Adele. *Poverty Is Not a Vice: Charity, Society, and the State in Imperial Russia*. Princeton, NJ: Princeton University Press, 1996.

Lyashchenko, Peter I. *History of the National Economy of Russia to the 1917 Revolution*. Trans. L. M. Herman. New York: Macmillan, 1949.

Maksimov, S. 'Gosudartsvennye prestupniki. Piataia chast'', *Otechestvennyia zapiski* 9 (September 1869): 229–72.

Maksimov, S. 'Sibirskaia sol'', in *Zhivopisnaia Rossiia. Otechestvo nashe v ego zemel'nom, istoricheskom, plemennom, ekonomicheskom i bytovom znachenii*. Ed. P. P Semenov. S.-Peterburg: Izdanie Tovarishchestva M. O. Vol'f, 1895, pp. 311–21.

Maksimov, S. *Sibir' i katorga*. 3 vols. S.-Peterburg: Tipografiia A. Transhelia, 1871.

Maksimov, S. V. *Sibir' i katorga*. 3rd edn. S.-Peterburg: Izdanie V.I. Gubinskago, 1900.

March, G. Patrick. *Eastern Destiny: Russia in Asia and the North Pacific*. Westport, CT: Praeger, 1996.

Martin, Janet. *Treasure of the Land of Darkness: The Fur Trade and Its Significance for Medieval Russia*. New York: Cambridge University Press, 1986.

Matkhanova, N. P. *Vysshaia administratsiia Vostochnoi Sibiri v seredine XIX veka: Problemy sotsial'noi stratifikatsii*. Novosibirsk: Sibirskii khronograf, 2002.

Michels, Georg Bernhard. 'The Violent Old Belief: An Examination of Religious Dissent on the Karelian Frontier', *Russian History* 19, nos. 1–4 (1992): 203–29.

Michels, Georg Bernhard. *At War with the Church: Religious Dissent in Seventeenth-Century Russia*. Stanford, CA: Stanford University Press, 1999.

Minenko, N. A. 'Obshchinnyi skhod v Zapadnoi Sibiri XVIII-pervoi poloviny XIX v.', in *Obshchestvennyi byt i kul'tura russkogo naseleniia Sibiri (XVIII–nachalo XX v.)*. Ed. L. M. Rusakova. Novosibirsk: Nauka, 1983, pp. 3–19.

Minenko, N. A. 'Pis'ma sibirskikh krest'ian XVIII veka', *Voprosy istorii* 8 (1983): 180–3.

Mirzoev, V. G. *Istoriografiia Sibiri (Domarksistskii period)*. Moskva: Mysl', 1970.

Monas, Sidney. *The Third Section: Police and Society in Russia under Nicholas I*. Cambridge, MA: Harvard University Press, 1961.

Morris, Norval and David J. Rothman, eds. *The Oxford History of the Prison: The Practice of Punishment in Western Society*. New York: Oxford University Press, 1998.

Mote, Victor L. *Siberia: Worlds Apart*. Boulder, CO: Westview Press, 1998.

Nikitin, N. I. 'Pervyi vek kazachestva Sibiri', *Voenno-istoricheskii zhurnal* 1 (1994): 77–83.

Nikitin, N. I. *Sluzhilye liudi v Zapadnoi Sibiri XVII veka*. Novosibirsk: Nauka, 1988.

Okladnikov, A. P. et al., eds. *Istoriia Sibiri s drevneishikh vremen do nashikh dnei*. 5 vols. Leningrad: Nauka, 1968–69.

Orlovsky, Daniel T. *The Limits of Reform: The Ministry of Internal Affairs in Imperial Russia, 1802–1881.* Cambridge, MA: Harvard University Press, 1981.

Parker, Geoffrey. *The Military Revolution and the Rise of the West, 1500–1800.* Cambridge: Cambridge University Press, 1996.

Pavlinskaia, L. P. 'Eshche raz ob etnicheskoi istorii Baikal´skogo regiona', in *Sibir´: drevnie etnosy i ikh kul´tury.* Ed. Pavlinskaia. Sankt-Peterburg: Rossiiskaia akademiia nauk, Muzei antropologii i etnografii im. Petra Velikogo (Kunstkamera), 1996, pp. 62–96.

Pavlov, P. N. 'Vyvoz pushniny iz Sibiri v XVII v.', in *Sibir´ perioda feodalizma, vypusk 1.* Ed. V.I. Shunkov, et al. Novosibirsk: Izdatel´stvo Sibirskogo otdeleniia AN SSSR, 1962, pp. 121–38.

Peizen, G. 'Istoricheskii ocherk kolonizatsii Sibiri', *Sovremennik 77,* no. 9 (1859): 9–46.

Perrie, Maureen. *Pretenders and Popular Monarchism in Early Modern Russia: The False Tsars of the Time of Troubles.* Cambridge; Cambridge University Press, 1995.

Petruchintsev, Nikolaj N. 'The Two Fleets of Peter I: Technological Possibilities'. Trans. Hans-Heinrich Nolte. [Unpublished TS in author's possession.]

Phillips, Edward J. *The Founding of Russia's Navy: Peter the Great and the Azov Fleet, 1688–1714.* Westport, CT: Greenwood Press, 1995.

Pintner, Walter McKenzie and Don Karl Rowney, eds. *Russian Officialdom: The Bureaucratization of Russian Society from the Seventeenth to the Twentieth Century.* London: Macmillan, 1980.

Pipes, Richard. *Russia under the Old Regime.* New York: Charles Scribner's Sons, 1974.

Platonov, S. F. *Boris Godunov: Tsar of Russia.* Trans. L. Rex Pyles. Gulf Breeze, FL: Academic International Press, 1973.

Pliguzov, A. I. 'Pervye russkie opisaniia sibirskoi zemli', *Voprosy istorii* 5 (1987): 38–50.

Pliguzov, Andrei I. 'Skazanie "O chelovetsekh neznaemykh v vostochnei strane"', *Russian History* 19, nos. 1–4 (1992): 401–32.

Poe, Marshall T. *'A People Born to Slavery': Russia in Early Modern Ethnography, 1476–1748.* Ithaca, NY: Cornell University Press, 2000.

Prikhod´ko, Mikhail. 'Sozdanie ministerskoi sistemy upravleniia v Rossii pervoi treti XIX veka', *Dva veka, zhurnal rossiiskoi istorii XVIII–XIX stoletii* 4 (2001). [Internet journal. Site now defunct, article in author's possession.]

Raeff, Marc. 'The Bureaucratic Phenomena of Imperial Russia, 1700–1905', *The American Historical Review* 84, no. 2 (1979): 399–411.

Raeff, Marc. *Michael Speransky: Statesman of Imperial Russia, 1772–1839.* The Hague: Martinus Nijhoff, 1957.

Raeff, Marc. *Siberia and the Reforms of 1822.* Seattle: University of Washington Press, 1956.

Raeff, Marc. *The Well-Ordered Police State: Social and Institutional Change through Law in the Germanies and Russia, 1600–1800.* New Haven, CT: Yale University Press, 1983.

Raleigh, Donald J., ed. *The Emperors and Empresses of Russia: Rediscovering the Romanovs.* Armonk, NY: M. E. Sharpe, 1996.

Remnev, A. V. 'Prokonsul Sibiri Ivan Borisovich Pestel´', *Voprosy istorii* 2 (1997): 141–9.

Reynolds, Robert L. *Europe Emerges: Transition toward an Industrial World-Wide Society, 600–1750.* Madison, WI: University of Wisconsin Press, 1967.

Rezun, D. Ia. *Russkie v srednem Prichulym'e v XVII–XIX vv. (Problemy sotsial'no-ekonomicheskogo razvitiia malykh gorodov Sibiri).* Novosibirsk: Nauka, 1984.

Roberts, Michael. *The Military Revolution, 1560–1660: An Inaugural Lecture Delivered before the Queen's University of Belfast.* Belfast: M. Boyd, 1956.

Robson, Roy R. *Solovki: The Story of Russia Told Through Its Most Remarkable Islands.* New Haven, CT: Yale University Press, 2004.

Rose, Lionel. *'Rogues and Vagabonds': Vagrant Underworld in Britain, 1815–1985.* London: Routledge, 1988.

Rothman, David J. *The Discovery of the Asylum: Social Order and Disorder in the New Republic.* Boston: Little, Brown, 1971.

Rowney, Don Karl. 'Structure, Class, and Career: The Problem of Bureaucracy and Society in Russia, 1801–1917', *Social Science History* 6, no. 1 (1982): 87–110.

Rusche, Georg and Otto Kirchheimer. *Punishment and Social Structure.* 1939; rpt. New Brunswick: Transaction, 2003.

Russkii biograficheskii slovar' v dvadtsati tomakh, 20 vols. Moskva: Terra-Knizhnyi klub, 2001.

Russkii biograficheskii slovar'. S.-Peterburg: Tipografiia I. I. Skorokhodova, 1905; rpt. New York: SPE Kraus Reprint Corporation, 1962.

Safronov, F. G. *Russkie krest'iane v Iakutii (XVII–nachalo XX vv.).* Iakutsk: Knizhnoe izd-vo, 1961.

Safronov, F. G. *Ssylka v vostochnuiu Sibir' v XVII veke.* Iakutsk: Iakutskoe knizhnoe izdatel'stvo, 1967.

Sapozhnikov, V. V. and N. A. Gavrilov. 'Zemli Kabineta Ego Velichestva', in *Aziatskaia Rossiia: Tom pervyi: Liudi i poriadki za Uralom.* S. Peterburg: Izdanie Pereselencheskago upravleniia glavnago upravleniia zemleustroistva i zemledeliia, 1914.

Schrader, Abby M. *Languages of the Lash: Corporal Punishment and Identity in Imperial Russia.* DeKalb, IL: Northern Illinois University Press, 2002.

Selishchev, A. M. *Zabaikal'skie staroobriadtsy. Semeiskie.* Irkutsk: Irkutskii universitet, 1920.

Semevskii, V. I. *Rabochie na sibirskikh zolotykh promyslakh: istoricheskoe izsledovanie.* 2 vols. S.-Peterburg: Tipografiia M. Stasiulevicha, 1898.

Sergeevskii, N. D. *Rech' v godovom SPB Iuridicheskago Obshchestva, 8 Marta 1887 goda, O ssylke v drevnei Rossii.* S.-Peterburg: Tipografiia Ministerstva putei soobshcheniia (A. Benke), 1887.

Shabanov, M. P. 'Rol' ssylki v protsesse russkogo zaseleniia Sibiri v XVII v.', in *Sibir' v istorii Rossii (k 100-letiiu Zinaidy Georgievny Karpenko): Materialy regional'noi nauchnoi konferentsii.* Ed. V. A. Volchek and A. M. Adamenko. Kemerovo: Kuzbassvuzizdat, 2006, pp. 62–6.

Shannon, Thomas R. *An Introduction to the World-System Perspective.* 2nd edn. Boulder, CO: Westview Press, 1996.

Shcheglov, I. V. *Khronologicheskii perechen' vazhneishikh dannykh iz istorii Sibiri: 1032–1882 gg.* 1883; rpt. Surgut: Severnyi dom, 1993.

Shebaldina, G. V. *Shvedskie voennoplennye v Sibiri: Pervaia chetvert' XVIII veka.* Moskva: Rossiiskii gosudarstvennyi gumanitarnyi universitet, 2005.

Shobodoev, E. B. 'Iz otcheta Gubernatora Treskina', *Zemlia irkutskaia* 4 (1995): 32–3.

Shunkov, V. I. *Ocherki po istorii kolonizatsii Sibiri v XVII–nachale XVIII vekov.* Moskva: AN SSSR, 1946.

Shunkov, V. I. *Ocherki po istorii zemledeliia Sibiri (XVII vek).* Moskva: AN SSSR, 1956.

Shunkov, V. I. et al., eds. *Sibir´ perioda feodalizma, vypusk 1.* Novosibirsk: AN SSSR, 1962.

Shunkov, V. I. et al., eds. *Sibir´ perioda feodalizma, vypusk 3.* Novosibirsk: Nauka, 1968.

Slezkine, Yuri. *Arctic Mirrors: Russia and the Small Peoples of the North.* Ithaca, NY: Cornell University Press, 1994.

Slovtsov, P. A. *Istoricheskoe obozrenie Sibiri. Stikhotvoreniia. Propovedi.* Ed. and intro. V. A. Kreshchik. Novosibirsk: Ven-mir, 1995.

Smirnov, Iu. I. *Orenburgskaia ekspedistiia (komissiia) i prisoedinenie Zavolzh´ia k Rossii v 30–40-e gg. XVIII veka.* Samara: Samarskii universitet, 1997.

Sokolovskii, Ivan Rostislavovich. *Sluzhilye 'inozemtsy' v Sibiri XVII veka (Tomsk, Eniseisk, Krasnoiarsk.* Novosibirsk: Sova, 2004.

Spierenburg, Pieter. *The Prison Experience: Disciplinary Institutions and Their Inmates in Early Modern Europe.* New Brunswick: Rutgers University Press, 1991.

Ssylka v Sibir´: ocherk eia istorii i sovremennago polozheniia. S.-Peterburg: Tipografiia S.-Peterburgskoi Tiur´my, 1900.

Stephan, John J. *The Russian Far East: A History.* Stanford, CA: Stanford University Press, 1994.

Stolberg, Eva-Maria, ed. *The Siberian Saga: A History of Russia's Wild East.* Frankfurt-am-Main: Lang, 2005.

Tolstoy, Leo. *Resurrection.* Trans. Rosemary Edmonds. New York: Penguin Books, 1966.

Tomsinov, V. A. *Speranskii.* Moskva: Molodaia gvardiia, 2006.

Treadgold, Donald W. *The Great Siberian Migration: Government and Peasant Resettlement from Emancipation to the First World War.* Princeton, NJ: Princeton University Press, 1957.

Vasilenko, Marina. ' "Bunt ot soslannykh zlodeev . . . " ', *Zemlia irkutskaia* 3 (1995): 27–9.

Waley-Cohen, Joanna. *Exile in Mid-Qing China: Banishment to Xinjiang, 1758–1820.* New Haven, CT: Yale University Press, 1991.

Wallerstein, Immanuel. *The Modern World-System: Capitalist Agriculture and the Origins of the European World-Economy in the Sixteenth Century.* New York: Academic Press, 1974.

Wallerstein, Immanuel. *The Modern World-System II: Mercantilism and the Consolidation of the European World-Economy, 1600–1750.* New York: Academic Press, 1980.

Weber, Max. *Economy and Society: An Outline of Interpretive Sociology.* 3 vols. New York: Bedminster Press, 1968.

Weber, Max. 'The Essentials of Bureaucratic Organization: An Ideal-Type Construction', in *Reader in Bureaucracy.* Ed. Robert K. Merton et al. Glencoe, IL: Free Press, 1952, pp. 18–27.

Weber, Max. *The Theory of Social and Economic Organization.* Ed. Talcott Parsons. New York: Macmillan, 1964.

Wood, Alan. 'Administrative Exile and the Criminals' Commune in Siberia', in *Land Commune and Peasant Community in Russia: Communal Forms in Imperial and Early Soviet Society*. Ed. Roger Bartlett. New York: St. Martin's Press, 1990, pp. 395–414.

Wood, Alan. 'Avvakum's Siberian Exile, 1653–64', in *The Development of Siberia: People and Resources*. Ed. A. Wood and R. A. French. Basingstoke: Macmillan, 1989, pp. 11–34.

Wood, Alan. 'Crime and Punishment in the House of the Dead', in *Civil Rights in Imperial Russia*. Ed. Olga Crisp and Linda Edmondson. Oxford: Clarendon Press, 1989, pp. 215–33.

Wood, Alan. 'Siberian Exile in the Eighteenth Century', *Siberica* 1, no. 1 (1990): 38–63.

Wood, Alan. 'The Use and Abuse of Administrative Exile to Siberia', *Irish Slavonic Studies* 6 (1985): 65–81.

Worobec, Christine D. *Possessed: Women, Witches, and Demons in Imperial Russia*. DeKalb, IL: Northern Illinois University Press, 2001.

Wortman, Richard S. *Scenarios of Power: Myth and Ceremony in Russian Monarchy*. Vol. 1. Princeton, NJ: Princeton University Press, 1995.

Yaney, George L. *The Systematization of Russian Government: Social Evolution in the Domestic Administration of Imperial Russia, 1711–1905*. Urbana, IL: University of Illinois Press, 1973.

Zacek, Judith C. 'A Case Study in Russian Philanthropy: The Prison Reform Movement in the Reign of Alexander I', *Canadian Slavic Studies/Revue canadienne d'études slaves* 1, no. 2 (1967): 196–211.

Zen´kovskii, Sergei. *Russkoe staroobriadchestvo: Dukhovnye dvizheniia semnadtsatogo veka*. Moskva: Tserkov´, 1995.

Name Index

Subject Index